SURVIVAL OF THE SAN
Order and Disorder in a Pre-trial Psychiatric Clinic

In this study of pre-trial clinical assessment, Robert Menzies examines a key element in our system of criminal justice and finds it wanting. His book calls into question the entire process by which the state determines that defendants are – or are not – mentally fit to stand trial.

The Metropolitan Toronto Forensic Service (METFORS) is a multi-disciplinary assessment agency which opened in 1978. During its first year of operation METFORS practitioners evaluated 592 defendants. Menzies has reconstructed medical and correctional records to trace the institutional careers of those men and women from their initial arrest, through their assessment at METFORS and the decision of the court, and finally through the two years following the initial assessment.

What emerges is an illuminating analysis of the character and outcome of forensic psychiatric decision-making; the relationship between clinicians and other criminal justice officials such as police, prosecutors, and judges; the ability of medical experts to shape judicial judgments about accused persons; and the long-term implications of these assessments for the psychiatric and carceral experiences of forensic patients.

Menzies presents a critical portrayal of pre-trial psychiatric assessment as an exercise in justifying, and even extending, the ambit of legal and therapeutic control over accused persons suspected of mental illness. He concludes that these remands can no longer be justified on medical, legal, or moral grounds.

ROBERT J. MENZIES is Associate Professor in the School of Criminology, Simon Fraser University.

ROBERT J. MENZIES

SURVIVAL OF THE SANEST

Order and Disorder in a Pre-trial Psychiatric Clinic

UNIVERSITY OF TORONTO PRESS
Toronto Buffalo London

© University of Toronto Press 1989
Toronto Buffalo London
Printed in Canada

ISBN 0-8020-5827-2 (cloth)
ISBN 0-8020-6737-9 (paper)

Printed on acid-free paper

Canadian Cataloguing in Publication Data

Menzies, Robert J., 1951-
  Survival of the sanest

Includes index.
ISBN 0-8020-5827-2 (bound)   ISBN 0-8020-6737-9 (pbk.)

1. Metropolitan Toronto Forensic Services.
2. Forensic psychiatry – Ontario – Toronto.
3. Pre-trial procedure – Ontario – Toronto.
4. Psychiatric clinics – Ontario – Toronto.
I. Title.

RA1151.M45 1989   614'.1   C89-094261-7

In memory of John P. Menzies
1912–1979

BIRON: What is the end of study?
KING: Why, that to know, which else we should not know.
BIRON: Things hid and barred, you mean, from commonsense?
KING: Ay, that is study's god-like recompense.

WILLIAM SHAKESPEARE   *Love's Labour's Lost* I, 1

And now here is my secret, a very simple secret: It is only with the heart that one can see rightly; what is essential is invisible to the eye.

ANTOINE DE SAINT-EXUPÉRY   *The Little Prince*

Contents

x Contents

Tables and Figures

FIGURES

Foreword

The most important sign of civility is how a society treats its marginal members. In particular, citizens assess the moral authority of the state in terms of how it deals with accused persons and criminal offenders. The state's record in this area serves as a barometer of all lesser exercises of authority.

There are signs that we in Canada are civilized, especially in comparison with other places and previous times. Even the most despicable people are not entirely written off: as a sign of our civility, we have abolished the death penalty. Indeed, I think analysis would show that in Canada, the more someone offends moral sensibilities through horrific acts of violence and disorder, the more health, welfare, and penal resources we devote to dealing with the offensive person. We mark our civilization by holding out eternal hope to the offender – and more significantly, to ourselves – that although he has gone wrong, our advanced scientific knowledge and enhanced legal system can remake him as a thoroughly respectable citizen. Even with the contemporary emphasis on the rights of victims, and the punitive mentality that emphasis urges, our moral sensibilities maintain respect for the offender's legal rights and rehabilitative potential.

Professor Robert J. Menzies' project is to question whether, in congratulating ourselves about our civility, we are letting our institutions do our thinking for us. He considers how the coercive power of the state is increasingly justified through claims to scientific expertise blended with expressions of legal authority. He queries whether these claims and expressions are directing our perceptions into grooves compatible with the social relations the institutions of state, science, and law wish to authorize. He contemplates how these claims and expressions might be fixing our gaze and thereby limiting the range of questions we ask and solutions we seek.

Menzies pursues his project by getting inside a pre-trial forensic clinic mandated to deal with, and provide recommendations about, some of the most wretched members of Canadian society. He lifts the veil of administrative decency that normally cloaks such institutions to pick its components apart, to learn about its organizations, its programs, its knowledges, and its communications. He shows that the clinicians, in concert with the police who feed them, and the prosecutors and judges whom the clinicians feed in turn, are primarily knowledge brokers. Their essential task is to manufacture formal knowledge that will articulate with exercises of coercive power. In analysing the manufactory at work – how its various agents make and move knowledge in the concrete circumstances of their daily tasks – Menzies documents the micropolitics of knowledge and power in meticulous and disturbing detail.

It is made evident that the formal knowledge of the clinicians, while based in common sense, is elite knowledge in that it is not part of everyday speech. As elite knowledge, the professional activities it authorizes and the decisions it legitimates are not open to participation by non-specialists, especially the accused persons who are the subjects of the clinicians' activities and decisions. As elite knowledge, the formal knowledge of the clinic is not democratic, and signifies the more general trend in society away from democracy and toward technocracy. Menzies feels that democracy should be at the heart of the clinic. He is centrally concerned with the ways in which the technical knowledge manufactured by the clinicians may not be serving justice, or fostering the human potential of those they capture and process.

The clinic is mandated to serve the needs of the accused persons it houses and to protect them from the more unjust and punitive excesses of the criminal law system. It is thus focused not only on the particular legal predicament of the accused, but also on his medical condition and moral character. As such the clinic is to operate with an individualized conception of good and evil, normality and abnormality, situating the causes of crime in the manners and morals of flawed individuals. It is to find out what is wrong with the individual qua human being and to activate whatever may be helpful in putting him right.

Menzies discovers an institution that exceeds its mandate in many ways. The clinic derives its primary legitimacy from the legal institution and therefore shifts its own institutional discourse and practice to meet the needs of the legal institution. For example, while the clinic's primary official function is to assess the fitness of accused persons to stand trial, it is preoccupied with making sentencing recommendations to judges even at the pre-trial stage. Central to these sentencing recommendations are assessments of the 'dangerousness' of the accused, even though such assessments are not officially mandated. 'Dangerousness' criteria are often paramount in spite of the well-established fact that psychiatrists and other clinicians cannot predict 'dangerousness.' Indeed, by means of a sophisticated follow-up investigation, Menzies discovers that psychiatrists are wrong more than half the time in predicting future violent conduct. In Menzies' words, 'In the peculiar alchemy of forensic discretion, clinical authority is largely founded upon a task at which practitioners are alarmingly inept.'

Clinicians offer such predictions routinely because the courts find them to be a powerful vehicle for justifying punishments. Clinicians tailor their knowledge to fit the formats of the legal institution to the point where their recommended prescriptions – whether for imprisonment, psychiatric confinement, or alternative dispositions – are routinely accepted by the courts. The concurrence between the clinicians' recommendations and judicial decisions increases with the intensity of the recommended punishment! Clinicians are expert advisers on punishment, helping the court to justify and legitimate its most coercive sanctions in terms of scientific knowledge and medical expertise. In the process clinicians fundamentally abandon their traditional medical orientations and commitments in favour of pre-trial confinement of criminal defendants, dramatizing the dangerousness of accused persons, rationalizing judicial labels, and legitimating the allocation of penal measures. Not incidentally, clinicians also help themselves, establishing a legitimate place and launching prestigious careers in the medico-legal complex.

Menzies finds an institution that is obsessed with itself. The organizations involved with the clinic are clients of each other, mutually dependent for referral of subjects and conferral of authority. The clinic's programs 'program' it to serve its own needs over and above its medical and legal obligations to both the accused and the public. Thus programmed, the clinic's only source of knowledge is itself. Like the journalist who turns to yesterday's newspaper to decide what is newsworthy and thus make more news, the clinician turns to the documents and classifications of the medico-legal complex to judge accused persons and to recommend what should be done *to* them.

While clinicians are well aware that reality is a fluid, they treat it as if it were a solid. They objectify their knowledge in documents in expressions of authoritative certainty to the courts. Disagreement about classifications is rare. When disagreement occurs, the accused is held in custody for an extended period in order to allow the clinicians an opportunity to get their act together and to forge a consensus for the courts.

Clinical assessment of the accused is characterized by clinicians reproducing each other's classifications as the case moves along in the pre-trial process. It is a process in which clinicians are primarily oriented to self-validation of knowledge, and self-confirmation of the wisdom of each other's decisions. The accused hardly matters at all, except as he might unknowingly offer verbal and visual signs that fit the existing classification scheme. Otherwise the accused's voice is silenced, and his personal identity is erased. As noted previously, for clinicians the crowning achievement is that the courts routinely validate their punitive judgments and, thereby, their professional authority.

While Menzies offers meticulous evidence that clinicians are unable to predict human behaviour with reasonable accuracy, this finding should not be taken to mean that human behaviour in general is unpredictable. When the wretched of Canada face Regina, the outcome is predictable indeed. Menzies concludes that the accused repeatedly emerge from the clinic 'in worse condition than they entered, as measured by their prospects for freedom, by their identities as criminal or psychiatric deviants, and by their vulnerability to the interventions of carceral and therapeutic control agents.'

In face of the overwhelming evidence he has assembled through a decade of scholarly research, Menzies is compelled to focus on the pathology of the institution itself. The medico-legal complex, in keeping with many other institutions in modern society, is apparently suffering from an acute case of megalomania. Borrowing the wisdom of Mary Douglas in her book, *How Institutions Think*, we can see that it is like 'the computer whose whole vision of the world is its own program.' As an institution that depends on scientific authority, legal authority, and punitiveness, its only reply to those who question it is more authority and more punishment.

The computer metaphor does not deny the fact that creative human beings make up the medico-legal institution. This book is replete with examples of creative clinicians telling stories and making cases out of myriad details of their subjects' lives. As such, the book testifies to the incredible capacity of humans imaginatively to justify the coercion they feel they must exercise over fellow humans. Indeed I believe few readers will be able to stretch their own imaginations to the point of visualizing a justification for control that has not been addressed within these pages.

While Menzies leaves the reader with the overwhelming sense that justice is primarily a matter of justifications, he also stresses that clinicians have finite capacities in this regard. The source of closure is of course the clinicians' institution, which does their thinking for them. While they are creative programmers, clinicians have to work within the parameters of the institutional 'computer.' All of their creative energy serves, in the long term and in the aggregate, to perpetuate the megalomania of the institution, as it feeds on itself in concentric spirals of amplification and intensification.

Menzies rejects reformist solutions because he appreciates that efforts to author different programs will only augment the institution's megalomania. Tinkering or repair work – changing some of the rules, adding new programs, undertaking further research, bringing in other forms of professional knowledge – will not change things but simply produce more doses of authority and punishment. Part of the difficulty in letting institutions do our thinking for us is that problems are seen as residing within individuals, and in the details of their organizing efforts. This vision creates the belief that if we change some individuals, and some aspects of organizing (rules, procedures, units, divisions), things will work better. They won't.

While Menzies would be the first to recommend against the death penalty for individual offenders, the death penalty is precisely his recommendation for the offensive institution. The pre-trial forensic clinic must be abolished in order to allow clinicians to extricate themselves from the institutional entanglements of law that force them into moral compromise and professional disgrace. Only when clinicians give up the key to their professional success as jailers on behalf of the legal system can they return to their proper place in 'the defence of sick people, the humanization of criminal justice, the presentation of alternatives to penal intervention, and the general blunting of control.' Only then will clinicians accord with our moral sensibilities of how marginal members of society should be dealt with, and thereby enhance our civility.

Richard V. Ericson

Acknowledgments

There are many to thank. This book has been published with the help of a grant from the Social Science Federation of Canada, using funds provided by the Social Sciences and Humanities Research Council of Canada. Other financial support came at various stages from the SSHRC Research Grants and Doctoral Fellowships programs, the Solicitor General Canada (through its unsolicited research grants competition), the Canadian Psychiatric Research Foundation, the Department of Justice Canada, the Ontario Ministry of Health, the Law Foundation of Ontario, the University of Toronto Centre of Criminology (through a contributions grant provided by the Solicitor General), and the Clarke Institute of Psychiatry. The index, ably compiled by Ken Garley, was produced through an allocation from the Simon Fraser University Publication Grants Committee. An abridged version of Chapter 2, entitled 'Psychiatrists in blue,' appeared in *Criminology* 25, no. 3 (August 1987), 901–25, and the Chapter 6 section on 'Forensic roulette and the phenomenon of multiple rewards' was published in different form as 'Cycles of control,' *International Journal of Law and Psychiatry* 10, no. 3 (1987), 233–49.

Roy Gillis, Val Cattelan, Carrie Broughton, and Steve Wellford contributed outstanding research assistance. Kay Cooper, Julie Hall, Donna Robertson, Mary Sutherland, and Aileen Sams helped in the presentation of tabular data. Alison Hatch and Dr William Glackman provided needed technical advice. Diana Sepejak and Jill Thurston were responsible for collecting much of the follow-up data from correctional and hospital files. The representatives of numerous mental health and criminal justice agencies co-operated far beyond the bureaucratic call of duty in allowing access to records and other documents under their jurisdiction. Special thanks go to Inspector R.C. Jackson of the Royal Canadian Mounted Police and to

Dr D. Craigen, Director General of the Medical and Health Care Services, Correctional Services Canada.

This study could never have been undertaken without the collaboration of the many police officers, psychiatrists, psychologists, social workers, nurses, and correctional officers whose activities are described below. The critical perspective of this book in no way dampens my genuine respect for the willingness of these professionals to subject their work to close scrutiny. As well, I owe an incalculable debt to the 592 METFORS patients whose experiences are recounted in the following pages. Their personal tragedies brought a poignant dimension to this study, and they spoke volumes about the resiliency of human identity against the depersonalizing forces that fuel modern institutions of social control.

Thanks go to past and present colleagues in the School of Criminology, Simon Fraser University, and for their especially valuable input on this book to Neil Boyd, Shelley Gavigan, Bill Glackman, Margaret Jackson, John Lowman, Ted Palys, and Simon Verdun-Jones. Commentaries on the manuscript were provided at various points along the way by Professors Anthony N. Doob, P.J. Giffen, A.R. Gillis, Timothy Hartnagel, Eric W. Single, Lorne Tepperman, and the three anonymous reviewers of the University of Toronto Press and the Social Science Federation of Canada.

Mr Virgil D. Duff, Managing Editor of the University of Toronto Press, has nurtured this book with a fine blend of tenacity and tact. Jim Polk was a virtuoso copy-editor, and Lorraine Ourom and Audrey M. Livernois provided much-appreciated support in editing and marketing.

Dr Christopher D. Webster, Head of Psychology at the Clarke Institute of Psychiatry, and Professor of Psychology, Psychiatry and Criminology at the University of Toronto, conceptualized, organized, and directed the project that spawned this book. Without his amazing energy, boundless intellectual curiosity, and friendly persuasion, the manuscript would have never been written. Dr Richard V. Ericson, of the University of Toronto Department of Sociology and Centre of Criminology, is more than anyone else responsible for the merits of what follows. I have benefited greatly and learned much from his intellectual integrity, critical understanding, good humour, and sound advice.

The final acknowledgment goes to Dr Dorothy E. Chunn, whose love, counsel, and tolerance have kept me sane.

SURVIVAL OF THE SANEST

Introduction

We have yet to write the history of that other form of madness, by which men, in an act of sovereign reason, confine their neighbours, and communicate and recognize each other through the merciless language of non-madness.

MICHEL FOUCAULT   *Madness and Civilization*

All seeing is essentially perspective, and so is all knowing. The more emotions we allow to speak on a given matter, the more different eyes we train on the same thing, the more complete will be our conception of it, the greater our 'objectivity.'

FRIEDRICH NIETZSCHE   *The Genealogy of Morals*

PSYCHIATRIC DISCRETION AND LEGAL ORDER

In recent years, sociologists have become increasingly concerned with the discretionary practices of legal officials. There has been an accumulating body of research that describes the decision-making work of police, prosecutors, lawyers, judges, probation and parole officers, and other agents involved in the judicial processing of criminal defendants (see generally Arkes and Hammond 1986; Emerson 1983; Ericson and Baranek 1982; Feeley 1979; Handel 1982; Hawkins and Tiedeman 1975; McBarnet 1981). This literature marks a radical movement in perspective among legal scholars. It departs from conventional portrayals of judicial process as a mirror image of the Law itself. It applies a more sophisticated approach to the relationship between action and structure. It represents legal officials as active participants in the construction of judicial decisions, and in the very structuring of legal control itself.

As a consequence, members of criminal justice institutions are increasingly being depicted as central figures in the organization of the criminal law. In shifting the focus from structural arrangements to human agency, socio-legal researchers have largely abandoned earlier functional and formalistic portrayals (e.g. Davis 1971; Kadish and Kadish 1973) of a rational-legal bureaucracy governed by immutable rules-from-above. They have become more sensitive to the situated and improvisational character of legal, extra-legal, and illegal decision-making. Judicial discretion is seen as a contextual and negotiated phenomenon, emerging out of the pragmatic and routine problem-solving activities of various occupational groups, and more specifically out of the immediate legal environment. As McBarnet writes 'deviation from legality is institutionalized in the law itself' (1979: 39).

Accordingly, individual agents are held to be directly responsible – functionally and morally – for the application of state power through the vehicle of the law. The legal ordering of criminal subjects is secured by the accumulating judgments of officials as they selectively enforce institutional rules (Carlen 1974; Davis 1975: 178), as they organize their occupational mandate (Freidson 1966; Johnson 1972; Simpkin 1979), and as they develop recipes for lending an appearance of authenticity, legality, and accountability to the products of their professional work (Leiter 1980; Pfohl 1978, 1979; Zimmerman 1974).

This study looks closely at the activities of one such collection of decision-makers working on the periphery of the criminal justice arena. As a professional body, forensic clinicians have evolved into a major force in the daily operation of the legal system. Over the course of this century, medical and penal models of justice have systematically fused into a relatively unified set of assumptions about the meaning of criminality and the organization of legal response (Castel, Castel, and Lovell 1982; Ingleby 1981; Rothman 1980; Turner 1987). In the process, psychiatrists and other 'helping' professions have increasingly assumed a central role in the classification and control of criminal subjects. They have adopted ideologies and mandates that are virtually indistinguishable from those held by more traditional practitioners of legal control. They have come to specialize in tasks that are principally oriented to the repression of crime. While psychiatry has always exercised powerful control functions, these trends have created an altogether different brand of medical agent – a clinician who is committed to punitive models of criminal justice, and who is integrally involved in a network of allegiances and transactions with police, prosecutors, lawyers, judges, and other legal authorities in the modern state.

The clinical professions have been integrated into the judicial system because they enhance its domination over offender populations. They offer a readily available body of 'scientific knowledge' that both magnifies the apparent deviance of legal subjects and rationalizes decisions made under the rubric of law. Through the expanding authority of forensic psychiatry, science has come to parallel law as an instrument of state power in 'the knowledge society' (Bohme and Stehr 1986). Much of what follows in this book is a demonstration of the similarities between law and science, both as general cultural frameworks for achieving legitimacy and as pragmatic tools of power in everyday decision-making (see Ericson and Shearing 1986; Gouldner 1976; Gusfield 1981; Habermas 1970). Through the mobilization of clinical categories and medical forms, the pathologies of defendants are made to appear factual and to merit intervention by mental health and criminal justice workers. The judgments of medico-legal officials, in turn, become authoritative because they are embedded in seemingly limitless displays of technical know-how and professional knowledge.

In the coalition between clinicians and courts, science and law are combined into a powerful reservoir of enabling resources. Medical agents are employed to conduct information work, to provide the raw materials that justify decisions made in the interests of the occupation, the organization, and the state, rather than for individual subjects. But because science is culturally viewed as value-free, as rational and based on indisputable facts, it functions to support the purported neutrality and benevolence of medico-legal agents. Science enhances law, since it contributes an ideological, cultural, and conceptual basis for maximizing legal accountability. Law enhances science, since it provides a receptive theatre of operation for psychiatry and related clinical professions.

In the following chapters I will be examining the medico-legal ordering of accused persons in the Metropolitan Toronto Forensic Service (METFORS), a pre-trial forensic clinic offering psychiatric assessments for the criminal courts in Toronto, Canada. The relationship between forensic discretion and legal order at METFORS will be addressed on numerous occasions in this book against the background of four interconnected themes. *First*, I argue that the nature and quality of psychiatric activities are framed largely against the expectations of legal officials with whom clinical classifiers persistently interact. The credibility of forensic professionals depends on their ability to demonstrate a special medical proficiency and value to their legal audiences. Such a relationship is infused with contradiction. Practitioners are professionally and ideologically suspended between court and clinic. On the one hand, clinicians are generally kept at arm's length from the realm of the court. Their distancing from the legal process means that psychiatrists can rarely assume a role as direct advocates for their claims. On the other hand, their relative detachment is enabling, since legal officials have little power of review over the process (as distinct from the output) of forensic activities, and since, in any event, legal standards for assessing 'medical' decisions are virtually non-existent.

This study examines the discretionary practices of forensic clinicians as primarily legal actors, whose allegiances and ideologies are in many ways interchangeable with those of police, prosecutors, probation and parole officers, and other officials. Psychiatric classifiers come to adopt a legalistic perspective nearly indistinguishable from that of their counterparts in other agencies. The distinctive features of medico-legal practice, by contrast, emerge from their use of the medical model as legitimating ideology. Despite socializing forces which impinge, forensic clinicians resist the inclination entirely to abandon their medical identity either to themselves or to outsiders. Credibility flows from issuing legally relevant judgments, yet these are perpetually formulated within the form and discourse of medical reality. Forensic discretion is indeed fashioned 'in the shadow of the law' (Mnookin and Kornhauser 1979), but the texture and shape of such decision-making is never devoid of medical content.

Second, forensic professionals are involved in a moral ordering process that reinforces and extends the labelling work of more traditional legal officials. Psycholegal decisions are primarily *matters of morals*, although they tend to be represented as *matters of fact* (Gouldner 1976: 262). Moral norms are infused in the practice of medico-legal decision-making. By impeaching the moral status of criminal defendants, the very character and 'soul' (Foucault 1977) of legal subjects can be made subject to scrutiny. Clinical and other specialist assessments are constructed around 'a moralization of minutiae' (Lofland 1969: 164).

In the context of forensic discretion, every facet of a person's criminal, cultural, and interpersonal biography is open to evaluation and valuation by expert classifiers. Clinicians strive simultaneously to upgrade their own moral status and to degrade their subjects' accounts (Garfinkel 1956). In order to accomplish 'respectability work' (Ericson 1975: 17), psychiatrists strive to establish respectability for themselves and disreputability for criminal defendants. Psychiatric assessments, in the most literal sense, are 'trials of moral character' (Emerson 1969). The activities of forensic professionals recurrently involve sifting through the elements of a person's moral career (Becker 1963), offering 'moral explanations' (Louch, in Giddens 1976: 44), and selecting a set of 'facts' that can be presented as indices of character, rather than the characterization and caricature that they 'in fact' represent (Emerson 1969: 101). Such stigmatization strategies constitute a major component of the METFORS diagnostic process described in the chapters which follow.

Third, the criteria for psychiatric discretion in legal settings, as for decision-making generally in the carceral system, are the emergent and reflexive products of professional problem-solving. Rules are embedded in the organizational conditions of their use: '... norms do not guide behavior as much as they provide people with after-the-fact justifications and explanations for behavior' (Hawkins and Tiedeman 1975: 23). Accordingly, rules do *not* exist before-the-fact, and hence clinicians are relatively free to improvise their decisions without the constraints of legal procedures or medical diagnostic schemes.

During the assessment of pre-trial forensic patients, psychiatric pathology, criminality and other categories are built up out of 'large masses of unintelligible data' (Cicourel 1968: 332). In the process of making sense out of forensic cases, professional classifiers learn to reify medico-legal 'facts' and to objectify the human experiences of their subjects. Such typification work, resulting in the distribution of 'processing stereotypes' (Hawkins and Tiedeman 1975), is accomplished in order to permit the communication of sensible and defensible accounts to legal audiences. The apparently coherent, comprehensive, and expert formulations sent to criminal court judges, as we will see, are in practice a carefully crafted set of images, invoked to justify the commonsense interpretive work of forensic clinicians. Psychiatric decisions often comprise simple restatements of prior judgments by other medical or legal authorities, reconstituted within the persuasive discourse of medical science. In everyday practice, the intuitive judgments of expert classifiers, cognitively and morally interchangeable with the decisions of non-clinical laypersons, are made to appear scientific, rational, just, and legitimate in the eyes of legal observers. What is typically a restatement of old knowledge is presented as if it were the discovery and property of current decision-makers. What is frequently a distortion and truncation of the authentic experiences and problems of criminal defendants suspected of mental illness is almost always represented by forensic practitioners as medically, legally, and ontologically 'real.'

Fourth, the ultimate test of psycholegal authority resides in the ability to produce persuasive accounts of subjects' clinical condition and criminal capacity – accounts that survive and resist challenge as official documents are passed across a succession of institutional levels. Forensic clinicians are alert to the central importance of written documents in sustaining their professional legitimacy. Their 'medical' autonomy, paradoxically, depends upon the systematic acceptance of their reality claims by legal authorities. Locked as they are into complex exchange networks with judges, prosecutors, and other officials, clinicians learn to adjust their signals to the particular frequencies of powerful audiences. And legal authorities are concerned with the pragmatic demands of adjudication and sentencing, rather than the (for them) esoteric problems of psychopathology and medical diagnosis. The acceptance of clinical judgments in criminal law is therefore dependent on psychiatrists' demonstrations that their efforts are directly relevant to criminal court concerns about legal order.

Working between the twin control systems of criminal justice and mental health, then, forensic clinicians must learn to extract from each those enabling norms and resources that maximize their psychiatric authority. Such professional authority, in turn, functions to reproduce wider processes of legal control. The pre-trial forensic assessment is advocated as a medical procedure designed to soften the blunt impact of judicial process; in practice it turns out to be an extension and proliferation of the state's criminal control apparatus. The relative autonomy, moral authority, and discretionary power of forensic institutions like METFORS derive from the central legitimacy of the legal system. In turn, these are reinforced by the techno-scientific ideology of the medical model. Together, these power sources combine in allowing legal control to cascade over entirely new categories of accused persons. Psychiatrists are enforcers, conscious or not, of an ordering process that extends beyond the walls of the clinic and, indeed, beyond the judicial realm altogether. In what follows I will be surveying the implications of these institutional patterns for the discretionary activities of the METFORS classifiers, and for the medico-legal careers of their forensic subjects.

RESEARCHING PSYCHIATRIC DECISION-MAKING AT METFORS

This book reconstructs the first year in the life of a pre-trial psychiatric assessment agency. METFORS was founded in September 1977 with the inauguration of a twenty-three-bed Inpatient Unit. The Brief Assessment Unit (BAU) of METFORS, described below, opened four months later on 23

January 1978. The research program depicted in this book, as a result, embodies an important *historical* component. It traces the development of METFORS, the activities and adjustments of its clinical personnel, and the experiences of its subject population during the clinic's first twelve months of full operation between January and December 1978.

This time-lag between the inauguration of METFORS and the publication of this account was necessary for two principal reasons. To begin, a follow-up component was built into the study design (see below, and Chapters 1 and 6) which permitted a two-year survey of subject experiences subsequent to assessment in the BAU. This outcome study extended the data collection process into 1980 and beyond (and, in fact, a supplementary project is currently under way that will eventually trace these medico-legal careers for a period of six years: see McMain, Webster, and Menzies, 1987). In addition, on ethical grounds – to minimize the identifiability of professionals and patients – it was important that a reasonable passage of time should intervene prior to publishing the METFORS case records. Since the original production of these materials, the majority of clinicians have left the facility, and their human subjects have dispersed widely throughout the community and the medico-legal system. This retrospective feature of the research is being used here, then, in concert with other measures to ensure the maximum feasible confidentiality for both authorities and subjects.

At the same time, this study of decision-making at METFORS should be viewed primarily as an effort to map the functioning of a *contemporary* control institution. Despite a major turnover in personnel, and despite some minor adjustments to the administrative structure and to the number of clinicians involved in BAU assessments (from five to three), the operation and medico-legal role of METFORS have changed little since 1978. Its current practices and programs represent, to a large extent, a consolidation of arrangements that were being worked out during the twelve months of this study. One of the recurring discoveries in research on discretionary control concerns the extraordinary capacity of authorities to adapt within their institutional environment, and to mobilize strategies for the efficient processing of legal subjects. Early into the first year of the agency's existence, as we shall see, the METFORS clinicians had already fixed upon a wealth of such enabling practices, which were rapidly incorporated as permanent guides to classification and related decision-making in the facility. Consequently the medico-legal activities described throughout this book, based on my analysis of 1978 documents, are not only relevant to the operation of forensic agencies in the current decade, but more generally they facilitate an understanding of discretionary practices that prevail throughout the crime control apparatus (see Berki 1986; Cohen 1985; Garland 1985; Lowman, Menzies, and Palys 1987).

During its first year of operation in 1978, the METFORS Brief Assessment Unit provided clinical evaluations on 592 separate individuals. Five different professional groups were involved in these brief assessments. In the majority of cases, subjects were transported to the BAU from one of the local pre-trial detention centres, underwent clinical team interviews, and were returned to jail on the same afternoon accompanied by a letter dictated by the presiding psychiatrist to the trial judge (see Chapter 1).

These remands were ostensibly geared to determine the fitness to stand trial of the METFORS subjects, under the provisions of the Criminal Code of Canada. But as I began to observe the diagnostic practices of the professional teams and to inspect the documents being generated out of the evaluations, it became apparent that clinicians were addressing a range of other issues that were not directly sanctioned by law. On a routine basis they were making decisions about the general mental condition of accused persons. They were determining the need for further psychiatric assessment and treatment. They were recurrently predicting the dangerousness of patients to themselves and others (Webster and Menzies 1987). In their letters to the courts, psychiatrists were routinely forwarding specific sentencing recommendations to judges, even when assessments were being conducted at a pre-trial stage. Moreover, an inspection of the documents being compiled by the METFORS clinicians – the psychiatric letters, and the reports of nurses, social workers, psychologists, and correctional staff – left a marked impression that fitness to stand trial, in the majority of cases, was at best a secondary consideration. Most of the defendants remanded to the Brief Assessment Unit were clearly capable of undergoing the criminal process. Although almost everyone received some manner of psychiatric label, fewer than one in five was found to be unfit. In fact, among the 592 subjects only six were ultimately confined under a Warrant of the Lieutenant-Governor (see Chapter 1) as unfit or not guilty by reason of insanity.

The inescapable conclusion was that psychiatrists and other clinicians were primarily being employed by the courts as 'experts' in the direct and indirect selection of legal sanctions. Judges were referring accused persons to METFORS in order to compile information that would assist in the sentencing of criminal offenders. These forensic assessments were providing an apparently scientific foundation of knowledge upon which judicial decisions could be legitimately constructed. For their part, and despite the medical mantle that clothed their credentials, discourse, and self-image, the METFORS classifiers in practice were voicing orientations and offering solutions that were primarily legalistic in content and function. The clinicians were clearly adapting to the conditions of their occupational environment. They were grounding their classification strategies and documentary practices in the context of a system that demanded concrete solutions to pragmatic judicial problems. The METFORS professionals were irrevocably implicated in the legal ordering of their subjects. Their prescriptions were being routinely converted by the courts into overt legal judgments that enhanced state control over criminal defendants.

Moreover, it was apparent that the criminality and potential violence of subjects were a principal concern among the clinical assessors. The transactions between clinicians and clientele, and the documents yielded from the assessments, were saturated with references to the subjects' presumed threat to the community. Members were alert to official records and informal signs of prior assaultiveness. They routinely registered their predictions about the future dangerousness of subjects, and incorporated these into recommendations concerning bail, hospitalization, and incarceration. Whereas dangerousness was a subterranean issue among the clinical classifiers – in the sense that it is not formally recognized as a legitimate mandate for pre-trial assessments – in practice this construct was the organizing focus for a substantial proportion of forensic cases at METFORS. Despite the abundant evidence demonstrating the inability of psychiatrists and others to predict dangerousness (see Chapters 3 and 4; also Hinton 1983; Menzies and Webster 1987; Monahan 1981; Webster, Ben-Aron, and Hucker 1985; Webster, Dickens, and Addario 1985; Webster and Menzies 1987), the clinicians displayed little apparent concern about assuming this function. They regularly diagnosed dangerousness in the Brief Assessment Unit, and included these predictions in more than half of all psychiatric letters to the courts (see Chapters 3 and 5). Dangerousness was clearly a central problem in the processing of forensic subjects.

On the strength of these early observations, this study began as an attempt to evaluate the accuracy of forensic predictions about dangerousness to others. This initial work on predictive accuracy evolved into the first of three major subjects that are woven together throughout this book. During its first year of operation, clinical team members in the Brief Assessment Unit completed research instruments following each of the 592 forensic interviews, indicating their predictions of dangerousness on a five-point scale. In order to validate these judgments, it was necessary to investigate the criminal and violent conduct of subjects subsequent to their assessment at METFORS. This was done by consulting a number of official documents, over a two-year follow-up period, including criminal records, medical files in psychiatric institutions, and reports of assaults and other infractions incurred during penal incarceration. It was then possible to generate quantitative analyses of the relationship between the predictions of METFORS professionals and the follow-up conduct of their subjects, which were intended to replicate and extend similar outcome research in the forensic field (e.g. Quinsey 1979; Steadman and Cocozza 1974; Steadman and Morrissey 1981; Thornberry and Jacoby 1979; Walker and McCabe 1973). Moreover, the predictability of patients could then be assessed by matching their socio-demographic and medico-legal attributes against their registered levels of violence during the outcome period. This work provided the principal impetus for the research project during its early stages. The findings and implications of these quantitative analyses are described in Chapter 6 below.

The second general subject of this book began to surface as the prediction-outcome analyses were drawing to a close. As expected, the METFORS clinicians had demonstrated no apparent expertise in forecasting the future violence of accused persons. The emphasis of the investigation began to shift instead toward the actual construction of these forensic decisions, during both brief assessments and more protracted in-patient evaluations. From my informal observation work in the Brief Assessment Unit during the summer of 1978, I was struck by the similarity between the discretionary activities of the METFORS clinicians and the judgmental practices described in the socio-legal literature on police, prosecutors, judges, parole boards, and other judicial authorities. It seemed that the medical experts were engaged in an endeavour that was primarily legalistic instead of therapeutic. They were involved in the manufacture of labels, categories, and communications that were grounded in occupational and institutional interests, and most particularly in their need to present themselves as rational, authoritative, and dependable participants in the sanctioning process.

At the same time, these discretionary judgments about forensic issues appeared to be based in commonsensical rather than scientific discourse (see Berger and Luckmann 1967; Cicourel 1968; Ericson 1981, 1982; Ericson, Baranek, and Chan 1987; Geertz 1983; Gusfield 1981; Lofland 1969; Pfohl 1978; Strauss 1978). The experts were recurrently reproducing prior official records and decisions by other agents, or alternatively they were responding idiosyncratically to the face-to-face presentations of subjects. Yet their documentary products – clinical reports, letters to the courts, and so on – were couched in the scientific language of discovery *as if* something new were being uncovered through the vehicle of medical knowledge and clinical discovery.

These observations raised a number of questions that consistently resurfaced in the writing of this book. On what categories, assumptions, dimensions, and heuristics were these decisions really based? What was the relationship between prior determinations by other clinical and legal practitioners (for example, the police – see Chapter 2; and Menzies 1987a) and the assessments formulated at METFORS? Did these practices follow any discernible pattern? Were they anchored in legal categories or psychiatric nosology? Did identifiable differences develop among the labelling practices across different clinical disciplines, or across individual members? Were decisions related to the socio-cultural attributes or medico-legal histories of the METFORS patients? Did these judgments change, over time, during subsequent assessments of the same subjects? How did these decisions affect the sentencing practices of the criminal courts, and the follow-up experiences and institutional careers of the METFORS patients?

In the pursuit of these research questions, it was possible to use the original quantitative data base developed for the evaluation of dangerousness predictions. A total of 135 variables had been assembled to measure background characteristics, clinical and legal decisions, and outcome experiences for the entire cohort of patients (see Chapter 1). These variables were incorporated into a statistical analysis of the above issues, and the results are presented in detail in Chapters 1 through 5 below. The prominent feature emerging from these computations was the relatively weak relationship between the attributes of subjects and the decisions of the METFORS practitioners (see especially Chapter 3). The situational, indexical nature of forensic discretion dominated these judgments and left cavernous holes of unexplained variance in statistical attempts to account for the activities of clinicians.

This led to the qualitative analysis of the METFORS medical records that will be merged with the statistical work that follows. I was able to consult the documents compiled by the practitioners for each of the 592 subjects – including police records, clinical files, psychiatric court letters, psychological test results, social work interviews, and in-patient ward notations. In the end, these became the principal focus of the investigation into psychiatric discretion at METFORS. These reports provided the raw materials for a retrospective documentary analysis of clinicians' perceptions, typifications, constructions, and accounts. They allowed a reading, a rendition of imputational strategies (see Lofland 1969) as they were recorded and announced by team members. They were saturated with references to the recipes, categories, moral criteria, and improvised understandings through which clinicians made sense of their subjects and conveyed information to other enforcers.

The documentary analysis in this book is used to cast light on the fabric and dynamics of these official constructions of knowledge. By reproducing the clinical reports of the METFORS practitioners, I allow members wherever possible to 'speak for themselves,' and they do so with eloquence. Their philosophies of punishment and treatment, their labelling strategies, their presentations of scientific knowledgeability, and their contextual viewings of subjects emerge inexorably from a reading of their documentary accounts. Despite the specialist language and medical rhetoric aimed at demonstrating scientific neutrality, it was the commonsensical, moralistic, and pragmatic character of forensic discretion that emerged as the overarching reality in these classification exercises.

The third major subject of this book embarks in a somewhat different, but related, direction. Once the follow-up profiles of the METFORS patients had been compiled and integrated with police reports and medical records, it became possible to chart the longitudinal careers of persons over a considerable period of time. For a substantial proportion of the patient cohort, these careers were characterized by recurrent confrontations with criminal justice and mental health authorities. Legal subjects appeared to be caught up in cyclical patterns of control, as they were repeatedly institutionalized, deinstitutionalized, and reinstitutionalized through prisons, mental hospitals, and the community (see Menzies 1987b; Menzies and Webster 1987). In many instances penal and psychiatric modes of response seemed virtually interchangeable as they mutually co-ordinated, supplemented, and augmented their respective control capacity. These relations among carceral institutions have been of increasing interest to socio-legal scholars over the past decade (Cohen 1985; Garland 1985; Garland and Young 1983; Henry 1983; McMahon and Ericson 1987; Scull 1983), as they attempt to chart the contours and terrain of the 'transcarceral system' (Lowman, Menzies, and Palys 1987).

Forensic populations are especially vulnerable to these organizational forces, as they are exposed to the definitions and enforcement strategies of parallel systems, which exercise similar levels of power to intervene in their lives. Agencies such as METFORS function as gatekeepers, by allocating subjects to one or another level of this loosely co-ordinated medico-legal system (Emerson 1969, 1983; Hochstedler 1986; March and Olsen 1976; Menzies 1987b; Ranson, Hinings, and Greenwood 1980; Silverman 1970). Much of what follows – particularly in Chapters 4 through 6 – deals with the systemic relationships among judicial and psychiatric agencies, with their intricate networks of surveillance and enforcement, and with their collective impact on the institutional experiences, conduct, and outcome careers of the METFORS patients.

ORGANIZATION OF THE BOOK

In the following chapters I draw together these interrelated subjects as they pertain to the operation and impact of the Metropolitan Toronto Forensic Service. Chapter 1 introduces METFORS, its members and its clientele, traces the development of the research project, and offers an initial case study that highlights the role of METFORS in structuring the careers of its subjects.

In Chapter 2, the arrest reports of the METFORS patients are scrutinized, and the analysis focuses on police strategies in mobilizing the forensic clinic as an institutional resource, and in developing quasi-psychiatric strategies for managing mentally disordered subjects.

Chapter 3 looks at psychiatric discretion in the Brief Assessment Unit, applies quantitative and qualitative analysis to the collective decision-making of team members, and reviews a number of recipes and tactics by which the experts attributed mental disorder and dangerousness to their patients.

Chapter 4 examines the protracted assessments of the 123 subjects who were immediately remanded to the METFORS Inpatient Unit. This discussion focuses on the use of psychological test instruments, on the role of informants enlisted by social workers, and on the monitoring of disorder and danger on the in-patient ward.

Chapter 5 investigates the relationship between psychiatric recommendations and judicial sentencing decisions, and provides a summary of issues addressed in forensic court letters.

Finally, Chapter 6 charts the aftermath of forensic assessments, by tracing the two-year follow-up careers of the METFORS subjects, by exploring the relationship between psychiatric and judicial components of the 'trans-carceral system,' and by considering the broader implications of this study for medico-legal practice and policy in Canada and elsewhere.

1

Setting the Stage:
Context, Subjects, and Method

Man can be seen as a person or a thing ... Even the same thing, seen
from different points of view, gives rise to two entirely different descriptions, and the descriptions give rise to two entirely different theories, and
the theories result in two entirely different sets of action. The initial way
we see a thing determines all our subsequent dealings with it.

R.D. LAING   *The Divided Self*

The essence of knowledge is, having it, to apply it; not having it, to con-
fess your ignorance.

CONFUCIUS

AN INTRODUCTION TO METFORS

The Metropolitan Toronto Forensic Service is a pre-trial psychiatric remand
centre located in Toronto, Ontario. It occupies two storeys of the Queen
Street Mental Health Centre, a modern mental health facility in the west
end of the city. The fourth floor comprises the Brief Assessment Unit
(BAU), a maximum-security unit specializing in brief, multidisciplinary clinical evaluations for the courts.[1] The BAU includes two interviewing rooms
(one supplied with a one-way mirror for outside observers), a holding cell,
a security room for disruptive patients, and several offices used by members
of the clinical team.

Five occupational groups are attached to the Brief Assessment Unit. During the tenure of this study, a total of four psychiatrists, three psychologists, three social workers, seven nurses, and fourteen correctional officers participated in the brief assessments.[2] All members except correctional officers are recruited and paid directly by METFORS. The latter are supplied through an arrangement with the Ontario Ministry of Correctional Services, and are primarily responsible for maintaining the security of the facility.

The fifth floor holds a 23-bed medium-security Inpatient Unit designed for the administration of thirty- to sixty-day protracted assessments. METFORS is administered through its parent institution, the Clarke Institute of Psychiatry, which is located in another building in Toronto. At any given time, there are between sixty and seventy-five employees salaried by the agency, including clinicians, administrators, researchers, psychiatric assistants, clerical/secretarial staff, dieticians, and cleaners. METFORS receives an annual operating budget of approximately two million dollars from the Ontario Ministry of the Attorney-General (METFORS Annual Reports 1977–86).

The establishment of METFORS in 1977 was pre-dated by half a century of forensic history in the Southern Ontario region. In 1925, the provincial legislature had enacted provisions for the commission of offenders to the Toronto Psychiatric Hospital for medical observation. The judge or magistrate was empowered to order forensic assessments for an indefinite period of time, and ten hospital beds were set aside for court cases. From 1926 through 1956, a total of 4895 accused persons were remanded for an average term of more than a month (Gray 1952), and the annual frequency of referrals consistently increased (Watson, Rich, and Gray 1957). Throughout the first half of this century, the psychiatric professions were becoming progressively entrenched within the everyday workings of the legal apparatus.

In 1956 the Ontario government provided for the establishment of a single clinic for the evaluation of criminal defendants. Part IX of the Mental Hospitals Act mandated judges to remand accused persons to the Toronto Forensic Clinic for both evaluation and treatment (Turner 1966). Throughout the 1950s and 1960s, the facility specialized in cases of 'sexual deviation,' and institutional psychiatrists continually lobbied to extend the purview of their authority (Turner 1960; Turner, Hutchinson, and Williams 1958). Increasingly, the Clinic became allied not only with the criminal courts, but also with probation officers, out-patient facilities, independent physicians, after-care agencies, and other in-patient psychiatric institutions. This expanding network received further impetus from the publication of a Canadian Royal Commission Report in 1958, which recommended inter alia that judges should be empowered to refer anyone convicted of an indictable offence for clinical assessment, and that 'diagnostic centres' should be developed to facilitate this objective (McRuer 1958).

Meanwhile, the Toronto psychiatric community was actively engaged in establishing a moral and scientific foundation for expansion, and in solidifying its relationship with institutions of criminal justice. In concert with clinical and academic researchers, for example, members of the Toronto Forensic Clinic began to produce a substantial body of published material on a range of forensic subjects. These included articles and books about pedophilia and exhibitionism (Mohr, Turner, and Jerry 1964), sexual deviation (Gigeroff 1964), alcohol and mental functions (Hutchinson, Tuchtie, Gray, and Steinberg 1964), homicide and mental illness (McKnight, Mohr, Quinsey, and Erochko 1964), and dangerousness (Stokes and Turner 1964). The psychiatric profession's entrepreneurial activities were enhanced by jurists who were more than willing to distribute authority into ancillary agencies, and by the general consolidation of medical models concerning the relationship between crime and insanity (Robitscher 1980). For their part, legal psychiatrists were advancing the view that such problems were best resolved by diluting the punishment response with copious measures of medical intervention. One forensic psychiatrist, writing in the 1964 Annual Report of the Toronto Forensic Clinic, phrased the matter in the following rhetorical terms:

Psychiatry is a body of knowledge with various applications in the fields of human and social disabilities: none is more significant than that concerned with the offender, and with the ways in which offences against the law emerge as behavioural problems ... [I]n terms of human conservation punishment alone is not the simple answer to the violation of the society's law and order. The possibilities of restorative measures, of returning the erring member to a rightful place in the social matrix, are worthy of rational, cool-headed explorations ... The Forensic Clinic provides this rational approach to the criminal, his offence and the circumstances in which the violation of the law occurred ... The Forensic Clinic has indeed been fortunate in the establishment of a strong collaborative relationship with the courts: the medico-legal confluence has not yet become a flood of mutual endeavour but has attained a stream of common understanding. (Stokes, in Turner 1980: 202–3)

On 1 July 1966, the Clarke Institute of Psychiatry was opened in Toronto under the jurisdiction of the Ontario Mental Health Foundation Act. 'The legislation provided for the Institute to develop as a teaching, research and service hospital under a Board of Trustees and responsible ... to the Minister of Health. The Institute was recognized as a public hospital ... and it was enabled to function as a teaching hospital by means of an agreement with the University of Toronto' (Menzies, Webster, Butler, Turner, and Jensen 1978: 25–6). A wide range of psychiatric programs were launched by the Clarke Institute, including the extension of sexual treatment, child and adolescent care, research activities, and both in-patient and out-patient facilities for general psychiatric and forensic patients.

Concurrently, several additional forensic units were established in and around Toronto during the 1960s and 1970s. The Lakeshore Psychiatric Hospital and Queen Street Mental Health Centre (the two major psychiatric institutions in Toronto) each reserved several beds for in-patients being detained on medico-legal remands. A number of general hospitals began to admit forensic patients on both an in-patient and out-patient basis. Within a 100-mile radius of the city, four major mental hospitals (Whitby, St Thomas, Hamilton, and Penetanguishene) reserved facilities for forensic populations. The hospital at Penetang included a maximum-security unit for the criminally insane (Oak Ridge), which had been operating since the 1930s, and which held about 300 men transferred from the correctional system, involuntarily committed, or institutionalized under Warrants of the Lieutenant-Governor as insane or unfit to stand trial (Quinsey 1979). St Thomas contained the only ward in the province for female forensic patients hospitalized under conditions of maximum security.

By the early 1970s, the forensic system servicing Toronto had proliferated to the point where several hundred patients were under psychiatric observation at any given time. Still, there was lingering dissatisfaction among psychiatrists with existing arrangements for the *brief* assessment of accused persons awaiting trial. Clinical examiners were generally obliged to conduct these mental assessments within the holding cells of local jails and lock-ups (Boyd 1964). Further, delays were incurred by administrative problems in finding trained specialists, and in-jail examinations were routinely being performed by general practitioners with no special psychiatric expertise. The pressures to systematize brief assessments were being applied by the forensic community (to fill a perceived void in the medico-legal structure), and by correctional administrators (to relieve the jails of their most psychotic and disruptive inhabitants: cf. Allodi and Montgomery 1975).

In 1972 a provincial legislative committee on the 'Health Care System in the Ministry of Corrections' (Botterell 1972) addressed the efficacy of forensic psychiatric services in Ontario. The resulting report suggested that treatment ideals were being subverted by the increasing demands for psychiatric assessments. 'The practice of utilization of Ministry of Corrections psychiatrists for adult courts depletes the already inadequate Ministry psychiatric services to sick prisoners. It also makes it difficult to obtain the services of psychiatrists interested primarily in the clinical care of ill prisoners' (Botterell 1972: 169). The apparent solution lay in further specialization, through training a sufficient number of clinicians to focus primarily on forensic assessments, in an environment separate from both jails and conventional hospitals.

An Inter-Ministry committee was struck, in accordance with the report's recommendations (Botterell 1972: 230), with the mandate to design the administrative framework for such an arrangement. After convening five meetings during 1974, and after visiting court clinics in the United States, the committee determined that a court assessment facility should be constructed in the context of a larger forensic service, and should be affiliated with the provincial court system, the University of Toronto, and other mental hospitals in the city (Turner 1980). It proposed that both a maximum-security unit for brief assessments (handling about 5 per cent of the court system's caseload) and a 25-bed medium-security in-patient ward be constructed (Turner 1980: 206).

The committee's recommendations were forwarded to the Ontario cabinet in September 1976. After further administrative amendments, the Metropolitan Toronto Forensic Service was officially established by Order-in-Council on 15 May 1977.[3] The provincial ministries of health and the Attorney-General distributed a joint press release, which endeavoured to portray METFORS as the prototypically modern forensic facility, as the rational culmination of reform efforts among policy makers and practitioners alike. 'A Brief Assessment Unit will provide rapid psychiatric assessment for those appearing in the courts who may be identified as having serious psychiatric and emotional problems. Some may be assessed whether they are mentally fit to stand trial and others may be assessed who become emotionally disturbed during the trial process ... This is recognized as a pilot project for possible expansion to other areas of the province' (in Turner 1980: 207).

Then Ontario Attorney-General Roy McMurtry officially opened METFORS on 15 September 1977. His inauguration speech was the model of progressive reformist discourse (cf. Rothman 1980). Benefits were seen by the minister to be yielded from this new service to authorities, subjects, and the public in equal proportion. Considerations of civil liberties and due process were conspicuously absent from the announcement. METFORS was portrayed as a professionalized reform institution. Its operations were favourably contrasted with prior arrangements, which were seen to have consistently thwarted the benevolent intentions of the law and its practitioners. McMurtry declared:

As a lawyer who practiced in the courts for almost 20 years and as Attorney-General for Ontario, I can proudly testify as to the need for and desirability of this facility ... The previous system of obtaining psychiatric assessments of persons before the courts has caused a number of problems for the people involved, for the courts, and for the Correctional Services and Health programs of this province. It is my belief that this facility will enable us to overcome many of these problems while providing the necessary protection for the public. We expect that during the first year, the staff will handle up to 1000 referrals from the courts. Eventually, the facility could handle up to 3000 referrals annually ...[4] Where in the past it has often taken the courts weeks or months to obtain such assessments, this facility will be able to provide assessment reports to the courts in many places in a matter of days ... The expediting of these reports will meet ... professional standards ..., will benefit the person before the courts, the judicial process and the public. The procedure will in no way infringe on the rights of a person before the courts. (In Turner 1980: 207)

The 23-bed METFORS Inpatient Unit was immediately opened in September 1977, but the Brief Assessment Unit was not operative until January 1978. Prior to that date, the attending psychiatrists continued to conduct brief assessments in the confines of the local jails. During the intervening period, the BAU physical layout was prepared, staff were recruited and trained, and meetings and workshops were held to inform the judicial, correctional, and police communities of the role to be assumed by the agency. The METFORS catchment area encompasses the entire criminal court system in Metropolitan Toronto. From the inauguration of the BAU on 23 January 1978, two to four persons daily have been assessed by the interdisciplinary team. Defendants suspected of mental disorder are typically remanded by the presiding judge under section 615.1 of the Criminal Code of Canada. The majority of forensic subjects are transported to METFORS, on the morning of their assessment, directly from one of the three pretrial detention centres in the city.[5] They arrive at about 9:00 a.m. in the company of correctional officers, and are detained in the maximum-security holding unit on the premises of the Brief Assessment Unit.

During the initial hour of their detention, the BAU nurse conducts a preliminary interview in order to assemble background information about accused persons. Prior to the formal evaluation, the team members meet in the nurse's office to review these data, along with the arrest report that generally accompanies the patient to the unit. The team interview itself is usually of short duration, and is generally concluded in about twenty to fifty minutes. The subject is led to the interviewing room by the correctional officer, and is seated across from the team leader (almost always the psychiatrist), with other members positioned in a half-circle about eight to ten feet away. Following the examination, the individual is returned to the holding cell, is provided with a lunch, and is ultimately returned to the jail at three or four o'clock in the afternoon. Meanwhile, the clinical team engages in a summary discussion of each case immediately subsequent to the interrogation. Interviews are usually completed by late morning (depending on the number of defendants present for the day). Each member prepares an individual report on the subject, and the psychiatrist dictates a letter to the judge that is returned with the accused to the detention centre. The team clinicians convene briefly once more in the afternoon to forze their recommendations, and these are usually communicated to the bject, prior to his or her departure, by either the psychiatrist or the nurse.

Three general dispositional options are available to the clinical personnel. In the majority of cases, the defendant is simply returned to the jurisdiction of the court to await trial, with or without a specific psychiatric recommendation. Alternatively, when the patient is perceived to be both mentally ill and imminently dangerous (to self and/or others), the psychiatrist may invoke involuntary hospitalization either to the METFORS Inpatient Unit, to another psychiatric facility in or around Toronto, or more commonly to the maximum-security unit at Oak Ridge (about 100 miles north of Toronto). Finally, approximately 30 per cent of patients are referred for an extended thirty- to sixty-day in-patient assessment at METFORS or another hospital (see Chapter 4). These subjects, unless they are perceived to be in need of immediate medical intervention, will be returned to the court with a recommendation for protracted assessment, and ordered to hospital by the judge at the next court appearance. Both the federal Criminal Code and Ontario's Mental Health Act empower the court to initiate long-term forensic remands. The relevant sections of both acts are summarized below:

CANADIAN CRIMINAL CODE

s.537 (1)(b) A justice acting under this Part may remand an accused to such custody as the justice directs for observation for a period not exceeding thirty days, where, in his opinion, supported by the evidence, or where the prosecutor and the accused consent, by the report in writing, of at least one duly qualified medical practitioner, there is reason to believe that

(iii) the accused may be mentally ill.

(2) Notwithstanding paragraph (1b), a justice acting under this Part may remand an accused in accordance with that paragraph (a) for a period not exceeding thirty days without having heard the evidence or considered the report of a duly qualified medical practitioner where compelling circumstances exist for so doing and where a medical practitioner is not readily available to examine the accused and give evidence or submit a report

(b) for a period of more than thirty days but not exceeding sixty days where he is satisfied that observation for such a period is required in all the circumstances of the case and his opinion is supported by the evidence or, where the prosecutor and the accused consent, by the report in writing of at least one duly qualified medical practitioner.

s.615 (1) A court, judge or provincial court judge may, at any time before verdict, where it appears that there is sufficient reason to doubt that the accused is, on account of insanity, capable of conducting his defence, direct that an issue be tried whether the accused is then, on account of insanity, unfit to stand his trial.

(2) A court, judge, or provincial court judge may, at any time before verdict or sentence, when of the opinion, supported by the evidence or, where the prosecutor and the accused consent, by the report in writing, of at least one duly qualified medical practitioner, that there is reason to believe that (a) an accused is mentally ill, by order in writing (b) remand the accused to such custody as the court, judge, or provincial court judge directs for observation for a period not exceeding thirty days.

(3) Identical to s.465(2), *mutatis mutandis.*

(7) Where the verdict is that the accused is unfit on account of insanity to stand his trial, the court, judge or provincial court judge shall order that the accused be kept in custody until the pleasure of the lieutenant-governor of the province is known, and any plea that has been pleaded shall be set aside and the jury shall be discharged.

s.681 (1,2) refer to the power of remand held by the court of appeal, *mutatis mutandis.*

s.803 (5) refers to the power of remand held by the summary conviction court, *mutatis mutandis.*

ONTARIO MENTAL HEALTH ACT

s.14 (1) Where a judge has reason to believe that a person who appears before him charged with or convicted of an offence suffers from mental disorder [defined in s.1(f) as 'any disease or disability of the mind'] the judge may order the person to attend a psychiatric facility for examination.

(2)   Where an examination is made under this section, the senior physician shall report in writing to the judge as to the mental condition of the person.

In the general context of this legal structure and institutional climate, the new facility received an enthusiastic response from the judicial, correctional, and psychiatric communities. During the first year alone, 686 brief assessments[6] and 226 in-patient evaluations were completed by the METFORS clinical staff. By June 1981, over 2500 assessments had already been performed, and over 350 patients had been interviewed on two or more occasions. Through the formalization of this co-ordinated forensic system in Toronto, and through the enlistment of co-operation from police and court personnel, the routine administration of brief assessments at METFORS was quickly accomplished. Significantly, scant attention was seemingly paid by practitioners to the social control implications of this new procedure. As the chairman of the METFORS Board wrote: 'None of us doubted that the staff ... would first and foremost obey their primary obligation as mental health professionals to the persons who become their patients, even when it is clear that there is also the obligation to report accurately and fully about their status to the courts. Similarly, none of us believed that the officials of the state would place pressure on health professionals of the sort that would put them in conflict with their consciences or their professional obligations' (METFORS Fifth Annual Report 1981: xiii–ix).

The practising clinicians emphasized the voluntary, therapeutic, ethical (Butler and Turner 1980), and non-coercive nature of the brief assessment. 'It should be pointed out that the patient's involvement in the process is quite voluntary[7] and, when requisite, we obtain the necessary Release of Information from the patient. We attempt to contact the patient's lawyer[8] and inform him about our assessment' (METFORS Third Annual Report 1979: 22). By the end of the first twelve months, twenty-two criminal court judges had each remanded at least ten of their defendants to the BAU (Webster, Menzies, and Jackson 1982: 15). The following comments of one Toronto provincial judge are representative.

During the past year, I had occasion to call upon the Brief Assessment Unit. After some ten days of a joint trial, submissions were made to me that a certain accused (who had been in custody for a year and had never in his life been seen by a psychiatrist) was unfit to continue with his trial because of insanity. Fortunately, I was able to remand that person to METFORS; in 4 days, after a brief assessment, the accused returned to court. The comprehensive report and its authors convinced me that although the accused might be a nominee for an 'Oscar', he was fit to stand trial and was not within the purview of Section 16 of the Criminal Code.[9] There is nothing that speaks as eloquently as the 'satisfied customer'; on the subject of the Metropolitan Toronto Forensic Service, there are scores of judges who, as I do, classify themselves as 'satisfied customers'. Since nothing succeeds like success, there is only one thing left for me to say to the Board of Directors at METFORS, its Director and all its personnel: ENCORE. (METFORS Fourth Annual Report 1980: vii)

By the early 1980s, then, METFORS was firmly entrenched on the terrain of the city's criminal court system. The 'good working arrangements' that developed between the clinic and the courts should be read as an index of wider adjustments and accommodations on the frontiers of psychiatric and legal control systems. Satellite agencies like METFORS come to emulate, in function and identity, the master institutions with which they interact. In the case of the Metropolitan Toronto Forensic Service, the clinicians rapidly learned to embrace goals and philosophies that are quite foreign to conventional therapeutic ideals. Yet they had little option, since the acceptance of METFORS within the judicial apparatus was based on the presumption that its members were, consciously or unknowingly, working to amplify state authority over criminal defendants. For all practical purposes, these forensic assessors were soon to become more legal than medical practitioners.

In response, METFORS has encountered vocal opposition from the civil liberties community (Levy 1980; Mewett 1980; Tacon 1979). Legal opponents have identified a litany of questionable practices. First, there is no statutory authority for *ordering* defendants to undergo a brief psychiatric remand in custody (Levy 1980: 1). Second, because a psychiatrist is not a 'person-in-authority' under Canadian law, there is no protection against self-incrimination during the course of the assessment (Schiffer 1978: 31–42; Tacon 1979; Verdun-Jones 1981). Third, the 'voluntary and informed' character of subject consent is highly problematic, given the awesome compliance pressures being applied by the legal system, and given the seriously psychotic and debilitated condition of many remandees (Tacon 1979). Fourth, pre-trial psychiatric diversion has historically functioned to extend rather than curtail the length of confinement for accused persons (McGarry 1971). Fifth, the routine acceptance of clinical recommendations by criminal court judges short-circuits any pretence of judicial review over psychiatric decisions (see Chapter 5 below). Sixth, METFORS personnel commonly address issues (for example, suitability for bail, need for imprisonment, dangerousness) which are outside of their statutory legal authority. Seventh, only a minority of METFORS patients are represented by legal counsel, and fewer still have attorneys present during their assessment. Eighth, the thirty- to sixty-day Inpatient Unit evaluation represents a period of confinement without a systematic program of treatment, and it often produces recommendations that are no different from those yielded by prior one-day assessments (Roesch and Golding 1980).

Levy suggests that remands to METFORS are engineered through an 'indirect back-door route which is used to get them to the hospital' (1980: 1). From this perspective, METFORS is a component of the pre-trial penal system (Feeley 1979), which is in real terms no less coercive than the post-sentence machinery. According to Levy, its legitimizing rhetoric notwithstanding, METFORS overtly operates to punish recalcitrant or uncooperative subjects. 'The "failure to cooperate" (even where the accused has refused to consent to the assessment in Court and even if the accused has been advised by Counsel not to cooperate) may well have the effect of inducing the judge ... to order that the accused be returned to METFORS for a thirty-day or thirty-to-sixty-day assessment ... This may even be done where the individual is charged with a trifling offence where there would have ordinarily been an immediate bail hearing' (1980: 3). Levy concludes that the expanding authority of METFORS practitioners must be curtailed: 'METFORS has taken on the impossible task of being a hospital/prison. The accused is being transformed into a new creature – a patient/accused/prisoner ... It is only one short step to the state imposing psychiatric examination at METFORS, or other such institutions, on individuals who have not even been drawn into the criminal justice system ... METFORS has been permitted to go too far too quickly' (Levy 1980: 6–7).

THE RESEARCH

From the opening of the Brief Assessment Unit on 23 January 1978, medical records were compiled on all patients evaluated by the clinical teams. These documents included the arresting police officers' report, the intake nurse's preliminary data sheet, reports of the forensic psychologist and social worker, the psychiatrist's letter to the court, and on occasion, files procured from other hospitals. Similar materials were collected on subjects remanded for protracted assessment in the Inpatient Unit. For the latter group, psychological reports digested the results of test batteries; in-patient social worker reports typically included summaries of interviews with family members; and psychiatrists maintained a log of their contacts with patients, the administration of psychotropic drugs, the results of medical examinations, electroencephalograms (EEGS), and so on. In addition, on the Inpatient Unit, detailed progress notes were compiled by nurses and psychiatric assistants, monitoring the behaviour of individuals on the ward, the occurrence of unusual or otherwise 'significant' events, and transactions with relevance for the medico-legal issues under investigation.

Supplementary to these medical records, one-page summary forms were developed for each of the five METFORS professions, which were to be completed immediately following each patient's assessment on the BAU (the psychiatrists' form is reproduced in Appendix A). These instruments allowed a rapid accumulation of quantitative data about the individual's socio-demographic status, his or her psychiatric and legal background, the nature of the current charge, his or her attitude and behaviour while on the unit, and other related epidemiological variables. As well, the BAU clinicians were asked to furnish judgments on a three-point scale (no, uncertain, yes) concerning such issues as fitness for trial and bail, mental disorder, certifiability, and the need for hospitalization, further assessment and/or custodial confinement. Attributions of dangerousness (to self and others, in the present and in the future) were elicited on a five-point scale (no, low, questionable, medium, high). Finally, the presiding psychiatrists used the forms to indicate their diagnosis of the subject (according to ICDA-9 classification),[10] and to make a recommendation concerning the individual's final disposition.

The METFORS medical dossiers (for brief and protracted assessments) and the BAU assessment instruments (brief assessments only) were compiled for every patient interviewed from 23 January 1978 until year's end. These materials constituted the major source of information on the patient's background and characteristics, and on the construction of clinical decisions by the METFORS personnel.

During the course of 1978, the METFORS research department received two major government grants to investigate, respectively, the pre-trial assessment process in Canada, and the prediction of dangerousness by forensic clinicians. As the year progressed, the BAU one-page assessment instruments were statistically analysed, and a number of reports were published on the dynamics of the assessment process (Menzies, Webster, Butler, Turner, and Jensen 1978), the characteristics of forensic patients (Webster, Butler, Turner, Jackson, and Menzies 1978), and the parameters of clinical decisions (Menzies, Webster, Butler, Jensen, and Turner 1980). This work also produced a study of 248 evaluations in six Canadian cities during July 1978 (Menzies, Webster, Butler, and Turner 1980; Webster, Menzies, Butler, and Turner 1982), an overview of legal issues involved in the forensic assessment (Menzies, Webster, and Jackson 1981), and a general book on the subject of forensic remands (Webster, Menzies, and Jackson 1982).

The decision to incorporate a follow-up of the 1978 assessments came as something of an afterthought. Originally, research on the subsequent careers of METFORS patients was focused on issues connected to the prediction of dangerousness, and was to be confined to a sample of 203 persons remanded from February through June 1979 (Menzies, Webster, and Sepejak 1985a). Eventually, though, we decided to expand the study to include a two-year follow-up study of the 1978 Brief Assessment Unit cohort.

The accumulation of outcome data, and the development of quantitative indices of dangerousness and other attributes, posed several difficulties. Early on, we elected to confine the follow-up search to official correctional and psychiatric sources only. The option of contacting and interviewing subjects was discarded for two reasons. First, the METFORS patients are a diversified and mobile population, and the logistics of locating and soliciting the co-operation of such a large group were clearly formidable. Second, serious ethical problems would inevitably surface during the collection of private knowledge about the criminal and violent conduct perpetrated by these people. Such data would not have been under the protection of legal privilege, and in a real sense such interviews would have presented a tangible threat to the subjects.

Conversely, the central problem in using these official sources emerges from the 'dark figure' of undetected conduct which tends to elude institutional records of any kind. For the purposes of an outcome study relying on correctional and hospital data, researchers have to assume that the curves of real and registered conduct run parallel, that subjects without official entries have indeed refrained from any form of disruptive or violent behaviour. This requires no small assurance about the comprehensiveness and authenticity of the follow-up data.

To combat these constraints, this project was geared to constructing outcome profiles that would incorporate the maximum pool of official information available on the METFORS patients. A total of 592 subjects were followed up during the outcome period. These comprised all consecutive brief assessments by the BAU clinical teams from 23 January to 31 December 1978 ($N = 657$), minus the second or subsequent assessments on the same individuals ($N = 54$), and minus 11 patients who were re-evaluated during the 1979 study mentioned above.[11]

The follow-up period was set at two years for all subjects. Exactly twenty-four months after each brief assessment (i.e. from 23 January to 31 December 1980), researchers consulted the computerized files of the Ontario Ministry of Correctional Services central registry. These data included the court's sentence for the original charge leading to assessment, all further arrests and convictions during the two-year follow-up, types and lengths of dispositions, and all institutional misconducts registered during confinement in Ontario provincial jails or prisons. Additionally, the medical records of METFORS, and of six other psychiatric hospitals within a 100-mile radius of Toronto,[12] were reviewed for evidence of in-patient or out-patient contacts with the patient cohort.

From the initial content analysis of correctional and hospital files, we found that 408 of the subjects had experienced at least one contact with either system, above and beyond those connected to the original criminal charge. These incidents were classified into four general categories: (1) criminal charges, (2) prison misconducts, (3) incidents leading to psychiatric in-patient or out-patient admissions, (4) incidents recorded on ward notes during hospitalization. Profiles were reconstructed from these data, and were used as the primary materials for several preliminary reports (Menzies, Webster, and Sepejak 1985b; Sepejak, Menzies, Webster, and Jensen 1983).

During 1982 and 1983, it became possible to supplement these data with follow-up materials extracted from other sources. One research assistant surveyed the Toronto Coroner's Office files for possible deaths among the 283 patients who had no further hospital or correctional contacts following the two-year outcome period. As it happened, ten subjects had in fact died, three by means of suicide. Next, the Medical and Health Care Services of the Canadian Penitentiary Headquarters furnished print-outs on the forty individuals who had spent at least part of the two years in the federal correctional system.[13] These documents included the dates and locations of imprisonment and transfer, the nature of offences leading to federal imprisonment, synopses of medical and other reports on the prisoners, and misconducts recorded against inmates during their institutional confinement. Finally, the Investigation Services of the Royal Canadian Mounted Police co-operated in supplying CPIC (Canadian Police Information Centre) records on 154 persons whose court disposition was missing and/or who could not be accounted for by hospital or correctional records during the entire twenty-four-month period. These files were especially useful in re-constructing the Canadian criminal records of subjects outside of Ontario.

All of the above materials supplemented the original data to generate the final two-year outcome profiles of the METFORS patients. Sample profiles are displayed in Appendix B. These encompass the court disposition for 587 subjects (five were missing), all criminal charges and violent behaviours registered against subjects, and a record of their institutional careers (including provincial and federal imprisonment, psychiatric in-patient and out-patient hospitalization, probation, parole, mandatory supervision, and time spent in the community). Missing from these profiles were an unknown number of hospital contacts outside of the 100-mile radius of Toronto, accurate correctional records at the provincial level outside of Ontario, as well as incarceration misconducts recorded in the nine other provincial systems. Further, twenty-one of the 592 subjects were excluded entirely from the outcome portion of the analysis. As mentioned above, ten had died. Four people failed to register on any of the data files, and seven left the country (see Appendix C).

The final step in developing the data base involved aggregating these various materials into discrete files for each patient, and developing a coding procedure for the generation of quantitative measures. These operations consumed the better part of a year, from August 1982 to September 1983. Research assistants photocopied and de-identified the patients' METFORS records, which comprised the police report, admission sheet, clinical progress notes, letter to the court, and in-patient records (including ward notes) where applicable. These were combined with the one-page assessment forms completed by the BAU clinicians, the record of court dispositions, and the full two-year outcome profiles to generate the final research files for each patient. Over 20,000 pages of data were accumulated and organized through this process.

Next, we formulated a coding manual in order to transcribe the file record information into a form suitable for computer analysis. A total of 135 variables were transferred onto Fortran coding sheets, and subsequently keypunched using the Michigan Terminal System (MTS) at Simon Fraser University. The data analysis enlisted the Statistical Package for the Social Sciences (SPSSX). There were twelve general categories of variables:

1 Demographic characteristics of patients, including legal and psychiatric histories.
2 Precipitating criminal charges and remarks of arresting officers concerning mental disorder and potential for violent behaviour.

3 Decisions of the BAU clinicians, extracted from the single-page summary forms.
4 Presentation and behaviour of subjects while in the Brief Assessment Unit.
5 Information about subsequent in-patient assessments, including behaviour on wards and length of time in hospital.
6 Content analysis of BAU and Inpatient Unit letters to the criminal court judge (diagnoses, recommendations, references to dangerousness, etc.).
7 Court dispositions.
8 Length of time between arrest and BAU assessment, and between assessment and sentence.
9 Further forensic assessments during the twenty-four-month follow-up.
10 Criminal and violent conduct recorded during the outcome period, and totalled after one month, three months, six months, one year, and two years.
11 Number of post-assessment hospitalizations, imprisonments, and length of time spent in hospital, in prison, on probation, and in the community.
12 Institutional status of subjects at the conclusion of the follow-up study.

These data needed to be worked into a multiple research design that incorporated both statistical and qualitative materials. The aggregate distributions of subject attributes, clinical decisions, and institutional experiences on their own could provide only a partial account of the forensic process. They had to be integrated with an interpretive reading of documents produced by legal and medical authorities. In Chapters 2 through 6, numerous case illustrations – from police reports, clinical records, progress notes, psychiatric letters, and correctional files – are employed to 'saturate' categories that emerged from the statistical analyses (cf. Glaser and Strauss 1967). This interplay of two methodological approaches provides an appreciative understanding of the structure of rules and resources and the system of organizational relations (Giddens 1979) as they were recognized and recorded by institutional members. By reproducing the accounts of clinicians, police, and others, aggregated summaries can be supplemented with a direct representation of inferential work conducted by these professionals (Denzin 1978a, b). An array of questions emerge from the analysis of institutional documents, that are fundamentally concerned with the ontological meaning of the thoughts and actions represented in these reports (Schatzman and Strauss 1973: 11).

At the same time, these official documents are still at best second-order constructions. Systematic field-work was not feasible as a research method

at METFORS, given the reluctance of clinicians to permit ongoing observations of their activities – and given our own concerns about intruding
on the interview process, and about violating the patients' rights to withhold voluntary and informed consent. As a result, we were unable to
monitor the everyday routines of members longitudinally over an extended
period of time.

In this sense, the study is governed by the limitations that prevail in
most sociological research based on official data. It would be untenable to
use the accounts of psychiatrists and other authorities as 'objective' descriptions of process, or to assume that they would be comparable with
the experiences of patients or of any third-party observer. Moreover, it
would be methodologically unsound and conceptually tautological to extract *causal rules* from these constructions, and then to invoke these rules
to 'explain' the sense-making practices of team members (Imershein and
Simons 1976).

None the less, these official accounts provide an important source of
materials for understanding the discretionary work of clinicians and other
officials. Categories and recipes for organizing medico-legal reality emerge
in the very production of these documents. If they did not describe transactions as they 'actually' occurred, these accounts did provide a construction of events as they were *seen* to occur by clinicians, and it was upon
these indexical versions of reality that patients were labelled, confined, and
launched into institutional careers of deviance. In other words, the METFORS
reports were *both* descriptive *and* justificatory, and these two functions
cannot be separated in the course of a documentary analysis. Research of
this kind must be sensitive to the processes through which official accounts
inevitably refract and reorder the 'facts' on which they are based. These
'facts' may be inaccessible or irretrievable, but this does not preclude an
appreciative understanding of the construction process itself. As subsequent chapters will demonstrate, clinicians and other officials expressed
their inferences and intentions with clarity and conviction. They routinely
exposed the construction process in the act of writing about it. By concentrating on the documentary accounts of forensic assessments, much can
be learned about the recipes and strategies informing the accounting process
itself.

THE METFORS PATIENTS

The personal and clinical attributes of pre-trial forensic patients have been
described in great detail by a number of authors (Geller and Lister 1978;

Gibbens, Soothill, and Pope 1977; Gostin 1977; Greenland and Rosenblatt 1972; Henn, Herjanic, and Vanderpearl 1977; Laczko, James, and Alltop 1970; Parker and Tennent 1979; Pfeiffer, Eisenstein, and Dobbs 1967; Roesch and Golding 1980). In general terms, these people present a wide diversity of behavioural, legal, and epidemiological backgrounds. Precipitating charges may range from 'Creating a disturbance' to 'First-degree murder'; their psychiatric diagnosis from 'Normal' to 'Chronic paranoid schizophrenia.'

The one consistent and common denominator can be found in the marginality of their social and institutional existence. Like criminal defendants in every Western jurisdiction, individuals facing psychiatric assessment are typically dependent, dispossessed, powerless people caught up in a system over which they exercise little knowledge or control (Baldwin and McConville 1977; Carlen 1976; Ericson and Baranek 1982; Feeley 1979). These are the semi-institutionalized and pre-institutionalized populations described by Scull (1983), Lerman (1982), Segal and Aviram (1978), Cohen (1979, 1985), and others, who are subjects of multiple interlocking control systems, and whose deviant careers repeatedly encounter the forces of criminal justice, mental health, and welfare (Chan and Ericson 1981; Cohen 1985; Donzelot 1979; Garland and Young 1983; Lowman, Menzies, and Palys 1987; Menzies 1982).

A survey of the 592 METFORS patients amply demonstrates both their marginal existence as fringe members of society and the frequency of their collective confrontations with control systems. Descriptions of the cohort are displayed in Table 1.1 and Appendix D. The METFORS patients were predominantly drawn from the population of young, disenfranchised, unemployed, often homeless urban poor. Over 90 per cent of the subjects were male. Their mean age was 29.3 years, with 61.4 per cent under the age of 30. Only one person in five had more than eleven years of education. Forty-one per cent of patients lived alone, in a boarding-house or institution; another 21 per cent had no fixed address at the time of arrest. Of 592 individuals, 364 (61.5 per cent) were single, and a further 134 were either separated, divorced, or widowed. Almost three-quarters ($N = 427$) of the subjects were unemployed at arrest; there were only 23 'skilled' workers, 14 white-collar workers, 4 professionals, and 21 students among the entire cohort. Just over a third ($N = 217$) had been born in Toronto; 202 patients were from elsewhere in Canada; the remainder had immigrated from Europe (83), the Caribbean and South America (28), Great Britain (24), the United States (16), Asia (9), and Africa or the Middle East (7).

An inspection of legal histories elicited similar patterns of social

TABLE 1.1
Characteristics of BAU patients

	Number	%	Mean
Gender			
Male	534	90.2	
Female	58	9.8	
Age			29.3
Less than 20	111	18.8	
20–29	252	42.6	
30–39	126	21.3	
40–49	67	11.3	
50–59	25	4.2	
60–69	9	1.4	
70 or greater	2	0.4	
Years of education			9.4
Less than 5	26	4.4	
5–8	163	27.6	
9–11	282	47.6	
12–13	93	15.7	
14 or more	28	4.7	
Marital status			
Single	364	61.5	
Separated	72	12.2	
Divorced	52	8.8	
Widowed	10	1.7	
Cohabiting	38	6.4	
Married	56	9.5	
Race			
White	522	88.7	
Black	44	7.5	
Oriental	4	0.7	
Asian/Other	7	1.2	
North American Indian	11	1.9	
Living status			
Alone	207	35.0	
With family	173	29.2	
With friend/lover	49	8.3	
Hostel/Boarding-house	24	4.1	
Institution	13	2.2	
No fixed address	125	21.2	
Occupation			
Unemployed	427	72.1	
Labourer	50	8.4	
Semiskilled	42	7.1	

TABLE 1.1 (continued)

	Number	%	Mean
Skilled	23	3.9	
White collar	14	2.4	
Student	21	3.5	
Management-professional	4	0.7	
Retired	4	0.7	
Mentally/Physically disabled	7	1.2	
Number of previous convictions			3.6
None	126	21.3	
1	90	15.2	
2	87	14.7	
3–5	180	30.5	
6–10	57	9.7	
11–20	48	8.1	
21 or more	3	0.5	
Number of prior violence convictions			0.8
None	350	59.2	
1	126	21.3	
2	53	9.0	
3–5	55	9.3	
6–8	7	1.2	
Juvenile record			
No	423	72.3	
Yes	162	27.7	
Previous post-sentence incarceration			
No	313	52.9	
Yes	279	47.1	
Psychiatric experience as juvenile			
None	483	82.3	
Out-patient	44	7.5	
In-patient	60	10.2	
Number of prior in-patient admissions			2.2
None	281	47.5	
1	96	16.2	
2	51	8.6	
3–5	86	14.5	
6–10	55	9.3	
11–20	19	3.2	
21 or more	4	0.7	
Previous suicide attempt			
No	433	73.1	
Yes	159	26.9	

TABLE 1.1 (continued)

	Number	%	Mean
Level of alcohol use			
None	44	7.5	
Low	154	26.1	
Medium	133	22.5	
High	259	43.9	
Level of drug use–other			
None	182	30.8	
Low	164	27.8	
Medium	98	16.6	
High	146	24.7	
Estimated IQ by psychologist			
Retardation	16	2.7	
Borderline retardation	50	8.5	
Dull normal	120	20.3	
Average	292	49.5	
Bright normal	100	16.9	
Superior	12	2.0	

marginality. Over one-quarter of patients ($N = 162$) had a juvenile arrest record prior to the age of seventeen. Only 21.3 per cent had not been convicted of a criminal offence previous to their current arrest. Eighteen per cent had more than five prior convictions, and 9 per cent had more than ten. Convictions for offences of violence had been registered at some time in the past against 242 individuals (40.8 per cent), and 259 (42.1 per cent) were at present accused of an offence of violence in their primary criminal charge. Almost one-half of the group ($N = 279$) had spent time in prison.

In Table 1.2, the breakdowns of charges, along with four other background descriptive variables, are compared for the METFORS patients, against a cross-section of all remanded accused persons housed in Ontario jails one month prior to the beginning of the study (Madden 1978: 20, 29). Clearly, the forensic patients were not entirely representative of remanded defendants in the province. The METFORS subjects were generally older than the general remand population, there was a higher proportion of women selected for psychiatric assessment, and patients were less likely to have a high school education. There were fewer METFORS patients than prison remand inmates with *no* previous conviction (21.3 per cent against 27.9 per cent). Finally, there was a substantially higher representation of

TABLE 1.2
Comparing METFORS patients with the Ontario in-jail remand population

	All remanded accused persons in Ontario (%)	METFORS patients (%)	% difference
Charge type			
Violence*	24.6	43.8	+19.2
Property	32.1	25.0	−7.1
Public order†	20.6	24.6	+4.0
Non-violent sexual	3.0	5.6	+2.6
Drugs/alcohol	14.2	0.7	−13.5
Traffic	5.5	0.3	−5.2
Gender			
Male	95.5	90.2	−5.3
Female	4.5	9.8	+5.3
Years of education			
8 or fewer	23.7	32.0	+8.3
9–13	72.5	63.3	−9.2
Post-secondary	3.8	4.7	+0.9
Age			
Less than 20	44.1	18.8	−25.3
20–29	32.8	42.6	+9.8
30–49	19.7	32.6	+12.9
50 or greater	3.4	6.0	+2.6
Previous convictions			
None	27.9	21.3	−6.6
1–2	25.6	29.9	+4.3
3–9	24.1	38.7	+14.6
10 or more	22.5	10.1	−12.4

* Robbery was originally coded as a property offence in the Madden (1978) report. This was relocated to the 'violence' category in the present table.
† 'Technical-administrative' offences were collapsed with public order offences for METFORS patients.

violent charges against the person in the Brief Assessment Unit (43.8 per cent, as opposed to 24.6 per cent among the prison remands). The proportion of non-violent sex offenders was somewhat higher in the BAU (5.6 per cent compared to 3.0 per cent), but neither drug, alcohol, nor traffic offenders were likely to be referred by the courts for psychiatric assessment.

Returning to Table 1.1 and to Appendix D, the METFORS patients also exhibited intensive clinical histories. Over one-half of the group had at least one previous in-patient admission to a psychiatric hospital. Ten per cent had been hospitalized while they were still under the age of sixteen. Seventy-eight individuals had more than five previous admissions, and twenty-three persons more than ten. There was a high level of alcohol and drug consumption evident throughout the group: 259 persons (43.9 per cent) were rated as 'high' alcohol consumers on a four-point scale by the clinical team, and 146 (24.7 per cent) used 'high' quantities of other drugs. Over one-quarter of the cohort ($N = 159$) had attempted suicide at some point in their lives. A total of 201 persons (34.0 per cent) were classified as personality disordered on their primary diagnosis, and 151 (25.5 per cent) as functionally psychotic. Only eight BAU patients emerged from the assessment with the label 'no mental illness.'

In total, the METFORS psychiatrists invoked eighty-four different clinical classifications on their subjects. Virtually no one exited from the process without at least one medical label, and the diversity of categories was impressive. Twenty separate types of personality disorder were identified, eight different kinds of paranoia. Neurotic disorders ranged from 'situational disturbance' to 'institutional neurosis' to 'stammering and stuttering.' The six most frequent diagnoses were in descending order: antisocial personality disorder (85), unspecified personality disorder (39), paranoid schizophrenia (32), chronic alcoholism (27), situational disturbance (26), chronic undifferentiated schizophrenia (25), and habitual excessive drinking (25).

Taken as a whole, the clinical labelling of the METFORS subjects combined with their socio-legal histories to depict a marginal population who had in many cases been free-floating for years between medical and legal institutions, and who were recurrently vulnerable to the powerful imputations of judicial and psychiatric authorities. In what follows we begin to explore the continuation of these medico-legal careers within the confines of the METFORS corridor.

A SUBJECT'S-EYE VIEW OF THE PROCESS

A Panoramic View of the Forensic Corridor
The Introduction to this book described some of the medico-legal conditions under which accused persons are engulfed by the forensic system. Defendants remanded for psychiatric assessment are institutional raw material, subject to a coding process that accentuates and distorts their experience of being deviant. The control structures of law and medicine merge

into a relatively integrated framework that absorbs participating authorities and conscript clientele alike. Any socio-legal analysis of these organizational forces must be sensitive to the progressive accumulation of official labels that are formulated around accused persons. Imputations of criminality and mental disorder pile up and are reinforced as individuals and information are conveyed from one subsystem to the next. The diverse institutions and agents in the medico-legal process are bound to and bonded by powerful ties, and their interactions sustain a continuity of control which is applied with increasing intensity toward the mentally ill offender.

This section surveys the 'progress" of the METFORS patients, first by tracking the entire cohort through the course of the study, and second by narrating in detail the case history of a selected individual. Figure 1.1 portrays the systemic channelling of the 592 METFORS patients through the interlocking judicial and clinical network. The ten columns identify the number of subjects who were assigned to various official categories at each successive stage in the process. This path diagram permits an initial panoramic view of the entire chain of events, which is subsequently broken down into component stages in Chapters 2 through 6. Moreover, Figure 1.1 provides a holistic perspective on the accumulative sequence of official responses, referrals, and discretionary decisions as they influenced the careers of the METFORS remand cohort.

In the leftmost column of Figure 1.1,[14] the correctional status of subjects at the point of their arrest broke down as follows: 293 (51 per cent) were at liberty, 149 (26 per cent) were on probation or parole, 97 people were on bail, 23 were unlawfully at large, and 7 were arrested while they were in prison.[15] Violent charges were laid against 280 of the BAU patients (49 per cent). Twenty-five per cent were charged with property offences, and the remainder were accused of offences against public order, non-violent sex crimes, and so forth (see Appendix D). Next, the arresting police officer(s) indicated that the accused person was mentally ill in 286 cases (56 per cent), and mentioned the defendant's potential for violence or dangerousness on 155 occasions (30 per cent: see Chapter 2).

Forensic decisions by the Brief Assessment Unit psychiatrists are reviewed in the fourth column of Figure 1.1. The majority of patients (386, or 72 per cent) were immediately found fit to stand trial, with 84 persons (16 per cent) considered unfit, and 57 (11 per cent) of questionable fitness. In addition, psychiatric judgments about dangerousness to others distributed as follows: 14 per cent 'high,' 30 per cent 'medium,' 14 per cent 'questionable,' 28 per cent 'low,' and 14 per cent 'no' (see Chapter 3).

FIGURE 1.1 Path diagram of legal status; police, clinical, and court decisions; and outcome

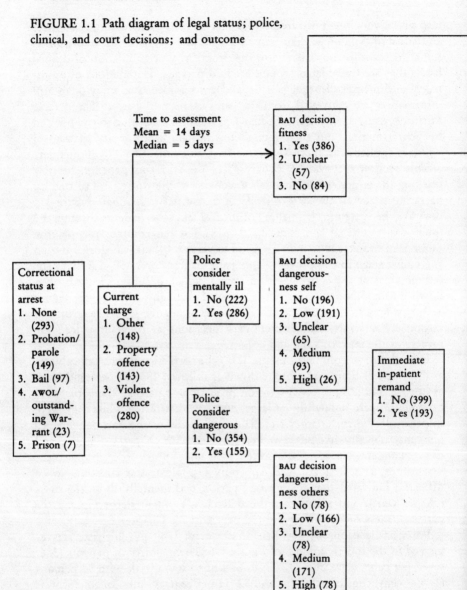

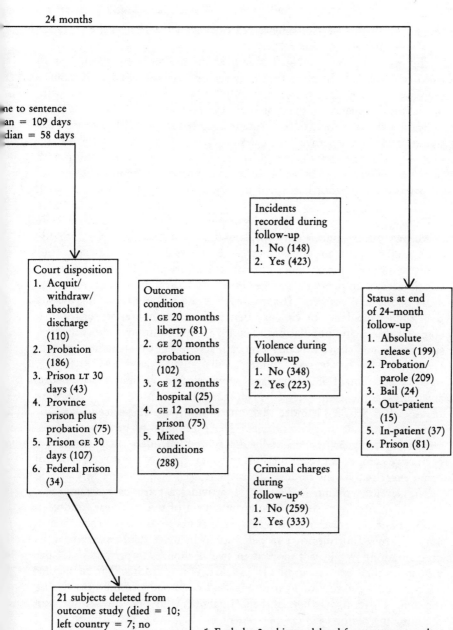

24 months

ne to sentence
an = 109 days
dian = 58 days

Court disposition
1. Acquit/
   withdraw/
   absolute
   discharge
   (110)
2. Probation
   (186)
3. Prison LT 30
   days (43)
4. Province
   prison plus
   probation (75)
5. Prison GE 30
   days (107)
6. Federal prison
   (34)

Outcome
condition
1. GE 20 months
   liberty (81)
2. GE 20 months
   probation
   (102)
3. GE 12 months
   hospital (25)
4. GE 12 months
   prison (75)
5. Mixed
   conditions
   (288)

Incidents
recorded during
follow-up
1. No (148)
2. Yes (423)

Violence during
follow-up
1. No (348)
2. Yes (223)

Criminal charges
during
follow-up*
1. No (259)
2. Yes (333)

Status at end
of 24-month
follow-up
1. Absolute
   release (199)
2. Probation/
   parole (209)
3. Bail (24)
4. Out-patient
   (15)
5. In-patient (37)
6. Prison (81)

21 subjects deleted from
outcome study (died = 10;
left country = 7; no
data = 4)

* Excludes 3 subjects, deleted from outcome study,
  who successfully suicided during follow-up.

Among the entire cohort, 193 subjects (33 per cent) were remanded for immediate in-patient assessment; 123 of these were seen in the METFORS Inpatient Unit (see Chapter 4).

The mean number of days between arrest and BAU assessment was 14 (median = 5), and the mean time between brief assessment and the court's sentence was 109 days (median = 58).[16] While direct comparisons with non-clinical remands for the time period were unavailable, there was every indication that the forensic assessment operated to extend the interval between arrest and sentence. For example, a survey of accused persons remanded in the province's jails (Madden 1978: 6), conducted one month prior to the commencement of the METFORS research, reported that over 66 per cent of persons had spent less than three months in jail awaiting trial.

Returning to Figure 1.1, the court dispositions for the BAU patients were as follows: probation, 34 per cent; acquittal, withdrawal, or absolute discharge, 20 per cent; provincial incarceration between one and twenty-four months, 18 per cent; provincial prison plus probation, 14 per cent; incarceration less than thirty days, 8 per cent; and federal incarceration for two years or more, 6 per cent. It appeared that the METFORS patients, despite their higher incidence of violent offences, received lighter sentences than comparable remand populations. The 1978 Ontario survey of accused persons mentioned above revealed a more severe level of sentencing than that experienced by the METFORS cohort. In that study (Madden 1978: 10–11), only 11 per cent of 555 defendants were released outright by the court, and only 14 per cent received probation; in contrast 66 per cent were sentenced to prison for more than one month, and 12 per cent were incarcerated in federal penitentiaries. These findings suggest that judges' sentencing practices for 'mentally disordered offenders' may embrace a corrective component that functions to counterbalance the carceral control being exercised via the forensic assessment itself (see Chapter 5).

The seventh column in Figure 1.1 provides a gross categorization of patients' institutional status during the course of the two-year follow-up study. Fourteen per cent of subjects were at liberty for more than twenty of the twenty-four months; 18 per cent spent more than twenty months on probation; 13 per cent more than twelve months in prison; and 4 per cent more than twelve months in psychiatric institutions. The remainder experienced a mixture of institutional and community conditions during the two-year term. Further, of the 571 patients who were tracked through the outcome period, 423 (74 per cent) had at least one officially recorded incident in correctional or hospital records, 333 (58 per cent) were charged with a criminal offence, and 223 (39 per cent) committed at least one act of violence. These base rates are extremely high in comparison to previous outcome studies of deinstitutionalized forensic patients (Quinsey 1979; Steadman and Cocozza 1974; Thornberry and Jacoby 1979). Finally, the rightmost column in Figure 1.1 lists the institutional status of subjects at the conclusion of the study. After two years, 37 per cent of patients were on probation or parole, and 35 per cent were at liberty in the community. The rest were in prison (14 per cent), were mental hospital patients (7 per cent), out-patients (3 per cent), or were on bail awaiting trial (4 per cent)[17] (see Chapter 6).

This schematic portrayal of the METFORS subjects' careers raised a number of related research questions that will be addressed in subsequent chapters. Through statistical analyses of variables associated with these various stages in the process, the following issues (among others) will be investigated in Chapters 2 through 6: To what extent could the forensic careers of patients be predicted from their prior behaviour and institutional background? What role was played by the original designations of arresting police officers in the production of psychiatric decisions about the METFORS cohort? Did original formulations about patients survive through the course of their institutional careers? Were there discernible relationships among decisions by METFORS clinicians about mental illness, treatability, dangerousness, and other forensic issues? Were the 193 persons remanded for protracted assessment in any way different from those who were immediately returned to the court? What influence did the METFORS recommendations exert on the court's disposition of individuals? Did these sentences have an impact on the subsequent institutional careers and conduct of the patient subjects? How accurate were the predictions of police, psychiatrists, and other clinicians concerning the future criminal and violent conduct of the METFORS cohort?

The Case of the Political Paranoid
This chapter concludes with a case study selected from the clinical records and outcome profiles of the METFORS patients. The narrative traces the path of a single patient, and the information being compiled about his case, as he is progressively arrested, remanded for psychiatric assessment, interviewed on the Brief Assessment Unit, transferred on Warrant of Remand to the Inpatient Unit, returned to court for sentencing, and monitored during the course of the two-year follow-up. Whereas Chapters 2 through 6 look at police, BAU, in-patient, and court decisions, along with outcome careers, as relatively discrete processes, this case history lends some per-

spective to the overall impact of the forensic system as a *totality* on the experiences of the METFORS subjects. This case is selected, not for its representativeness or statistical reliability, but because it brings focus to the powerful official resources at work, and because it demonstrates the basic continuity of a longitudinal labelling process that incrementally cements and intensifies the deviant identities of forensic patients.

The case involves a fifty-two-year-old married man of Swiss descent, who had been living in a small town in northern Ontario for the previous twenty-seven years. For several months prior to his arrest, the accused had been embroiled in a dispute with the Ontario government, over payment he claimed was owed for contract work that he had performed some years earlier. Eventually, he drove his car to Toronto, and proceeded to unleash a fervent one-man protest action against the provincial ministry. He dogged the legislative offices with phone calls for a period of two months, and having been rewarded with the usual level of government non-response to such an approach, he launched a more decisive plan of assault. The police report read:

On December 19, 1978, at 6:00 pm[18] the accused before the court entered the office in the Ontario [government] buildings. The accused who indicates that he has a dispute with the Government of Ontario then proceeded to chain himself to a round coffee table with heavy link chain and two padlocks. Then, with the chain locked to his leg the accused exited the office, travelled to the ground floor on the elevator, exited the building by way of the front door and placed the coffee table on the front hood of a police vehicle which was parked outside. The accused then waited to be arrested by the police who returned a short time later. (PR 578)[19]

The subject was thereupon charged with 'Theft under $200.' While the arresting officers noted that Mr M. had no previous criminal record, the circumstances of the incident apparently warranted that a show cause hearing be convened to determine his suitability for bail,[20] and that a psychiatric examination be made. Tactically, the police attempted to frame the case against what would be considered 'normal behaviour' in the context. 'The accused appears to be acting in a manner that in a normal person would be considered disorderly ... In the officer's opinion the accused should submit to a psychiatric examination prior to a show cause hearing' (PR 578). No further evidence was offered to justify the need for assessment. It appeared that the 'facts' of the transaction were deemed sufficient to support the police recommendations.

Three days later Mr M. was escorted to the METFORS Brief Assessment

Unit from the Don Jail in the downtown east side of Toronto. He was detained in the holding area of the BAU at 9:00 a.m., and two hours later was interviewed by the five-member clinical team. By the end of the day, it had been ascertained that 'the patient suffers from a severe form of mental illness,' and that a 30-day assessment at METFORS was needed 'to assess fitness and potential for dangerousness' (NR 578).

The psychiatric assessment unit is a context where normal rules of discourse are rendered inoperative, where patient utterances are not allowed to pass unchallenged, and where the discovery mission demands close scrutiny of every detail and shade of meaning (see Chapter 3; Allen 1987; Pfohl 1978; Scheff 1966). It is a dangerous place for the loose-of-tongue. No biographical item, and no verbal or behavioural gesture, can be allowed to pass without consideration as potential evidence of pathology or criminality. In the following passage taken from the BAU nurse's report, such qualities as being talkative, humorous, dramatic, and concerned with the environment were framed by the reporter against the perceived background of Mr. M's psychiatric condition.

Mr. M. was oriented to time, place and person and remote and recent memory appeared good. The patient was very talkative during the interview and throughout his stay on the Brief Assessment Unit. He seemed euphoric, but was able to be rational when he was directed to focus on topic. Generally, the patient was very tangential and exhibited pressure of speech. He laughed, made jokes and presented in a dramatic fashion. The patient was distractable and seemed obsessed with his ideas of environmental improvement, etc. (NR 578)

The psychologist in the interview developed a line of theorizing more directly related to the defendant's potential for dangerous behaviour. First, the psychologist issued a multiple classification of the patient based on clinical observation. 'Mr. M. presented himself clinically as an obsessive-compulsive personality with hypomanic features; i.e., pressure of speech and euphoria. On several occasions Mr. M.'s thinking was characterized by loose associations and thought blocking' (POR 578). Having worked out a provisional profile, the psychologist merged this reasoning with the theory that Mr. M was immersed in progressive patterns of violence that would continue to escalate. The psychologist noted that the patient had in sequence separated from his wife and children, criticized the government in letters to newspapers and officials, set up a tent on the grounds of the Ontario legislature, committed the present offence of 'Theft Under,' and, if still unsuccessful in securing a favourable outcome, 'planned to chain himself to a government building and "shoot some windows out with a 300 Savage" ' (POR 578). The BAU psychologist concluded: 'It is the opinion of this examiner that while Mr. M. is presently fit to stand trial the medical evidence suggests that he may be experiencing the onset of a mood disorder – manic depressive type. Further, the plan he mentioned concerning the rifle may represent an escalation which can prove harmful to himself or others' (POR 578).

The social worker pursued a similar trajectory of logic. Having found the patient's story 'somewhat amusing but frightening,' the social worker concluded that insufficient data had been elicited to permit the formulation of a decisive assessment. None the less, the 'escalation' hypothesis was endorsed. 'I do feel that one should look very carefully at how much escalation in terms of dangerousness is occurring within this man' (SWR 578).

In the METFORS Brief Assessment Unit, the attending psychiatrist holds the ultimate responsibility for communicating the 'team decision' to the presiding judge. In this instance, it had been determined that the subject's mental condition and potential for violence warranted a protracted assessment in the METFORS Inpatient Unit. Previous analyses of psychiatric court letters (Allen 1987; Forst 1980; Konečni, Mulcahy, and Ebbeson 1980; Pfohl 1978; Steadman 1973) have noted the stylized and standardized content of these disclosures. Evidence of incongruity, indecision, discrepant meanings, multiple realities, and discordant data is abandoned, as the psychiatrist enjoins the court to accept the clinical documentation in order to secure desired outcomes. Such strategies are singularly successful (see Chapter 5). The medical reality is routinely endorsed as the appropriate basis for legal response. In the present case, the psychiatrist's letter was one-half page in length. It comprised four pointed themes: the professional authenticity of the report; the severe mental condition of the defendant; the patient's marked potential for violence; and the need for extended clinical evaluation.

This man was examined today by our assessment team consisting of psychiatrist, psychologist, social worker, psychiatric nurse and correctional officer. On examination today he was extremely voluble, talkative and euphoric. It is quite apparent that he suffers from a cyclothymic personality disorder that is progressing into a manic depressive psychosis. His psychotic condition is at present in its early stages since his contact with reality is quite good and he is able to be rational when he puts his mind to it. However, he is markedly discursive in his replies to questions and it is difficult to keep him to the point.

He does suffer from a severe form of mental illness and it is necessary to examine this man further in an in-patient setting in order to assess his fitness to proceed and certainly in the matter of his potential for dangerousness in the community. Our assessment team had considerable concerns with reference to the latter consideration.

I would therefore recommend that he be remanded to our Inpatient Unit for a period not exceeding 30 days at the completion of which time a full report will be submitted to the Court. (PL 578)

At the conclusion of the brief assessment, the subject was returned to the Toronto Jail for a further six days until his next appearance in court, whereupon the judge remanded him back to METFORS for a thirty-day assessment. The in-patient evaluation, according to the attending psychiatrist, was arranged to elicit a wider spectrum of data about the patient's mental status. Specifically, this broadening of perspective was to involve three sources of material: the deployment of psychological testing instruments; a social work profile, including interviews with significant others in the patient's life; and behavioural observations on the ward by psychiatric assistants and nurses.

The psychological testing in this case was a pivotal documentary resource (see Chapter 4). Personality inventories and projective tests provide a technology which lends a pseudo-objective rigour to the evaluation process. These instruments typically result in a proliferation of interpretive possibilities. In practice, such tests are subjective in the most literal sense, given the open-ended nature of possible lines of inquiry, and given the ability to fit conclusions to the most organizationally enabling hypotheses. In this instance, the Inpatient Unit psychologist concluded that the test results indicated an astounding diversity of clinical pathologies. Few diagnostic stones were left unturned. Having secured Mr M.'s results on the Minnesota Multiphasic Personality Inventory, Bender Gestalt, Wechsler Adult Intelligence Scale, Rorschach, and Thematic Apperception Test, the psychologist categorized him as manic, neurotic, hysterical, antisocial, and psychotic.

At least four distinct areas of pathology are suggested by the test results. The first is *mania* as indicated on the MMPI and also by his tangential speech and the flight of ideas. The second is in terms of *neurosis*. The MMPI indicated high degrees of both hysteria and depression in this man. Neurotic tendencies were also evident on the W.A.I.S. in that his verbal scores were significantly higher than his performance scores ... Such a pattern is also indicative of such anxiety. A third characterological tendency in this man is an anti-social one. This is suggested both by the MMPI and a sub-test of the w.a.i.s. These anti-social elements have a flavour of paranoia to them as well. Finally the fourth area of pathology is thought disorder suggestive of a major mental illness namely that of schizophrenia. A disorder in thinking and a disturbed contact with reality are strongly suggested by the picture arrangement test of the w.a.i.s. and by Rorschach. (IPOR 578)

As a result, the proliferation of psychiatric labels was enhanced by the multidimensional nature of these test results. The sense of science implied in these tests conveyed an impression of value-neutral objectivity. The MMPI 'indicated' mania, hysteria, depression, antisocial paranoia, and schizophrenia. The w.a.i.s. 'suggested' neurotic tendencies out of the patient's strong verbal performance. Consequently, the psychologist's conclusions appeared to represent a logical continuation of this 'discovery' process. 'Mr. M. is a highly intelligent individual with marked manic and neurotic tendencies. It is likely that there is an underlying psychotic process to his personality which he defends against by his mania and intelligence. In fact the label pseudo-neurotic may well be applied to him. It can describe a person showing an active search for identity, a constant frenetic engagement with their world in attempts either to comply or to rebel yet they are usually endowed with enough strength to resist psychotic disintegration.' (IPOR 578)

The in-patient assessment also afforded the opportunity to contact and interview the subject's relatives and acquaintances in the community. The METFORS social worker located and interviewed a Toronto resident who had known Mr M. some two decades earlier, but who had had little further contact with the patient since that time. Nevertheless, an avalanche of retrospective data was accumulated from the informant and entered into Mr M.'s profile. The informant recalled that in the late 1950s 'Mr. M. was protesting against the government in much the same fashion as he is at the present time ... People in the community saw Mr. M. as "crazy" because of his action and his constant government protests' (ISWR 578). According to the informant, the patient's wife 'had been trying to commit her husband to a psychiatric hospital for some years.' The materials extracted from the interview were adeptly used to support the hypothesis that Mr M.'s pathology was rapidly deteriorating. 'This young man [the informant] has been acquainted with Mr. M. for several years, both as a young boy and an adult. He indicates that the patient has not changed a great deal over the years with the exception that his protests are more visible and now his family are included in the long list of individuals who are apparently trying to take advantage of him. Mr. C. [the informant] does not see Mr. M. as a particularly dangerous man, but is fearful that the patient may, in fact, be dangerous to individuals connected with the government.' Even the reluctance of the informant to maintain contact with the accused was noted as a harbinger of things to come. The social worker concluded: 'I would be concerned about the extent this man may, in fact, act if his demands were not met by the government. This concern would also be exemplified by the fact that the patient has no support system in the community with the exception of Mr. C. who is now indicating his fear of further long term involvement with Mr. M.' (ISWR 578).

During the patient's twenty-eight-day confinement on the METFORS In-patient Unit, detailed progress notes were compiled (47 pages) monitoring his activities and verbalizations on the ward. Nurses and psychiatric assistants appeared to select documentary evidence out of the vast range of conduct and utterances exhibited over the course of one month, in order to push lines of theorizing and to consolidate the hypotheses of the professional clinicians. The following illustrations are extracted from the ward observations of Mr M.

30 December 1978: Hypomanic. Kicked copatient in rear. Sense a long-standing maladjustment to life problems which has produced considerable frustration and depression ... Patient unable to deal with reality, therefore skims surface and is easily distracted from topic.

6 January 1979: Realizes utopian society an unlikely reality, acknowledges own powerlessness and is pessimistic re. man's humanity. Connections in strands of arguments loose, even vague. For one who confesses ignorance of Marxist thought, patient's method of analysis bears a close resemblance.

9 January 1979: Unrealistic future plans. Discounted political-legal system, no form of protest other than tenting, wants to sue government officials for marriage breakdown. More patient was confronted, more agitated he became. Patient's protests = elaborate defence against frustrating and depressing past life and current bleak situation. (IPN 578)

These cryptic ward notes were packaged into a powerful document asserting the hopelessness of the patient's social and mental condition. Mr M.'s 'detachment from reality' was viewed to render him depressed, frustrated, maladjusted, powerless, pessimistic, and Marxist.

The in-patient psychiatrist's letter to the court provided the final clinical articulation of the subject's illness and dangerousness. The letter was prefaced with a careful inventory of the scientific procedures employed in the accumulation of evidence:

1 Mr. M. received psychiatric interviews from Dr. C. and Dr. G.
2 Mr. M. received a physical examination from Dr. F., routine blood tests and urinalysis, an electro-cardiagram, and X-rays of chest and abdomen.
3 A psychologist carried out a number of psychological tests.
4 A social worker spoke with a friend of Mr. M.
5 Mr. M. himself provided written material about his thoughts and preoccupations.
6 Mr. M. was under daily observation by the nursing staff. (IPL 578)

These materials, as in the case of the BAU letter, were compacted into a standardized version of the patient's clinical profile that left little room for ambiguity or doubt. The letter represented a symbolic testament to the authenticity of the diagnosis. The background reasoning process itself was virtually absent from the letter. The psychiatrist confined himself to affirmations and declarations about Mr M.'s medical condition. 'Mr. M. suffers from a major mental illness characterized by marked suspiciousness with emotional lability. In patients with paranoid thinking there is always some risk of future dangerousness depending on the emotional contexts in which they find themselves. In his present state it is not felt that he is in immediate danger, but we have serious concerns about the future ... I feel that as his paranoid thinking develops he may well act-out in an aggressive and dangerous manner' (IPL 578).

Mr M. was returned to court on 24 January 1979, and sentenced to forty days' imprisonment (for the original charge of 'Theft Under') on the same day. He served twenty-seven days of the sentence in the Toronto Jail. During the two-year follow-up period, Mr M. showed that he was not to be easily deterred from his campaign against the Ontario government. But the official response to his protests intensified apace. On 5 June 1979, he was brought to the Queen Street Mental Health Centre by the police, after pitching a tent in front of a local newspaper building. He had painted a sign on his car proclaiming that 'The Toronto [   ] prints only half truths.' For his troubles, his car was impounded, and he spent one day in jail and one night in hospital. On 7 June 1979, Mr M. was charged with 'Mischief to Private Property.' Further charges ('Breach of Municipal Bylaws,' 'Breach of Highway Traffic Act,' 'Theft under $200,' and 'Assault with Intent to

Cause Bodily Harm') ensued in late fall of the same year, and resulted in 108 days of imprisonment during the winter of 1979–80.

On 4 June 1980, Mr M. was convicted of the earlier mischief charge and sentenced to twelve months' probation. On 11 June 1980, he was arrested for 'Being Unlawfully in a Dwelling Place' and transferred to the Oak Ridge maximum security unit at Penetang for the next four months, where ward notes indicated that he was 'sarcastic with staff,' 'excessively talking and arguing,' 'subject to fits of uncontrollable rage at political issues,' 'prepared to engage in a physical fight with a copatient,' and, on one occasion, he 'spit and threw water on staff.' He was returned to the Toronto Jail on 26 November 1980, and was still incarcerated in that institution, awaiting trial, when the outcome period terminated on 21 December 1980.

SUMMARY

This chapter has provided an introduction to the Metropolitan Toronto Forensic Service, its institutional history and context, its organizational members, and its subject clientele. The development of Toronto's forensic system was traced over a fifty-year period. The legal and structural ecology of METFORS was examined as an enabling framework that fostered 'good working relationships' between the psychiatric practitioners and the courts, while at the same time allowing for potential breaches of formal law, medical ethics, and civil liberties.

The research design of the current study was surveyed. The project entailed a longitudinal summary of the forensic careers of 592 patients from the point of their initial arrests, through their clinical assessments, court dispositions, and twenty-four-month follow-ups tracing further deviant, criminal, and violent activities recorded by the mental health and correctional systems. Data analysis involved triangulation between documentary examination of subjects' arrest reports, medical records, and outcome contacts, and statistical exploration of 135 metric and categorical variables abstracted from the files. Particular attention was paid to the demographic and psycho-legal characteristics of the patients, the decisions of police, clinicians, and courts, the content of the medical documents and letters to the judges, the frequency and intensity of criminal and violent behaviour exhibited by patients during the follow-up period, and the ability of members to identify and predict this outcome conduct.

Finally, a case history was abstracted from the medical and correctional records, giving some indication of the forensic patient's unique view of the ordering process as he or she is funnelled through the myriad channels of interlocking official agencies. From the subject's vantage point the system is very much experienced as a holistic control enterprise (Emerson 1983), in which deviant imputations are incrementally built up, initial judgments are routinely rubber-stamped at late junctures in the process, and the informational product is virtually always accepted as factual, unproblematic, and real.

Having sketched out this panoramic view, we now begin the process of surveying the various individual stages of the forensic corridor, as the METFORS patients are channelled from the streets to the precincts, through the clinics to the courts, and beyond.

2

Opening the Door:
Police Encounters with the
METFORS Patients

The policeman, like the trusty sentinel, must go to his post and be prepared to meet all kinds of dangers ... He has to encounter the hidden, and stealthy, and desperate foe.

AUGUSTINE E. COSTELLO   *Our Police Protectors*

The police provide a frontline definitional coding system through which large numbers of persons are processed and referred to other cooperating or symbiotically dependent agencies of control. Two consequences result: the police act as 'trend-setting' definers of deviance (or controllable offenses), and they enjoy the supportive coding supplied by other agencies within a social control network.

PETER K. MANNING   *Police Work*

POLICING THE MENTALLY DISORDERED

The police occupy the front end of the 'carceral continuum' (Foucault 1977). Because of their strategic placement as institutional gatekeepers, police are able to exercise control over the distribution of subjects, knowledge, and symbolic messages to other locations in the judicial network. They can harness and selectively deploy 'facts' and images about accused persons – signals that adhere and survive as police interpretations of reality are sent on to allied legal officials.

Police work to present their activities and interventions as both just and justifiable. To this end, individual patrol officers come to absorb a broad inventory of institutional, normative, and cultural guidelines for ordering their cases, for extracting those informational elements with maximum payoff and persuasive force, and for organizing an official account that will impress and influence legal audiences. They accomplish these goals through the situated and creative deployment of legal categories. 'The police make sense of the legal categories of crime: they use them to get the "job done adequately," as they define this, and they *see* the situational contingencies as defining the nature of the "job" and its "adequate" performance, hence, as necessarily defining how one should *use* the legal categories' (Douglas 1971: 104).

Like other members of the judicial system, police learn to *mediate* between the structural constraints of legality and the occupational demands for expedient and accountable imposition of the law (McBarnet 1981). By producing relevant and answerable renditions of their control work, the police are able to justify – in legal, moral, and organization terms – their personal responses to criminal cases. The law and its enabling resources become pivotal categories for the production of powerful messages about accused persons (Ericson 1981, 1982; Manning 1977; McCabe and Sutcliffe 1978). 'Police justifications may be a distortion of the spirit of legality but they are an exact replica of the spirit of the law' (McBarnet 1981: 48).

Police are involved in the reconstruction of legal and other normative realities for the sake of the organization, and for themselves. They come to rely on their reportorial abilities to generate the 'official paper' (Manning 1979: 25) that will satisfy superiors, administrators, and members of the court bureaucracy. In their efforts to maximize professional autonomy and accountability, patrol officers come to rely heavily on these reportorial skills, which permit recurrent transformations of ambiguous police-citizen transactions into definitive depictions of conformity to law. They frankly acknowledge that the case is only as good as the paper on which it is written (McCabe and Sutcliffe 1978). As Manning contends, '[officers] work to do two things: to accomplish work within the premises of the work as they understand them, and to create, if necessary, the proper official paper which will represent events within the official, sanctioned format for such events as they are administratively understood' (1979: 25).

In the process of assembling such selective and monochromatic records of what went on in their encounters with citizens, police learn to accommodate facts to rules, to highlight the legality of their methods, the culpability of their subjects, and the desirability of their recommended institutional outcomes. 'Officers "patrol" the facts about the disputes they are called upon to deal with. What initially appears a complex matter with as many shades as a chameleon in a box of crayons ends up black and white ... [T]he many possibilities are reduced to one version which will influence decisions about ... the category used in the final version' (Ericson 1982: 131).

Police accounts impose a sense of rationality on their interventions into the lives of criminal defendants. Police attempt to assimilate their cases into conceptual packages that display the logic and legality of their official actions (McCabe and Sutcliffe 1978). In their search for admissible explanations, patrol officers are continuously engaged in the mutual elaboration of specific 'facts' about defendants and their rule violations, and organizational policies and categories that allow justifiable official responses. Police actions and accounts are simultaneously grounded in a retrospective comparison with the past treatment of similar cases and a prospective speculation about the impact of their responses and judgments on other legal authorities.

Such practical decision-making involves 'drawing the line' so that some 'pattern' or 'type' is produced that allows for a course of action consistent with general policies or rules laid down by penal, welfare, and institution code statutes, and the everyday practices of the agencies involved. Thus the particulars – the contingencies of the case – are always being interpreted vis-a-vis past reports or encounters, present depictions ..., and the general policies or rules to be found in statutes and departmental activities. The officers must somehow articulate the particulars or contingencies of present caess with general policies, rules, or typologies they utilize for 'making sense' of emergent social interaction over time. (Cicourel 1968: 163)

Consequently, police accounts are used to satisfy standards of authenticity that are announced or tacitly held by other members of the judicial system. In making a case for their control activities, and for the definitions they impose on incidents and defendants, police attempt to minimize possibilities for rebuttal or reinterpretation by other officials (Emerson 1983). In so doing, police learn to rely on a number of reportorial tactics for communicating the seriousness of incidents that warrant their intervention, and for optimizing the potential for desired outcomes. The influence of these accounts hinges on the ability to dramatize and highlight the saliency of such events (Manning 1977: 26). Thus, the police rendition of reality represents a pragmatic transformation of 'facts' into symbols and messages that are designed to stress the 'operative legality' (Skolnick 1966: 14) of their activities; to amplify the 'strength of the signal' (Manning 1977: 267); and to demonstrate conclusively the need for exercising appropriate legal control over accused persons.

In order to cast the relationships with which they deal into legal terms that provide their legal force with legitimacy, the police symbolically transform facts into legal elements, rules of law, and hence create cases. Legal rules are used by the police and their legal allies to guide the reconstruction of facts to facilitate entry of cases into the legal system. In so transforming these facts, they state and make visible the official (legal) consequences of certain sequences of behavior. They create predictability in the anticipation of sentencing. (Manning 1977:100).

This chapter explores the accounting practices of police in their initial apprehension of the METFORS subjects. Through a documentary analysis of the official paper that emerges from these encounters, I examine the typification strategies that accompany police depictions of mental illness and dangerousness among this sample of pre-trial forensic patients.

As will become clear, the police encounter a number of difficulties associated with the arrest of apparently mentally disordered subjects. Superimposed on their decisions about the need to impose legal sanctions is their need to deliberate on the costs and benefits of initiating psychiatric diversion. They must learn to assess situationally the mental condition of their subjects, and to develop sufficient linguistic skills for communicating such 'diagnoses' to superiors and other officials. The presence of apparent mental disorder adds further complexity to the discretionary work of line officers, as they come to assume a quasi-psychiatric function, rendering judgments about the level of pathology being manifested by their subjects, and about optimal strategies for exercising medico-legal control over such persons (Yuille 1986). The possibility of psychiatric diversion opens up an entirely new line of procedural prospects, and the police find it increasingly necessary to make choices among divergent judicial and clinical channels of response.

Police are not well-equipped to discharge this function (Schiffer 1978: 15). They are exposed to an array of contradictions and strains associated with their management of the mentally disordered (Bittner 1967; Matthews 1970; Monahan, Caldeira, and Friedlander 1979; Murphy 1986; Teplin 1984a, 1984b). Traditionally, police have been reluctant to participate in the psychiatrization of accused persons. Their efforts to secure the clinical diversion of the mentally ill have been constrained by the unavailability of sufficient specialist knowledge, and by the institutional barriers that have marked off mutually exclusive zones of criminal and psychiatric intervention. The police have been threatened by the reluctance of clinical officials to validate their decisions. In yielding to psychiatric modes of response, they have risked losing their jurisdiction over the disposition of criminal defendants.

> The police ... disavow all competence in matters relating to psychopathology and seek to remain within the lines of restraint that the disavowal imposes. Accordingly, the diagnosis they propose is not only emphatically provisional but also, in a sense, incidental ... From their point of view, it is not enough for a case to be serious in a 'merely' psychiatric sense. To warrant official police action a case must also present a serious police problem. As a general rule, the elements that make a case a serious police matter are indications that if a referral is not made, external troubles will proliferate ... Estimating the risk of interior deterioration of the psychiatric condition as such is perceived as lying outside of the scope of police competence and thus not an adequate basis for making emergency apprehensions. (Bittner 1967: 279)

Yet despite their resistance to assuming this function, the police have been thrust by circumstances into the maelstrom of the mental health referral system, through their application of both civil commitment legislation (Rollin 1969; Warren 1977) and the crime control apparatus itself (Teplin 1984b). 'When people feel threatened or annoyed by the bizarre or irrational conduct of another, they usually call the police. So the mentally ill's first official contact with the criminal process is often in the person of a police officer' (Law Reform Commission of Canada 1976: 24).

Consequently, in the course of their everyday activities police have been forced to accept a public role as 'psychiatric medics,' and to develop ongoing relationships with a variety of mental health authorities. But as Tucker has documented, such encounters tend to be characterized by competing territorial claims and contradictory expectations. Police objectives are not always accomplished through the practice of psychiatric diversion. '[T]he labels of the police officers did not seem to affect the diagnosis given by the psychiatric residents ... It appears that ... decisions of psychiatric residents were made on information other than that mentioned ... in the police reports' (Tucker 1972: 15–16).

In their study of hospital referrals by police in Toronto, Fox and Erickson (1972) found that over a quarter of the subjects were refused admission after having been transported by police to psychiatric facilities under the auspices of the Ontario Mental Health Act.[1] Moreover, discussions with police revealed their general reticence towards discharging such a mental health function. 'Most police interviewed, while accepting the disposition of suspected mentally ill persons as part of their work, did not particularly like it and would have been pleased if others assumed their function in this area' (Fox and Erickson 1972: 171). Finally, police in this study routinely applied imputations of dangerousness to legitimize their psychiatric referrals, even in the absence of violent conduct on the part of subjects. In the face of legal constraints and psychiatric opposition, police were frequently induced literally to invent a state of dangerousness in order to satisfy statutory criteria for commitment to civil hospitals (Fox and Erickson 1972: 174).

Yet in recent years, this conflict-ridden process appears to be undergoing a dramatic change. Such impediments to policing the mentally ill have been clearly diminishing in recent years, in response to the increasing presence of pre-trial forensic clinics which are attached directly to the criminal courts. The emergence of such agencies as the Metropolitan Toronto Forensic Service, offering routine psychiatric intervention within the ambit of the criminal law, has provided an important resource for police in cases of suspected mental disorder. Where the law has been violated, police can maintain legal jurisdiction over defendants by initiating arrest proceedings with a recommendation for forensic assessment, instead of undertaking the less predictable process of civil psychiatric commitment. By first securing arraignment under criminal legislation, and then attaching labels of mental illness and dangerousness as psychiatric 'kickers' in their official reports, police can potentially expand their scope of influence over the subsequent institutional careers of defendants believed to be mentally ill.

In addition, under the auspices of criminal instead of civil procedure, mental health practitioners are less equipped to negate the psychiatric referrals of police, since pre-trial assessments are being ordered directly by the presiding criminal court judge. Consequently, with the expansion of such facilities police may be increasingly disposed to adopt a psychiatric approach to their transactions with citizens, since mental health 'diversion' is more likely to be viewed as a supplement rather than an impediment to their control function. Under the facilitating conditions afforded by pre-trial forensic clinics like METFORS, police may become much more proactive in the formulation of psychiatric labels; in the identification of clinical dangerousness; and in the successful redirection of arrested persons into the forensic system.

THE POLICE CONSTRUCTION OF PSYCHIATRIC CATEGORIES

The remainder of this chapter focuses on the role of arresting police officers in defining the pathologies and structuring the subsequent pathways of the METFORS patients. As will become apparent, the initial contact between defendants and police was pivotal in the construction of facts and images about these 'mentally disordered offenders.' Such data became the principal outcome of police practices, and other officials – the METFORS clinicians included – were reliant on these arrest reports in the formulation of their own professional judgments. By undertaking a documentary analysis of arrest reports concerning the METFORS patients, it was possible to evaluate the substance and influence of police decisions, and to gauge their relevance for the determinations of other legal and medical authorities.

The METFORS patients were accompanied to the Brief Assessment Unit by a copy of the police arrest record. In most cases these documents included the arrest report itself (providing data about the accused person, the offence, and relevant circumstances surrounding the incident), a supplementary description of the alleged offence (typically one or two pages in length), and a 'show cause' report (containing the officer's justifications for detaining the defendant in jail prior to his or her trial).[2] As a matter of routine, the arrest and prison records of the accused found their way into the reports, and information about his or her current legal status (on bail, on probation, etc.) was made available. On occasion, the written statements and anticipated testimony of police, complainants, and witnesses were enclosed, as well as synopses of confessions extracted from the defendant(s).[3] Prior to the convening of interviews with the METFORS subjects, the Brief Assessment Unit clinicians met on a daily basis to peruse and discuss these various documents. Altogether, for the 592 subjects, 528 police reports of some description were contained in the METFORS medical record files. Of these, 504 could be viewed as 'completed' (that is, including information above and beyond the one-page arrest report). These records, then, provide the raw materials for this chapter's look at police decision-making leading to the arrest and subsequent forensic remand of the METFORS subjects.

Table 2.1 provides a summary of police perceptions about these patients. In the eyes of arresting officers, this was apparently a highly disturbed and dangerous group. In 94 per cent of cases, the police completed a 'show cause' report on the accused person.[4] In other words, it appeared from these data that only about one patient in twenty was considered suitable for pre-trial release. On the assumption that these recommendations would

TABLE 2.1
Decisions by arresting police officers

	N	Per cent no	Per cent yes	Missing cases
1 Completion of show cause report by police*	538	6.2	93.8	64
2 Police mention a mentally ill file† or previous psychiatric contact	496	62.3	37.7	96
3 Police consider suspect to be mentally ill	525	42.7	57.3	67
4 Police recommend a psychiatric assessment	504	61.9	38.1	88
5 Police consider suspect to be suicidal/ dangerous to self	526	89.5	10.5	66
6 Police consider suspect to be violent/ dangerous to others	526	69.4	30.6	66

* A show cause report is completed when the police desire to retain the suspect in custody prior to trial on either primary grounds (to ensure attendance in court) or secondary grounds (in the public interest; for example to prevent the commission of a further offence). See Chapter 1, note 20.
† Record of previous mental illness contained in police files.

not be universally endorsed by prosecutors or the court, the show cause reports generally included suggestions about the conditions to be attached to bail release; these often entailed, among others, recommendations for psychiatric assessment and/or treatment.

As Table 2.1 also indicates, police mentioned records of previous psychiatric contacts for 37.7 per cent of defendants. Since in fact 52.5 per cent of the METFORS patients had been hospitalized as psychiatric in-patients at some point in their lives (see Chapter 1), these findings suggest that mental histories regularly found their way into police files. For the majority of these cases, the words 'M.I. ON FILE' were entered prominently at the top corner of the arrest report. In over 57 per cent of the 525 cases for which sufficient data were available, the arresting officers wrote that the defendant was mentally ill and/or in need of psychiatric treatment. Further, for 38.1 per cent of the accused persons, the police recommended a pre-trial psychiatric assessment. Increasingly over the duration of the study, officers indicated that METFORS should be the venue of that assessment.

This evidence graphically illustrates the psychiatrization of the police in the METFORS catchment area. Over the twelve months of the study, there was a general increase in the proportion of police reports recommending psychiatric assessment. In the first quarterly period (January through March), there were 89 completed police reports and 23 assessment recommendations (25 per cent). The percentages for the subsequent three-month periods were 39.5 for April through June (58 of 147), 35.5 for July through September (50 of 141), and 48.0 for October through December (61 of 127).[5] Moreover, direct references to METFORS began to surface in police reports as the study progressed. Although there was no mention of the clinic during the first quarter (January through March), the following three-month periods contained, respectively, 2, 5, and 8 reports that specified METFORS as the preferred venue for psychiatric remand.

Accordingly, patrol officers in Metropolitan Toronto were frequently responsible for the application of psychiatric labels to criminal defendants. For a substantial proportion of the METFORS patients the initial documentation of pathology arose on the occasion of their arrest.

Police were also alert to the potential dangerousness of their arrestees. Over 10 per cent of police reports indicated that the defendant was suicidal or otherwise at risk of harming himself or herself. References to potential for violence were usually contained in the show cause reports. In 30.6 per cent of cases, the police overtly declared that the accused was violent and/ or dangerous to other persons. These judgments about the individual's dangerousness were connected with the desire to hold the suspect prior to trial, to secure a psychiatric assessment, or to communicate to the court the need for a custodial sentence (see below).

Table 2.2 looks specifically at the construction of police decisions about the potential violence and dangerousness of subjects. Dangerousness is a pivotal consideration in police discretion concerning the mentally ill, since it is a central component of decisions to invoke emergency commitment under the Ontario Mental Health Act, and to detain arrested persons in jail prior to trial.

This dichotomous variable ('dangerousness is / is not specified in the reports') is associated in Table 2.2 with background characteristics of the defendant, the nature of current charges, police judgments about mental illness, subsequent clinical and judicial determinations, and subject behaviour during the two-year follow-up period. Among thirteen measures of subject background and offence type, four were statistically related to police pronouncements about dangerousness. Specifically, judgments about violence potential were higher for defendants with an officially recorded history of violence and with more prior violent offences, for those currently charged with an assaultive crime, and for those demonstrating a lower level of drug use (based on a four-point scale estimate by the BAU clinicians). Clearly, police ascriptions of dangerousness and violence were directly

TABLE 2.2
Police judgment of suspect dangerousness/potential for violence with background, clinical decisions, and court disposition*

	Suspect not dangerous (%)	Suspect dangerous (%)	N	Statistic χ^2	df	p
Previous violence				29.79	1	<0.0001
No	80.3	19.7	269			
Yes	58.0	42.0	257			
Present charge				77.70	2	<0.0001
Property	92.5	7.5	133			
Other	79.7	20.3	138			
Violence	51.8	48.2	255			
Police consider suspect mentally ill				22.95	1	<0.0001
No	60.7	19.3	223			
Yes	60.8	39.2	301			

	Mean	Mean		t†	df	p
Drug use	2.42	2.20		−2.05	522	0.04
Number of prior violence convictions	0.63	1.21		4.88	523	<0.001
BAU psychiatrist dangerousness rating	2.73	3.64		7.84	524	<0.001
BAU psychologist dangerousness rating	3.14	3.76		4.98	453	<0.001
BAU social worker dangerousness rating	3.16	3.98		5.97	389	<0.001
BAU nurse dangerousness rating	2.83	3.61		6.14	522	<0.001
BAU correctional officer dangerousness rating	3.05	3.58		4.08	509	<0.001
Total number of follow-up incidents	5.14	3.57		−2.92	507	0.004
Total number of follow-up criminal charges	2.73	1.66		−3.16	507	0.002

* No significant interactions with the following variables: previous incarceration, previous suicide attempts, employment at arrest, age, number of prior hospitalizations, number of follow-up violent incidents, number of prior arrests, gender, years of education, alcohol use, court disposition.
† Number of cases in categories for t-tests: for 'Drug use' to 'Correctional officer rating', not dangerous = 365, dangerous = 161; for 'number of follow-up incidents' to 'number of follow-up criminal charges', not dangerous = 354, dangerous = 155.

correlated to the suspects' records of prior violence. They were not typically related to such defendant characteristics as age, gender, employment status, or number of previous arrests for non-violent offences.

Police judgments about dangerousness were, however, significantly connected to their designations of the suspects' mental illness. Accused persons viewed to be mentally disordered were more likely than others to be recorded as potentially violent in the police reports. Of 301 individuals considered mentally ill, 39.2 per cent were labelled as dangerous; only 19.2 per cent of the 223 *not* viewed as disturbed received this notation.

Next, police attributions of dangerousness were compared with the predictions of dangerousness to others recorded on a five-point scale (see Chapter 1) by the forensic clinicians in the METFORS Brief Assessment Unit. For all five professional groups involved in psychiatric evaluations, designations of the accused person's dangerousness significantly agreed with the original judgments of the arresting officers. Those defendants characterized as potentially violent by the police routinely received higher clinical predictions of dangerousness than other persons. For example, the mean 'dangerousness to others' score assigned by the BAU psychiatrists was 3.64 for the group defined as dangerous at arrest, compared with 2.73 for others. Given the concordance between police and clinical assessments of dangerousness, it would seem that forensic specialists were especially reliant on initial police designations in structuring their own 'medical' decisions about this issue. As Blumberg writes, ' ... psychiatric reports reaffirm and re-circulate the same knowledge about the accused originally furnished by the police ... refurbished in the patois and argot of social work and psychiatry' (1967: 67). In short, police officers wielded substantial leverage in the generation of official images about dangerousness and other forms of clinical and legal deviance. The confluence of police and clinical decisions about dangerousness was testimony to the accumulation of definitional power at the front end of the carceral continuum.

However, such definitional power on the part of police was apparently unwarranted. The final set of statistics in Table 2.2 correlates the judgments of arresting police officers with the follow-up conduct of METFORS patients during the two-year outcome period. Those subjects considered potentially violent or dangerous by police were on average no more dangerous than others during the twenty-four months, as measured by the total number of violent incidents recorded in hospital and correctional records. In fact, individuals viewed by police to be potentially violent were each involved in 1.57 fewer officially documented incidents, and in 1.07 fewer criminal charges, than those not so categorized. Apparently, to the extent that the

METFORS clinicians incorporated police assessments into their decision-making on the subject of dangerousness, the accuracy of their assessments was not likely to be enhanced.

POLICE STRATEGIES FOR MANAGING MENTAL CASES

The Forensic Clinic as an Institutional Resource
Police officers, as noted above, have traditionally shown a reluctance to impose psychiatric labels on citizens in conflict with the law (Bittner 1967; Fox and Erickson 1972; Matthews 1970; Teplin 1984a). The referral of subjects to hospital for civil confinement has been viewed by police as an inefficient and time-consuming practice with little occupational payoff. They have risked losing credibility with mental health officials, losing jurisdiction over criminals who might be returned to the streets within hours by the hospital, and losing ground in maintaining their primary self-defined identity as crime fighters rather than social service personnel.

The development of forensic units such as METFORS has therefore been strategically advantageous for the police. Such medico-legal agencies have permitted line officers to exercise both psychiatric and judicial control over criminal defendants. They circumvent the need to channel disturbed individuals directly into an unpredictable and unrewarding psychiatric system. Instead, charges can be laid according to established routine, subjects can be escorted to jail with a recommendation for clinical assessment, and the forensic evaluation can often be convened within twenty-four hours of arrest. By keeping the psychiatrist at arm's length, while at the same time invoking mental health interventions for troublesome cases, the police (and of course the courts) can virtually ensure both a criminal disposition and a medical prescription for the accused.

In their reports about the METFORS patients, Toronto police officers expressed a deeply entrenched frustration with the perceived roadblocks to securing psychiatric confinement through civil mental health procedure. In Case 261, for example, the suspect was arrested on a charge of 'Weapons Dangerous.' The police had responded to a call about a man who was threatening to kill himself with a butcher knife. When they arrived on the scene the suspect was standing in a driveway wielding the weapon in front of him, and as they drove up, he threw the knife in the general direction of the vehicle and was thereupon apprehended. The individual was then escorted by the police to Queen Street Mental Health Centre, where he was refused admittance by the attending psychiatrist. The police then escorted the subject to the local station, laid criminal charges, and wrote the following in their show cause report:

The arresting officers attempted to have him admitted to the facility – but were advised by the staff doctor that they didn't want to admit him – because he was dangerous to the nursing staff. They wished him remanded to the court – so that he could be kept and assessed under the METFORS system used at the facility for violent persons.

The doctors further advised that the accused subject is on medication and as long as he takes this medication he is all right. They are under the impression however that when he's taking it – and is getting better the family interferes and influences him not to take the drugs.

Irregardless of the opinion of the mental facility – it is the opinion of the investigating officers that the accused subject is dangerous – and should not be released from custody – is obviously mental – and should be remanded by the court for a mental assessment under the METFORS system for remanded prisoners. He is very lucky that he was not seriously hurt by the police officers when he attacked them with the knife. (PR 261)

Four days later, the subject in this case was referred by the court to the Brief Assessment Unit. He spent fifteen of the following seventeen months in psychiatric hospital, first on a protracted forensic remand, and later as an involuntary patient. The court disposition for the original 'Weapons Dangerous' charge was eighteen months' probation.

METFORS clearly provided a valuable mechanism for detaining individuals charged with relatively minor offences who would otherwise have been immediately released on bail. Case 050 involved a youth in a pool hall who smashed a window when ordered to leave by the police. Noting that the suspect had a 'mental illness' card on his file, the officers wrote in their show cause report: 'It is apparent that the accused has a mental problem and this was confirmed by his father and it should be taken into consideration when bail is set the mental condition of the accused' (PR 050).

In some instances police would refer to the 'best interests' of accused persons in justifying the mental confinement of defendants. The subject's need for treatment could be invoked as a justification for referral (although in practice treatment is not among the mandates of pre-trial clinical assessments: see Webster, Menzies, and Jackson 1982). At times, the reasoning of police could take on rather odd configurations. In one such case, the officers arrested a twenty-five-year-old man for 'Watch and Beset' after he was found loitering outside the home of his former woman friend. In their report, they observed that 'he is in a very depressed state and is emotionally upset,' and they concluded that 'he is just not mentally capable at this time to handle any type of institution.' Based on this premise, the police recommended that 'this man should be in ... a Hospital where the proper help can be given to him' (PR 523). The glaring contradiction of logic apparently escaped the reporting officers.

On other occasions forensic psychiatrists were able to influence the referral patterns of police and, by extension, of criminal court officials. In the conduct of their daily practice, clinicians could earmark candidates for future psychiatric assessments, and alert legal authorities to these possibilities. Case 467 involved a man accused of 'Indecent Telephone Calls,' most of which were unwisely directed to the downtown headquarters of the Metropolitan Toronto Police. The accused's father reported him to the arresting officer, who was able to initiate clinical referral on the basis of prior psychiatric input. The officer wrote:

The accused has a long history of mental illness and has been in and out of several institutions. During the recent investigations the writer has found that he is a very insecure individual and readily admits that he has problems getting sex with women ...

The investigating officer feels that this man should be examined by some Institution directed by the court. I have spoken with his father and he advises me that a Doctor X ... at the Clarke Institute of Psychiatry has available space for him and would like to have him for a thirty day assessment. (PR 467)

After being referred to the Clarke Institute by the presiding court judge, the defendant spent almost three months on the in-patient ward (on the strength of a relatively minor charge with only a remote possibility of yielding a prison sentence).

In the apprehension of the METFORS patients, it was evident that a consistent institutional ecology developed around police motives and practices. In order to discharge their crime control mandate, the police employ the forensic hospital as a detention facility. To justify these psychiatric referrals, they adopt and master a quasi-medical lexicon that provides clinical reasons for legal outcomes. Alerted to the advantages of forensic dispositions, police learn to merge criminal and clinical criteria in classifying their subjects. Mental illness and criminality are increasingly difficult to disentangle in police accounts of perceived mentally disordered defendants. Moreover, police are inclined to view the clinic as an unproblematic resource for removing troublesome people from the streets. For the police,

METFORS offered a complementary blending of psychiatric and social ordering functions for enhancing their authority over legal subjects.

Moral Assessments and Normal Outrage

From the police perspective, the METFORS patients displayed abundant signs of moral as well as mental defect (Emerson 1969). Arrest records and show cause reports were littered with detailed renditions of the subjects' reprehensible and unconscionable conduct. By mobilizing the 'facts' about defendants' moral careers, police were able to demonstrate not only that these people were miscreant and mad, but also that they *merited* the full force of their forensic dispositions. Degradation strategies of this type functioned as instruments of depersonalization, as they facilitated the construction of 'essential character,' external to the subject's current troubles and circumstances. Such characterizations were incorporated into an authoritative demonstration that the accused person failed to satisfy even the minimal standards of social virtue. By so doing, police depictions provided a powerful set of materials for the rationalization of subsequent decisions throughout the course of the medico-legal process.

This imagery was typically produced by police through the narration of subjects' marginal and intransigent 'moral careers.' Such depictions were based largely on the socio-economic and class occupancy of the accused person, and they figured prominently in recurrent police denunciations of homeless, impoverished, or institutionalized suspects. Police predicated their moral designations largely on the presumption that individuals without emotional or social attachments would continue to wreak havoc on the public peace. Illustrations of this process were recurrent in the METFORS police documents. When reporting the source of income for one individual on welfare, the police inserted 'the good folks of Canada' (PR 520), offering a tacit view concerning the 'real' source of the accused's troubles. In describing a defendant charged with shoplifting a 57-cent tin of anchovies and a 55-cent package of noodles, the arresting officer wrote:

In the interest of the public good a show cause hearing should be commenced and the accused be held in custody ... The accused has a history of mental illness. He rents a room at [ ] Mackenzie Street but has yet to stay there. He is a transient and sleeps where ever he can. He is not married or employed. He has no roots in the community and it is felt that he will not appear for trial ... He has a past history for robbery, offensive weapons, break and enter, theft, fraud, and failing to appear ... A residence check shows that the accused man does not live at [ ] Mackenzie Street, in fact he has no fixed address. (PR 430)

In a case that received extensive coverage in the local media, a twenty-nine-year-old male, a few days after being released from the Oak Ridge Unit at Penetanguishene, was arrested for fondling a seven-year-old girl in her backyard. The police recommended both a show cause hearing and a psychiatric examination. They reasoned that the defendant's extensive institutional history, coupled with the nature of the charges, provided adequate justification for his civil commitment in a mental institution.

This is the first time the subject has been out of the hospital in his life. He left [the hospital] with enough money to get to the city and 1 meal. He has lived in public parks, sleeping on benches and in fact has gone to the washroom in his pants on several occasions ... This subject has no friends, no relatives and since his release from hospital is existing like an animal.

It is quite obvious the subject is not fit to be on the street, he is not capable of looking after himself. A psychiatric examination should be held and I feel that this subject might very well be found certifiable. If not a detention order should be sought in this matter, the grounds are pretty obvious, he has no place to stay, no money, no ties in the community, in fact he is a pretty sorry case to say the least. (PR 502)

Police recurrently characterized their subjects as remorseless and disaffected criminals with no deference to moral or legal authority. One accused was arrested for 'Weapons Dangerous' after he had entered the back kitchen of a neighbourhood restaurant brandishing a knife. The police requested a show cause hearing, declaring '[i]t would appear from this man's previous criminal record that he has very little respect for law and order and also has a drinking problem. He is a burden on the tax payer, being supported entirely by welfare payments. It would seem that if this man is released he will continue with his life of crime to the detriment of the public' (PR 369). Another accused was facing four charges of 'Indecent Exposure.' In the show cause report, the police announced: 'The time has come for the accused to be detained ... He is making a fool out of the law and the court system' (PR 407). A woman on probation assaulted an officer while being arrested on a liquor charge. The synopsis of the occurrence read: 'This accused does not understand the meaning of Keep the Peace and be of good behaviour when bound by a probation order. She apparently has no regard for authority of law ... It is obvious that if released the accused will in all probability due to her addictions and fear of Gaol, not appear in Court as required. And it is requested that she also be required to seek PSYCHIATRIC help' (PR 057).

Failure to convey the proper degree of remorse or respect was also interpreted by police as a harbinger of present mental illness or future violent behaviour. In the mini-trials conducted at the scene of the crime and later in the precinct station, the moral credibility of defendants was largely based on their ability to convey an impression of rueful penitence. The subject in Case 288 was charged with 'Wounding' when, in a drunken condition, he struck a friend on the head with a baseball bat. In the show cause report, the police wrote: 'The accused stated he had struck the man because he was making fun of him at a party. The accused does not appear to be aware of the seriousness of his act and displays no emotion what-soever ... Because the accused does obviously not realize the consequences of his act a similar act could occur if in fact the accused were angered with devastating results' (PR 288). The future possibilities were left to the imagination of the reader.

Given the restrictions on their management of time and resources, and given the limited availability of specialist knowledge about mental disorder, police were led to register judgments based on what were for them familiar categories. Mental illness manifested itself as disrespect, recalcitrance, moral defect, and silence, instead of the more subtle indicators of pathology that in police eyes were more properly monitored by psychiatrists and other mental health professionals. In the above examples, officers were able to gloss over the complexities of defendants' presentations, to focus on a very few master cues that would explain and explain away the subjects' bizarre behaviour. Police were able to make sense by making sensible use of moral and legal concepts that they well understood. The more problematic and esoteric interpretation of troublesome cases was left to the 'experts.'

Tactical Drama and Tacit Messages
The police were the authors of dramatic communications designed to magnify the subjective madness and dangerousness of their subjects. By fashioning such compelling depictions, police sought to validate their interpretations of defendants' conduct, and to impress upon other officials the validity of their inferences. In spite of a formal commitment to objectivity and detachment, in effect these reports were laden with expressive rhetoric that reflected and reinforced the occupational interests of police. As Young suggests, dramatic messages are intended to confirm the interpretive schemes developed by their authors. 'In contrast to scientific communication, which attempts to find an hypothesis that fits a situation, dramatization creates a situation that predetermines the hypothesis' (1965: 151; cf. Burke 1945; Gusfield 1981).

Five different expressions of dramatic rhetoric were apparent in the police accounts of the METFORS subjects. First, officers strove to accumulate a wealth of deviant knowledge about accused persons. As Skolnick writes, 'in the absence of clear goals or specific criteria of competence, police in fact collect enormous quantities of data. Primarily, these data serve as a point of reference, the equivalent of a "set of books" ' (1966: 166). The arrest reports were extensive, one-sided versions of the individual's socio-legal condition, in which multiple descriptions were compiled into master deviant categories of criminality, mental disorder, and dangerousness. Accused persons were characterized not only as lawbreakers, but also as pathological, immoral, unwanted, unconcerned, irredeemable, untreatable, undaunted, and unwell.

These depictions were particularly convincing when they could be framed as integrated biographies about the subject in custody. By documenting the progressive development of pathologies and delinquencies, police could retrospectively arrange the chain of events in order to explain the occurrence and foreclose alternative interpretations. In one such case a nineteen-year-old youth had been placed in a residence operated by a local church group. After he had gone missing on the day of his arrival (along with a sum of money belonging to the church), he was caught and arrested for 'Theft Under.' From available records and testimony, the police pieced together a convincing rendition of the defendant's spiralling moral career.

- single
- no fixed address
- placed at the [home] by members of the [Church group] – stayed one day
- at 9 years of age parents divorced
- at 10 years made ward of the Children's Aid
- placed in a number of group homes
- continually ran away
- placed in the [   ] Training School as a result
- self-admitted mentality of a 10 year old
- attained grade 10 at [   ], a school for slow learners
- received a number of mental assessments – results: slow learner, incompetent
- admits to convictions ... for theft under
- subject is retarded to a degree
- led life of being unwanted
- appears unable to cope with life on his own

— REQUEST A MENTAL EVALUATION BEFORE PROCEEDING WITH THIS CHARGE.
(PR 302)

A second tactical device permitted officers to amplify the deviance and danger attributed to defendants in their transactions with official personnel. At the disposal of police was a vast range of vitiating knowledge that could be translated into powerful messages about the character and conduct of the accused. These accounts were mobilized to convey all that was wrong with these people, and the resulting dramatic narratives could range from pathetic comedy to classical tragedy to theatre of the absurd.

In the following case, two young women were observed by patrol officers throwing glass bottles onto a roadway. The police account of ensuing events, literally and functionally, spoke for itself.

The officer approached the two accused to find out what was going on, and at this point the accused started to swing at the officer ... The accused then swung her purse striking the officer on the right side of the head knocking him unconscious. The officer's partner had called for back up, and was engaged in a struggle with the accused when help arrived and the two were arrested. The accused before the court was arrested on a charge of 'Assault Causing Bodily Harm' and then taken to [the precinct station], there her purse was searched and a steak knife found inside it. She was asked why she had the knife and stated she had the knife to stab pigs like the officer and his partner.

[T]he accused before the court requested the use of washroom facilities. This request was complied with, and the accused was escorted from the office where she was being processed out into the hallway. The accused then ran into the main office where she embraced the co-accused. She was requested to break it up and continue on to the washroom to which she replied to the officer, 'Go fuck yourself'. The officer took hold of the sleeve of the accused's blouse and told her to come along, at which time the accused pulled away from the officer and pulled right out of the blouse leaving it held by the sleeve in the officer's hand. The co-accused then started shouting rape, and started to cause a disturbance. The co-accused was subdued and the officer entered the office where this accused was. He handed the blouse to the accused whereon she punched the officer and grabbed his tie, causing it to tighten and choke the officer. She resisted all effort to cause her to release the tie, and the officer was forced to punch the accused to prevent his being choked. Once struck the accused released the tie and was subdued. The officer was not seriously hurt, but the tie had to be cut off as the knot could not be undone. (PR 137)

In requesting a detention order in this case, the officer showed an ingenuous talent for understatement, writing: 'She has a violent nature and does not like police' (PR 137). The subject was remanded to METFORS twelve days later, where three of the four examining clinicians coded her as 'highly dangerous.' She received three and one-half months in prison and two years probation for the offence.

Such dramatizations of people and events were especially salient in the police portrayal of sex offences, and in their attempt to demonstrate the psychiatric features of bizarre sexual conduct. Case 580 involved a twenty-three-year-old male, a transient in the city, who was arrested by the Metropolitan police on a charge of 'Bestiality.' The arresting officers recorded the complainant's account of the alleged crime:

About a week and a half ago ... I met the accused man on the streets. He had no place to stay and I felt sorry for him so out of Christian Fellowship I invited him to stay at my apartment for the time being. When I met him he had a white dog ... He brought the dog with him when he came to stay at my apartment. Some days after he came to live at my apartment I saw that he was occasionally interfering with his dog in an indecent manner by touching it on its private parts. During the early morning hours of [one night] I was awakened by the whining of M.'s dog. M. was sleeping in the same room as me, in a sleeping bag on the floor. When I was awakened I saw that M. had his dog under the covers with him and he was holding the dog to him. It appeared that he was having intercourse with the dog. M. was making groaning noises and the dog was whining ... The next morning I spoke to M. and I told him what I suspected and that I did not want anything like this going on under my roof. M. then said to me that the dog was his wife and that he would do what he wanted with it. He also said that he loved the dog and that he loved to 'Fuck his dog'. He also said 'I'll fuck my dog if I want to'. I did not report this to the police at this time as I hoped that I could help this man. However I did not think that I was making any headway so I came to see the police and spoke to the Staff Sergeant there ... Later that evening two plainclothes officers came to the apartment and they took M. and the dog away ... (PR 580)

The police developed this episode into a vivid account of the subject's psychotic condition and sexual perversity. 'In the opinion of the investigating sergeants the accused man should be held in custody for the purpose of psychiatric assessment. He apparently has had psychiatric help in the past ... In addition to this his conduct, when in the company of the investigating officers would indicate that he should be examined by a duly qualified medical practitioner, for example he refers to the dog involved in this matter as "his wife" ' (PR 580). This document established a point of departure for subsequent official management of the defendant. Although the charge of bestiality was eventually suspended by the court, he was remanded to METFORS where he was diagnosed as a chronic paranoid schizophrenic. He spent ten of the next twenty-four months in various mental institutions.

A third operational strategy invoked by police involved the reproduction of 'moral panics' (Cohen 1972; Hall, Critcher, Jefferson, Clarke, and Roberts 1978) through identifying subjects with subcultures 'well known' for dangerousness in the community. Subcultural identities could be forwarded as pivotal categories (Lofland 1969) that 'explained away' the bizarre and violent actions of accused persons. Dangerous attributes were thus reinforced by their membership in a wider class of group affiliations. These people were viewed as particularly threatening, because *all such persons* were generally feared by the public. One defendant, a sixteen-year-old black male, had been arrested for an especially violent knife attack for which he eventually received seven years imprisonment. During a street fight, he had stabbed a bystander in the neck, severing the spinal cord and leaving the victim a permanent quadraplegic. The police noted that the assault was unprovoked, and that the subject 'had no remorse for the victim's plight ONLY HOPING THAT THE VICTIM WOULDN'T DIE, SO THAT HE, THE ACCUSED, WOULDN'T HAVE TO GO TO JAIL' (PR 353).

To make sense of the subject and his conduct, and to construct an irrevocable rendition of his dangerous condition, the police fixed upon the cultural affiliations of the accused. For the police, the actions seemed comprehensible, and indicative of enduring risk, given the subject's membership in a particularly 'dangerous' religious and cultural 'sect.' 'The accused has by his own admission affiliated himself with a group of blacks, both young and old, who refer to themselves as "Rastafarians", "Rastas", or "Dreds". This group of individuals express very antisocial attitudes and have been involved in a large number of serious violent crimes in the Toronto area over the past few years – these crimes run from Murder to Attempting to Obstruct Justice by threatening Crown witnesses' (PR 353).

Fourth, trouble could be regularly translated into danger by reference to subjects' disruption of official routines. Judgments about insanity and violence in these instances were grounded not so much in the nature of the offence itself, but in the usurpation of scarce police and other official resources. Such persons were seen to be disordered or dangerous because they violated officials' perceptions about their own value to the community. In one case, a man had been recently discharged from a psychiatric hospital, where according to the police report he had 'received insurmountable doses of medication.' At 1:30 on a weekday morning he pulled a fire alarm located on a street corner in the south end of the city. The police wrote:

Activation of the fire signal box was recorded at the fire department which resulted in three fire trucks and a fire departmental vehicle to be dispatched to the scene from the fire hall assigned to that particular area. This irresponsible action on behalf of the accused meant that the units and trained firemen responding to his false alarm could not be utilized elsewhere in the event that a fire of a serious nature occurred simultaneously and a fire unit, or units, from another hall more distant had to be summoned resulting in valuable time lost in the preservation of lives and property.

The units responding to this particular call ascertained after some time that their attendance was not required. The police car which also attended to this needless call located the accused about 100 yards east of the location of the signal box ...

It appears that the accused ... seems to suffer from mental disorder in the opinion of the police. He was ... taken to the police station where he was charged with this offence in the hopes that he will continue to receive psychiatric treatment for his condition as there seems to be no doubt the accused will continue his actions until some danger is encountered. (PR 336)

Condemnation of this kind was a direct product of transactions where enforcement efforts were frustrated and police 'lost face' in bringing off the arrest. The defendant in another such case had locked himself in his apartment and telephoned the police threatening to shoot his parents. A two-hour stand-off ensued, during which time the police were unable to make contact with the suspect by either phone or loudspeaker. When they finally entered the apartment, they found that the man was alone, had no weapon, and in fact was in the middle of an abortive suicide attempt using his gas stove. Subsequently, the officers wrote: 'A total of five divisional uniform cars with 2 men each were tied up, as well as 3 E.T.F.[6] units with 6 men, 5 oldclothes officers, 2 Investigative Sergeants, 2 uniform sergeants, and 3 ambulances were tied up from approximately 7:20 p.m. until the time of his arrest at 9:30 p.m. This is a grand total of 14 vehicles tied up and 26 men tied up for approximately 2 hours' (PR 357). On investigation, the police found that the defendant had a history of mental disorder and two prior criminal convictions. These provided sufficient reason for interpreting his actions as indicative of imminent danger: 'The accused's mental background, and criminal record clearly indicate that the accused is in need of psychiatric assessment, and if released in his present state is a definite danger to the public' (PR 357).

A fifth police tactic involved incorporating into reports a tacit message directed at prosecutors, clinicians, and judges. These documents offered courses of action to other officials, based on police inferences about the need for official intervention. Signals took on an especially retributive quality when the defendant was seen to have escaped the appropriate judicial tariff merited by past deeds. In such cases messages were laden with ominous overtones, and they underscored the prior indiscretions of overly permissive officials. In Case 487, for example, the police arrested the accused on charges of 'Theft Auto,' 'Criminal Negligence – Auto' and 'Failure to Remain.' He had attempted to steal a car in a shopping mall, but lost control of the vehicle, striking a parked car and a fire hydrant. The police undertook to establish a causal link between the subject's dangerousness to the public and the unduly lenient judicial treatment he had previously experienced from the courts. Further, they were able to impart a psychiatric interpretation of events into the account as a 'kicker' to reinforce these inferences. They wrote:

There is little doubt that this accused man has no regard for the law. He is on 3 bails and 2 terms of probation. He is unable to live with any members of his family and has in the past stolen from his parents and aunts and uncles. He appears to have no direction and is a menace to the public.

A MENTAL ASSESSMENT OF THIS MAN IS NEEDED

CONVICTIONS:

October/72: Indecent Assault Female, fail to comply 2 counts, 18 months probation on each charge.
June/77: Unlawfully in a dwelling, possession over, suspended sentence and 18 months probation and 100 dollars cash.
December/77: Break and enter with intent, suspended sentence 2 years probation.

NOW YOU KNOW WHY HE IS STILL GETTING INTO TROUBLE. (PR 487)

Police were especially driven to convey these messages when the defendant was viewed to be a public danger. At the distant end of the normalcy continuum, violence and madness were approached as interchangeable phenomena, and extraordinary measures were needed to secure the containment of such persons. One defendant, eventually remanded to METFORS, was accused of pushing a woman onto the subway tracks for no apparent reason. The victim had narrowly escaped being struck by a passing train. The investigating officers determined that they were dealing with a 'deranged' subject. They wrote: 'The man denies all knowledge of this occurrence. He is erratic and goes from a very quiet mood to very talkative and loud with crying fits ... He stated "WHORES ARE ALWAYS MOCKING HIM" ... LENGTHY MENTAL HISTORY ... Police are recommending a mental assessment on this accused and feel he is a grave danger to the public in his present condition' (PR 172).

Such cases were relatively unproblematic for police, since the drama implicit in their accounts of events required little enhancement. Police could enlist readily available criminal and medical histories to establish a biography of dangerousness, as in Case 197, where the defendant was charged with two counts of 'Assault Causing Bodily Harm.' The police report read:

The accused before the court approached the victim (11 year-old boy) who he has known for some time at the rear of his apartment building ... The accused took the victim to his apartment telling the boy he would let him see his budgie. Upon entering the apartment the accused took the boy to the bedroom. Before leaving the living room area the accused bunched a tea towel up in his hand so the victim would not see same. The accused then told the victim to lie down on the bed which he did. The accused then told the victim he was going to scare him and quickly pulled out the towel. The accused then wrapped the towel around the victim's neck and squeezed until the victim went unconscious. The boy was released and upon arriving home was taken to ... hospital. The victim suffered severe abrasions to the neck area and burst blood vessels in one eye.

The accused before the court is a danger to the public at large and as such should not be released from custody ... The accused ... informs investigating officers that he feels a sense of power during the choking act. There is no doubt that on some occasion if this man is released from custody that the choking act could very well result in asphyxiation and a homicide charge ... There is no doubt this accused requires further psychiatric assessment. (PR 197)

Four months prior to his arrest, this defendant had been an in-patient at METFORS.[7] During that remand, the psychiatrist had written that his 'risk [to the community] is low at this time and it is my opinion that Mr. K. is suitable for both bail and for probation.' On the strength of the above police report, the BAU psychiatrist was induced to alter his prognosis on this second assessment: 'The above opinion supporting bail and probation for Mr. K. in the past, is modified in light of his recent behaviour. It is my opinion that Mr. K. does represent such a substantial danger to the community, that he is not a candidate for bail or probation' (PL 197). Subsequently, the subject was remanded for extended assessment, recommended for 'testicular enucleation' (castration) by a sexologist at another hospital,[8] and ultimately sentenced to five years in penitentiary.

On rare occasions, this police preoccupation with dangerousness could be modified, and officers could be induced to 'go easy' in their recommendations for medico-legal disposition. In Case 118, the defendant had been charged with threatening a shopkeeper with a knife. The reporting police officer offered an inspired account of the suspect's medical condition, and of its relevance to the case. It seemed that the accused had sustained extensive burns on his legs two years earlier, after being shot in the stomach and crashing his car during a failed robbery attempt. He was still undergoing skin grafts on his legs, and was scheduled for further surgery within two weeks of his current arrest. The charging officer opined, on the basis of this information, that medical procedures in the case might in fact operate in the interests of public safety: 'The investigating Officers feel this man is a danger to the public if released ... However the man is to go into hospital shortly. If a doctor's certificate was produced he could possibly be released on a cash bail. He is to have his legs grafted together so it is unlikely that he would run' (PR 118).

SUMMARY

This chapter has reviewed the front-line assessment of the METFORS subjects by arresting police officers. The discretionary practices of police were closely related to subsequent medico-legal decisions about these forensic patients. In their depictions of mental disorder and dangerousness, the police were able to present convincing arguments for the psychiatric and carceral confinement of accused persons. Patrol officers recurrently supplied formidable packages of clinically and legally relevant data that were routinely incorporated into the diagnoses and dispositions of forensic agents and judicial authorities. They successfully translated their complex transactions with suspects into coherent, consistent, and convincing portrayals of delinquency and disorder.

In the reports reviewed in this chapter, police were primarily concerned with maximizing the ambit of institutional control over defendants perceived to be mentally ill. Their adoption of psychiatric rhetoric and reasoning has been encouraged by the development of forensic agencies such as METFORS, which allow police simultaneously to secure psychiatric intervention *and* retain criminal jurisdiction through the exercise of their powers to arrest. Consequently the police have come to appreciate and to seek the occupational payoffs associated with clinical solutions to legal problems. These reports were replete with references to the psychiatric history, mental pathology, and clinical dangerousness of forensic subjects. Police were able to legitimate their actions and to secure desired outcomes by structuring their efforts according to the anticipated responses of clinical experts and legal officials. Police accounts of disorder and danger were systematically related to the diagnostic and dispositional judgments of other authorities, and their initial formulations were likely to survive relatively unaltered throughout the course of the subjects' institutional careers.

In sum, the arresting officers were able to establish an explanatory framework for making sense of the irrational conduct displayed by the METFORS patients. As forensic gatekeepers, they offered persuasive accounts of madness and violence that were prospectively geared to maximize control over subjects, and over the subsequent judgments of psychiatrists, prosecutors, judges, and other medico-legal authorities. By focusing on the bizarre, outrageous, and uncontrollable features of criminal conduct, the police were routinely successful in manufacturing powerful images that demanded therapeutic or carceral intervention or both. They alerted other medical and legal officials to the 'essential' character of criminal defendants, and hence laid the groundwork for the ensuing forensic careers of the METFORS patients.

3

The Forensic Corridor 1: The METFORS Brief Assessment Unit

Sir, though I am not splenetive and rash,
Yet have I in me something dangerous.

WILLIAM SHAKESPEARE   *Hamlet* v, 1

It is with our judgments as with our watches: no two go just alike, yet
each believes his own.

ALEXANDER POPE

DISCRETION AND DISORDER IN THE BRIEF ASSESSMENT UNIT

The METFORS Brief Assessment Unit was the nerve centre of the forensic
remand system in Metropolitan Toronto during the period of this study.
During their single-day confinement in the BAU, the 592 criminal defendants
were subjected to a concentrated round of clinical activity designed to
expose their deviant identities, and to portray their pathologies as legally
relevant and objectively real. This chapter enters this first stage in the
'forensic corridor' in an effort to chart the diagnostic practices of team
members in the BAU, and to discern their implications for the forensic
experiences of the METFORS subjects. Through an integrated quantitative
and documentary analysis of the medical records generated by presiding
clinicians, I will be surveying the discretionary strategies enlisted to di-

agnose psychiatric disorder and impose legal order on this group of accused persons.

As described in the Introduction and Chapter 1, the Brief Assessment Unit clinicians were relatively free to improvise their characterizations of forensic patients. Following a ten-minute perusal of police reports, and a diagnostic interview that seldom exceeded forty-five minutes, team members were able to formulate powerful accounts of mental disorder among the METFORS cohort. These expert notations harboured a formidable arsenal of legal, psychiatric, and moral denunciations. Whereas they appeared to be rule-governed and grounded in the formal logic of diagnostic reasoning, these brief assessments were more often a loosely assembled production of ad hoc theories about madness and criminality. They were facilitated by the ambiguity of such open-ended constructs as mental disorder and dangerousness. They were mediated by the low visibility of clinical determinations which were at least partially insulated from the scrutiny of the courts. Moreover, they gained legitimacy from the willingness of judicial officials to delegate responsibility for discretionary powers that they were themselves loath to assume.

Forensic experts are in the business of making sense (Handel 1982). Professional classifiers are involved in the routinization, regularization, and normalization of images that impart a sense of structure to their daily activities, and that maintain an impression of orderliness in their occupational environment. To make sense, clinical and other authorities continuously compress a seemingly indigestible array of stimuli into manageable packages that will enable decision-making 'in the here and now' (Hawkins 1981: 107). They normalize by reducing information to levels of complexity and intensity that will be acceptable to themselves, to their more powerful audiences, and often even to the subjects of their inquiries (Scheff 1972; Sudnow 1965).

Forensic decisions are based on the truncated packages of official data that are acknowledged by their clinical authors. The volumes of records and dossiers, assembled and stored in medical libraries and computer files, become impressive (and expensive) window dressing used to demonstrate the legitimacy of professional opinion. In practice, the fate of subjects is often sealed long before their face-to-face encounter with their psychiatric judges (Allen 1987; Pfohl 1978). The salient themes in forensic assessments are usually established prior to the conduct of the clinical interviews themselves (Arkes and Hammond 1986; Kahneman, Slovic, and Tversky 1982). The process is devoted less to diagnosis than to legitimation (Habermas

1975), to ' ... the discovery of something new (or old) on the basis of what is already known' (Leiter 1980: 146).

Given the limited flexibility of control institutions and the frequent inability of their members to manage complexity, 'routinization schemes' (Waegel 1981: 274; see Roth 1977) become the professional's cognitive tools for making sense and appearing sensible. Official designators work to attain consistency, to establish an 'essential self' for subjects (Blum and McHugh 1971: 108) that will inform all further organizational response to problematic cases. As Lofland notes (1969: 123), such official categories tend to cluster into pivotal indicators of deviance. Whereas clinicians seek to maximize the list of stigmatizing labels applied to their subjects, these multiple indicators are merged into master categories through the process of imputing pathology and criminality. '[C]oding as deviant is facilitated if there are available for use in small numbers a large number of alternatively sufficient indicators. One of the most effective features of some psychiatric coding schemes is their ability to use only a few of a very large number of alternative indicators in order to code Actor as pivotally deviant' (Lofland 1969: 141).

In the act of reducing clinical complexity, expert classifiers are able to project a kaleidoscope of deviant images about criminal defendants, to select only the most colourful attributes of such profiles, and to portray the final product of assessments in simplified and monochromatic tones. This decolourization of complex and multihued forensic cases represents a direct response to the pragmatic concerns of legitimacy work. Pivotal categories allow a professional mastery over otherwise unintelligible phenomena. They also facilitate the compression of data into forms that will be comprehensible to legal audiences (Gusfield 1981: 98).

Moreover, such discretionary practices reduce the risk of committing official classification 'errors.' Pivotal categories are so broadly defined, so enabling, that no cluster of deviant attributes could ever entirely miss the mark. Diagnoses of mental disorder, incompetency, psychopathy, dangerousness, and so on, are fail-safe categories. They may be recurrently disputed or challenged, but they are virtually invulnerable to meaningful or lasting invalidation.

These imputation practices assume similar patterns at every stage of the medico-legal corridor, and they take on a number of recognizable features throughout the process. Initial records (police reports, case histories) are selectively read by official classifiers (Cicourel 1968). Only data relevant to the attribution work of professionals are compiled by line personnel

(Garfinkel 1967). Psychological tests and other diagnostic instruments are applied to facilitate the closure of master categories (see Chapter 4). Lines of inquiry pursued during interviews tend to be stylized and pre-packaged (Pfohl 1978; Warren 1982). Final reports gloss procedures and particulars in order to magnify the few pivotal labels that are seen to 'really apply.' Medical meaning and criminological commonsense are institutionally achieved by denying the authenticity of subjects' own accounts, by relying on intuition disguised as science, and by attaching properties of legitimacy and permanency to resulting official versions of forensic reality. This is the foundation of psychiatric discretion in the METFORS Brief Assessment Unit, for making sense of forensic subjects undergoing one-day clinical evaluations. The remainder of this chapter is concerned with both a statistical account of these decisions and a documentary analysis of medical records compiled by the BAU team members.

AN AGGREGATE ANALYSIS OF DECISION-MAKING IN THE BAU

This section examines the construction of forensic judgments by the Brief Assessment Unit professionals. The following data extracted from the MET-FORS documents are used to explore in detail the clinical designation of mental disorder, dangerousness, and related constructs, and to associate these decisions with background and contextual factors, and with the characteristics of clinicians and clientele. This analysis is meant to complement the handful of published studies (e.g. Allen 1987; Cocozza and Steadman 1976; Forst 1980; Hiday 1981; Konečni, Mulcahy, and Ebbesen 1980; Pfohl 1978; Roesch and Golding 1980; Scheff 1972; Steadman and Morrissey 1983; Warren 1982) that have been concerned with reconstructing and accounting for the discretionary activities of forensic clinicians. By incorporating quantitative materials abstracted out of the Brief Assessment Unit reports and the single-page instruments completed by professional staff following each interview conducted during 1978 (see Chapter 1 and Appendix A), I attempt to map the contours of forensic classifications applied to the 592 METFORS defendants.

Initially, the various decision variables yielded from clinical team members were computed to determine the frequency distribution for such judgments as fitness to stand trial, dangerousness, and related issues. From the outset it was clear that the attribution of dangerousness was a central feature of METFORS brief assessments. An examination of the 583 available intake forms completed by the attending nurse revealed that dangerousness was mentioned as a clinical concern in 375 cases (64.3 per cent). Moreover, the presiding psychiatrist referred to the dangerousness of subjects in all 592 summary assessment forms, and in 55.7 per cent of letters to criminal court judges (see Chapter 5).

In Table 3.1, decisions about dangerousness to self and others, and fitness to stand trial, extracted from assessment forms, are presented for each occupational group. As measured by its perceived incidence among the METFORS patients, dangerousness to others substantially outdistanced the other two issues as a relevant concern. For example, psychiatrists assigned 43.1 per cent of their BAU patients to 'medium' or 'high' categories of dangerousness to others. In comparison, only 20.8 per cent of subjects were located in the medium or high ranges of dangerousness to self, and only 16.1 per cent were viewed as unfit to stand trial. Similar distributions among categories held across all five clinical professions, with social workers registering a slightly higher level of perceived dangerousness than other occupations.

Following this, the decisions of BAU psychiatrists concerning fitness to stand trial, dangerousness to others, and dangerousness to self were cross-classified. To facilitate these computations, 'unclear' decisions were deleted, and categories were collapsed to produce two levels of perceived dangerousness ('no/low' and 'medium/high'). Among those 385 patients assigned by psychiatrists to the 'low' end of the dichotomized dangerousness-to-self variable, 160 (41.6 per cent) were ranked in the 'high' range of dangerousness to others. In contrast, a full 89 of 117 persons viewed as dangerous to themselves (76.1 per cent) were also ascribed as dangerous to others. This pattern reflected a positive and statistically significant relationship between psychiatric imputations of dangerousness to self and others ($\chi^2 = 41.38$, df $= 1$, $p < 0.0001$). Interestingly, when the dichotomized depictions of dangerousness to others were disaggregated across decisions about fitness to stand trial, there was little difference in the percentage of 'dangerous cases' between 'fit' subjects (49.6 per cent of 365 cases) and 'unfit' patients (49 per cent of 365 cases). However, a substantially higher 69 per cent of the 42 individuals described as 'questionably fit' by psychiatrists (and typically remanded for protracted assessment – see Chapter 4) were rated as dangerous to others ($\chi^2 = 5.83$, df $= 2$, $p = 0.05$). It appeared that psychiatric attributions of potential dangerousness to others were associated with high rankings on potential suicidal or self-injurious behaviour, and with marginal or middle-range judgments about fitness.

A second series of research questions were concerned with the structural arrangements among the various clinical judgments rendered by the MET-

TABLE 3.1
Assessments of dangerousness and fitness by BAU clinicians

	Per cent no	Per cent low	Per cent unclear	Per cent medium	Per cent high	Number of cases	Mean*
Dangerousness to self							
Psychiatrists	33.8	34.0	11.5	16.2	4.6	592	2.24
Psychologists	27.7	28.7	16.8	19.3	7.6	513	2.51
Social workers	21.3	49.9	9.4	13.0	6.4	437	2.33
Nurses	44.4	20.5	21.4	10.5	3.2	590	2.08
Correctional officers	25.4	21.9	27.7	18.4	6.5	566	2.59
Dangerousness to others							
Psychiatrists	13.7	29.4	13.9	29.6	13.5	592	3.00
Psychologists	10.7	17.9	19.9	30.0	21.4	513	3.34
Social workers	6.4	28.9	11.0	28.3	25.6	438	3.38
Nurses	21.2	12.9	22.7	25.6	17.6	590	3.06
Correctional officers	14.1	12.0	33.4	21.4	19.1	566	3.19

	Per cent yes	Per cent questionable	Per cent no	Number of cases	Mean†
Fitness					
Psychiatrists	72.8	11.1	16.1	548	1.43
Psychologists	79.8	8.3	11.9	471	1.32
Social workers	83.0	5.9	11.1	406	1.28
Nurses	76.0	9.3	14.7	546	1.39
Correctional officers	75.9	8.2	16.0	526	1.40

* Where no = 1; low = 2; unclear = 3; medium = 4; high = 5.
† Where yes = 1; questionable = 2; no = 3.

FORS professionals in the Brief Assessment Unit. Altogether the attending psychiatrists recorded their decisions, following brief assessments, on ten separate issues relating to the forensic process: fitness for trial, mental disorder, certifiability, need for in-patient treatment, need for further assessment, fitness for bail, need for out-patient care, need for custodial confinement, and dangerousness to both self and others. These diagnoses were recorded on a three-point scale (no, questionable, yes) with the exception of dangerousness, which was rated on a five-point scale (no, low, questionable, medium, high – see Chapter 1 and Appendix A).

In Table 3.2, the results of correlational and factorial analyses are presented in an effort to elaborate on the internal relationships among these various psychiatric judgments. The matrix in the upper section of Table 3.2 displays the Pearson product-moment coefficients among all zero-order combinations of decision variables. Several patterns are brought into relief in this matrix. First, psychiatrists' endorsements about the dangerousness of their subjects to others were positively correlated with decisions concerning dangerousness to self, unfitness for bail, certifiability, and need for a custodial setting ($r = 0.273, 0.345, 0.122,$ and 0.344 respectively); they were inversely associated with recommendations for out-patient treatment ($r = -0.214$). Second, variables measuring the perceived mental status of METFORS patients (general mental disorder, certifiability, recommendations for in-patient treatment and further evaluation) were all positively correlated, with coefficients ranging from 0.43 to 0.76. Third, psychiatric recommendations against pre-trial bail release were correlated with both mental disorder and dangerousness assessments, suggesting that the METFORS classifiers were advising pre-trial detention not only for patients whom they considered dangerous, but also when they detected manifestations of clinical pathology among their patients (see Chapter 5). Fourth, prescriptions for out-patient treatment were negatively correlated with all items except 'mental disorder' and 'dangerousness to self.' Apparently, psychiatrists were willing to recommend treatment in the community only where an absence of serious mental illness was accompanied by negligible levels of dangerousness to others.

In the second half of Table 3.2 these ten decision variables were subjected to a principal component analysis, resulting in the identification of three factors which accounted for just over one-third of the variance. It seemed that psychiatric decisions in the BAU were roughly aligned along three basic dimensions: (1) 'Mental Disorder' (subsuming judgments about fitness to stand trial, general mental disorder, certifiability, need for in-patient treatment, and need for further assessment); (2) 'Suitability for Release' (cor-

TABLE 3.2
Principal component analysis of decisions by BAU psychiatrists

Correlation matrix

	TFIT	MDIS	CTABL	INPAT	FURTH	BFIT	OUTPAT	CUSET	DSF	DOF
TFIT	—	.565	.665	.755	.590	.381	−.287	−.181	.193	.015
MDIS		—	.473	.572	.468	.240	.016	−.159	.203	−.010
CTABL			—	.591	.434	.325	−.252	−.073	.216	.122
INPAT				—	.577	.353	−.262	−.187	.220	.068
FURTH					—	.339	−.205	−.188	.224	.064
BFIT						—	−.444	.427	.196	.345
OUTPAT							—	−.223	−.032	−.214
CUSET								—	.066	.344
DSF									—	.273

Loadings on principal components

	Mean	Standard deviation	Component 1 Mental disorder	Component 2 Suitability for release	Component 3 Dangerousness	Communality
TFIT	1.43	0.75	0.877			0.807
MDIS	1.95	0.96	0.739			0.595
CTABL	1.32	0.72	0.749			0.597
INPAT	1.55	0.85	0.864			0.758
FURTH	1.72	0.95	0.750			0.573
BFIT	2.26	0.92		0.735		0.708
OUTPAT	1.57	0.85		−0.756		0.678
CUSET	1.72	0.84		0.696		0.671
DSF	2.28	1.21			0.825	0.743
DOF	3.03	1.30			0.620	0.613
Eigenvalue			3.760	1.924	1.059	
% of variance			37.6	19.2	10.6	

Note
N = 547 (listwise deletion of missing data)
TFIT = fitness to stand trial
MDIS = mentally disordered
CTABL = certifiable
INPAT = in-patient treatment needed
FURTH = further assessment needed

BFIT = fitness for bail
OUTPAT = out-patient treatment needed
CUSET = custodial setting needed
DSF = dangerousness to self
DOF = dangerousness to others

relating positively with unfitness for bail and need for custodial confinement, and negatively with recommendations for out-patient treatment); and (3) 'Dangerousness' (including ascriptions about danger to both self and others). According to this analysis, then, the various clinical judgments rendered by psychiatrists in the Brief Assessment Unit could be reduced to these three fundamental categories. Beyond the generic considerations of pathology, dangerousness, and need for confinement, further elaboration of the formal medical and legal issues themselves seemed to add little to an understanding of forensic decision-making.

Next, Table 3.3 disaggregates psychiatrists' decisions about dangerousness to others, dangerousness to self, and fitness to stand trial across twenty-four variables measuring the socio-demographic and medico-legal attributes of METFORS subjects. Results are displayed only for those t and F scores that surpassed 0.05 levels of significance, and for product-moment coefficients above an absolute value of 0.10. Seven of the background variables (gender, employment status at arrest, occupation, race, marital status, living status, and estimated IQ) failed to reach the criterion threshold for any of these three psychiatric decisions.

For judgments about dangerousness to others, a full twelve of the twenty-four background attributes surpassed the criterion level of association (years of education, number of previous psychiatric in-patient admissions, history of post-sentence incarceration, number of prior convictions, previous convictions for violence, evidence of past violence in official records, type of charge precipitating the psychiatric remand, clinical diagnosis, level of alcohol use, level of drug use, conduct in the Brief Assessment Unit, and presence of delusions during the interview). In contrast, decisions about dangerousness to self were related to only four background variables (number of prior in-patient hospitalizations, evidence of a previous suicide attempt, level of drug use, and behaviour in the Brief Assessment Unit).

Psychiatric determinations about fitness to stand trial tended to be positively associated with general indicators of a mental health history, but were mostly correlated negatively with evidence of criminality and violence. For example, patients found unfit to stand trial were more likely to have exhibited delusions or hallucinations, to be diagnosed as psychotic, to have behaved in a psychotic, angry, or depressed manner while in the BAU, to be charged with a non-violent offence, to have been born outside Canada, to have a record of prior hospitalizations, and to be older than persons considered to be fit for trial. Conversely, there were fewer unfit subjects with histories of juvenile court involvement, violence, or incarceration, and this group collectively yielded fewer prior convictions and convictions for violence, and lower levels of alcohol consumption.

On the basis of the above statistical work, one might be led to conclude that forensic decisions about fitness to stand trial and dangerousness were significantly associated with a range of patient characteristics, including prior criminality, mental status, substance abuse, and general socio-demographic circumstance. However, it was also evident that these many background variables were relatively powerless as predictors of clinical decisions in the Brief Assessment Unit. Among all of the statistically significant relationships documented in Table 3.3, the most efficient predictor of psychiatric judgments was the type of charge precipitating the METFORS assessment, which accounted for only 13.5 per cent of the variance in dangerousness designations. Decisions in the BAU were at best only loosely aligned with the 'objective' stimuli presented by criminal defendants and their medico-legal environment. By extrapolation, the clinical judgments of forensic professionals had to be grounded in criteria and considerations largely independent of their patients' attributes.

Moreover, these vagaries in patterns of decision-making were compounded by discrepancies among the inferential practices of individual psychiatrists. Table 3.4 displays the outcome of a multiple classification analysis comparing the mean ratings of dangerousness to others assigned to patients by the four attending METFORS psychiatrists, controlling for prior violence, behaviour in the clinic, previous incarcerations and hospitalizations, and level of alcohol use. The degree of perceived dangerousness assigned to subjects was largely contingent on which psychiatrist was making the decision in any given case. Adjusted mean ratings for the four BAU psychiatrists were: 3.12 for Psychiatrist 1, 3.06 for Psychiatrist 2, 2.98 for Psychiatrist 3, and only 2.37 for Psychiatrist 4. All other factors in the analysis being held constant,[4] Psychiatrist 1 rated patients almost a full point higher on dangerousness to others than did Psychiatrist 4.

Clear inter-rater differences were therefore evident in the dangerousness ratings of the Brief Assessment Unit clinicians. In general terms, psychiatric designations at METFORS represented more than the simple transformation of input data into scientific outcome. They were the product of active clinical interpretations, the selective incorporation and reconstruction of background materials, and the application of diagnostic categories that all functioned to dissociate the attributes of subjects from the content of judgments defining their legal and medical status. The remainder of this chapter will focus on these discretionary strategies and contextual forces

TABLE 3.3
Associations between background variables and psychiatrists' decisions

Background variable	Dangerousness to others			Dangerousness to self			Fitness to stand trial		
	t	df	p	t	df	p	t	df	p
Gender									
Prior suicide attempt	4.42	590	<.001	7.14	590	<.001			
Prior incarceration	10.13	590	<.001				−3.51	546	.001
Prior violence							−3.83	546	<.001
Employed at arrest									
Juvenile court record							−4.56	539	<.001
Hallucinations							12.33	546	<.001
Delusions	2.32	589	.02				17.75	545	<.001
	F	df	p	F	df	p	F	df	p
Behaviour in BAU	5.51	5,541	<.001	10.97	5,541	<.001	69.32	5,541	<.001
Occupation									
Race							3.34	5,536	.006
Place of origin									
Marital status									
Living status									
Current charge	42.46	2,545	<.001				6.23	2,545	.002
Diagnosis	9.41	5,541	<.001				71.11	5,541	<.001

	Pearson r	Pearson r	Pearson r
Estimated IQ			
Level of alcohol use	.159		−.194
Level of drug use	.112	.150	.108
Age			
Number of prior convictions	.114		−.169
Number of prior violent convictions	.298		−.152
Years of education	−.108		
Number of prior hospitalizations	.109	.181	.249

Note

For dangerousness to self and others: 1 = no; 2 = low; 3 = unclear; 4 = medium; 5 = high.

For fitness to stand trial: 1 = yes; 2 = - questionable; 3 = no.

The *t* statistic was generated for dichotomous background variables, *F* for non-metric variables with three or more categories, and *r* for metric variables. Only significant results are shown for *t* and *F* statistics. Only Pearson coefficients above |.10| are included. *N* = 592.

TABLE 3.4
Multiple classification analysis: psychiatrists' predictions of dangerousness to others

	SS	df	MS	F	p
Explained	205.09	12	17.09	12.59	<.001
Residual	781.81	576	1.36		
Grand mean = 2.99		$R = .456$		$R^2 = .208$	

Variable and category	N	Unadjusted mean	Eta	Adjusted mean for independents and covariates	Beta	F	p
Psychiatrist			0.17		0.17	7.03	<.001
Psychiatrist 1	242	3.15		3.12			
Psychiatrist 2	134	2.98		2.98			
Psychiatrist 3	150	2.99		3.06			
Psychiatrist 4	63	2.40		2.37			
Previous violence			0.39		0.35	70.25	<.001
No	306	2.51		2.55			
Yes	283	3.51		3.47			
Behaviour in BAU			0.21		0.17	3.94	.002
Co-operative/pleasant	249	2.83		2.83			
Depressed/despondent	150	2.88		2.92			
Angry/hostile	72	3.67		3.50			
Psychotic/delusional	96	3.02		3.11			
Refused to co-operate	10	2.90		2.94			
Violent/acted out	12	2.56		2.61			
Previous incarceration			0.18		0.02	0.23	NS
No	312	2.77		2.97			
Yes	277	3.24		3.02			
Level of alcohol use						17.05	<.001
Number of previous hospitalizations						6.91	.009

that contributed to the wide variations in medico-legal decision-making among the BAU professionals.

THE IMPUTATIONAL DYNAMICS OF BRIEF ASSESSMENTS

The METFORS clinicians were empowered by the courts to construct official renditions of criminal pathology – accounts that reflected not only the deviant status of accused persons, but also the special knowledge and authority informing the professional practices of their authors. Forensic discretion in the Brief Assessment Unit was anchored in the creative mobilization of recipes and exemplars (Imershein and Simons 1976) that first and foremost served organizational goals and occupational interests. The BAU clinicians worked to mediate between their environment of medicolegal systems and rules, and their own pragmatic goals in producing acceptable versions of psychiatric reality. The experts' diagnoses emerged from the interplay between their individual apprehensions of pathology and criminality and the more general organizational framework of problems and solutions within which they worked (see Goffman 1983: 4). The power of psychiatrists and other clinicians to define forensic reality was shaped by members' strategies in managing this environment and using its enabling features to further their occupational interests (see Blumer 1969; Giddens 1976; McBarnet 1981).

The remainder of this chapter comprises a reconstruction, from the medical records compiled by clinicians in the METFORS Brief Assessment Unit, of the recipes and rules-of-thumb that were mobilized to facilitate the discovery of madness and criminality among the 592 criminal defendants. Eight general discretionary practices emerged in the analysis of these documents.

First, psychiatrists and other experts were alert to signs of resistance on the part of subjects, and they worked to neutralize such gestures, often interpreting them as symptoms of mental illness.

Second, team members endeavoured to maintain a united front in their official portrayals of collective decision-making. All evidence of dissensus, contradiction, and conflict was routinely erased from written documents and from reports distributed to legal audiences.

Third, clinicians regularly conducted 'trials of moral identity' (Benson and Hughes 1983: 143). Their evaluations of pathology and violence were informed by global judgments about the moral character of accused persons. Forensic decisions embraced the totality of an individual's 'personality structure,' and were saturated with references to the inherent deficiency, depravity, and degeneracy of subjects' value systems.

Fourth, clinicians routinely suspected their patients of denial, contrivance, and deceit. The behaviour and utterances of accused persons were continuously open to challenge, credibility was withheld, and their claims to normality were reformulated by clinicians into symptoms of pathology.

Fifth, forensic decision-makers worked under the assumption that mental illness and criminality were frequently covert and subterranean phenomena, which could be exposed only by probing into the hidden depths of mind and consciousness.

Sixth, wherever possible, clinicians imposed stereotypical categories upon their subjects, producing reified and one-sided caricatures of their psycholegal condition. Given the ready availability of labels that were widely accepted in the popular and professional culture, the BAU classifiers could apply their diagnoses with minimal cognitive expenditure, while maintaining the appearance that their judgments were governed solely by the application of scientific principles to medical problems.

Seventh, clinical diagnoses were organized according to the legalistic ecology of the METFORS clinic. Affiliated with and dependent upon the criminal courts, psychiatric authorities recurrently applied a crime-responsibility-punishment model for interpreting 'medical' cases. The correctionalist mentality of forensic clinicians was a prominent feature of their official responses to patients, and was characterized by frequent references to the efficacy of punishment, to the value of imprisonment, and to the need to exercise constraint over disruptive and predatory clients.

Eighth, the determination of dangerousness was a prominent mandate for the Brief Assessment Unit team members. Despite the apparent focus upon fitness to stand trial, clinical diagnosis, and related issues, in practice the METFORS professionals were consistently alert to indications of potential violence among subjects, and they developed a range of strategies that facilitated the identification of dangerousness in the BAU. As official definers of psycho-legal reality, the clinicians were particularly attentive to the verbal and behavioural cues that could be assembled during clinical exchanges, merged with available medical and legal reports, and offered as evidence for the presence of imminent danger.

Deactivating Subject Resistance

The METFORS clinicians invariably responded in negative terms to overt displays of resistance on the part of accused persons in the BAU. Efforts to delegitimize the assessment process, or to devalue the professional expertise of team members, were commonly interpreted as signs of mental illness or manifestations of criminal character. Forensic patients were ill-advised to oppose or challenge the authority of their psychiatric judges.

The degree of co-operation exhibited by subjects was a critical element in the production of clinical judgments in the Unit. Patients who assumed an adversarial position against their evaluators, who maintained their innocence and normality, or who remonstrated against the activities of clinicians, were typically subjected to a barrage of negative labels. Forensic authorities at METFORS moved to negate, to sanction, and otherwise to suppress the protests of obstreperous individuals. This strategy could, for example, be applied by invoking a general diagnosis of mental pathology: 'He felt that the assessment process at METFORS was part of the police and the "system's" general harassment of him ... There was definitely a paranoid flavour to his conversation' (NR 367). In other cases, the patient's reticence was interpreted as an attempt to manipulate the outcome to his or her advantage: 'He is very smooth and manipulative. I felt that he was not a reliable informant and was somewhat irresponsible in relation to himself and those around him. He attempted to play on the sympathies of the interview team. When he was not successful, some hostilities did begin to show through' (SWR 475); 'The patient ... refused to give a consent for release of information, stating that this was his lawyer's advice ... He appeared not to be telling the truth and was a very unreliable historian. His insight was nil and his judgment was poor' (NR 239).

When defendants refused to participate in psychological testing, their refusal could be attributed to paranoiac tendencies: 'Psychological testing was attempted but not completed because of his preoccupation with the assessment process' (POR 263). Alternatively, failure to partake in the clinical agenda was sometimes viewed as a harbinger of underlying hostility toward authority and the law. 'The results of the MMPI are invalid as Mr. G. sabotaged the test by responding in a stereotyped fashion on the last several hundred items. Rather than overtly refusing to take the test, he passive-aggressively sabotaged the test ... On the surface he is willing to comply with any request we make so as to avoid time ... This young man appears to be headed toward a personality disorder' (POR 311); 'he presented as a very unreliable historian and appeared to be doing some game playing when it came to presenting the facts ... His attitude towards the assessment was that of indifference. He appeared to have no regard for the law' (NR 170). Even a reluctance to discuss one's alleged criminal charges could be used to support clinical denunciations:

This young man was extremely difficult to interview. He was very hostile during the interview. He was slow to answer questions ... He would not elaborate at all on the charge against him (SWR 398) ... There appeared to be much underlying anger, particularly when he was asked about his past criminal record ... He appeared to be an unreliable historian, not giving an honest picture of himself. He was uncooperative to questioning, volunteering no additional information and giving monosyllabic responses. (NR 398)

Throughout the course of brief assessment, clinicians engaged in a proactive search for 'significant' conduct and utterances that were consistent with emerging definitions. Within such an enabling context as the Brief Assessment Unit, even an appearance of amiability and civility could be viewed as indicative of deviant character. 'He had an unwarranted feeling of well being during the interview' (NR 475); 'One received the impression that butter would melt in this man's mouth' (POR 379). Clinicians were invariably suspicious of patients' motives. 'I interviewed Mr. V. at 0930 at which time he was pleasant, polite and cooperative, although he was somewhat guarded in conversation ... During the interview he appeared to be observing me at times in a seductive fashion' (NR 055); 'Late in the afternoon when I was leaving the unit Mr. A. asked to speak to me. It was somewhat startling since he had refused to speak all day ... I felt that the real reason he decided to speak was because he wanted me to mail a letter and thought I could be manipulated into bypassing the jail system' (SWR 546).

When subjects aggressively rejected the overtures of forensic authorities, they sometimes courted official reactions that were more than just symbolically reciprocal. The following passage, recorded by the METFORS nurse, narrates the efforts of two detention centre officers to 'manage' a psychotic defendant:

CO T. and CO U. entered the security room with CO R. and CO M. from METFORS. At this time [the subject] was lying on the bed covered with the sheets. His clothes were off and he appeared to be masturbating. Mr. T. told him to 'get up and put on your clothes right now'. The patient did this. As CO T. and CO U. began to handcuff the patient, he swung out at Mr. T. with his fist. Mr T. was not struck. The patient was restrained on the security room bed by COS T., V., R. and M. while Mr. T. and Mr. U. applied the handcuffs and the leg-irons. The patient was struggling to break free during this process and Mr. U. said, 'Don't struggle or I'll break your fucking neck. I mean it, I have my black belt you know, and I can do it'. It took approximately 4 minutes to secure the patient in handcuffs and leg-irons. The patient was then taken to the holding area. The cut on [the patient's] nose was slightly bleeding at this time but he was cooperative and subdued. Mr.

T. and Mr. U. escorted the patient from the BAU. In the hallway just outside the BAU Mr. T. stomped on the patient's right foot and then Mr. U. put his foot in front of the patient's left foot thus the patient lost his balance and fell on his knee with his arms cuffed behind his back. The patient ... was then escorted to the elevator and down to the van. (NR 261)

Maintaining a United Front

In concert with their recurrent efforts to short-circuit and sanction the resistance of forensic patients undergoing assessment in the BAU, the MET-FORS professionals were also reluctant to document evidence of conflicting judgments or accounts in their official reports. With minor variations, the records produced by nurses, social workers, psychologists, and psychiatrists sustained an impression of consensual decision-making in the Brief Assessment Unit. The circulation of reliable and stable images about accused persons was an important instrument of legitimacy, as it concealed from legal audiences the ambiguity and complexity inherent in the judgmental process. The contradictions, professional conflicts, and inconsistencies characteristic of group clinical discretion (Pfohl 1978) rarely surfaced in the final METFORS documents. When dissensus was apparent, clinicians typically endeavoured to hold subjects for extended periods of assessment (see Chapter 4) in order to forge a purportedly unanimous opinion:

It was difficult to determine whether he was suffering from mental illness or whether in fact he was being manipulative and lying outright. I felt that he was an anti-social personality. The rest of the team tended to feel that perhaps he was suffering from a schizophrenic illness. I would have seen him go back through the court system, however I believe the final recommendation was that he be sent to METFORS for a 30 day assessment (SWR 372) ... Mr. J was somewhat of an enigma. The interview data was inconclusive in respect to the possibility of Mr. J. having some sort of mental disorder ... However test data seem to indicate strongly that there is an incipient schizophrenic process in this young man ... It is felt given the current test data as well as the interview data that Mr. J. should be recommended for a 30 day assessment. (POR 372)

Although there was some division of opinion among the members of the group interview team, it was my feeling that Mr. E. appears to be suffering from some kind of paranoid ideation concerning alleged implantations of units in his head. Some of the members felt that this was best accounted for as malingering, but I felt, given the fact that he had chopped off a finger at one point, malingering might not be the most suitable explanation ... In view of the degree of disagreement among the various team members, it was felt that Mr. E. should be returned for a 30 day assessment. (POR 381)

The Brief Assessment Unit evaluation could also be organized to avoid conflict with the diagnoses of professionals outside of METFORS. In Case 407, for example, the BAU clinicians declined to offer a decision about dangerousness because the patient was in the process of charging another psychiatrist with rendering a false diagnosis. As the METFORS social worker indicated:

[The patient] began the interview by stating that he is here because of Dr. Z. He states that it is alleged that he is a danger to his ex-wife and his children. He states that he has charged Dr. Z. before the [Medical Association] and that Dr. C. is the psychiatrist who is working on behalf of the patient. Dr. U. [the METFORS attending psychiatrist], being familiar with the alleged charges against Dr. Z. felt that we were not in a position to make any assessment on a one-hour interview of the dangerousness or potential dangerousness of this man. (SWR 407)

The METFORS clinicians were apparently concerned in this and other cases about the prospects of entering into an adversarial relationship with a fellow professional. Their position underlined the consensual basis of forensic discretion, and led to the recommendation that Patient 407 be remanded for an extended assessment. The METFORS psychiatrist reported to the presiding judge:

This examination was incredibly brief. Mr. D. indicated to us that a colleague of mine had assessed him and this is the reason why he is here. He indicated that Dr. Z. and also Dr. C. had assessed him and it sounded ominously as if there was a lot of confusion in this area. In view of the involvement of other psychiatrists ... I immediately recommended that Mr. D. be admitted to the Inpatient Unit at METFORS ... This would enable us to gather all previous information. At the end of this time or when our assessment is completed we shall forward a more comprehensive and binding report to Your Honour. (PL 407)

Trials of Moral Identity
The evaluation of remanded forensic patients in the Brief Assessment Unit extended beyond the legal and medical categories available to clinical members. These assessments were organized to highlight the disreputability of subjects, and to elicit in global terms the most salient features of their 'essential character.' The METFORS documents represented a polymorphous

blend of clinical, legal, and moral stigmas. The discretionary power of psychiatric classifiers was reflected in the extraordinary diversity of standards against which the value and values of subjects could be measured. Moralistic constructions of deviance were pivotal to the exercise of forensic decision-making, as they were sufficiently diffuse, penetrating, and abstract to encapsulate the entirety of the individual's ascribed personality. By appropriating widely distributed cultural norms, clinicians could demonstrate that their realm of expertise transcended the more narrow concerns of diagnosis and adjudication. More than this, every available item of knowledge about defendants was potentially subject to moral assessment in the BAU. 'Because psychiatric diagnosis is inherently evaluative and hence in a way necessarily arbitrary, application of the mental illness designation is, if unchecked, almost infinitely expandable' (Schur 1980: 30). The METFORS clinicians were therefore engaged in 'respectability work' (Ericson 1975: 17). Their sense-making activities were, like those of other social control agents, intimately connected with wider social processes of moral ordering (Douglas 1970: 21).

Members of the METFORS assessment team organized their moral attributions around a number of interdependent themes. Subjects were frequently characterized with reference to their nonconformity, disrepute, disrespect, inadequacy, and resistance to the overtures of social control and 'helping' agents. One such individual – an eighteen-year-old male accused of breaking and entering – was described in these terms by the BAU psychologist: 'His anchorings in relation to society are minimal. He has little respect for the rules and regulations of society. He is not very concerned about the results of his actions. He views his actions as appropriate to his end, that is securing money that he needs for what he wants' (POR 496). In another case the social worker fixed upon the defendant's apparent failure to profit from prior lenient treatment. 'It would seem that he has been given the benefit of the doubt by the courts in previous situations but has not responded to his present probation by staying out of trouble. He does tend to present himself as "poor me". He appears to be an inadequate, hostile man' (SWR 065). Clinicians were especially alert to signs of irresponsibility and dependency among patients. 'Mr H. is an inadequate individual who has difficulty in coping with responsibility in the community. He becomes dependent on drugs as a way of coping with real life difficulties and expects to be taken care of by the system' (PL 007); 'He presented himself during the interview as a demanding, intimidating individual who is insistent on wanting to know what we were going to do for him' (SWR 513).

Other persons were stigmatized as poor patients, as recalcitrant and unresponsive to therapeutic overtures. 'Psychologically, this man presents as someone who remains underdeveloped emotionally ... Many opportunities have been available to him, according to Ms. L. [social worker], who worked with him intensively for over a year, but to no avail' (POR 031); 'We felt that he had been given every chance to alter his lifestyle and a lot of very valuable staff time has been spent with this young man trying to get him to change his modus operandi ... It is felt that Mr. O. does not want to alter his lifestyle' (PL 031). Conversely, a subject's claim to *being* mentally ill and to *requiring* assistance could be read as an irresponsible attempt to justify delinquent conduct: 'He comes across as a ... manipulative young man. He displayed several characteristics in keeping with a dependent personality. He depends on others to manage his affairs, he depends on others to keep him out of trouble, and to get him out of any difficulties. We all agreed that he appeared to be using his illness as a crutch. He was informed that there are many, many people with his illness who are under adequate control with medication and are able to lead normal lives. He insists, however, that he is different' (PL 539)

Brief Assessment Unit team members were accomplished in the conversion of seemingly positive attributes into harbingers of disorder. One such case involved a subject whose psychological test results attested to his 'strong moral principles.' The psychologist wrote: 'Test scores indicate that Mr. D.'s response-set was strongly influenced by his need to be seen as a virtuous man of strong moral character. Such a position is not uncommon among psychologically naive persons who rely on denial and repression to deal with psychological difficulties' (POR 295). Remarking on this man's orderly appearance, the social worker added: 'He was exceptionally well-groomed for someone coming from the ... jail, in fact one wondered how he was able to be so neat and tidy. This would support an obsessional type of personality' (SWR 295). If psychological test endorsements happened to collide with global impressions of pathological identity, the positive findings could be discounted or simply ignored. This strategy was evident in the evaluation of a twenty-two-year-old male diagnosed as an 'explosive personality disorder.' The psychologist's reasoning was charted in the medical report:

Mr. Y.'s test endorsements have him depict himself as energetic, alert, optimistic and coping with life's problems in an acceptable fashion. Such a picture is in marked contrast to the impressions gained from the clinical interview and police report concerning the alleged offence ... Responses during the clinical interview suggest to this examiner that Mr. Y. is a young man of at least average intelligence who is fit to stand trial and presents no symptoms of a major mental illness. However, it is the opinion of this examiner that Mr. Y. suffers a personality disorder characterized by impulsivity, immaturity, low frustration-tolerance and a disposition towards antisocial acting-out without regard for the consequences of his behaviour. (POR 121)

Such methods of moral ordering were widely available. With the assistance of legal documentation and interview data, clinicians could provide a retrospective, biographical narration of the individual's deviant career, establishing the continuity and progression of character defects (see also Chapter 4). In Case 186, the BAU social worker charted the deviant biography of a young woman accused of 'possession under $200.'

She states that she has no full siblings and she is the youngest of the 14 children born to her mother. She states that she spent [time] from the age of about 9 in all kinds of foster homes ... At age 12 she states that her father came around and she loaded a gun and ordered him off the property. She states that she also had a gun charge in 1975 for which she served 15 months in prison. She states that when she was 8 she drank Javex in an attempt to kill herself. She states that she also has attempted to kill herself by overdosing and by hanging. She indicates that she has been in institutions off and on since she was about 10 years old. Her mother sent her to Training School at age 10 as unmanageable ... From the Training School system she graduated into the adult prison system and into psychiatric hospitals. She has been in [four different psychiatric institutions] at various times ... She has a long history of drug abuse including heroin and cocaine, but at age 17 she was heavily involved in speed and shot speed every day for approximately 6 years. She supported herself by writing cheques and using credit cards. She also sold drugs to support her habit. She states that she hung around with bikers, including Satan's Choice ... [She] is now addicted to alcohol ... She has been in one serious fight [in prison] where she apparently attempted to choke one of the other inmates and the woman was apparently seriously injured. She says that when she gets angry she goes 'rangy' and beats people up. Physical abuse by her is not unknown. She says that she almost killed her mother but they were able to talk mother out of laying charges ... We see in this young lady a very disturbed, deprived woman who has led an extremely difficult life where she has abused her body, has abused other people, and has been abused by other people ... Certainly she is able to state very clearly that she is seeking revenge and expects to find it. I would see this woman as a very impetuous woman and in many ways a very unpredictable person. (SWR 186)

To amplify the scope of their response, clinicians could concentrate on devalued attributes that were entirely unrelated to the precipitating criminal charges. Particularly in the event of sexual 'deviance,' the focus of moral evaluations in the BAU often shifted toward a more global labelling process. In Case 285, a twenty-year-old male charged with 'Fraud' found himself the subject of an inquiry into his sexual identity. The social worker's report was primarily devoted to a rendition of the defendant's homosexual 'career,' although this account had no apparent relationship to the charges precipitating the forensic remand:

G. states that he had his first sexual experience with a cousin when he was approximately 7. He said it began as a show and tell relationship but over the years grew into a sexual relationship.. He states that he then had further sexual relationships when he was attending [a private boy's school] and he said by the time he was 16 he was hustling downtown. He said that he looked older than his age so he was able to hang out in the bars without any difficulty. He said at that time he was making approximately a thousand dollars a week by hustling. He said that he enjoyed it because he liked to have lots of jewelry and clothes. He indicates that he has had heterosexual relationships and at the present time he believes he is homosexual but in fact can go either way ... He feels he is primarily a homosexual and plans to pursue this career. He has been hustling in the Toronto area for four years and supporting himself in this way ... I felt that this man's patterns of behaviour have been well established. (SWR 285)

Finally, forensic team members could project a wide range of negative images that galvanized the moral and mental inadequacies of remanded subjects. Adjudications of moral character were most successful when they relied on the quantity as much as on the content of deviant labels. The most remarkable feature of the METFORS BAU reports was the sheer volume of discrediting attributes that could be generated in the context of a brief assessment. Individually and collectively, clinicians commanded an encyclopaedic reservoir of negative descriptions. Witness the BAU psychologist's assessment of a defendant accused of failing to comply with a probation order:

Mr. J. depicts himself as a socially isolated, depressed, anxious and tense young man who is very discouraged with himself. Persons responding in a similar fashion are often seen as restless, distractable and talkative. They have a low frustration-tolerance and are frequently angry with others but cannot express such feelings in a modulated fashion. Under psychological stress such individuals are apt to obsess and ruminate over their problems with no alleviation of their misery. Favouring projection, isolation and rationalization as ways to defend themselves against unacceptable thoughts or feelings, such persons are apt, when under prolonged stress, to display hyperactive thought patterns and act-out in a hostile, explosive, antisocial fashion. Mr. J.'s capacity for interpersonal intimacy, data would suggest, is severely limited because of conflicts surrounding emotional dependency. Most of his relationships would be characterized by superficiality and a self serving nature. (POR 243)

Suspending Credibility

The 592 METFORS patients were subjected to a cumulative series of 'credibility assessments' in the Brief Assessment Unit (Bonnie and Slobogin 1980: 508). Members worked from the assumption that subjects' accounts were not to be trusted, that mental and criminal pathology was marked by a divergence between the appearance and essence of psychiatric reality. The expressions of persons defined as mentally ill or dangerous were not generally taken at face value in the context of forensic interviews. Recurrently, positive assertions by accused persons were officially recorded as 'claims,' negative responses as 'denials.' The discovery mission of the METFORS classifiers required that they uncover the contradictions in patients' testimony, that they identify the discrepancies between their subjects' narrations and those recorded in official documents, and that they challenge the authenticity of claims to normality.

In the context of brief assessments at METFORS, these practices amounted to, in Lofland's terms, 'a tendency to view Actor's phenomenology as epiphenomenal' (1969: 297). The forensic patient is constantly denied access to acceptable explanations for prior conduct and current problems. As Friedenberg writes, 'his [or her] own wishes and purposes are not considered except as symptoms' (1975: 19). In the absence of normalizing strategies that sustain coherence in everyday conversation (Goffman 1983; Leiter 1980), credibility becomes a scarce resource: 'As with all relationships between clients and professionals, the element of trust is normally "one-way" from the client to the professional rather than reciprocal ... [E]xperts ... tend to give their evidence in the context of official reports which creates an objectification of their evidence. The accused, however, is not allowed any of these props and instead gives descriptions in everyday language which ends up sounding like a story' (Ericson and Baranek 1982: 94, 195–6).

Clinicians are thus able to annihilate the accounts of their subjects by exposing them to unattainable standards of validity, and by transforming them into overt symptons of deviant identity. Their informational control affects not only the content and quality of officially recognized knowledge, but also the very acceptance of these data as factually 'real.'

The METFORS professionals consistently withheld credibility from the evidence supplied by subjects during clinical interviews. On numerous occasions the BAU staff recorded their scepticism about the truthfulness of patients' assertions. In Case 188 the four responding clinicians were unanimous in rejecting the testimony of a thirty-four-year-old black 'chronic schizophrenic' accused of bodily assault. The attending nurse noted his failure to discuss the alleged criminal offence leading to the forensic remand. 'He did not present an honest picture of himself and was very evasive in conversation stating "I don't remember" to most questions. He ... refused to talk about his previous criminal charges or his present charge ... He appeared suspicious (thinking that the psychiatrist was too young to be a real psychiatrist) ... At times he became angry when questions were pursued. He appeared rather indifferent towards the assessment process' (NR 188). The social worker's comments addressed the style and content of this man's narrative: 'He was quite repetitive and his thinking appeared to be quite disorganized. I felt that he frequently was not telling the truth [and] that the information given by this young man was not too reliable ... He tells a rather garbled story ... and it would appear that in fact he is being evasive' (SWR 188). The psychologist's reasoning followed a similar theme: 'Indications in terms of confusing answers and discrepancies within the data indicate that he is probably not a reliable historian and his stories must be treated with some degree of objectivity. However, despite these indications of problems in cognitive functioning, there does appear to be an element of manipulation or malingering about it ... This individual's characteristic life style is ego-syntonic and therefore not subject to change' (POR 188). Lastly, the presiding psychiatrist credited the patient's reticent conduct to an assumed mental illness: 'Mr. G. showed some disordered thinking, including circumstantial and tangential thinking ... Mr. G. was hostile to questioning and accused me of being like the Crown Attorney. Mr. G.'s judgment appeared impaired and his insight ... was markedly limited' (PL 188).

In their role as forensic lie detectors, the BAU clinicians invoked a variety of cognitive tactics to refute or revise the reality claims of subjects. Claims to innocence could be reconciled with imputed deviant categories: 'He completely denies the charges of indecent assault and this certainly would not be unpredictable and would fit generally with the pattern of men who molest their own children' (SWR 175). Attempts by patients to elaborate on their replies to interrogation met a similar fate: 'He was at times evasive and extremely circumlocutionary. He had difficulty in answering questions in a simple fashion and would preface any reply with a long 'position-statement' prior to giving an answer. This reveals a rigid, compulsive nature and gave rise to the impression that he was at times frankly untruthful' (PL 572).

Team members were especially alert to the possibility that defence counsel might have 'gotten to' the subject prior to the assessment and thereby 'modulated the information flow' (POR 437). According to the social worker's report on a male patient charged with breaking and entering, '[h]e was verbally very smooth and appeared to be well-coached for today's assessment. He was very manipulative [and] showed little affect ... He presented himself as "poor me" which led to my feeling that he had been well coached' (SWR 526). Clinicians apparently believed that patients could secure legal advantage from the METFORS brief assessment. Even in the absence of overt indications of deceit, this possibility weighed heavily in the construction of credibility assessments. In Case 346 the BAU psychologist wrote: 'I had great difficulty giving much credence to much of the testimony of this young man in the interview situation. I admit I have no hard evidence to back this up but I think that he was being less than honest in many situations. Obviously, he has much to gain in this particular interview with respect to his charges' (POR 346).

At times, the suspected manipulative, malingering, or miscreant demeanour of subjects could be decoded by members as surface manifestations of sexual pathology: 'Mr. L. presents himself in a very controlled, well-mannered and well-rehearsed fashion. Mr. L. would seem to make an effort to elicit the listener's sympathy. There is a strong manipulative quality to this young man's presentation of himself and this writer queries his sexual identity' (NR 074). It could suggest inherent flaws of character: 'Insight into her difficulties was defended against through rationalization and intellectualization. The examination noted that there was substantial narcissism in this woman's elements. Beneath the armour was considerable hostility which was observed to be displaced inappropriately sometimes upon herself and more frequently upon others' (POR 134). It might represent distortions of ego-identity: 'He sees himself in somewhat of a Robin Hood image, states that he will only steal from institutions not from people ... He's probably not as smooth as he thinks he is and will have difficulty if he pursues his career of fraud because people will begin to see through him' (SWR 041). Alternatively, it could be seen to reveal a contempt for social mores: 'At times she gave bizarre statements [which] appeared to be attention-seeking mechanisms consistent with this woman's rejection of any of society's values' (PL 105).

Moreover, psychiatric diagnoses of BAU patients were often shaped by members' credibility judgments about interview presentations. One such case involved a fifty-one-year-old man, with an extensive criminal history, who was labelled a 'chronic undifferentiated schizophrenic' by the METFORS assessment team. This designation was principally based upon the subject's 'paranoid' claims about his role as a police informant. 'His mood was slightly hypomanic and some grandiose delusions were noted. For example, he claimed ... that he was an underground agent for the police ... There appeared to be some evidence of psychotic thought disorder' (NR 104); 'He says that he's an investigator for the police [and] that he was working for [　] Division at the time [of the alleged offence] to obtain information for them. He ... obviously had some paranoid ideation [and] is potentially a dangerous man' (SWR 104). The psychiatrist relayed this information to the presiding judge: 'He expresses delusional ideas ... [H]is ideas flowed rather disjointedly in a tangential manner. On occasion he expressed strange ideas about his role as an investigator for ... detectives in [　] Division' (PL 104). Four days following the METFORS brief assessment, the social worker reported a telephone conversation with the staff sergeant of [　] Division, who had proceeded to corroborate the subject's 'delusional' account: 'Sergeant J. states that they have known Mr. L. [for six months]. At that time he arrived at the police station stating that he had been investigating for them and had information to pass on to them. As it turned out, the information regarded a counterfeiting ring and Sergeant J. states that they in fact were able to make arrests as the result of the information that Mr. L. had given them' (SWR 104). Despite this disconfirming report, the patient's diagnosis was not amended. In the official letter conveyed to the court, the subject's diagnosis as a 'chronic undifferentiated schizophrenic' remained firmly in place.

Probing for Secret Knowledge

In their accounting practices, forensic clinicians demonstrate to patients, peers, and powerful others that they have access to significant knowledge about defendants that is unavailable to uninitiated outside observers. Psychiatric discretion is supported by the presumption that important medico-legal 'facts' are not easily yielded, that symptoms of pathology and criminality must be probed and pressured into existence ... that 'knowledge is not only secret but secreted' (Ericson and Baranek 1982: 83). By deploying clinically accepted categories and techniques, professional classifiers create the appearance that they are exploring the depths of their subjects' character and consciousness. They learn to apply an aura of esoterica to common-sense 'discoveries' about medico-legal patients. They preserve a monopoly over 'tacit knowledge' (Polanyi 1958) that enhances their power to dominate the psychiatric labelling of accused persons. As Giddens suggests, '[t]he reflexive elaboration of frames of meaning is characteristically imbalanced in relation to the possession of power, whether this be the result of the superior linguistic or dialectical skills of one person in conversation with another; the possession of relevant types of "technical knowledge"; the mobilization of authority or "force," etc. "What passes for social reality" stands in immediate relation to the distribution of power' (1976: 113). The 'deep structure' of clinical deviance is thus open to the scrutiny of medical adjudicators and becomes their property (Christie 1977). Their subcutaneous investigations pay dividends in the proliferation of clinical ascriptions and the preservation of professional power.

In the METFORS Brief Assessment Unit, members displayed an aptitude for reading, and reading into, the 'character structures' of their patients. Consistently, their reports reflected a professed capacity to scan beneath the surface appearances of subject presentations. Subtle nuances observed during exchanges between interviewers and patients were seen to harbour meaningful 'facts' about the attributes of defendants. 'He gave positive evidence of what we call thought blocking. He appeared to be actively hallucinating and this also prevented him from communicating with us. His long pauses to us indicated that he was carrying on a private conversation with the voices that he is hearing ... In other words, what we are seeing here is a man suffering from chronic paranoid schizophrenia' (PL 080). Information solicited from defendants during interviews could provide 'clues' in the search for hidden deviance, as in the case of an individual charged with 'Weapons Dangerous': 'He is quite obsessional about giving details and dates. He volunteered that he has been accused by other people of aggressive and molesting acts with children and with a woman in his apartment building. He says that he was never involved in any of these activities, denied them profoundly, despite the fact that he was the one who raised them. One became very suspicious of this and wondered if he was not asking for help around the whole sexual area' (SWR 236).

Moreover, defendants' reactions to staff members could be seen to manifest underlying disturbances and concealed criminal activities. 'He did not appear to relate well to female staff during the interview as noted by his decreased eye contact and increased hostility and rigidity when female staff asked him questions ... There was much underlying hostility noted and he appeared to be quite obsessional and over-controlled' (NR 523); 'When we asked her about drugs she asked if this information could be given to the courts. When we said it could she said she really didn't want to talk about it so I do feel that the information of drugs is not reliable information and it is likely that she is much more into the drug scene than she has admitted' (SWR 109).

The METFORS specialists routinely probed into the secret lives of their subjects. In the BAU context every potentially relevant item of information, however private or intimate, became the property of clinical examiners. This practice was especially noticeable in the assessment of sex offenders, where the personal lives and public transgressions of accused persons were viewed as medically and legally inseparable. In Case 569, the subject was accused of indecently assaulting a woman whom he had picked up in a downtown Toronto bar. On the day of this man's assessment, the METFORS social worker telephoned the defendant's wife in an effort to solicit information about his sexual history. In response, the informant volunteered an abundance of sordid details that charted the patient's history of promiscuity:

She said that she has had some feeling that there had been sexual problems, and that they have had some sexual difficulties in their marriage. She stated that when they were first married R. [the patient] had been charged with 'Rape'. He explained to his wife that he had given this girl a ride and that she yelled rape and the charges were dismissed. Mrs. E. is also aware that R. has had an affair very early in the marriage and the couple have maintained contact with this girl and her new husband. She says that sometimes when she did not feel like becoming involved in a sexual relationship he would be very persistent and she would give in. R. seems to be wanting to have group sex. He likes to have his wife reach climax and take pictures of her while she is having a climax. Mrs. E. says that she has had some concerns about what R. does with the pictures and hopes that he does not sell them. She says that this all started when he was travelling to California. He has also encouraged her on occasion to make love to another girl or to go out and find another guy. He likes to buy his wife fancy underwear, such as nylon bras and garter belts, and buys a lot of sexual books and pornographic pictures. (SWR 569)

In particular, the Brief Assessment Unit clinicians relied on psychological testing as a vehicle for uncovering covert knowledge about deviance and disorder (see Chapter 4). These tests were incorporated into the assessment process because they lent a technical authority to official pronouncements about the internal workings of patients' minds. Interpretations of subjects'

test results capitalized on the assumption that these were valid representations of fixed character traits. They served to generate pseudo-scientific
'profiles' that stockpiled negative descriptions for use by the METFORS team.
Following the administration of an ink-blot test, the METFORS psychologist
described one patient in the following terms: 'A Rorschach protocol noted
that Mr. Y. is a sensitive, suspicious individual who is highly dependent
on his environment. A preoccupation with sex and a violent fantasy life
lower the form level of this protocol. Together with features of someone
who has difficulty with controlling his impulses when placed in highly
charged emotional situations, the record is suggestive of someone who is
thought disordered. The record is more than someone making a difficult
transition from adolescence to adulthood' (POR 093).

In another case, the psychologist's insights were based upon a completed
Minnesota Multiphasic Personality Inventory profile. Characteristically,
the subject – a twenty-one-year-old woman charged with fraud – was
identified as belonging to a generic class of persons all exhibiting similar
traits:

Miss M.'s endorsements have her describe herself as socially isolated, depressed,
distrustful of others and suffering a deep sense of personal inadequacy. Feeling
hard done-by and 'picked upon', she has difficulty accepting responsibility for the
consequences of her own behaviour. Persons responding in a similar fashion are
often described as irritable, aggressive, egocentric and self-indulgent. When confronted they are often evasive, resentful and argumentative. Immature, insecure,
indecisive and passively manipulative, they often exhibit poor judgment, are suspicious and have exaggerated needs for affection and attention. Under stress defences such as projection, displacement, reaction-formation and somatization prove
to be inadequate and they are prone to impulsively acting-out their aggressive and
sexual impulses without regard for the consequences. Following such a pattern
they often experience depression and/or an exaggerated sense of guilt which is
relieved either by manipulation of the environment or another acting-out episode.
Suicide attempts among persons presenting this profile are not uncommon ... That
such characteristics are not syntonic with her self-image is reflected in her job
history, community support and anxiety-reactions to some of her own behaviour.
(POR 380)

Cultural and Other Stereotypes
Forensic psychiatric decisions are nested in commonsensical categories that
are widely shared in the public domain. When seen apart from its role as
a discourse of power, there is nothing particularly special about the specialist knowledge of medico-legal experts. Clinical theories and pro-

nouncements about the condition of legal subjects are anchored in cultural beliefs and value systems that are distributed throughout and beyond the numerous institutions of social control in modern society. 'Stereotyping is ... elaborated at the levels of public decision-making and organizational processing ... [O]rganizational practices, particularly the selection and processing of individuals by formal agencies of control, often reflect common public stereotypes or more specific organizational ideologies grounded in stereotyped thinking' (Schur 1971: 51). Criteria for clinical decision-making and the classification of defendants reflect the individual theorizing of experts and the organizational needs of the agency. This results in arbitrary and idiosyncratic renditions of the psycholegal status of accused persons. In practice, forensic judgments often degenerate into mere speculation (Bottomley 1973: 220).

The typification work of the BAU clinicians revealed the impact of common cultural stereotypes on the formulation and closure of diagnostic labels. This practice of 'substituting the self-explanatory for the questionable' (Schutz 1964: 95) was especially evident in medical explanations advanced to account for the conduct and status of 'alien' and other marginal patients. When subjects could not be located within standard diagnostic formulae, clinicians were obliged to rely on ad hoc theorizing that reflected their idiosyncratic value systems and cultural beliefs. The result was an array of inventive accounts that virtually erased the distinction between commonsense and nonsense.

Brief Assessment Unit team members were sometimes required to explain the psychotic symptoms displayed by recent immigrants from foreign countries. In Case 441 the psychiatric nurse charted the delusional utterances of a former citizen of the Soviet Union. 'He talked about Russian spies, British Intelligence Agents and the K.G.B. ... He said that "they", i.e., the Secret Police, are putting "mental pressures" on him, and "they" follow him constantly. He said that he interprets "signs" from the Secret Police' (NR 441). Revealingly, the BAU clinicians were able to normalize and explain away this man's apparent mental state with reference to the political state of the Soviet Union. 'These may have been paranoid delusions, but this is difficult to determine as he had escaped from Russia, and people indeed may have been watching him or bothering him here in Canada ... There may have been a core of reality present in this man today' (NR 441); '[G]iven the uniqueness of his background, it is difficult to determine whether this paranoia around the Russian Secret Police has any basis in reality' (POR 441) ... 'Whether in fact he is being followed by Russians one cannot be certain' (SWR 441).

In a similar case the defendant's aversion to psychiatric professionals was incorporated into clinicians' 'knowledge' about the 'uncharacteristic' role of psychiatrists as social control agents in the Soviet Union. The defendant was a thirty-six-year-old immigrant who was charged with 'Theft under $200' and 'Failure to Appear.' The BAU nurse described his behaviour during the team interview: 'He was angry and refused to shake hands with the doctor and several times throughout the interview his eyes darted one way or another. He did think the room was "bugged." Of course if he had been involved with the police in Russia then this could be a cultural problem and not paranoia' (NR 057). The psychiatrist's court letter elaborated on this idea: 'Mr. O. would not discuss his previous life in Russia. It is possible that experiences in that political system have left Mr. O. markedly suspicious about police motives, and that this is the basis for his suspiciousness. If this were the case it is not surprising that he would be uncooperative to mental health professionals whom he would regard as agents of the state' (PL 057).

The socio-cultural identity of METFORS patients was a prominent factor in forensic explanations about deviant behaviours. Membership in 'religious cults,' for example, could be mobilized as evidence for suspected law-breaking activities. This reasoning was evident in the case of a Rastafarian immigrant from Jamaica who was facing criminal charges for threatening a hotel employee. The BAU psychiatrist was motivated to speculate about the subject's possible use of marijuana in the context of religious ceremony. 'He denies indulgence in alcohol but he is an extremely knowledgeable man about marijuana. It is well known that people from Jamaica belonging to this particular cult are very heavy smokers of the stuff which is given several other names by them ... [T]here is no psychiatric diagnosis that we can put on him except that we suspect he has been heavily involved in marijuana. For this we have no absolute proof, it is a suspicion as far as his life story and his knowledge of marijuana go' (PL 550).

In another instance, a recent Jamaican immigrant to Canada, charged with 'Watch and Beset' by his estranged wife, was judged by the BAU psychologist to be suffering from similar cultural contingencies. 'Mr. W. represents a bit of an enigma in terms of pathology. It is difficult on a short term basis to determine whether he is indeed suffering from a mental illness, putting on some kind of a charade, or displaying a culturally pre-determined behaviour pattern ... [T]here has been an extensive history of pot abuse which seems tied in with his Rastafarian religion' (POR 368).

Patients could also be classified by virtue of their departure from commonly held racial stereotypes. A twenty-year-old native Canadian, diagnosed under the category 'Habitual Excessive Drinking,' was found by the social worker to be 'quite open' during the assessment ... 'much more so than we would ordinarily find in the Canadian Indians that we interview' (SWR 466). Further, the cultural distance between clinicians and subjects could even lead to recommendations that patients be returned to their country of origin, ostensibly for their own good. The following is an excerpt from the psychiatrist's court letter concerning an immigrant from India, whose final METFORS diagnosis was 'Eccentricity':

This man has lived a fairly eccentric existence for many years. His demeanour reminds one of the several holy men one sees in India who are supported by the community and by the villagers. We felt that this man has not got accustomed to the North American way of life, which apparently has been too difficult for him to adopt ... He is a very peculiar man ... Indeed, he may be almost called ascetic and this characteristic can annoy or even provoke people who are unacquainted with people like him. He is very naive about North American or Canadian customs, re. welfare, legal aid, etc. ... If the opportunity arises for him to return to India then this should be taken with great speed so that he can feel more comfortable in the community in which he actually grew up.(PL 433)

In their efforts to construct reasonable explanations for the delinquent, delusional, and disreputable conduct of their subjects, the METFORS professionals displayed an extraordinary ability to probe into the minutiae of official data and to extract 'significant' themes. These were regularly offered to legal audiences as authentic causal accounts. In reality, they were improvised lay theories, couched in psychiatric jargon, and used to legitimate the overall clinical profile yielded from the brief assessment.

The METFORS records were rife with such apparent insights into the psycho-social forces that had purportedly precipitated the downfall of patients. For example, it 'made perfect sense' to associate the criminal behaviour of a car thief with the profession of his father: 'It is interesting to note that a number of his alleged offences involved automobiles. His father is a car dealer and Mr. G. notes considerable friction between him and his father around his father's interest in cars' (PL 292). Data yielded from the individual's biography could be converted into causal explanations, as in the case of a derelict accused of setting fire to trash-cans: 'The patient had previously ... worked in the mining industry and had been involved particularly working with the boilers. One had to wonder if there is a connection between this and the present fire setting incident' (SWR 207).

A prototypical theme involved the rejection or transgression by subjects of parental, familial, institutional, cultural, and political values. '[I]t is apparent that he had "opted-out" of his family's upwardly mobile life style. Instead of assuming the parental values, he has chosen an alternative lifestyle which they do not approve ... Dynamically, it appears that this young man's lifestyle is a passive but hostile attempt to deal with his parents whom he remains emotionally close to' (POR 115); 'Mr. W.'s early development and development throughout adolescence has not been conducive to the internalization of controls. His early life in terms of parental discipline was not consistent. As a result, Mr. W. tends to do what he wants when he wants to do it' (POR 522). And finally, in the case of a young Caribbean immigrant to Canada: 'He has made only a marginal adjustment to Canadian culture ... and has not integrated any positive benefits from his experiences in group homes. He shows indications of low self esteem ... and has been associating with a delinquent peer group as a means of coping with these feelings. He would appear to have benefitted from a period up north and he might be encouraged to live in such an area, if only to separate himself from his peer group' (POR 388).

Punitiveness and Responsibility

The Brief Assessment Unit clinicians frequently adopted a correctionalist approach to the ordering of forensic cases. Their organizational alliance with judicial authorities was a powerful influence on forensic decisions at METFORS. Traditional medical ideologies and constructs tended to dissipate in the shadow of the courts. The marginal autonomy of individual justice agencies is experienced throughout the judicial process, as noted by Feeley: '[T]he interdependencies of the separate components of the system and their collective relationship with the larger environment have important effects on how justice is perceived and administered' (Feeley 1979: xviii). At METFORS, clinicians were principally involved in the formulation of dispositional recommendations for consumption by court authorities. Their role as medical experts was supplementary or even incidental to concerns about punishment, responsibility, and legal disposition. Although clinicians were able to maintain their symbolic status as therapeutic agents, in practice the METFORS brief assessments reflected their primary function as adjuncts to the criminal process.

Clinicians recurrently subscribed to the crime-responsibility-punishment model (Ericson 1975) in their classification of criminal defendants. Irrespective of their mental status, individuals were usually held accountable for their criminal conduct. According to the METFORS professionals, psychiatric pathology was seldom an exculpatory attribute. The true measure of their moral condition was to be found in patients' demonstrations of remorse, repentance, and responsibility. When such displays were not forthcoming, clinicians responded in retributive terms. Such persons needed, accordingly, to face the consequences of their actions, and were typically returned to the court with a recommendation designed to elicit a punitive disposition. Brief Assessment Unit team members could furnish compelling arguments in favour of such responses:

I felt that he seemed quite set in his pattern of behaviour. It would appear that he has only done time once despite the long periods of charges and that he does not seem to be aware that he must face the consequences of his behaviours. For this reason I think he should go back through the court system ... It would appear that it is unlikely that he is motivated to obtain any kind of professional help at the present time. (SWR 287)

It is the opinion of this examiner that Mr. J. ... does have a basic personality disorder characterized by poor moral development, low frustration-tolerance and hyperactivity in thought and action. Further, it is the clinical opinion of this examiner that the nature of the charges ... reflects a general disregard for the rights of others. Inasmuch as it is likely that Mr. J. will continue his present lifestyle of anti-social activity perhaps deportation to his country of origin would be appropriate. (POR 156)

On examination, Mr. Q. demonstrated little anxiety or remorse for his alleged act, or for other acts which he was found guilty of in the past. Insight into his alleged anti-social activities was judged to be minimal ... Mr. Q. has had difficulties associating with authority figures for a long period of time ... [I]t was this examiner's opinion that Mr. Q. was attempting to manipulate the interview situation to meet his own needs, such as receiving a positive psychiatric assessment in which to return to Court. It is also in this examiner's opinion that Mr. Q.'s needs would best be found in a secure setting where controls would be internalized over a long period of incarceration. (POR 534)

Other more idiosyncratic factors were also found to be related to the punitiveness exhibited by BAU team members. For example, assessors reacted in profoundly negative terms to the hedonistic attitudes of some patients: 'He had presented himself to be an individual who is emotionally immature, shallow in interpersonal relationships and limited in situations requiring sound judgment. Internal controls are considered poor. Conscience development is also limited. Behaviourally, this individual may periodically demonstrate flagrant excesses in his search for pleasure' (POR 228). The social irresponsibility of welfare recipients could provoke especially animated denunciations: 'At present he suffers from gross immaturity in his personality development. Apparently he holds the view that if he does not receive a welfare cheque that he can do exactly as his own wishes dictate, that is, get money from somewhere else ... indicating to us, therefore, that he may repeat patterns of behaviour that have got him into trouble ... If he were granted bail he may get himself into a similar kind of trouble' (PL 132).

A final feature of clinical retributiveness was the interpersonal emnity toward patients that sometimes manifested itself during BAU assessments. It was evident that team members simply disliked a number of their subjects, and this global animosity was carried over into their formulations of clinical profiles. The antipathy and 'counter-transference' of assessors toward accused persons surfaced from their readings of biographical documents, from their responses to the alleged criminal offences, and from the interpersonal dynamics of clinical interviews. The final product of brief assessments was inextricably linked with the emotional reactions of team members. Although clinicians were reluctant to express their aversion and rancour in direct terms, these sentiments were nevertheless a prominent feature in the construction of forensic decisions:

I feel that this young lady is a very inadequate, immature girl of borderline intelligence. She has no insight into the excessive drinking that she has become involved in. She seems quite satisfied with her style of life. She was not aware that the people she had [struck with her car] had been injured and although she was shocked, she immediately responded with concern that she would have to spend more time in jail. I felt that this woman would be highly dangerous under alcohol [and] is obviously not motivated to seek help (SWR 111) ... Her impulsivity, poor socialization, low frustration-tolerance and a predisposition towards acting-out her conflicts combined with the disinhibiting influence of excessive alcohol and drug abuse suggest that it is highly likely she will continue to present problems ... (POR 111)

With respect to the [current] charges, Mr. G. feels no remorse about hitting his father ... [This is] a young man of borderline intelligence whose personality integration is both primitive and immature. Mr. G. is largely unaware of his own emotional conflicts and tends to displace or project them onto his environment ... Lacking in motivation and naive, Mr. G. demonstrates poor social judgment: 'I'll get Welfare and just hang around on the streets'. In light of his family's inability to control his behaviour and lack of resources with which to cope with a foreign culture, perhaps consideration could be given to the idea of sending him back to [his country of origin]. (POR 129)

Deciding about Dangerousness to Others

Depictions of dangerousness were a prominent and recurrent feature of clinical discretion in the Brief Assessment Unit. The construct of dangerousness was an especially salient concern for the METFORS clinicians, as they were involved in the delivery of practical courses of action to court authorities, and sentencing decisions were frequently dependent on the alleged threat presented by criminal defendants to themselves, to specified others, and to the community in general (see Chapter 5). But labels of dangerousness, like other forensic constructs, were only indirectly related to the prior violence or current criminality of accused persons (Menzies 1986; Webster and Menzies 1987). Instead, these judgments emerged from the discretionary practices and occupational interests of BAU assessment teams, and they tended to vacillate between commonsensical renderings of violent histories and stereotyped inferences about the dangerous capacities of sexual offenders and the mentally ill.

In the former category were those persons who were 'simply dangerous' (Pfohl 1978, 1979; Webster and Menzies 1987). Such persons were generally categorized according to biographies of violence or the nature of precipitating charges. Typically, the BAU clinicians classified these defendants as personality disorders, and they documented their formulations with official accounts of assaultive conduct. These assessments were relatively unproblematic for the METFORS experts, as they required a simple updating of criminal histories into the present and future tense. The current dangerousness of subjects could be established as a continuation of progressively spiralling violent careers. One standard heuristic method involved the merging of clinical data with informant testimony to amplify the perceived dangerousness of patients (see Chapter 4). The following report concerns a man charged with 'Mischief to Private Property':

Persons responding [to psychological testing] in a similar fashion have difficulty expressing hostility in a modulated fashion and are often described as irresponsible, immature, demanding, egocentric and impulsive. They often react to stress with irritability, temper tantrums and destructive behaviour. Information drawn from the interview and correlated with the police report ... indicates to this examiner that Mr. A. is denying responsibility for his behaviour and projecting said responsibility onto his environment ... [H]is wife indicates that over the past six months Mr. A. has become increasingly difficult to live with. He has frequently been abusing alcohol and has used physical force on her on several occasions ... His denial, impulsivity, low frustration tolerance and disposition towards aggressive acting-out when combined with the disinhibiting effect of alcohol abuse make Mr. A. significantly dangerous to others. Further, it is the opinion of this examiner that without some kind of intervention, it is likely that Mr. A. will continue acting-out aggressively and that such a pattern, from his wife's perspective, suggests that there may be an escalation. (POR 470)

A related signpost in the identification of 'simply dangerous' defendants was the police account of the alleged offence. Brief Assessment Unit professionals frequently classified dangerousness on the basis of unsubstantiated arrest reports prior to the criminal conviction of METFORS patients. As the BAU psychiatrist reported in one letter to the presiding judge: 'If the description by the police of the alleged incident is true, then it is obvious that one has to think that this man is potentially dangerous' (PL 548). Often the assessment team members relied on extensive narrations of the alleged incidents – once again, prior to legal adjudication by the court – to legitimate their findings and to dramatize the seriousness of the subject's condition, as in the following excerpt:

Mr. K. presented himself as an effeminate individual who claimed that he attempted to 'get even' with his male lover for abandoning him for someone else. Details of the alleged offence noted that this individual wantonly and recklessly threw a set of burning matches into a locker area of a building and calmly went upstairs for a coffee before leaving the burning building. He gave little or no evidence that he was concerned about the welfare of other tenants in this building. Further elaboration into this act noted that his ex-lover was not in the apartment during the incident and when confronted about this Mr. K. just smiled ... Clinical impressions based upon the interview and MMPI suggest that Mr. K. is basically an anti-social personality with associated features generally descriptive of individuals suffering from schizophrenia. Together these features suggest that he is a danger to others. (POR 070)

The Brief Assessment Unit clinicians were particularly sensitive to the potential dangerousness of alleged sex offenders, even in cases where violence was absent from the precipitating incident. Those subjects diagnosed as 'sexually disordered' received significantly higher rankings of dangerousness than all other diagnostic categories on the BAU research instruments. Sexual dangerousness was routinely imputed to persons accused of minor sex crimes. One such case involved a seventeen-year-old male charged with 'Common Assault.' The incident was described in the police report as follows: 'At about 1:00 p.m. the accused was in an elevator coming down from the 11th floor along with a female. At this time the accused youth approached the victim, stood very close to the victim, looked her in the face, studied her for a while and then said "I LOVE YOU". As a result of his general appearance and the tone of voice the victim became quite scared. The victim then pushed her way past the accused and ran to the superintendant who called the police and apprehended the accused leaving the building via a rear exit' (PR 165). Following his arrest, court appearance, and psychiatric remand to the Brief Assessment Unit, the subject received the following evaluation from the participating METFORS psychologist: .

Adolescents responding in a similar fashion are often brought to society's attention because of emotionally inappropriate behaviour. They are usually described as socially isolated, emotionally distant and have inter-conflicts concerning sexuality and emotional dependence. These individuals usually adopt denial, projection and regression to deal with their emotional conflicts and are described as lacking in empathy and in psychological insight. It is the impression of this examiner that V. is seriously disturbed. His inability to empathize with others, his feelings of being hard-done-by, and his inability to express his anger in any modulated fashion combined with poor impulse control could result in sudden aggressive acting out to the surprise of those around him. Without therapeutic intervention, it is the judgment of this examiner that V. will continue to act out. Escalations of these patterns in addition to some risk of suicide could also become part of this man's future if he does not receive assistance. (POR 165)

Other cases of sexual offending engendered similar patterns of response among the METFORS specialists. In Case 349, an eighteen-year-old male was facing a charge of 'Indecent Assault – Female' subsequent to the incident described below: 'He noticed the victim (a ten year-old girl) driving her bicycle up a hill ... and when she reached the top of the hill the accused walked up behind her and sat on the bicycle behind her. He then placed his hand inside the girl's pants and said "I'm going to feel you up". After placing his hand inside the girl's pants he got off the bicycle and ran away' (PR 349). On the basis of these data and the clinical interview, the BAU social worker was able to extract a profile of progressively spiralling sexual dangerousness. 'It would appear that his sexual behaviour is escalating from exposure charges to indecent assault.[5] I feel that this is very significant in terms of his potential for danger in the future' (SWR 349).

On another occasion, a sixty-year-old retired writer was arrested after propositioning two women who had responded to his newspaper advertisement for a live-in housekeeper. To his detriment one of the complainants was an undercover policewoman. The arrest report read: 'At 9:30 p.m. the policewoman arrived at the apartment and was invited in by the accused wearing a loose fitting bathrobe. She stated that she was answering the ad and the man asked her to be seated on the couch. The man immediately sat down tightly beside her and the robe fell open exposing his privates to her view. He immediately suggested that what he really wanted was a sexual companion and reached over and touched the woman's hair. The officer moved away and the man reached out and stroked her arm. The officer got up and opened the apartment door allowing other officers into the apartment at which time the man was arrested' (PR 079). The defendant was charged with 'Forcible Confinement' and 'Indecent Assault – Female' and was remanded two days later to METFORS. While the subject was described by the majority of team members as a 'passive introspective individual' (POR 079), the attending social worker was able to conclude without apparent evidentiary basis that he showed a serious potential for violence. 'This man is an alcoholic who is confused as a result of drinking. However, he could become angry and violent if a female he approached panicked or became hysterical' (SWR 079).

Finally, the forensic assessors at METFORS recurrently manifested the belief, despite an abundance of contradictory research findings (Menzies and Webster 1987; Menzies, Webster, and Sepejak 1987), that mental disorder and dangerousness were often interchangeable, that insanity was a potential precursor to violent aggression. When delusional patients had previously engaged in assaultive conduct, the METFORS professionals were especially inclined to draw causal connections between madness and violence. Mental illness was seen to render such persons both out-of-touch with reality and out-of-control. In cases of 'pathological dangerousness' (Webster and Menzies 1987), clinicians typically proceeded by documenting the psychotic symptoms of subjects, and supplementing these with peremptory conclusions about their potential for future dangerousness. The following two examples are characteristic of members' reasoning in the identification of 'dangerously psychotic' patients:

Mr. H. is acutely disturbed. This disturbance is characterized by a pre-occupation with the abstract such as theoretical and religious beliefs. Excessive fantasy has been incorporated by him and often used to escape the direct expression of aggressive impulses. Psychological defence mechanisms are incorporated to adapt to these unusual thoughts and feelings and thus help him to justify to himself that periodic behavioural outbursts are ego-alien. Projection and intellectualization distort reality to the degree that reality takes on a new form, having delusional ego-syntonic features ... [H]e is considered to be the type of disturbed individual who may perceive that someone is a threat to him and to avoid personal harm will react with behaviour which he thinks is self-preservative. This behaviour exhibited to protect himself could become very aggressive, leading perhaps to serious injury to others. (POR 172)

This young man presented himself to be a former psychiatric patient who had a long involvement with mental health professionals. During the course of the interview, it was observed that his hold on reality was marginal [and] functions related to attention and concentration were noticeably impaired ... He seems to be suffering from a thought disorder. He told a long involved story of his family punching him in the head, wiring him to a go-cart, hitting him with a sledge hammer, pouring gas down his throat, etc. He also talked about catching little white fleas and people breaking down the doors to get them. This young man is obviously mentally disturbed and in need of treatment at the present time. It is possible, because of his disturbed thinking, that he may, in fact, be quite dangerous to others or to himself in the future. (SWR 168)

SUMMARY

This chapter has surveyed the discretionary practices of forensic clinicians in the METFORS Brief Assessment Unit. Decisions about the psychiatric and criminal condition of accused persons have been shown to be indexical products of the cognitive strategies, ad hoc theorizing, and moral choices of team members. BAU practitioners were able to improvise their solutions to medico-legal problems by incorporating the most enabling features of official documents, psychiatric categories, and the behavioural presentations of accused persons in the BAU. They contributed to the individualization of deviance by divorcing the conduct and utterances of subjects from their legal and cultural context. The clinical accounts yielded from brief assessments at METFORS were selective and concentrated renditions of forensic reality that maximized the imputed pathology of defendants as well as the imputational authority of clinical classifiers. They functioned to reinforce the validity, objectivity, and benevolence of medical knowledge, at the same time as they consolidated the pathological identities and institutional careers of mentally disordered defendants.

The METFORS clinicians were grounding their decisions in a number of situated strategies that could not be accounted for solely through statistical correlations of background and decision variables. These judgments emerged instead out of the indexical and commonsensical discretionary activities of BAU members. These were essentially trials of moral identity which comprised global judgments about the conduct and values of forensic patients. Accused persons were subjected to credibility assessments designed to challenge claims to innocence and normality. Clinical evaluations were conducted under the assumption that pathological symptoms were often covert phenomena that could be exposed only by probing into the deep structure of consciousness and conscience. These typification practices were supplemented by ad hoc reasoning that reflected the cultural biases and idiosyncratic theorizing of individual clinicians.

Moreover, forensic imputations at METFORS were fundamentally juridical rather than therapeutic. The legalistic ecology of the Metropolitan Toronto Forensic Service was associated with a wholesale abandonment of traditional psychiatric orientations, and with an emphasis instead upon conceptions of responsibility, correctionalism, and penality. This perspective was especially salient when patients resisted the probative overtures of team members or when they refused to assign credibility to their decisions. In these cases forensic experts were inclined to mobilize the full force of their legal authority to ensure an appropriate institutional outcome.

In general, these case studies have illustrated the role of one-day pretrial psychiatric assessments in facilitating the ordering of criminal defendants, in rationalizing judicial labels, in establishing the essential pathology and dangerousness of accused persons, and in providing an apparent medical framework for the allocation of penal measures. In this capacity, the BAU evaluations were integral to the sanctioning authority of the criminal justice system. They transported medico-legal subjects far along the pathways of the forensic corridor.

4

The Forensic Corridor II:
The METFORS Inpatient Unit

'But I don't want to go among mad people,' Alice remarked.
'Oh, you can't help that,' said the Cat: 'we're all mad here. I'm mad.
You're mad.'
'How do you know I'm mad?' said Alice.
'You must be,' said the Cat, 'or you wouldn't have come here.'

LEWIS CARROLL *Alice's Adventures in Wonderland*

Although they are called 'clients,' members of conscript clienteles are not
regarded as customers by the bureaucracies that serve them, since they
are not free to withdraw or withhold their custom or to look elsewhere
for service. They are treated as raw material that the service organization
needs to perform its social function and continue its existence.

EDGAR Z. FRIEDENBERG *The Disposal of Liberty and Other*
Industrial Wastes

FROM BRIEF TO PROTRACTED ASSESSMENTS

Of the 592 METFORS patients, 193 (almost one in three) were remanded by
the court for extended assessment, or were immediately certified by BAU
psychiatrists for involuntary pre-trial hospitalization. The in-patient evaluation is clearly a central feature of the pre-trial forensic process. In Canada, both the federal Criminal Code and the provincial Mental Health Act

empower thirty- to sixty-day remands for the purpose of clinical assessment (see Chapter 1). Some observers suggest that the protracted assessment furnishes 'a more satisfactory procedure' for medico-legal authorities, since 'it enables continuous observation of the suspect by trained psychiatric personnel' (Macdonald 1976: 110). According to this view, the in-patient remand is purportedly a last-resort procedure, to be reserved for those who are not amenable to brief screening evaluations at the pre-trial level (cf. Law Reform Commission of Canada 1976).

In other circles, however, the extended court-ordered assessment has been the subject of great controversy. The socio-legal research on the practice of in-patient remands (e.g. Geller and Lister 1978; Gibbens, Soot-hill, and Pope 1977; Greenland and Rosenblatt 1972; Jobson 1969; Kun-jukrishnan 1979; Pfeiffer, Eisenstein, and Dobbs 1967; Roesch and Golding 1980) has identified a number of potential abuses of process stemming from the activities of medico-legal officials. For example, the evaluation may be conducted within an unnecessarily secure institutional setting, in cases where less restrictive conditions would otherwise be indicated (Greenland and Rosenblatt 1972). The length of pre-trial confinement may be dispro-portionate to both the clinical objectives and the nature of the offence, especially when defendants are charged with relatively minor crimes (Pfeif-fer, Eisenstein, and Dobbs 1967). In-patient assessments may curtail the prospects of securing bail, and may cause lengthy delays in the criminal trial process (Gibbens, Soothill, and Pope 1977).

The potentially coercive elements of extended pre-trial evaluations have been underscored in a number of studies (Halpern 1975). In their review of 787 cases committed to twelve hospitals in Ontario, Greenland and Rosenblatt (1972: 400–01) reported that a sizeable proportion of such re-mands were either unnecessary or ineffectual, and that a large percentage of subjects spent one to two months in hospital following relatively trivial offences that did not eventuate in prison terms. Roesch and Golding (1980) indicate that an extension of the assessment period has at best a marginal impact on the clinical findings of forensic professionals. Roesch directly compared brief and protracted assessments on competency to stand trial, and found that 'judgments made on the basis of a brief interview were highly related to judgments made on more lengthy institutional evaluations' (1979: 548). This result is consistent with research data demonstrating that 'as the amount of information about a case increases, the confidence of the clinician in the accuracy of his judgment increases but the validity of the inference does not' (Klein 1976: 112; see Mischel 1965; Sarbin 1986).

Faulk and Trafford (1975) suggest that in-patient remands, with their compulsory institutionalization of accused persons, are routinely invoked to ensure pre-trial detention and the presence of defendants in court. This is a recurrent theme in the research on psychiatric assessments (Gibbens, Soothill, and Pope 1977; Laczko, James, and Alltop 1970; Sparks 1966). There are also indications (Geller and Lister 1978; Stone 1978) that forensic in-patient hospitalizations have become a substitute for involuntary civil commitment procedures (Gostin 1979). As the number of formal commitments has diminished in recent years in response to legal reforms, the use of extended pre-trial assessments has increased in direct proportion. Court-ordered remands may be developing into an alternative system for regulating the mentally ill (Allodi and Montgomery 1975; McGarry, Curran, Lipsitt, Lelos, Schwitzgebel, and Rosenberg. 1974). The availability of facilities and resources provided by forensic hospitals may encourage courts to direct the flow of human traffic towards these institutions, in order to effect control and to solicit clinical data about such issues as psychiatric diagnosis, fitness for trial, suitability for bail, treatability, dangerousness, and recommended disposition (Menzies, Webster, Butler, and Turner 1980: 474).

These patterns also reflect on the relative success of 'gatekeeping' facilities like the METFORS Brief Assessment Unit in regulating the numbers of forensic in-patients. There is no evidence that the BAU has managed even to slightly diminish the forensic population in the Metropolitan Toronto area. On the contrary, it would seem that the introduction of METFORS has instead contributed to the growth of pre-trial hospitalizations. Since about one-third of these 'screening' evaluations result in pre-trial institutional confinement (see Chapter 1), and since some 600 to 800 people are processed by METFORS in a given year,[1] the Brief Assessment Unit has ironically come to offer a convenient service for facilitating psychiatric *confinement* instead of diversion. In turn, the METFORS Inpatient Unit has enhanced the holding capacity of the Toronto medico-legal system, by providing an additional twenty-three beds for the detainment of mentally disordered offenders. The Brief Assessment Unit and In-patient Unit (as well as other forensic facilities in the jurisdiction) have functioned to expand the web of state jurisdiction over such groups. They have become symbiotically allied, and they are linked together by the referral practices of the BAU staff and the courts.

What can we learn about the characteristics of criminal defendants who become in-patients, and about the process of detaining accused people for extended pre-trial remands? Table 4.1 cross-tabulates psychiatrist recommendations for immediate in-patient assessment (extracted from a content analysis of BAU court letters) with the actual referral decisions of criminal court judges. Above all else, these data demonstrate the prominence of long-term hospitalizations in the institutional careers of METFORS patients. In 215 out of 592 cases (36.3 per cent) the BAU psychiatrist either requested an in-patient Warrant of Remand from the court, or directly certified the accused person to hospital. The majority of these recommendations ($N = 146$) nominated METFORS as the appropriate site for in-patient assessment. Other hospitals were typically mentioned when the defendant had been previously detained in these institutions, or when (s)he lived within their catchment area. As it turned out, 193 of the 592 subjects (32.6 per cent) were in practice either remanded or certified to hospital. Most of these assessments occurred at METFORS ($N = 123$), Queen Street Mental Health Centre ($N = 34$), or the Oak Ridge Unit at Penetanguishene ($N = 13$).

There was also a close correspondence between psychiatric recommendations and judicial decisions to funnel subjects into forensic facilities. Overall the court acted on the clinical prescription in 166 of 197 cases (84.3 per cent);[2] 156 (79.2 per cent) of these referrals resulted in hospitalization at the institution named in the psychiatric letter. Of the 128 defendants recommended for assessment at the METFORS Inpatient Unit,[3] 105 (82.0 per cent) were indeed subsequently admitted to METFORS.

Consequently, over a third of accused persons were subjected to an extended period of hospital confinement following their 'screening' in the Brief Assessment Unit. Moreover, judges systematically upheld the recommendation of METFORS psychiatrists concerning the need for further evaluation. There appeared to be at best a minimum of judicial review over these decisions; only thirty-one patients failed to be hospitalized after being earmarked by psychiatrists for in-patient assessment.

A related issue concerns the characteristics of defendants receiving protracted remands, and the nature and consequences of these in-hospital assessments. Table 4.2 presents a list of seventeen variables that significantly differentiated among three patient cohorts: those 123 subjects remanded to the METFORS Inpatient Unit, the 69 people remanded elsewhere for in-patient evaluation, and the other 399 who did not receive a pre-trial hospital assessment. Several useful findings emerged from these bivariate analyses.

First, persons referred to hospital for a protracted remand exhibited a much less extensive history of criminality than other subjects, as measured by prior violence, number of convictions (for violence and otherwise), past imprisonment, and the presence of a juvenile record.

Second, measures of psychiatric history and mental disorder were significantly related to in-patient referral patterns. Forty-one per cent of METFORS in-patients and 63 per cent of in-patients assigned to other hos-

TABLE 4.1
Frequency and location of in-patient assessments subsequent to METFORS BAU remand

Psychiatric assessment conducted	Assessments requested by BAU psychiatrist								
	No assessment requested	METFORS	Queen Street	Lake-shore	Clarke Institute	Penetang	St Thomas	Whitby	TOTAL
No assessment	368	18	7	4	1	0	1	0	399
METFORS*	0	123	0	0	0	0	0	0	123
Queen Street	1	2	31	0	0	0	0	0	34
Lakeshore	0	0	1	4	0	0	0	0	5
Clarke Institute	5	1	0	0	3	0	0	0	9
Penetang	1	2	3	0	0	7	0	0	13
St Thomas	1	0	0	0	0	1	4	0	6
Whitby	1	0	0	0	0	0	0	2	3
TOTAL	377	146	42	8	4	8	5	2	592

* Of 123 METFORS in-patients, 105 (85.4 per cent) were ordered for protracted assessment by the court under a Warrant of Remand. The remaining 18 (14.6 per cent) were certified directly by the psychiatrist to the METFORS In-patient Unit under the terms of the Ontario Mental Health Act.

pitals were diagnosed to be psychotic, compared with only 12 per cent of the brief assessment-only cohort (over half of the latter group were identified as personality disorders). In-patients were also much more likely than others to have been found unfit to stand trial, or questionably fit, during the Brief Assessment Unit interview.

Third, persons channelled away from METFORS to other hospitals seemed to comprise a unique category, ranking high on both criminal conduct and clinical pathology. These defendants were apparently viewed by BAU clinicians to be both dangerous and mentally ill, and were generally remanded to the maximum-security unit at Penetang. The implicit METFORS policy was that subjects with dual ascriptions (pathological *and* violent) were better dealt with elsewhere.

Fourth, in-patient assessments were associated with a substantial prolongation of legal process (cf. Geller and Lister 1978; Jackson 1978; Kunjukrishnan 1979; Schreiber 1970; Verdun-Jones 1981; Webster, Menzies, and Jackson 1982). The average number of days from arrest to sentence was 88 for those returned to court, compared with 150 for METFORS in-patients and 141 for those assessed in other hospitals. In-patients typically waited five months for the resolution of their criminal case, in contrast to less than three months for other defendants in the sample.

Fifth, although there were no inter-group differences in types of precipitating criminal offences, those referred for in-patient assessment were disproportionately *less* likely than others to be sentenced to prison. For in-patients, the period of pre-trial hospital confinement was perhaps viewed by criminal court judges as a kind of 'dead-time tariff' for the purposes of sentencing, and hence the courts might have been balancing dispositions against time already served in hospital. This would also account for the large percentage of charges withdrawn for in-patients assessed outside of METFORS (27 out of 69 cases). Alternatively, it could be argued that the extensive judicial delays for in-patients constituted a simple abuse of process, and violated subjects' rights to equality of treatment. When accused persons were immediately hospitalized and ultimately imprisoned, they were subjected to a form of double jeopardy through the sequential application of medical and legal sanctions.

Sixth, the data revealed marked differences in the follow-up criminal and violent conduct of the three groups. Those subjects remanded to an institution other than METFORS for in-patient assessment comprised the most 'dangerous' cohort during the two-year outcome period, followed in order by non-in-patients and METFORS in-patients. For instance the average num-

TABLE 4.2
Comparing subjects referred for in-patient assessment with other BAU patients

	METFORS in-patient assessments (N = 123) (%)	In-patient assessments in other hospitals (N = 69) (%)	No in-patient assessments (N = 399) (%)	χ^2	df	p
Prior incarceration				13.10	2	<.001
No	65.0	60.6	47.8			
Yes	35.0	39.4	52.2			
Previous violence				21.20	2	<.001
No	69.9	51.5	46.3			
Yes	30.1	48.5	53.7			
Employed at arrest				10.92	2	.004
Yes	32.5	10.6	25.7			
No	67.5	89.4	74.3			
Juvenile court record				13.78	2	.001
No	81.3	84.1	67.6			
Yes	18.7	15.9	32.4			
Diagnosis				134.63	10	<.001
None-neurosis	10.6	1.5	12.2			
Psychosis	40.7	63.1	12.4			
Sex disorder	2.4	1.5	1.7			
Mental retardation/organic	9.8	9.2	2.2			
Alcohol/drugs	9.8	3.1	20.9			
Personality disorder	26.8	21.5	50.5			

Disposition								χ^2	df	p
Acquit/withdraw/absolute discharge	24.0		38.7		17.5					
Probation	41.3		41.9		28.9					
Prison LE 30 days	1.7		1.6		10.3					
Provincial prison plus probation	13.2		8.1		14.2					
Prison 30 days–2 years	10.7		8.1		23.5				48.10	10	<.001
Federal penitentiary	9.1		1.6		5.7					

	Mean	N	Mean	N	Mean	N	F	df	p	R/ beta
Age	28.8	123	32.9	68	28.8	398	4.07	2,587	.018	.117
Previous convictions	2.29	123	2.74	68	4.14	398	9.78	2,587	<.001	.180
Previous violence convictions	0.41	123	0.66	68	0.94	398	8.40	2,587	<.001	.167
Number of prior hospitalizations	1.41	123	5.16	68	1.97	398	26.46	2,587	<.001	.288
Alcohol use	2.81	121	2.80	65	3.15	359	7.21	2,542	.001	.161
Psychiatrist–fitness	2.00	121	2.26	65	1.09	359	189.78	2,542	<.001	.642
Psychiatrist–danger to self	2.79	121	2.37	65	2.09	359	16.35	2,542	<.001	.239
Days from arrest to sentence	149.5	123	141.1	62	87.7	378	10.93	2,560	<.001	.194
Number of follow-up violent incidents	0.76	121	1.74	64	0.95	385	6.08	2,567	.002	.145
Number of follow-up days in prison	99.2	121	40.7	64	136.6	385	9.58	2,567	<.001	.181
Number of follow-up days in hospital	89.5	121	229.4	64	24.5	385	95.95	2,569	<.001	.501

No significant differences among in-patient and other assessments for the following variables: estimated IQ, current charges, psychiatrist–dangerous to others, occupation, level of drug use, number of follow-up incidents, marital status, years of education.

ber of violent incidents was 0.76 for METFORS in-patients, 0.95 for non-in-patients, and 1.74 for persons receiving in-hospital remands elsewhere.

Seventh, and finally, there were significant variations in the patterns of institutional confinement during the follow-up period for in-patient and brief-assessment subjects. The latter group averaged 137 days in penal institutions over the two years, but only twenty-five days in psychiatric hospital. In-patient assessment subjects, in contrast, spent more time in hospital and less in prison. Overall, the subsequent patterns of patient conduct and official response, like the attributes of METFORS subjects and the judgments of medico-legal professionals, were strongly associated with decisions to order a protracted in-patient assessment before trial.

STRATEGIES FOR SECURING IN-PATIENT ASSESSMENTS

According to the Canadian Criminal Code, extended pre-trial in-patient assessments can be ordered *only* for the purpose of evaluating fitness to stand trial (see Schiffer 1978; Verdun-Jones 1981; Webster, Menzies, and Jackson 1982). Yet a large proportion of accused persons were being re-manded to the METFORS Inpatient Unit for other reasons. A content analysis of the 1978 Brief Assessment Unit court reports revealed that psychiatrists had cited the diagnosis of *dangerousness* as a rationale for recommending a protracted remand in 62 (50.4 per cent) of the 123 cases subsequently referred to the Inpatient Unit. In various instances psychiatrists had also recommended extended assessments to establish a clinical diagnosis, to evaluate suitability for treatment, to gauge the subject's potential for sui-cide, or to establish an appropriate hospital or correctional placement (see Menzies 1985).

Overall, criminal court judges tended to endorse such in-patient rec-ommendations, whatever the rationale cited by forensic professionals. As indicated in Table 4.1 above, more than four out of five prescriptions for extended warrants of remand were successful in enlisting judicial consent. For their part, the METFORS psychiatrists consistently managed to recruit an ample supply of in-patient clientele (even when legally invalid criteria such as dangerousness were being cited). They experienced an exceedingly low refusal rate, and they were clearly able to inspire the court's confidence in the validity of these assessments.

The clinical focus on establishing legitimacy was evident from a content analysis of court letters written by the BAU psychiatrists. When recom-mending an extended evaluation, the METFORS clinicians consistently re-ferred to the benefits that would be yielded for both the accused person and the criminal court. In the case of a youth charged with 'Attempted Rape' and 'Indecent Assault,' the BAU psychiatrist underscored for the court the defendant's willingness to participate in the assessment process. 'It was unanimously agreed between us that Mr. O. can benefit from a 30 day assessment at the METFORS Inpatient Unit. When he was asked whether he would consent to that he indicated that anything that would help him would be acceptable' (PL 200).

In other instances the psychiatrist would overtly suggest hospitalization for the purpose of administering psychiatric treatment prior to trial. Generally, such recommendations were framed so that the individual's 'best interests' were attached to questions about potential dangerousness. Case 452 involved a middle-aged, middle-class woman charged with wounding her husband in a domestic dispute. The patient was diagnosed as acutely depressed, and the Brief Assessment Unit team determined that further evaluation was in order. The BAU psychologist concluded: 'Current assessment suggests that Mrs. G. may be a potential risk to herself and/or her husband if allowed out on bail on Monday, the rationale for this being that she has few supportive figures in the community and little in the way of plans of where to live. Because of this, it is felt to be in the patient's best interests to admit her to the METFORS Inpatient Unit for a period of 30 days. This time will allow her to begin to develop some composure, develop a constructive plan about what to do if she does receive bail, and at the same time, give her the opportunity to find a lawyer' (POR 452). This formulation was mirrored in the BAU psychiatrist's court letter: 'Due to Mrs. G.'s present mental disturbance (i.e. acute depression), we would request that your Honour grant a 30 day remand to the METFORS Inpatient Unit so that further assessment and treatment may take place. This assessment would also allow an opportunity to assess Mrs. G's potential for future dangerous behaviour towards herself and/or others in the community' (PL 452).

In order to secure judicial Warrants of Remand psychiatrists frequently expressed dissatisfaction with the quantity and content of data accumulated from the initial brief assessment. Here the need for further medico-legal knowledge was coupled with assurances that the in-patient evaluation would provide important supplementary information. For example, in the case of a youth accused of a minor indecent assault, the psychiatrist expressed confidence in the need for and diagnostic utility of in-patient confinement, despite the fact that the subject was neither psychotic, certifiable, nor unfit.

Mr. L. is not psychotic and is not certifiable ... Although he is fit for trial by the usual criteria, it is felt by us all that he needs a further period of inpatient assessment. During that inpatient stay we can determine more accurately his degree of retardation, his potential for dangerousness, the possibility of recurrence, and whether or not his actions have escalated over the past few years. He has already indicated that he has never hurt anyone ... but he is not sure in which direction things are going. (PL 349)

Alternatively, METFORS psychiatrists sometimes reasoned that an extended hospitalization would elicit data that were temporarily being suppressed by the subject's mental illness or hostile attitude: 'He admitted to hallucinations, he showed marked thought blocking, his expression was pained and painful, his speech was mainly halting and he admits also to being depressed. He tried hard to be cooperative and communicative, but I think his illness restricts him from being as cooperative and communicative as he would like' (PL 144).

Another patient, with no history of violence, was charged with possession of a stolen credit card. In the Brief Assessment Unit, he refused to discuss his charges with the clinical team. The nurse observed: 'He appeared to understand the nature of his alleged charges, however he did not talk openly about the surrounding circumstances with us. He was very vague and evasive about his alleged charges. It was unclear as to whether this man would be able to advise counsel' (NR 332). Meanwhile the psychiatrist apparently detected a potential for violence that required further scrutiny: 'On examination this man was found to be withdrawn, tense, suspicious and significantly depressed ... [H]e would not or could not give a full account of himself ... I would recommend that he be remanded to our Inpatient Unit here at METFORS for a period not exceeding 30 days for a full psychiatric assessment. A particular issue to which this assessment will address itself is the issue of possible dangerousness in the community as the material elicited at this examination would suggest that this is a significant area for investigation' (PL 332).

Subsequently, the defendant in this case spent fifteen days in jail, followed by twenty-three days in the METFORS Inpatient Unit. Upon the subject's final discharge to the court (where he received six months' probation) the in-patient psychiatrist wrote to the judge: 'Mr. H. is fit to stand trial, he is not certifiable ... Mr. H. represents no danger in the community, unless his depression, while untreated, would deepen and compel him to destructive behaviour to himself or others' (IPL 332). This latter qualification is noteworthy, as it is an apparent attempt retrospectively to legitimate the original justifications for five weeks of pre-trial confinement based on a relatively minor charge. By proposing the *possi-*

bility of dangerous behaviour, however remote, the in-patient letter was able to endorse the rationale for the original decision to admit, despite the subject's obvious fitness, non-violence, and trivial offence, and apparently because of his reticent demeanour in the Brief Assessment Unit.

A related clinical strategy for enlisting judicial warrants of remand centred on documentation of the subject's violent history and dangerous propensities. For instance, potential violence could be directly linked with the subject's imputed mental illness: 'It is my opinion that he may be suffering from a mental disorder and I would recommend that he be remanded to our Inpatient Unit for a period not exceeding 30 days for full neurological and psychiatric assessment. Because of this possible mental disorder he could constitute a danger in the community' (PL 148).

When the defendant was facing charges of a sexual nature, the perceived need for long-term assessment of dangerousness was particularly acute, as with a man accused of raping his daughter: 'Mr. Y. did indicate that he was experiencing long-standing sexual difficulties and felt concerned about his problem. In order to more fully assess the relationship between Mr. Y.'s depression, and sexual concerns, with the alleged behaviour of rape, I would request Your Honour remand Mr. Y. to the METFORS Inpatient Unit for a more complete assessment. I believe this to be in the interest of both the court and Mr. Y' (PL 420).

Referrals for in-patient dangerousness evaluations could even be anchored in unfounded evidence unrelated to the alleged offence. One subject was remanded on a charge of 'Weapons Dangerous,' but the recommendation for hospitalization appeared to be based upon unrelated incidents concerning his sexual conduct – information that was volunteered by the defendant during the METFORS brief assessment (PL 236: see Chapter 3).

Through the vehicle of these reports, then, the Brief Assessment Unit psychiatrists were able to introduce a total of 123 defendants to the Inpatient Unit during 1978. I now turn to the process and practice of these in-patient assessments at METFORS. The remainder of this chapter will focus on the role of psychological testing in the detection of disorder and criminality, on the enlistment of informants by forensic social workers, and on the sustained monitoring of subjects by nurses and psychiatric assistants on the ward of the Inpatient Unit.

MOBILIZING THE PSYCHOLOGICAL REPORTS

Almost all of the METFORS Inpatient Unit subjects were exposed to a battery of psychological tests, which typically were administered over the course of an entire day (see Appendix E). The procedure usually took place in a room reserved for this purpose, and the various components of the tests (both written and oral) were supervised by the in-patient psychologist who was assigned to the patient in question. Selections from the resulting psychological reports were routinely incorporated into psychiatrists' letters to the court.

These tests were, in strategic terms, the raison d'être for the in-patient forensic psychologists. Their findings and conclusions were framed in a stylized discourse that both documented the pathological condition of patients and affirmed the specialist knowledge of its authors. The multitude of psychometric, projective, cognitive, and intelligence tests provided a legitimating resource for accentuating the status of psychologists as integral participants in the assessment process. Forensic psychologists used these tests as multi-purpose implements for the moral devaluation of their subjects. These were not 'tests' in any real sense, since their very administration meant that the patients must inevitably 'fail.' Favourable evaluations and positive interpretations were virtually non-existent. Psychologists adopted a 'proclamatory style' (Goffman 1981) in using these instruments to confirm rather than to examine. While lip service was paid to rituals of 'discovering' the internal characterological flaws of subjects, in practice psychologists were simply reproducing old labels in a new discourse.

Psychologists thus held considerable discretionary power. They could orchestrate their results to highlight incipient theories about subjects, to illustrate the 'high technology' of their science, and to co-ordinate their findings with those already voiced by other authorities in the medico-legal system. They could adopt a variety of strategies for maximizing their definitional control over test results, and for monopolizing the resulting labelling process.

One such strategy involved the compression of multiple negative evaluations into a single diagnostic report. A number of psychological tests could be co-ordinated so that each was seen to locate a separate pathological condition. The result was often the presentation of 'multi-dimensional' images about in-patient subjects that both reflected and yielded composite profiles of mental disorder and dangerousness. In one typical case, the in-patient psychologist interviewed a twenty-six-year-old woman who was facing a relatively minor 'arson' charge along with 'fraud accommodation.' While on the Unit, the patient completed three psychological tests: the Minnesota Multiphasic Personality Inventory (MMPI), the Rorschach (Ink Blot), and the Thematic Apperception Test (TAT). No fewer than twenty-one negative descriptions emerged in the psychologist's interpretations of these results:

Ms. M.'s psychological makeup may be viewed from several angles. On the one hand, the MMPI suggests that she is basically an immature, egocentric, demanding and highly dependent young woman who is likely to develop somatic complaints as a reaction to stress ... [I]t is likely that her many preoccupations are superficial and short lived. Also indicated by the MMPI and the TAT are certain antisocial tendencies. It is likely that Ms. M. can be a highly suspicious and distrustful individual with few qualms about manipulating those around her in order to further her own needs. Many of this patient's responses on the Rorschach are suggestive of some form of thought disorder or schizoform process. Indeed, the MMPI also indicates the presence of unconventional thinking patterns suggestive of schizoid tendencies ... She appeared as a grandiose, self centred and highly dependent individual who has a strong Machiavellian component to her personality. It becomes clear that she enjoys being the centre of attention and will step on a few toes to gain this position. (IPOR 581)

In this way, deviant categories could be arranged in psychological reports to achieve maximum dramatic effect. These labels were so compelling that there was little apparent need to develop a biographical context – psychological records seldom conveyed more than just the test results and interpretations. The reports tended to comprise a simple recitation of deviant categories, as in the following psychological account of a subject arrested on a non-violent indecent assault charge: 'Mr. P.'s endorsements on personality tests have him depict himself as depressed, tense, irritable, suspicious, impulsive, self-depreciating, ruminative, over ideational and subject to quick mood swings ... Distrustful of people, Mr. P. utilizes regression, projection, rationalization and displacement to avoid close interpersonal contact. Persons endorsing test items in a similar fashion are often seen as resentful, hostile, dependent, worried, low in self-esteem and frustration tolerance as well as prone to acting-out psychological conflicts ...' (IPOR 152).

In-patient psychologists also benefited from their flexible management of deviant classifications. Given the enabling context of psychological testing, neutral and even positive information could be made consistent with the deviant master images being transmitted to other medico-legal authorities (Lofland 1969: 149). The METFORS subjects underwent a systematic deletion of their positive attributes as these were transposed into the official psychological discourse of the clinic. Obedience, respect, conformity, passivity, and related 'virtues' were routinely collapsed into, and became symbols for, the mental pathology and intransigence of the accused. The following passage presents a typical conversion of 'pleasant and cooperative' behaviour into indices of personality disturbance and potential violence: 'Mr. A. on the whole has been pleasant and cooperative with staff and patients. His behaviour if anything is somewhat passive and dependent ... One suspects that this man, although seemingly meek and eager to please, has a strong undercurrent of explosive anger and hostility in reaction to his present life circumstances. It is conceivable that he may deal with this anger through anti-social behaviour' (IPOR 404).

Like other clinicians, psychologists were engaged in the interrelated tasks of reducing complexity, eliminating ambiguity, and highlighting the mental pathology and criminality of subjects. Typically, the personality categories resulting from these transactions were similar to those developed at other levels of the system. They were ad hoc, subjective, discretionary, non-replicable expressions of the individual clinician's biases. But when these judgments were integrated into the clinical rhetoric of discovery, they appeared to be, in Garfinkel's terms, 'clear, coherent, planful, consistent, chosen, knowledgeable, uniform, reproducible [and] rational' (1967: 34). They were crafted in an effort to 'persuade and convince' (Gusfield 1981), as in the following depiction of a patient arrested for robbery.

The tests and interview data present a picture of a very depressed individual with strong anti-social and paranoid tendencies. Generally speaking this is a man who harbours a basic fear and distrust of his fellow man. He states that people make him feel 'self conscious and paranoid' ... The defences available to him are primitive ones of displacement and projection. These combined with low impulse control and poor social judgment suggest a potentially explosive personality who is likely to act out his negative feelings towards others particularly under the influence of alcohol. Although motivated to change his hopes and expectations in this area are basically grandiose and unrealistic ... The anti-social, immature and hostile elements in this man's personality suggest an individual who is resistant to any meaningful change. This man's prognosis for change is poor. (IPOR 455).

Psychological testing therefore contributed to the amplification of deviance in the forensic classification process. Whereas these instruments appeared on the surface to be technical and value-free, in practice the test results were impressionistically merged with intuitive notions about the mental and moral condition of subjects. In spite of disclaimers to the contrary, test results seldom harboured surprises about accused persons. They functioned instead to confirm what the psychologist 'knew all along' from documents, prior accounts, and subjective evaluation (Garfinkel 1967: 186–207). They stamped these accumulated 'facts' with the authenticity of scientific procedure. And these procedures were almost universally used to denounce, to externalize (Berger and Luckmann 1967), and to establish the essential deviance of subjects as inherent, stable, habitual flaws of character. Psychological tests were viewed to be valid indicators of personality *structures* that persisted over time, and hence they complemented and rationalized the presumably more ephemeral views of other clinicians.

In the Inpatient Unit, the attending psychologists routinely applied psychometric tests *as if* they were objective yardsticks of deviancy, *as if* their skills were principally technical rather than interpretive. Pfohl suggests that [u]nlike psychiatrists, who are taught to rely more heavily on their clinical judgments and past professional experience, psychologists tend to be professionally socialized into the use of more refined or structured approaches to investigating a client's "inner life" ' (1978: 87). But whatever their unique style, in content the psychological accounts were virtually interchangeable with those of psychiatrists and other clinicians. Accused persons were, in either case, subject to such a wide variety of negative attributions that the reported results were naturally selective, and were constituted not in scientific method, but in the indexical expectations and moral evaluations of the professional classifiers.

These strategies were particularly apparent when psychologists were dealing with 'dangerous' people. Psychological testing in the METFORS Inpatient Unit was recurrently targeted upon the identification of potentially violent subjects. Despite the lack of evidence supporting the validity of psychometric predictions about dangerousness (Megargee and Bohn 1979; Menzies, Webster, and Sepejak 1985a), the METFORS psychologists relied heavily on their test instruments to formulate estimates of future conduct. When defendants entered the Unit with a serious violent history, and when common sense pointed to a finding of dangerousness, the test interpretations seldom digressed from this theme. In Case 376, the subject had a prolonged history of violence, had been arrested for 'Weapons Dangerous' and 'Assaulting Police,' and had been considered certifiable as both mentally ill and dangerous by the BAU psychiatrist. On the Inpatient Unit, the attending psychologist administered the MMPI with predictable results. The test interpretations concentrated exclusively on the dangerousness theme, and resulted in an unambiguous collection of violent imagery about the accused person.

Persons responding in a similar fashion are often seen as highly rebellious, inadequate, apprehensive, impulsive and under-controlling in their hostility. They are chronic worriers with strong compulsive and obsessive features who are apt to act out their psychological conflicts in an anti-social fashion. It would appear that Mr. S.'s defences of somatization, regression and displacement are proving to be inadequate in the face of day-to-day stress. Under stress he is apt to become hyperactive in thought and action. Such hyperactivity when combined with impulsivity, hostility and the use of displacement or projection to ward off his own aggressive impulses, makes Mr. S.'s behaviour unpredictable and likely to be of an anti-social nature. Under conditions of stress it is quite likely that Mr. S.'s contact with reality becomes seriously impaired and his thought processes are apt to take on delusional features which evoke acting-out as a response. Persons presenting a similar profile are often diagnosed as suffering a major affective disorder. It is the opinion of this examiner that Mr. S. is in serious psychological difficulty and in his present condition represents a danger to himself and others. Perhaps medication and treatment at a psychiatric facility would reduce the likelihood of his continued acting-out behaviour. (IPOR 376)

In cases where the potential for violence was less overt, psychologists could still invoke various strategies for charting and communicating 'discoveries' about dangerousness. They could focus on the 'anti-social personality' of the accused person: 'Mr. R. has an underlying personality disorder of the dis-social type. Many of his thoughts and attitudes are anti-authoritarian. He can be quite rebellious and headstrong. He is capable of flouting society's rules at will' (IPOR 269). They could supplement their data with items extracted from the patient's biography, as in the case of a paranoid patient who had once served in the army: '[H]e may well represent a danger to the community in the future. Due to his military background he could be capable of responding in an aggressive manner to someone who is perceived to be an agent of the enemy' (IPOR 441). They could rely exclusively on intuition, in the face of discrepant test information: 'He may not be a danger to others, but I suspect he is' (IPOR 225). They could portray their subjects as under-controlled beings, driven by primal impulses, and inadequately constrained by their internal and external environments: 'Personality assessment depicts him as a narcissistic and egocentric individual with limited ego controls ... Mr. P., in the opinion of this examiner, suffers from "superego lacuna", which has been a precipitating developmental factor in his anti-social behaviour' (IPOR 154).

Hence, psychologists actively pursued lines of theorizing about patients, and embellished their results with moral rhetoric, while managing to display their reports as definitive, standardized, and authentic descriptions of subjects' 'inner states.' Psychologists relied heavily on these instruments to sustain their expert status. Because of their monopoly over this technology, the forensic psychologists, more so than other clinicians, were dependent on the perceived validity of such 'scientific' methods. Their willingness to apply, in good conscience, such denunciative ascriptions to their subjects was a function of their accommodation to what Ellul terms a 'technological morality,' where '[t]here is in the concept of the normal a concern for precise knowledge, for the rationale of behavior, for the adjustment to ... objective conditions ... , since in the final analysis it is the clinical technician who decides what is normal' (Ellul 1975: 167).

The test interpretations of psychologists made sense contextually, given their professional mandate to maximize signs of pathology and criminality (Hawkins 1981: 112). Dominant themes about madness and dangerousness were continuously used to submerge alternative points of view. For their part, the METFORS Inpatient Unit psychologists were induced to mobilize these enabling features of their work environment, in order to preserve their professional authority and accountability. Psychologists were both empowered by the credibility extended to their technical know-how, and constrained by the limitations imposed by and upon these instruments. Caught (like all medico-legal officials) in the delicate balance between autonomy and irrelevance, psychologists worked to construct dramatic accounts of deviance – accounts that would underline the expert status of the authors, while amplifying the pathological imagery within which their subjects were being enclosed.

SOCIAL WORKERS AND THEIR INFORMANTS

On the Inpatient Unit, psychiatric social workers were primarily responsible for accumulating data about the METFORS patients' family background and social experiences. In order to extend their informational reach beyond the walls of the institution, social workers enlisted the co-operation of informants. These included family members, employers, co-workers, co-students, and a variety of other participants in the subjects' personal web of affiliations. In a typical case, the presiding social worker would arrange an appointment with informants, and would conduct the interview in his or her office on the METFORS premises. If in-person interviews were not possible, information would be collected over the telephone. These interviews could touch on a wide range of issues concerning the subject's personal history. At the conclusion of such exchanges, the social worker would compose a report, usually several pages in length, to be inserted into the patient's medical file.

A number of studies have charted the complex chain of transactions through which family and official agents collaborate in the social control of mental patients (Horwitz 1982: 36–47). Goffman (1961) describes the deployment of 'betrayal funnels' which are forged over time between family and clinic. Others have documented the tendency for mental illness to be first recognized within the family unit (Clausen and Yarrow 1955; Fox 1978; Horwitz 1977; Linn 1961). Much of this work has focused on the initial attempts among intimates to normalize early symptoms of pathology (Gove and Howell 1974; Sampson, Messinger, and Towne 1964; Yarrow, Schwartz, Murphy, and Deasy 1955). Rule transgressions and bizarre conduct are typically met by a 'nothing unusual is happening stance' (Emerson 1970; Laing and Esterson 1964) and a resistance to psychiatric definitions of the situation (Horwitz 1982: 32). However, this early ambivalence typically evaporates, once the subject has been externally categorized as deviant by clinical authorities: '... the tendency of intimates to deny the presence of mental illness holds only for the *initial* recognition of mental illness. While family members may normalize unusual behaviors for many months or years, after a formal label of mental illness has been applied to a member they are less reluctant to view behavior within a mental illness framework' (Horwitz 1982: 41; see Angrist, Lefton, Dinitz, and Pasamanick 1968).

Three conditions are necessary for the mobilization of a familial 'lay referral system' (Freidson 1961). First, the disturbing words and deeds of the subject must be defined and accepted, within the daily round of family and intimate transactions, as essentially a mental health problem beyond the remedial resources of the group. 'In this way, the friend, relative, or acquaintance can confirm recognition of a problem and encourage professional counsel without risking antagonism, rejection, or personal entanglement. Furthermore, the layman may honestly perceive that physicians ... are appropriate and suitable choices; or, at least, that they *might* be able to take care of the problem' (Hawkins and Tiedeman 1975: 132).

Second, the diagnosis of psychopathology by a professional tends to foreclose alternative interpretations of disturbing conduct on the part of an intimate relation. Family and peers will be persuaded to abandon their denial mode, and to unite in support of the expert imputation.

Once a psychiatric professional has labeled someone, instead of exhibiting the normalizing tendencies that existed before the initial hospitalization, family members often interpret unusual behavior as indicative of mental illness. While before the formal label was applied, responders were likely to interpret strange behavior as stemming from a variety of sources, once a professional made a formal diagnosis of mental illness any future incidence of strange behavior would be explained within an illness framework ... [T]he label provides a perceptual framework that offers a more crystallized explanation of the symptoms. (Horwitz 1982: 41)

Third, the incidence of violent or criminal behaviour tends to break down the defence system of the intimate circle of family and friends. When the member is seen to cross the threshold into public rule-breaking or overtly threatening activities (Kadushin 1969; Sampson, Messinger, and Towne 1961), close relations are inclined to surrender control over his or her deviant identity. Formal labels applied by official agencies begin to supersede and redefine the informal control practices of family and peers. Supporters are co-opted into the betrayal funnel, and become willing informants and contributors to the institutional labelling process. They are rewarded by assurances that their participation is in the best interests of the individual, and that the subject has by his or her actions forfeited any moral right to guardianship. Intimate others become converts, supplying data that are vital to the stigmatization of their member, and facilitating the official construction of criminal and pathological identity (Cockerham 1981: 240–46; Hawkins and Tiedeman 1975: 205).

In the METFORS Inpatient Unit, clinicians seldom needed actively to persuade significant others to 'testify' against the subject. Prior to being interviewed, family members, friends, neighbours, and others had generally reached consensus with the official characterization. Social workers were able to take advantage of long-standing conflicts between subjects and informants in soliciting significant data from the latter. Often, the subject's lengthy history of deviant conduct had erased any reservations held by the informant. Sometimes, the interviewee had been a direct victim of the defendant's transgressions, and clinicians could mobilize his or her desire for retaliation. The social work interviews yielded, as a result, an abundance of powerful and intimate data, collected under seemingly benign circumstances, that added to the documentation being compiled in the subject's official record.

Friends and family members were ostensibly enlisted to fill in omissions in the patient's official biography. This was a highly selective and arbitrary process, as informants predominantly dwelt on those historical 'facts' that were consistent with the damning details available in institutional accounts. In Case 275, for example, a nineteen-year-old youth was accused of striking his sister with a piece of furniture while she was asleep on the family's living-room couch. He was diagnosed in the Brief Assessment Unit as 'personality disordered, with schizoid and antisocial traits' (PL 275), and remanded to the Inpatient Unit for twenty-eight days. During the patient's confinement on the Unit, the psychiatric social worker conducted an extensive interview with his mother. She recounted a lengthy history of deviant conduct perpetrated by the accused, none of which had previously appeared in the criminal or hospital record, but all of which was now documented in the social worker's report. Some excerpts from the file are presented below:

According to Mrs. L. the patient was a behaviour problem as a very young child. Before he was even 5, he had done things such as scratch a store owner's car with a nail, beat up a crippled boy, set a fire, throw pop bottles at the police and steal from stores. She gave several examples to illustrate how devious he was at such a young age. She says he used to take a little girl into the store with him who would talk to the manager while he loaded his pockets with stolen goods ... The patient has been living with his mother since November of 1977. She says that since that time he has acted out in many ways. He has stabbed a love seat in her home about 6 times. He has burned a couch several times with the end of his cigarette. He has put his fist through a closet door. He stabbed his sister's teddy bear. She says that practically everything in the living room is broken. She feels that he did something to hurt the cat because the cat was terrified of him. She thinks that he hit [his sister's] baby because she heard a loud smack when he was feeding the baby in the kitchen ... Both the patient's mother and the patient's sister are afraid of him. The sister has said that she will leave if he is allowed home. (ISWR 275)

These details were recorded in the social worker's report, and at the conclusion of the evaluation they were incorporated into the psychiatric formulation conveyed to the criminal court. The in-patient letter to the presiding judge read: 'Mr. L. ... exhibit[s] a long standing pattern of maladaptive behaviour characterized by impulsivity, aggressive outbursts with low tolerance to frustration, inability to follow through on goals or learn by experience as well as anti-social behaviour. This pattern of behaviour ... is in keeping with a diagnosis of personality disorder-immature type with anti-social features' (IPL 275). Three weeks after being discharged from the Unit, the patient was sentenced to six months' imprisonment and two years' probation.

Informants willingly offered a wealth of legally relevant materials, in the context of interviews that were supposed to be driven by 'social service' motives. They provided, in Goffman's terms, 'a means of synthetically building up a picture of the patient's past that demonstrated that a disease process had been slowly infiltrating his conduct until his conduct as a system was entirely pathological' (1961: 375). In the case of a twenty-four-year-old male facing a serious arson charge, both family and neighbours were interviewed by the in-patient social worker. The parents of the patient reported that he had been involved in fire-setting from the age of four years, and that his behaviour had been progressively deteriorating. A telephone interview with the subject's next-door neighbour elicited an array of data that brought his pathological identity into clearer focus.

[A]mong his own age group he was always considered to be a loser. Apparently until he entered training in the armed forces, he was always very fat. He never did well in school, and does not have friends now, primarily because they see him as a braggart and a person who lives in a fantasy world. Apparently, he tells people stories that they know are not true. V. [the patient] ... was never able to do anything right. He was fat, did poorly in school, and was always into 'boy troubles'. Mrs. J. [the informant] feels that throughout his life, V. has been begging for extra attention, at least in recent years V. seems to buy friends by being the big spender. As far as Mrs. J. knows, V. has never had a girlfriend as a lover, although he has had female friends as buddies. She stated that her own daughter and her daughter's husband cleared out the patient's apartment after his arrest, and found a large amount of hard-core pornography. When I asked her to explain 'hard-core', she said 'much more than one would see in Penthouse magazine' ... [S]he felt he had caused a fire [several years earlier] in the [armed services]. She stated they were able to trace the fire to him because he had left matches from his father's company on the scene of the last fire he had set. (ISWR 451)

Social workers were able to capitalize on such accounts to impose a sense of continuity onto the personal history of subjects, while managing simultaneously to rationalize current psychiatric theorizing. Another patient had been arrested on a 'Weapons Dangerous' charge after chasing his wife around their apartment with a butcher knife. He had been subsequently certified by the BAU psychiatrist as psychotic and suicidal, and immediately admitted to the METFORS Inpatient Unit. The clinical team was faced with the task of producing a consistent profile that would account for the subject's recurrent violence and suicidal ideation. Once again, this profile was in large part supplied by the testimony of significant others in the defendant's personal life. The social worker's interview with the subject's uncle located this missing clinical thread in the fabric of his childhood upbringing:

Mr. N. [the informant] began by describing the deprived family background in which P. [the patient] was raised. He says the nine children were brought up like a 'pack of wild dogs'. The father beat the children and their mother, and P. was apparently abused even more than the others because he did not look like [the father]. According to Mr. N. the family has lived by their own laws on a farm ... ever since being thrown out by neighbours ... They marry as many times as they wish without getting a divorce. One of the daughters has apparently had five husbands. According to Mr. N., P. too has had more than one wife. He was in Georgia for a while and brought back a hillbilly girl who couldn't read or write and was age 14 ... Mr. N. says that at one time there were 25 people living on the farm. The children often stick to the floor from being wet. He says that one child died from pneumonia from lying in his own urine. (ISWR 033)

In such accounts, informants mediated between the personal troubles of patients and the active construction of dangerous and pathological categories by the METFORS clinicians. The co-operation of close relatives and friends was therefore a central component in the imputation process. These were the 'expert witnesses' who were privy to private manifestations of deviant conduct – to information that often cemented the clinicians' tentative hypotheses about the defendant's medico-legal status.

This function was especially pivotal in cases of sexual deviance, where the testimony of intimates could literally 'break the case open' for the clinical assessment team. Elusive and private conduct could become public knowledge, allowing diagnoses of sexual 'disorders' to become grounded in a foundation of empirical evidence. Such cases were commonplace. The sister of a young man charged with violently assaulting a woman provided a graphic description of his predilection for obscene telephone calls and for masturbating on his nephew's teddy bear (ISWR 172). The aunt of a seventeen-year-old male accused of serious rapes and bodily assaults reported that his mother had dressed him in girl's clothing to the age of twelve (ISWR 061). The wife of a man facing criminal charges for fellating his three sons recounted in detail his bizarre sexual fantasies and recurring difficulties with premature ejaculation and impotence (ISWR 082). In the aftermath of a brutal knife attack on a female friend of the accused, the subject's father corroborated initial clinical diagnoses of sexual psychopathy.

The patient's father first stated, 'I have no son G., I disowned him ... Mr. D. was not at all surprised by the offence and feels that his son is very dangerous. Mr. D. has received calls from teachers from [   ] School saying that G. has been there threatening people with knives and one time with a gun. Apparently a resident ... who lives in the home where G. was staying has told Mr. D. that his son has threatened a few young men at the residence. Mr. D. feels that the patient has manipulated ... the Director of the residence, and that [the director] has no idea of the patient's real behaviour. Mr. D. feels that the patient should be locked up and away from civilization. He feels that the only reason that G. was not convicted of his previous 'Attempted Rape' charge was because the victim did not show up in Court. (ISWR 445).

As these cases demonstrate, strategic alliances repeatedly developed between clinicians and informants, wherein the latter were recruited to bear witness against defendants, to provide testimony that might not be so easily elicited within the more inhibiting environment of the criminal court. Yet this reportorial licence was never absolute. Data furnished by family and friends tended to be glossed, reconstructed, or otherwise neutralized whenever their evidence or opinions directly contradicted clinical impressions about the accused person. When conflict arose, informants risked being incorporated into the pathological picture being developed by the clinical team. When they displayed a denial mode, or when they refused to participate in the betrayal funnel, their role could be abruptly modified. When they declared themselves as advocates for the interests of the accused, their accounts could be openly challenged or discredited by the social worker. Informants were enlisted as supplementary biographers, and hence their narratives about subjects had to support and converge with the agency's emerging formulations (Lofland 1969: 150). Otherwise, they could find themselves targets of, rather than contributors to the labelling process.

The METFORS in-patient records were rife with examples of the validity control exercised by clinicians over their informants. In Case 445 (see above) the youth's parents, a teacher, and the arresting officer had all endorsed the clinical view that he was extremely dangerous. However, the supervisor of the patient's group home struck a discordant note in the social work interview: 'Mr. A. noticed very little strange behaviour by the patient during [the] three weeks [prior to the alleged offence]. He stated that there were no black outs, no memory loss, no confusion, no bizarre behaviour and no sleeping problems ... Mr. A. stated that during the time [the subject] was at the house he seemed to be very popular with girls. He would talk to many girls on the phone [and had] managed to match up boys in the house with girls that he knew ... Mr. A. had never heard the patient mention the victim of the offence' (ISWR 445).

This testimony collided with evidence supplied by the other witnesses, and if unchallenged might have complicated the otherwise uniform assessment of psychopathy and extreme dangerousness. The social worker, however, successfully neutralized these supportive images, not by openly denying their veracity, but instead by throwing into doubt the motivation and credibility of the informant. Mr A. was evaluated as an unreliable witness, and the social worker concluded that Good Samaritanism was incompatible with effective denunciation: 'During this brief interview it was difficult to do an adequate assessment of Mr. A. [the informant]. He did seem to be sincere in his desire to help young people and from his own description, seems to be quite successful in filling a need. I question his motivation simply because it is hard to believe that one person could donate so much of his personal time and financial resources to helping problem adolescents' (ISWR 445).

When family members denied the necessity or value of the in-patient hospitalization, similar clinical defences were usually mobilized. Such a response dominated the case of a twenty-year-old male accused of fondling a young girl in a public park. The subject's parents were openly sceptical about the need for clinical confinement. Following her interview with the parents, the social worker reported: 'It was difficult to determine whether [they] fully understood the charges or considered J.'s charges as minor offences. Mr. U. clearly gave the message that he didn't like the attitude of the police and said "you could just touch somebody nowadays and get arrested for indecent assault". I got the feeling that he was trying to blame the police for arresting J. and causing family difficulties. They both stated ... that they would like J. to come home because he was only getting worse staying here' (ISWR 349).

The parents were violating a ground rule for such exchanges, namely that the very fact of hospitalization confirmed the seriousness of the offence and its attendant pathology. These two informants were therefore perceived as adversaries to the forensic process, and were dismissed as contributors to the patient's criminality: 'It was difficult to obtain specific information from this family ... I got the feeling from Mr. U. that he was being inconvenienced by coming to the interview. He seemed to take no responsibility for J.'s problem, in fact, he thought J. would be fine if they just kept him busy. My concern would be that he may, in fact, be passing the same message on to J.' (ISWR 349).

When they were unable to 'convert the nonbelievers' (Hawkins and Tiedeman 1975: 122; Kadushin 1969: 75), social workers converted them into clinical cases themselves. Efforts to defend the subject were read as active resistance, and as cover-ups that were designed to subvert the clinical process. In Case 373, a woman's reluctance to disclose intimate details about her marital relationship with the patient was viewed as meaningful symptomatology:

She was very elusive, very defensive. She would talk about problems in the marriage but when we got to details it became much more difficult to elicit information from her. I felt that this couple are playing 'we have a secret' and that until they can begin to talk about some of these issues, they are probably not going to get too far in dealing with the problems in the relationship ... [T]he fighting that goes on in the relationship is part and parcel of their method of dealing with each other ... I think the situation is deteriorating very rapidly and is probably going to get worse as time goes on. (ISWR 373)

Alternatively, the social worker might turn the diagnostic lens directly on the hostile witness himself or herself. The informant in Case 385 was the mother of a twenty-five-year-old man charged with 'Theft Auto.' Much of the social worker's questioning was initially focused on the personal history of the *informant* rather than the subject. 'When I asked her why she got married she laughed and said "what does all this have to do with [my son]?" She refused to respond to many questions concerning her marital and family history, and it was difficult to determine whether she was in fact being genuinely uncooperative or talking about her marriage brought back many unresolved feelings for her' (ISWR 385). The informant's reactions provided ample indication, according to the social worker, of 'genuine' recalcitrance, and of the mother's contribution to the problems being experienced and perpetrated by the son.

Taken as a whole, these social work documents revealed a routine, extensive, expedient, and legitimate network of informants that was regularly harnessed by forensic clinicians. Whereas the majority of socio-legal research on informant systems focuses on police work (e.g. Skolnick 1966), here is evidence of an organized round of collusion between authorities and citizens that is equally penetrating and efficient. Social workers were able to extend the assessment process beyond the walls of METFORS, and into the daily experiences of subjects, by developing these channels of communication with intimate others. In virtually every in-patient remand, they could rely on these networks to support their emerging inferences about psychopathology and related forensic problems. For their part, informants actively collaborated in performing much of the information work for clinicians, and they were selectively rewarded for their role in the consolidation of deviant labels. As in most information networks, both groups stood to benefit from these exchanges – the informants by finding medical support for their grievances against patients, and the clinicians by tapping a fertile source of pertinent data.

Social work consultations facilitated forensic ascriptions of mental disorder. They appeared to humanize these labels, by enlisting the support of close relations, who were ostensibly 'on the side' of patients. Moreover, the breadth of available documentary knowledge was staggering, and far surpassed those accounts of life histories contained in judicial records or conventional medical files (Goffman 1961: 159). To gain authenticity, every official attribution must have a history, and must be grounded in concrete, mundane descriptions of everyday behaviour. The METFORS social work interviews were instrumental in breathing life into these designations, in merging institutional categories with the longitudinal biographies of forensic patients.

MONITORING MADNESS ON THE WARD

The 123 METFORS in-patients spent an average of twenty-eight days each on the Unit. As with psychiatric hospitalizations elsewhere, the administration of clinical treatment was a generally accepted feature of these extended remands (despite questionable legal authority: see Chapter 1). The majority of patients were routinely given a variety of psychotropic drugs. Subjects attended group therapy sessions presided over by a psychiatric assistant or nurse; they were interviewed by psychiatrists and clinical psychologists; and a recreational therapist and part-time medical doctor were attached to the unit.

However, both staff and patients were aware of the overriding custodial and observational focus of these assessments. These protracted remands were principally used to produce forensic recommendations for the courts, and hence line personnel were centrally concerned with surveillance, and with the simple documentation of pathology among forensic inmates (cf. Schiffer 1978; Webster, Menzies, and Jackson 1982). The daily round of activities in the In-patient Unit was designed to facilitate the continuous scrutiny of patients. Prevailing therapeutic discourse notwithstanding, professionals and attendants were primarily responsible for accumulating and relaying legally relevant data to criminal court judges.

The conduct and utterances of subjects were systematically charted through three forms of documentation: consultation records kept by psychiatrists following each interview with patients; observations made during group therapy and recreation sessions; and progress notes maintained by psychiatric assistants and nurses during the course of each eight-hour shift. In addition, an admission form was completed for each patient (along with a statement of objectives for the assessment), and a discharge summary was filed at the conclusion of an individual's confinement.

The METFORS Inpatient Unit progress notes were critical to the entrenchment of forensic labels about mental illness. The line staff (psychiatric assistants and nurses) accumulated extensive inventories of pathological behaviour and rule-breaking that transpired on the ward. These notations often exceeded 100 pages over the course of a thirty-day assessment. They were important instruments in the attribution process, since they helped to contextualize, and to bring into the present tense, the official medico-legal accounts of pathological and criminal careers. As Goffman writes, 'the nursing notes kept on the ward ... chart the daily course of each patient's disease, and hence his conduct, providing for the near present the sort of information the case record supplies for his past' (1961: 159).

The task for psychiatric assistants and nurses was not only to maintain order and security on the Inpatient Unit, but to participate directly in the assessment by recording behavioural manifestations of the patient's condition (Schur 1971: 54). Out of the extraordinary range of transactions, among dozens of staff members and as many as twenty-three patients, emerged a systematic dossier on each subject that relied on interpersonal and impressionistic sources of data (Goffman 1959: 249). Entries could be selectively read to validate and finalize clinical labels. Such informational items are described by Garfinkel as 'tokens – like pieces that will permit the assembly of an infinitely large number of mosaics' (1967: 202). In this sense, the record-keeping of line personnel was functionally equivalent to the typification work of psychiatrists and related forensic specialists. Like other workers, in-patient staff were responsible for developing and sustaining deviant imagery in the form of official dossiers. The Inpatient Unit documents were characterized by an accumulation of descriptions and interpretations that accentuated the pathological status of patients, while fulfilling the legal role of METFORS as knowledge broker for the courts.[5]

The documentary activities of in-patient personnel comprised a number of working strategies that shaped their written accounts. One such practice involved the proactive solicitation of 'meaningful' data during every possible transaction between staff and patients. This work was facilitated by repeated assurances to subjects that assessments were in their own best interests, that their willing participation was an important pre-condition for a favourable evaluation. When one METFORS in-patient complained to staff that 'he does not like people picking at his mind,' the nurse came to the defence of her observational activities: 'It was explained to him that we are here to assess him and to record even the most obvious explanations so as to give as accurate an assessment as possible' (IPN 147). Another individual was heard to protest his treatment at the hands of the in-patient psychiatrist: 'I'm not crazy. I'm normal. Dr. L. mixes me up.' The nurse recorded her response: 'Explained to him that Dr. L. can't help him if he doesn't level with him and tell him the truth' (IPN 047). It seemed that effective therapy in this case was contingent upon a full confession.

In other instances, the patient's failure to disclose was interpreted as a sign of malingering or mental illness, as with a twenty-six-year-old woman charged with 'Arson' and 'False Pretences': 'Brushes off confrontations as meaningless. Skilfully avoiding *any* interview. Denial, avoidance and projection ... Extremely manipulative' (IPN 581). Alternatively, mental disorder could be viewed to impede the subject's ability to co-operate with the evaluation: 'Appears anxious ... does not seem to understand his role as a patient' (IPN 335). Whatever the perceived source of their recalcitrance, it was clear that in-patients courted potentially serious repercussions when they failed to comply.[6]

Psychiatric assistants and nurses probed aggressively for evidence of pathology and criminal disposition. Such proactive search tactics concentrated on the discovery of 'underlying contributors' to medico-legal problems. In the process, the claims and conduct of subjects came to be viewed as epiphenomenal, as imperfect representations of hidden psychogenetic forces. 'Patients' statements are not taken for granted as accounts of things as they really are. Instead, they are to be treated as possible projections of things as they "unreally" exist in the minds of the mentally ill' (Pfohl 1978: 138).

In one particularly vivid case, a thirty-five-year-old male was on vacation in Toronto when he was arrested for impaired driving. The following morning (having smashed the toilet in his jail cell after the arrest, receiving a second charge of 'Public Mischief' for his trouble) he was remanded to the Brief Assessment Unit and involuntarily certified to the Inpatient Unit by the psychiatrist ('He showed marked euphoria with flight of ideas and difficulties in concentration and attention. This was associated with an inappropriate joking and a high level of nervousness' [PL 278]). Once the subject was admitted, the in-patient staff moved to document this diagnosis. The progress notes two days later read: 'Claiming various academic degrees and corporate executive positions. Excessive demands. Grandiose, paranoid, tangented with flight of ideas, angry with current situation, undermining with patients' (IPN 278). On the following day, the in-patient social worker was contacted by a friend of the accused, who proceeded to confirm most of his 'paranoid' claims. It turned out that he held two university degrees (one a Master of Business Administration), he owned his own company in another Canadian city, and he previously had been the vice-president of a corporation in the United States. Three days later the subject was discharged to the court; his confinement had lasted only five days. The in-patient psychiatrist's court letter read: 'Since admission to hospital Mr. A. has settled significantly and he is no longer certifiable. Hence, I am returning him to court' (IPL 278). The sentence was three months' probation.

This was an extreme illustration of the conceptual mirages that could distort observations made by personnel in the Inpatient Unit. But it was by no means unique. Patient 035 was a twenty-six-year-old male accused of wounding his mother's tenant in a knife attack. His sexual overtures toward a female co-patient were interpreted by staff as indications of a 'reaction formation' against his underlying homosexuality (although there was no other mention of sexual orientation anywhere in the clinical record). 'Patient initiates conversation re. sexual attractiveness of [female] copatient. [Quoting subject] "But if I am sexually attracted to [ ], why would all you people think that I am a homosexual?" ' The reporter merged these denials with a written account of the patient's sexual inadequacies. 'It would be interesting to observe whether J.'s seeming attraction to peer [ ] is of genuine interest or a concoction on his part to prove his manhood.' Other items appeared to confirm this depiction. 'Protective of mother ... description of self as being a person with both "ruthless and charming forces" ... Feels he is not masculine ... In writer's opinion, patient appears to be experiencing a gradually increasing level of sexual frustration. This frustration may be partly due to the confusion he appears to be experiencing relating to his own sexuality. Appears to have fear that he will be labelled as a homosexual and continues to insist that he is not' (IPN 035).

Another routine reporting strategy among line personnel involved the consistent discrediting and discounting of claims to normality. When observations were inconsistent with clinical accounts, they tended to be reformulated, through a number of remedial practices, into evidence that confirmed official renditions of psychiatric reality. Patients were literally caught in a Catch-22, where virtually any performance on their part was eligible for inclusion in their pathological profile. Basic prerequisites for normal communication – trust, reciprocity, mutuality – were at a premium in this environment. The organizational system of rewards and sanctions on the Inpatient Unit contributed to the objectification of subjects and their accounts, rendering them less than authentic in the eyes of professional observers.

Staff members were hence inclined to confront the reality expressions of their subjects. When patients verbalized their doubts about the benevolent objectives of METFORS, their words could be viewed as emblematic of criminal potential or intent: 'Says staff do not trust the patients and that some staff get a hard time if they treat patients with respect. Says guards at the Don Jail told him what METFORS was like – get patients to talk then use it against them in court ... Be aware of potential for hostility and anti-authority attitude ... Some paranoid ideation – "You people all ask me the same things – are you trying to trip me up?" ... Continue to probe gently for more information' (IPN 269).

Similarly, patient experiences and expressions could be displaced from their institutional context. A subject with a history of psychiatric hospitalizations was observed to be constantly sniffing his orange juice in the morning – probably not an entirely inappropriate action, given the very real possibility that medication could be administered in this way. In her notes relating to this observation, however, the reporter glossed over this possible motive, in favour of a more ominous conclusion: 'Expressing paranoid ideation. Underlying anger evident. Projecting hostility to staff. Refused medication [stating that] medicine is poison ... Very negative, hostile and suspicious re. situation. Testing staff. Manipulative re. abuse of diet' (IPN 236).

The activities of patients could be comprehended and made to fit clinical expectations through a variety of related practices. Co-operative conduct could be transformed into symptoms of alleged deviance: 'Quiet wandering around unit continues with patient being involved in very little socializing and leisure activity. Since this behaviour is quite typical for this person it would suggest a lack of concentration being preoccupied within himself. When dealing with copatients and staff patient is very cordial and urbane to the point of excess, suggesting an underlying disrespect or hostility' (IPN 172). Apparently 'normal' relationships that developed among patients could be viewed as less than authentic, as in the case of a twenty-year-old woman who became involved with a male co-patient while on the Inpatient Unit: 'During patient's assessment, she was almost constantly in the company of one male copatient ... A pseudo romantic relationship grew from their mutual assessment periods ... It would appear that although [the] patient sees the need for help, [she] has at this time misplaced her priorities. Presently being male companionship' (IPN 446). Finally, patient verbalizations about their personal life outside the institution were routinely dismissed by staff, and were often used to support official accounts of the subject's pathology. One such case involved a former member of a motorcycle gang, who was being assessed on charges of 'Wounding' and 'Weapons Dangerous.' During the day shift, his conversation with a psychiatric assistant was charted in the progress notes:

Recounted past relationships with girlfriends. Spoke of one woman whom he admired for her involvement in criminal activities. At the same time he was living with her, he had another girlfriend whom he appreciated for her body. Apparently when he was young he was engaged to be married, however he broke it off. His present girlfriend is also interested in marriage, however L. [the patient] feels he is not ready to 'settle down' ... Above statements indicate further antisocial characteristics, unable to become emotionally involved with others. (IPN 147)

When patients exhibited a 'displaying mode' instead of a 'denial mode' – when they were floridly psychotic and expressed their symptoms openly (Pfohl 1978) – relatively little effort was needed to establish deviancy for the record. Staff members required no more than a brief anecdotal description of conversations and events. Case 184 involved a thirty-seven-year-old male, diagnosed as a paranoid schizophrenic, who had been arrested for 'Threatening Telephone Calls.' On the evening of his admission to the in-patient ward, the patient's psychotic monologues were captured in the progress log:

Patient remains grossly delusional. 'I was J. Edgar Hoover's bodyguard. Do you happen to know that both Robert and John F. Kennedy are still alive? I saw them once in Angola' and on and on. *Grandiosity*: 'Do you KNOW what it is like to have a million dollars?' Cooperative, but reality contact poor. Flight of ideas, grandiose delusions, looseness of associations, tangential, some delusions of persecution. '*They* must be here – I am under hypnotic control ... I am the son of Kaiser Wilhelm and my mother was the real developer of the atomic bomb. I graduated from Annapolis with President Carter' ... [The patient] explained that contrary to popular belief, Adolph Hitler did not die at the end of World War II, rather in 1962. He also claimed that Chinese leader Mao Tse Tung is alive and well in the Himalayas somewhere under an assumed name. He was sure of this, as he had spoken to him personally. (IPN 184)

A 21-year-old male charged with 'Petty Trespass' was admitted to the ward on a Warrant of Remand after being diagnosed as a manic-depressive in the Brief Assessment Unit. His remarks were documented by the admitting nurse:

'I hate people' ... 'I love sunshine, beaches, sports, but I hate people. I am going to kill that judge. He sent my mother to Queen Street Hospital and it killed her. I am going to blow him apart – he knows it was in that paper. I'm going to blow up the CN Tower – we built it. I don't like it ... My brother is going to blow this building up in fifteen minutes, he doesn't care ... He's killed people ... I belong to the Mafia and I have 500 vagabonds outside' ... Patient related grandiose ideas stating he was to inherit 10 million dollars when his grandmother dies. (IPN 047)

In many cases, the Inpatient Unit staff actively solicited information about the criminal offence allegedly committed by accused persons. This practice was both legally and ethically problematic, since defence attorneys were rarely present on the ward, since these progress notes were potentially subject to subpoena by the court, and since there was no written indication that patients were warned about the legal status of these confessions. Sometimes, patients themselves expressed concern about divulging such evidence prior to their criminal trial. One dossier read: '[Patient] stated that third party information was given to the doctor about his past legal history, and is concerned as to how same occurred, since he signed release of information forms only for "open information".' The staff member's written response to this protest illustrated the high priority assigned to such materials: 'Allow ventilation, with hope that patient will divulge secretive information about self, that staff can work through with him' (IPN 094).

More frequent were instances in which patients ingenuously revealed the circumstances of their alleged offences, to the point of providing open confessions to clinical staff. Patient 072 was charged with 'First Degree Murder,' following the bludgeoning death of his business partner. The inpatient remand had been ordered for the purpose of gauging the subject's dangerousness, as well as to investigate the possibility that he was insane at the time of the alleged offence. While on the ward, his numerous conversations focused on the events surrounding the crime. During one such exchange, the psychiatric assistant not only recorded a rough description of the homicide, but also went so far as to offer an interpretation of the subject's motive for the killing:

He had had nobody he could open up to, and he had been 'scared' to speak to his family about his financial and mental conditions. His confusion, depression, and anger would rise overpoweringly at [his] partner's apartment at the time of the charge-related incident when (as has been charted before) partner would request patient to mortgage his property for business financing. Patient would refuse to do so, partner would abuse patient and his family, take up a stone from desk to strike patient. The fight would start, patient would lose control and became 'like a madman'. 'Sometimes I think it's a dream ... that this couldn't be happening to me'. He could not recall further data of charge-related incident ... Saying more quantitatively, but not qualitatively ... Writer sees this man as a very troubled, introverted, diffident ... person, whose frustration, anger and disappointment existed at a high intensity for some time prior to the charge-related incident, and finally getting the better of his controls in said incident ... (IPN 072)

In the course of interviewing patients about their crimes, staff members also endeavoured to neutralize accounts that conflicted with the 'official version' of such incidents. When such contradictions arose, observers were openly incredulous about patient accounts, and they depicted the 'stories' of subjects as tarnished reflections of what had 'really' transpired. In Case 154, the patient was charged with the first-degree murder of a milk-store clerk during an attempted robbery (for which he ultimately received life imprisonment). During the in-patient assessment the subject consistently maintained that he had been too high on drugs at the time of the robbery to have formed criminal intent. The following notation relates an exchange on the Inpatient Unit, during which the psychiatric assistant attempted to discredit this defence by highlighting contradictions in the subject's account.

[The patient] indicated he felt [the] charge should be dropped to 2nd degree murder because of (a) diminished responsibility because he was 'stoned' at the time of alleged offence (indicating he took some valium, Tylenol and whisky prior to the incident to calm himself down) (b) indicated that he didn't intent to hurt anybody ... Indicated that he planned to commit a robbery in order to get money to go out west. Claimed that he took a gun along, which was supplied by his co-accused, so that he would not be 'challenged' during the hold up ... Told writer that he doesn't remember alleged incident and phoned his co-accused the day following said incident to ask him what had happened. YET indicated that he recalled what he said to his co-accused when asked 'What happened?' immediately after alleged incident happened (NOTE: Apparently co-accused was waiting in car outside premises where incident occurred). Said that he answered latter question by asking 'Can't you smell it' Meaning – 'can't you smell the gunpowder?' ... Agreed with writer's suggestion – that alleged incident may have happened because he panicked during the course of a robbery. (IPN 154)

Through the use of these surveillance strategies, METFORS in-patients were closely monitored for symptoms of potential dangerousness. In their identification of apparently dangerous defendants, staff members were especially alert to evidence of psychopathy and moral deficiency, and to the failure of subjects to experience remorse about their victims and deeds. The progress notes for an accused rapist read: 'Feels no sorrow for his victims. "I can't feel sorry for them. They weren't people to me. I enjoyed stalking them. It was exciting. I would probably do it again. It's difficult for me to see them as people. They were just bodies ... If I did it again I'd make sure I wouldn't get caught' (IPN 061). A twenty-three-year-old male accused of molesting young girls was described in similar terms:

No remorse for his young victims. He described how gentle he was with the young girls – he specifically mentioned that there was no violence (physical harm) or 'penetration' – he didn't think that they (the victims) would be unduly affected by their specific experience with him. When it was pointed out reversed and he was a victim then how would he feel – minimal response (couldn't absorb this concept) ... Appears to be talking all he can about sex saying he knows he has a problem, but showing no remorse or insight, is very unrealistic about his future ... Only concern[ed] about his personal needs and satisfaction related to fulfillment. (IPN 200)

Focus on the dangerousness of in-patients was always accentuated when they appeared to be directing hostility towards the observers themselves.[7] 'Though patient appears sincere ... he also is very smooth ... [My] subjective feeling/opinion [is] that this patient is trying to manipulate his assessment. Is convinced he is intelligent enough to play one role before staff and another with co-patients. This could present a serious problem in terms of acting out – there is enough anger and covert hostility present, to query whether this patient presents an elopement or other risk on the unit' (IPN 154).

In another case, the staff members continuously returned to the theory that the patient was ensnared in a progressively accelerating spiral of sexual deviance that would probably lead eventually to seriously assaultive behaviour (he was accused of a minor indecent assault at the time of assessment). The following reported transactions ensued over the course of several days:

Wednesday: Indicated to writer that if he gets out on the street that 'it could get worse' as once he gets 'the urge' he doesn't 'want to stop' ... Indicated that he was not going to do anything here until he was 'spanked' ... Potential for acting out in order to 'appease' his desires for a 'spanking'.

Saturday: When asked about if he would repeat the same incident, L. stated 'no, I can masturbate if I feel the urge' – when confronted that it didn't stop him with this charge – L. didn't have anything to say.

Sunday: Patient was asked about his charges becoming more serious. L. then said 'you mean rape someone' – 'no I never thought about that' – *then laughed inappropriately.*

Monday: Stated that he enjoyed 'touching [the victim]' and may do so again but does not want to go to jail ... Said he should get help because 'I may do something worse' – refused to elaborate. (IPN 349)

Through a number of observational and interpretive strategies, then, in-patient ward activities at METFORS presented clinicians and line staff with a wealth of signifying data. By maintaining continuous scrutiny over their patients, and by applying a selective filter to transactions on the unit, members were able to enhance the information work of professional classifiers. These documents were merged with data yielded from legal records, clinical reports, and social work investigations to produce powerful accounts about defendants' mental and criminal status. Throughout the hierarchy of the institution, staff members were united in their mandate to consolidate psychiatric depictions, and to register their relevance for judicial decisions. Psychiatrists and other professional clinicians supplied the 'specialist knowledge' and scientific rationality. Nurses, psychiatric assistants, and other line staff provided the raw materials that shaped and supported these accounts. In the process, the conduct and utterances of METFORS in-patients were selectively heard, neutralized, and reconstructed to promote official presentations of clinical reality.

SUMMARY

In-patient assessments at METFORS afforded clinicians the opportunity to reproduce and validate their emerging depictions of psychopathology among forensic patients. They provided a valuable context for the transmission of powerful labels to criminal justice authorities. Clinicians were proficient in securing the court's compliance in the ordering of protracted assessments. Over 80 per cent of their recommendations for pre-trial hospitalization were endorsed by a judicial Warrant of Remand. Overall, a third of the METFORS patients were remanded to an in-patient forensic clinic. This occurred in spite of questionable legal authority, in cases where the confinement was clearly ordered to evaluate dangerousness or treatability, or when the length of mandatory detention surpassed the expected judicial tariff for minor criminal charges.

In the context of the METFORS Inpatient Unit, patients were subjected to a variety of interviews, tests, and continuous observation by professionals and line staff. Members compiled dossiers in an effort to produce meaningful representations of the defendant's conduct and utterances during confinement. Psychologists deployed an arsenal of psychometric and projective instruments (see Appendix E) that facilitated the construction of deviant categories. Social workers conducted extensive interviews with close relations, who supplied 'significant' biographical data consistent with clinical and legal accounts. The line personnel closely monitored the daily round of activities on the ward, selectively recording those events and transactions that confirmed and amplified prior forensic descriptions.

The final product of the METFORS in-patient evaluation, like the Brief Assessment Unit remand, was a refined and 'scientific' document, reconstructed out of this reservoir of medico-legal knowledge, which was forwarded to the court by the presiding psychiatrist. These letters were careful articulations of the ideal, which typically jettisoned all signs of contradiction and complexity that were characteristic of the METFORS assessments. They displayed the experts' ability to convert multifaceted presentations of forensic reality into unidimensional renditions that could survive legal scrutiny. In the following chapter, then, I look at the practical consequences of these reports, by considering the impact of BAU and Inpatient remands on judicial sentencing, and more generally by surveying the broader patterns of medical and legal judgments about the METFORS patients.

5

The Forensic Corridor III: Sentencing the METFORS Patients

The criminal will undergo the punishment which has been merited, not by a doubtful faculty of his mind, but by all that which constitutes his personality, his psychic organism, his instincts, and his character.

RAFFAELE GAROFALO

Harken ye judges! There is another madness besides and it is *before* the deed, *Ah*, ye have not gone deep enough into this soul!

FRIEDRICH NIETZSCHE

THE FORENSIC CLINIC AND THE CRIMINAL COURT

This chapter explores the relationship between METFORS clinical decisions and the sentencing practices of Toronto criminal court judges. Forensic classification work is oriented toward the production of criminal sanctions (Geller and Lister 1978; Shah 1975; Stone 1978). In order to establish their professional authority – and to effect desired legal outcomes for mentally disordered defendants – clinicians at METFORS and similar clinics come to adopt ideologies and strategies that are forged 'in the shadow of the law' (Mnookin and Kornhauser 1979). The following examination of METFORS psychiatric recommendations and judicial sentencing is focused particularly on the strategies invoked by clinicians for securing favourable criminal dispositions. These analyses will involve a detailed scrutiny of BAU letters to the court, along with the court sentences imposed on the 592 METFORS defendants.

In the course of delivering assessments for the court, forensic decision-makers learn to recognize the organizational, occupational, and symbolic advantages that are gained by assuming a quasi-judicial function (see Warren 1982). Psychiatric reports to court officials are not only imperfect reconstructions of medical reality (Chapters 3, 4), but they are also based in constructs and discourse that are more legalistic than therapeutic in content. Forensic accounts conveyed to the court reflect the collusion between clinical and judicial agents (Ericson 1976; see Feeley 1979). The 'juridification' of medical classifiers has been the hallmark of organizational relations in the forensic system, and this socialization process has solidified the position of psychiatric authorities and reinforced their ability to influence the course of criminal dispositions. In the interests of producing pragmatic solutions to concrete legal problems (Soothill 1974: 189), forensic clinicians have come virtually to abandon traditional psychiatric models of practice, and consequently they have acquired increasing authority over the selection of criminal sanctions against mentally disordered defendants.

Research on the judicial impact of clinical assessments has consistently demonstrated the deference of judges to the recommendations of forensic professionals. In civil commitment proceedings, competency hearings, criminal trials, and evaluations of dangerousness, the decisions of legal authorities only rarely depart from the prior judgments of clinical practitioners. The close correspondence between recommendations and dispositions suggests that judges are at least partially reallocating their sentencing authority to psychiatric experts – that clinical assessments have become the fulcrum of the trial process for cases involving alleged mental disorder. By rubber-stamping forensic decisions, judicial authorities are able to merge criminal dispositions with therapeutic justifications (Szasz 1956: 310). As the presiding judge held in a recent Canadian dangerous offender hearing: '[o]n this issue, the courts really have nowhere to turn except to those who have expertise in the field of psychiatry.'[1] In the process, forensic clinicians have become sentencing authorities in their own right, and their 'medical' opinions have become a catalyst for the application of penal sanctions.

A number of studies during the past two decades have examined the high rates of concurrence between clinicians and judges in criminal cases (see Campbell 1981; Menzies, Webster, and Jackson 1982). Most of this work has originated in Great Britain. De Berker (1960) surveyed the mental status reports written by medical staff at Brixton Prison Hospital during 1957, and found that 92 per cent of sentencing recommendations were apparently followed by the courts. Bearcroft and Donovan (1965) reported that judges endorsed nine out of every ten psychiatric prescriptions offered during 1963 by forensic professionals in a London mental institution. This level of agreement was replicated by Sparks (1966) over a one-year period in two central London courts. In a study of 638 women remanded for assessment to Holloway Prison during 1967, Dell and Gibbens (1971) found that magistrates concurred with clinical recommendations in 91 per cent of cases. Prins (1976) discovered rates of 86 per cent for adults and 95 per cent for juveniles assessed during 1968 and 1969. Woodside (1976) reported that 48 of 66 psychiatric prescriptions for treatment (73 per cent) were accepted by criminal court judges in Edinburgh during 1972. The corresponding figure coming from a retrospective study of remands in 18 London and 34 Wessex courts (Gibbens, Soothill, and Pope 1977) was 77 per cent, although the authors noted that no specific dispositional recommendations had been offered in 40 per cent of cases. Finally, a replication of the de Berker (1960) investigation, involving a three-month sample of remands to Brixton Prison in 1975, yielded an 80 per cent agreement rate between clinicians and judges (Bowden 1978).

Several North American studies have produced similar findings. On the subject of fitness to stand trial, for example, Vann (1965) reported that criminal court judges had endorsed psychiatric competency assessments without a single exception. Pfeiffer, Eisenstein, and Dobbs (1967) found a 90 per cent rate of agreement between medical recommendations and judicial decisions about competency. Steadman's study of 178 competency hearings in New York City during 1971 and 1972 recorded an 89 per cent concurrence level (Steadman 1979). This latter figure was matched in a more recent Florida study (Williams and Miller 1981).

In their research on the correspondence between clinical decisions and general court dispositions, Jablon, Sadoff, and Heller (1970) found that judges acted upon 220 of 240 psychiatric recommendations (92 per cent), in a patient sample for which over half of medical reports prescribed in-patient treatment. In Canada, two studies have noted that the level of concordance is at least partially related to the nature of the psychiatric findings. In a survey of 787 forensic remands in Ontario (Greenland and Rosenblatt 1972), recommendations for in-patient treatment were accepted in about four out of every five cases, in contrast to a concurrence rate of only one-in-three following recommendations for outpatient treatment. Likewise, Menzies, Webster, Butler, and Turner (1980) examined 248 pre-trial assessments in six Canadian cities over a one-month period in 1978, and found that concurrence increased with the intensity of recommended criminal sanction. In 73 per cent of cases where psychiatrists prescribed prison, judges selected a carceral disposition. The courts accepted clinical judgments for 59 per cent of subjects recommended for hospitalization. Finally, 54 per cent of defendants recommended for out-patient care were sentenced to a term of probation (where out-patient attendance could be attached to the probation order).

Researchers have documented similar patterns in judicial decisions about dangerousness and involuntary certification. A high correspondence between psychiatric and judicial findings of dangerousness was revealed in Steadman's study of competency assessments in New York (1973), where 87 per cent of 256 clinical recommendations based on apprehended dangerousness were endorsed by the courts. Altogether there were only thirty-four disagreements between psychiatrists and judges, and six of these involved positive court findings of dangerousness to others where the clinician had originally found the subject not dangerous. Steadman was critical of the organizational framework of procedures under which these dispositions were secured.

It is not clear on what actual bases psychiatrists are predicting the occurrence of such behaviour ... Throughout these reports and the cross-examinations at the hearings there is consistent omission of any documentation that the stated criteria have been shown to be associated with what is being predicted. The courts do not demand specificity in the level of seriousness of the predicted behavior, the imminence of the predicted behavior, or the probability that it will occur at the predicted level. Despite the gaps in psychiatric presentations and lack of documented expertise to make predictions, there was an 87 per cent concurrence rate ... It is because of this extremely high concurrence rate that psychiatric predictions of dangerousness are so important. (Steadman 1973: 420–1)

The dispositional power of mental health professionals has been especially evident in the adjudication of mentally ill persons for the purpose of securing involuntary civil commitment (Coleman 1984; Warren 1982). In one study, Scheff concluded that the introduction of psychiatric testimony was serving to undermine the adversarial nature of these proceedings. Clinical evidence in commitment hearings permitted judges to 'justify their decisions by referring to the recommendations of the psychiatrists, and thus use the psychiatrists as "fronts" for their own purposes' (Scheff 1975: 324). As a consequence, the process of legal decision-making was being systematically undermined by assumptions about the alleged scientific superiority of expert witnesses.

In other American research on civil commitment proceedings, the rates of concordance between recommendations and decisions to hospitalize have generally ranged from 96 to 100 per cent (Rock, Jacobson, and Janopaul 1968; Wegner and Fletcher 1969; Wexler et al. 1971; see Teplin 1984a). In the context of near-unanimous endorsement of medical opinions about mental disorder and dangerousness, it has been apparent that judges are relinquishing their prerogative to impose or reject commitment applications. In North Carolina, Hiday found that in over a third of *contested* cases neither the judge nor the defence counsel requested even minimal evidence to establish the defendant's 'imminent dangerousness' (the commitment criterion in that state). Indeed, more than 20 per cent of commitments were ordered 'without a showing, by a preponderance of the evidence, that there was imminent danger due to mental illness' (Hiday 1977: 664; see Boyd 1980: 165; Hiday 1981, 1983). Finally, the judicial receptivity to clinical diagnoses was mediated by the adversarial reactions of defence counsel (see Wegner and Fletcher 1969). The overall concurrence rate of 75 per cent dropped to 57 per cent when psychiatrists were pressed to substantiate their evidence for dangerousness, and rose to 100 per cent when no such challenges were forthcoming. The average court hearing in this study lasted five minutes. A typical exchange between judge and defence counsel, presented below, illustrates the court's disinclination to dispute the expertise of psychiatrists in commitment hearings:

Judge: 'I know we have no evidence of respondent's danger, but the psychiatrist says here that he is schizophrenic and imminently dangerous.'
Counsel: 'How can he say my client is dangerous? There is no evidence.'
Judge: 'They have ways of knowing – tricks and tests not known to us.' (Hiday 1977: 655)

Clearly, then, the translation of clinical labels into judicial outcomes is a routine feature of the forensic system. Both criminal and civil court judges are favourably disposed toward enlisting the services of forensic assessors (Bohmer 1973, 1976; Hogarth 1971). In Justice Bazelon's words, they have successfully managed 'to throw this particularly hot potato into the collective psychiatric lap' (1975: 188). Despite continuing ambiguities and problems of communication and jurisdiction (Geller and Lister 1978: 58; McGarry, Curran, Lipsitt, Lelos, Schwitzgebel, and Rosenberg 1974: 99; Schiffer 1978: 216; Stone 1978: 62–3), the clinical judgments of mental health experts are routinely endorsed by criminal court judges. The juridification of forensic experts has been paralleled by the psychiatrization of the judiciary, and by their delegation of discretionary authority when confronted by apparent mental illness. In making sentencing decisions, judges have been moved increasingly to incorporate the expert opinions of their clinical colleagues (Blumberg 1967: 124–5, 137).

METFORS RECOMMENDATIONS AND JUDICIAL DISPOSITIONS

The letters written by METFORS psychiatrists were their principal instruments for securing judicial compliance with forensic recommendations. Given their infrequent attendance in the criminal courts, psychiatrists relied on these reports to impress judges with the validity, relevance, and scientific authority of their formulations. Hence, court letters were pivotal to the legitimacy strategies of the METFORS classifiers. Their written presentations were designed to reinforce their right to broach issues of penal disposition, and to minimize the possibility of legal challenge or rebuttal. In their efforts to 'achieve practical decidability' (Garfinkel 1967: 18), psychiatrists mobilized a variety of editorial and reportorial strategies that affirmed their discretionary authority (see Emerson 1969: 265–6).

From this study it was evident that criminal court dispositions were closely in accord with the recommendations of METFORS psychiatrists. In Table 5.1, the recommendations extracted from a content analysis of Brief Assessment Unit letters are tabulated against the ultimate sentences selected by the presiding judge. To begin, it was common practice for psychiatrists to indicate a specific preferred disposition in their reports. Of 587 letters included in the analysis,[2] 394 (67.1 per cent) contained a dispositional recommendation. Of the remainder, 66 (11.2 per cent) involved a general request that the defendant be returned to the court for sentencing, and 127 (21.6 per cent) contained no specific prescription. The 394 BAU psychiatric recommendations distributed as follows: 193 for protracted clinical assessment (see Chapter 4); 83 for imprisonment (37 of these suggesting treatment during incarceration); 82 for probation (59 included a recommended provision for treatment); 33 for immediate psychiatric hospitalization; and 3 for release. The actual sentences imposed by the court, in order of absolute frequency, are presented below:

1. Probation	189 (32.2%)
2. Acquitted–Withdrawn–Absolute Discharge	121 (20.6%)
3. Provincial Prison 1 Month to 2 Years	109 (18.6%)
4. Provincial Prison Plus Probation	76 (12.9%)
5. Provincial Prison 30 Days or Less	43 (7.3%)

TABLE 5.1
Recommendation in BAU letter by court disposition

Disposition	No specific recommendation	Trial/ through court system	Probation with treatment	Probation no treatment	Prison with treatment	Prison no treatment	Further psych. assessment	In-patient treatment	Release	TOTAL (PER CENT)
Acquit/withdraw/ absolute discharge	21	9	9	2	5	5	53	15	2	121 (20.6)
Probation	42	10	33	8	3	6	74	12	1	189 (32.2)
Incarceration LE 30 days	12	9	5	4	4	2	7			43 (7.3)
Provincial prison plus probation	19	10	6	6	5	6	21	3		76 (12.9)
Incarceration 31 days–2 years	27	22	4	2	14	20	18	2		109 (18.6)
Federal incarceration	6	2			6	7	12	1		34 (5.8)
Fine		2								2 (0.3)
WLG							6			6 (1.0)
No disposition yet		2	2	1			2			7 (1.2)
TOTAL (PER CENT)	127 (21.6)	66 (11.2)	59 (10.1)	23 (3.9)	37 (6.3)	46 (7.8)	193* (32.9)	33 (5.6)	3 (0.5)	587

* Less than the 215 requests for in-patient assessment indicated in Table 4.1, as the recommendation for 22 subjects was coupled with a more specific prescription for treatment.

6. Federal Penitentiary (2 Years or More)	34	(5.8%)
7. Disposition Pending (after 2 Years)	7	(1.2%)
8. Warrant of the Lieutenant Governor	6	(1.0%)
9. Fine	2	(0.3%)

As in several of the recommendation-disposition studies reviewed above, the judicial acceptance of METFORS psychiatric reports was apparently predicated at least partially on the nature of the recommendation. Judges were especially receptive to clinical prescriptions for carceral confinement. In 64 of 83 cases where the BAU letters recommended imprisonment (77 per cent), the subject was incarcerated. In comparison, only 41 of 82 recommendations for probation (50 per cent) were endorsed by the court, and a further 11 defendants (13 per cent) received probation supplementary to a prison term.

In addition, a substantial proportion of METFORS subjects recommended for in-patient assessment or treatment were subsequently either released or placed on probation by the court. Among the 226 defendants earmarked for hospitalization by BAU psychiatrists, 154 (68.1 per cent) were acquitted, discharged, or sentenced to probation (compared with 43.2 per cent of all other groups). As suggested in Chapter 4, judges may have been compensating for the term of in-patient hospitalization to which defendants were being subjected. The relative 'leniency' of sentences imposed on these individuals could have been a response to the tariff of 'time served' in psychiatric confinement. Alternatively, the clinic's recommendation for hospitalization could be interpreted as an unnecessary intrusion upon the liberty of these individuals, given that the courts viewed them as appropriate candidates for release into the community (see Geller and Lister 1978; Greenland and Rosenblatt 1972; Webster, Menzies, and Jackson 1982: Ch. 4).

Table 5.2 provides a cross-tabulation between recommendations contained in the court reports compiled by the METFORS Inpatient Unit psychiatrists and the subsequent dispositions rendered by the criminal courts (see Chapter 4). A comparison of these in-patient letters with the content of brief assessment reports (from Table 5.1) revealed systematic differences in the distribution of psychiatric recommendations. For example, only six of 123 in-patient assessments (4.9 per cent) resulted in 'no specific recommendation,' against 21.6 per cent of BAU letters. Psychiatrists were moved to include some form of dispositional reference, however vague, following the added expenditure of time and resources associated with thirty- to sixty-day clinical remands. Inpatient letters were also more likely

TABLE 5.2
Recommendation in in-patient letter by court disposition

Disposition	No specific recommendation	Trial/ through court system	Probation with treatment	Probation no treatment	Prison with treatment	Prison no treatment	Further psych. assessment	In-patient treatment	Release	TOTAL (PER CENT)
Acquit/withdraw/ absolute discharge	2	11	4		1		2	8	1	29 (23.6)
Probation	1	14	24	4			4	3		50 (40.7)
Incarceration LE 30 days			2							2 (1.6)
Provincial prison plus probation	1	6	3	1	1	1	3			16 (13.0)
Incarceration 31 days–2 years		6	2	1	1	1		2		13 (10.6)
Federal incarceration	2	2			3	2	1	1		11 (8.9)
WLG		1							1	2 (1.6)
TOTAL (PER CENT)	6 (4.9)	40 (32.5)	35 (28.5)	6 (4.9)	6 (4.9)	4 (3.3)	10 (8.1)	14 (11.4)	2 (1.6)	123

than BAU reports to recommend probation (41 cases, or 33.4 per cent) and psychiatric hospitalization for treatment (14 cases, or 11.4 per cent), and they were less inclined to contain recommendations for imprisonment (10 cases, or 8.2 per cent). Interestingly, even at the conclusion of such extended periods of psychiatric evaluation, 10 of the subjects (8.1 per cent) were recommended for yet another term of in-patient assessment.

The congruence between psychiatric recommendations and court dispositions appeared to increase following protracted remands at METFORS. For example, 9 of 10 persons recommended for carceral confinement received a period of imprisonment. Further, 28 of 41 subjects (68 per cent) were sentenced for probation in compliance with METFORS recommendations for this sentence; another 4 persons (10 per cent of those recommended) received probation in addition to a prison term. These general patterns suggest that the criminal courts may have conferred some added legitimacy to clinical pronouncements following extended in-patient assessments. Whatever the validity of clinical decisions in the METFORS In-patient Unit, the additional resources expended during protracted remands seemed to pay dividends in securing increased compliance among criminal court judges.

PSYCHIATRIC SENTENCING IN THE BRIEF ASSESSMENT UNIT

The psychiatrist's court letter is a 'purified distillate' (Hughes 1958: 71) of the forensic assessment process. Like other reports reviewed in earlier chapters, the final message to the judge represents a highly selective and truncated version of clinical findings in the Brief Assessment Unit. As Matza suggests, 'the very act of writing or reporting commits the author to a *rendition* of the world, and a rendering is a sifting' (1969: 9). The authenticity of psychiatric letters is secured through the conveyance of powerful messages about accused persons. Such images are unidimensional, categorical, and directly geared to serving the perceived interests of the criminal court. They are also imperfect records of what actually transpired. '[The summary report] is a transformation of what members did and concluded into a highly specialized professional language which presents itself as an "objective" and "expert" description of a patient's individual psychiatric reality. Gone are all traces of the interactional process by which members formulated "senses", "hunches", and "theories" about patients. Remaining is an impressive array of terminology, which describes the patient in terms of "syndromes" and "symptoms" ' (Pfohl 1978: 212).

In the everyday practice of clinical classification at METFORS, the psychiatrist's letter was the pivotal concern for the BAU team. Much of the evaluative task was prospectively oriented toward the distribution of persuasive messages to legal audiences. In the process, the prospects of a fair hearing could be jeopardized. 'The production of these reports becomes their raison d'être ... [T]he organization seems to generate decision-making criteria which relate more to smooth functioning and efficiency and protecting the organization from real or potential criticism' (Shover 1974: 355). More generally, forensic psychiatrists succeed in converting their medical recommendations into court dispositions by exercising editorial discretion over the vast reservoir of knowledge potentially available to the court; by magnifying selected informational items into one-sided depictions of subjects' troubles; and by framing the final account in the convincing discourse of clinical diagnosis. In so doing they are able to persuade criminal judges that the psychiatric version of reality is more valid, scientific, and legally relevant than alternative interpretations.

Psychiatric court letters tend to be truncated, stylized, and limited in their presentation of tangible evidence. Their power to persuade is based on the professional legitimacy of the writer more than the special contribution of the report itself. According to a defence lawyer interviewed in one Canadian study: 'The sort of thing which upsets me is the letter that they sent back ... with the accused ... [E]ach of the letters say exactly the same thing with the arrangement of the letters identical. I feel that it's just a pro forma letter which is typed up to appear to be ... an in-depth thing, but it really isn't' (Ericson and Baranek 1982: 17; see Roesch and Golding 1978: 426).

The forensic letter is a vehicle for impression management (Blum and McHugh 1971: 108). It functions as an 'informational funnel,' whereby 'potentially relevant data are abandoned while recorded data are subject to increasing reification and typification' (Hawkins and Tiedeman 1975: 197). In the editorial process that is central to letter-writing, clinically relevant items with no pragmatic utility tend to be deleted from the official record, while materials consistent with the generic picture are given undue prominence and medico-legal significance (Goffman 1961: 375). The forensic assessment is depicted in these letters as a technical, scientific, and orderly enterprise. Complexities, inconsistencies and dissensus (see Chapter 3) are erased or collapsed into a linear judgment that is bereft of troublesome overtones. 'The infinite colours and shades of the real world, its nuances and subtleties, are transformed into bold blacks and whites' (Hawkins 1981: 113; see Garfinkel 1967: 199). Forensic psychiatrists, as 'suppliers of facts,' use these letters to 'absorb the ultimate decision makers into their own moral universes' (Hawkins 1981: 107). Accordingly, they are able to achieve a high level of concordance between psychiatric recommendations and criminal court sanctions.

Like the forensic documents described in other studies (see above), the METFORS psychiatric letters were typically brief (one to two pages in length), they were standardized in format, and they contained a preponderance of conclusionary statements (often with scant reference to supporting evidence). Despite these limitations, the METFORS psychiatrists readily offered overt dispositional recommendations to the criminal court. In only 127 cases (21.6 per cent) was there no direct reference to sentencing in the Brief Assessment Unit letter. Moreover, these court letters were saturated with claims to specialist knowledge. Psychiatrists recurrently used arcane terminology and proclamations about the unique contributions to be offered by medical expertise. The METFORS letters were an extension of the denunciation strategies invoked throughout the assessment process. They reproduced negative labels that had been formulated in the forensic clinic or elsewhere, and they left judges with little doubt about the moral inferiority, pathological identity, criminal propensity, and potential dangerousness of accused persons before the court.

Typically, the persuasive power of psychiatric letters was enhanced by the proliferation of diagnostic labels intended to impress legal authorities. Psychiatrists supplied not only the medical category, but also its translation into a generally understandable idiom. They portrayed themselves as doubly indispensable to the court, as both definers and interpreters of psycholegal reality. Frequently, this took the form of esoteric theorizing about the pathology being attributed to the accused person.

In one such case a woman charged with fraud was found by the BAU team to have a twin brother. This item of information was incorporated into the court letter to demonstrate the psychiatrist's prowess for uncovering latent disorder, and to justify a recommendation for further psychiatric intervention:

Miss G. gives a fascinating history of being involved in over-indulgence in alcohol for some time. However, although this is the presenting problem, there is much more behind this than at first appears. She is one of twins and her twin brother ... is currently in fourth year university ... apparently being quite a success. ... The so-called anti-social activities in which she has indulged are the equivalent of acting-out her depressive feelings following ... the psychological loss of her twin brother. It is well known that twins, whether they be identical or non-identical, have an uncanny attachment to each other, even though at times they refuse to acknowledge this ... [W]e are willing to offer our services and follow her up in a therapeutic programme designed by [the METFORS] social worker and myself, psychiatrist. (PL 380)

More commonly, BAU psychiatrists were able to reinforce status claims by the simple enclosure of medical jargonese in their court reports. In summarizing his evaluation of a sixty-eight-year-old woman accused of 'Nuisance – Cockroaches' and 'Failure to Clean Premises,' the psychiatrist wrote to the judge: 'Mrs. L. shows features of a major mental illness, specifically involutional paraphrenia.' He then proceeded to define this obscure label for the benefit of the legal audience: 'This mental illness is characterized by a single delusional idea in an otherwise intact individual, the onset of which occurs in the late middle-life period' (PL 570). In other cases the psychiatric reporter could be even more forthright in his or her declaration of specialist knowledge. '[W]e believe that he has what is often called a schizoid personality; that is, he does not suffer from schizophrenia, but his personality tends to make him somewhat withdrawn' (PL 549) ... 'Test material reveals him as being immature and as being field dependent. That is to say, he leans very heavily on the views of his peers rather than of his parents' (PL 127); 'When we started on the list of, as she calls them, problems, it was clear that she would admit to almost anything I suggested as far as an illness was concerned. To this one gives a label and we call it hypochondriasis' (PL 135).

The METFORS psychiatrists almost never forwarded court letters that were in any sense tainted by tentative diagnoses or recommendations (see Chapter 3). Instead, their reports were populated with unequivocal declarations, couched in dramatic language, that deflected and denied the counterclaims of subjects and medico-legal adversaries. Often, this strategy entailed a wholesale assault on the defendant's credibility as a witness or informant. By establishing the mendacious and manipulative character of patients, psychiatrists could short-circuit the authenticity of opposing accounts.

For instance, a reluctance to co-operate could be offered to the court as evidence of personality disorder: 'On examination today this man was tearful and highly manipulative. It was difficult to obtain from him a clear account of his past and his tearfulness was associated with considerable hostility and petulance at not receiving immediate psychiatric attention. He claimed that he needed treatment but was reluctant to answer any questions that would make treatment possible' (PL 564). A discrepancy between subject testimony and official documents, however mundane, could be conveyed as proof of the person's perjurious potential. 'Some of the information she gives does not correspond with the other information we have from the police record. For example ... [s]he stated that she finished Grade 11 at age 18, but the other information we have is that she finished Grade 10 ... She has a personality structure which is fundamentally anti-social and ... she does not always listen to ... sound medical advice given to her ... We also felt that she does not have as much respect for authority as she may be able to use to help keep herself out of trouble' (PL 358).

In other cases, the BAU psychiatrist could proactively seek out and point the court toward contradictions and gaps in the forensic subject's account. 'He hinted that without the use of alcohol he is unlikely to get himself into trouble, but at the same time he stated that before he started drinking he used to be in all sorts of difficulties concerning authority figures' (PL 408); 'He gave a story of his father having committed suicide four years ago but this story was not supported by his mother who was spoken to on the telephone eventually. Mother stated that T.'s father had killed himself two years ago not four years ago ... He led us to believe that he had a fiancee, then he corrected that by saying that she is his girlfriend, age 15' (PL 169); 'He stated that he liked to camp, fish, go hiking and sometimes play baseball ... We were not sure how much time he has had to do these things' (PL 262).

Psychiatrists' letters were also used as vehicles for conveying powerful depictions of moral character that had been formulated in the Brief Assessment Unit. The messages enclosed in these reports were clear and convincing. A twenty-two-year-old subject charged with 'Common Assault' was described in the following terms: 'He is on welfare and has, in the past, worked very little. In fact, he stated that the longest time he has worked is a couple of months. He lives in a rooming house, does little and as far as we could tell, he spends his time walking around and drinking when he feels like it. He further stated that he has a girlfriend who is also on welfare' (PL 398). In the case of a chronic alcoholic accused of indecent assault, the psychiatrist reported that 'he is probably destroying some of the few brain cells that he has' (PL 133). To reinforce the denigration of moral character, the METFORS psychiatrists could project evidence of deficiency and pathology into even such innocuous interests as music and chess: '[H]e talked about being musically inclined and possibly having a career with guitar playing and with painting but we felt that this man had a rather exaggerated sense of his own abilities and of his possibilities for establishing such a magnificent career' (PL 074); 'His hobbies, he says, are reading, going to symphony concerts and chess and it was not quite clear whether he has opponents with whom he plays chess or whether he solves chess problems or whether he uses himself as his own opponent. He did say, however, that he gets bored with his existence at this time' (PL 431).

Psychiatric letters at METFORS were therefore infused with negative ascriptions that supported punitive responses and legitimized the psychiatric sanctions being imposed by forensic specialists. These demonstrations of clinical authority and subject deficiency served as catalysts for securing desired judicial outcomes. They were pivotal to the production of clinical prescriptions on a number of specific forensic issues, which will be reviewed in the remainder of this chapter. Yet at the same time these court letters comprised a systematic distortion of psychiatric reality, by recurrently misrepresenting the medico-legal predicaments of criminal defendants and the organizational process of clinical assessments.

The legal audience which received the expert opinions of psychiatric team members missed much by only receiving opinions worded in objective diagnostic nomenclature. This nomenclature was more than professional short hand. It was also a disguise for the subjective inferences and social interactions which produced it ... transform[ing] loose indexical theorizing into a tight, reflexively realized 'fact.' The interactionally determined basis for a conclusion is lost in the reading of the expertly stated conclusion itself. Ad hoc theories become objective findings. The many steps which generate a finding are disguised by the one step which announces that decision. (Pfohl 1979: 74)

I now turn to the specific content of psychiatric opinions forwarded to the criminal courts, by individually addressing the seven principal forensic issues contained in the METFORS Brief Assessment Unit letters. These were: fitness for bail and penal confinement, probation, psychiatric detention, fitness to stand trial, criminal responsibility/insanity, dangerousness to self, and dangerousness to others.

Fitness for Bail and Penal Confinement
Among the 587 METFORS BAU patients for whom data were available, 83 (14.1 per cent) received a recommendation for penal confinement in the psychiatrist's letter to the court. In 144 cases (24.5 per cent), the attending psychiatrist directly indicated that the subject should not be granted bail prior to trial. Forensic clinicians were clearly willing to assume responsibility for judgments that restricted the liberty of their patients. They were addressing pre-sentence issues at a pre-trial level (Menzies, Webster, Butler, and Turner 1980), and they were providing opinions in support of carceral imprisonment in the absence of statutory authority. Recommendations for

penal confinement and denial of bail were unique among forensic decisions in the extent to which they catapulted the METFORS classifiers onto ethically contentious and legally problematic terrain.

An examination of BAU court letters revealed three principal justifications for recommending penal detainment. Psychiatrists urged a prison sentence for the 'benefit' of the individual; as a preferred alternative to therapeutic intervention; or because the subject presented an apparent danger to the community.

There were those who impressed psychiatrists as potentially redeemable, who from the clinical viewpoint could be straightened out through their experience in prison. For some of these, correctional confinement was seen to bear therapeutic properties. 'I believe it is important to prevent this development [of an antisocial personality disorder] by exposing this youth to what therapeutic facilities are available in a correctional setting' (PL 127); 'It is possible that within a correctional setting Miss V. will be able to deal with her own underlying feelings of inadequacy. A closed setting would assist Miss V. in structuring her day and prevent her from escaping into antisocial behaviour or alcohol abuse' (PL 044). For other subjects the psychiatrist recommended incarceration as a valuable opportunity for occupational training. '[T]o put a diagnostic series of labels on him, he can be called a chronic alcoholic and an inadequate anti-social personality ... However, it is quite possible that he can benefit from an opportunity for training in a correctional centre' (PL 340); 'It would appear to us that he would benefit from being in a custodial setting where he may attempt to learn a trade. He has indicated that what he wants to learn to become is a mechanic' (PL 063).

Ironically, the BAU subjects could also receive prison recommendations if their official histories indicated a *failure* to co-operate with or respond to psychiatric interventions. On these occasions carceral confinement was often advocated as a last-resort strategy. Clinical efforts to secure a prison sentence were geared to demonstrations that accused persons could not be adequately restored to normality in the mental health system. 'It is unlikely that psychiatric treatment would significantly alter Mr. C.'s present life style given the long history of rejection and failure to cooperate in psychiatric institutions' (PL 590); 'He is a poor treatment risk for either alcoholism, or drug involvement, or other problems associated with his personality structure ... It was considered by this team that he is not fit to be granted bail at present and being such a poor treatment risk, he should go through the court and correctional systems' (PL 259); 'Mr. Z. shows evidence of a long-standing personality disorder of an antisocial type. Such an emotional disturbance is extremely difficult to treat successfully. Although Mr. Z. requests psychiatric treatment, he noted that he did not benefit from his involvement at the [ ] Institute. At the present time he is not a good candidate for psychiatric treatment. When he is released from detention he is free to seek psychiatric assistance' (PL 412).

Psychiatrists were frequently inclined to prescribe carceral sentencing on the basis of explicitly punitive reasoning. At times this practice was associated with the presumed deterrent impact of prison. 'I cannot recommend a psychiatric disposition to this girl's problems in that I am not convinced she is amenable to this approach. It may be that a short period of incarceration will serve to advise her of her responsibility in her own behaviour' (PL 484); 'I would recommend that Your Honour consider reinforcing the reality of the situation that Mr. A. finds himself in. I believe the threat of incarceration could be a strong deterrent on Mr. A.'s future anti-social behaviour' (PL 027).

Alternatively, custodial confinement could be regarded by METFORS psychiatrists as a just response to prior miscreance, as a necessary preventative measure, or as a rational method for dealing with dangerousness.[3] Psychiatric reasoning in these cases hinged on the uncontrollable conduct attributed to such defendants, and on predictions about the dire consequences of less restrictive dispositions. 'Our team concluded that Mr. Y. has an anti-social personality disorder and he has been also involved in deviational sexual activities ... We also felt that Mr. Y. should go through the court system and since these alleged charges took place while he was on parole, he will need to face the consequences' (PL 437); 'Mr. M. had no hesitation in telling us that he has had a long history of uncontrollable behaviour ... We consider his fundamental personality structure to be antisocial. In view of the information we have received it seems inadvisable for him to be granted bail at this time as he is likely to get himself into all kinds of other trouble' (PL 323); 'She is unlikely to cooperate with conditions set by the court if she were freed, for example, on bail or probation for she has very little respect for authority' (PL 137); 'Under the influence of alcohol suppressed hostility could be released and I believe he could act out aggressively towards others. This behaviour could not be sufficiently checked by normal considerations for the feelings of others because of his particular personality type. Hence probation may be a risky business' (PL 201).

When the METFORS psychiatrists attributed a condition of dangerousness to their subjects, their recommendations for imprisonment were particularly intense, and were typically buttressed with overt references to the defendant's propensity toward violence. In the case of a middle-aged man accused of indecently assaulting the eleven-year-old son of his next-door neighbour, the psychiatrist assimilated the defendant's sexual history into a diagnosis of extreme dangerousness, hinting that the subject himself was ambivalent about being released from prison:

Mr. S. indicated a number of perverse sexual experiences as a child. His grandfather sexually assaulted him when he was 11 years of age and at age 20 he had sexual involvement with his mother. Mr. S. has had a wide variety of sexual experiences with women, including a number of prostitutes. He noted that his sexual attraction to young boys has been present for over 20 years ... He requires psychiatric assistance within the correctional setting ... Mr. S. represents a significant risk to the community given his lack of social stability and impaired judgment while under the influence of alcohol. In addition, his sexual deviation renders him a significant risk to young boys. Mr. S. has insight into this and does not wish to be released from custody ... He is not a good candidate for release on bail at this time and is not a suitable candidate for probation in my opinion. (PL 416).[4]

Probation Orders

The Brief Assessment Unit psychiatrists recommended probation in eighty-two of the court letters (14.0 per cent). Among these reports, fifty-nine included the suggestion that subjects undergo psychiatric treatment as a term of their probation. In prescribing a probationary sentence, psychiatrists displayed abundant faith in the rehabilitative potential of this disposition. Probation officers were viewed as therapeutic counsellors who were capable of organizing and monitoring the subject's community activities. Accordingly, a sentence of probation was often recommended in court letters as an end in itself. Following the assessment of a youth charged with 'Assault Causing Bodily Harm' the METFORS psychiatrist advised the court to consider this 'soft' alternative:

Despite Mr. K.'s behaviour in these assaults causing bodily harm, we do not view him as an aggressively dangerous individual. He has no previous history of any significant anti-social behaviour, and his attitudes and ideas as expressed in the interview are basically pro-social. Despite his disturbed behaviour in these assaults, I would consider him a suitable candidate for probation. A lengthy period of probation with strict controls could provide the necessary structure for Mr. K. to successfully resolve some of his own adolescent concerns. (PL 167)

In other instances, probation was prescribed as a method for establishing a sympathetic interpersonal environment for co-operative patients. 'I would support Mr. E. being granted probation on these charges in that, perhaps, he could benefit from regular contact with an adult male outside the family. This relationship could assist him in dealing with some of the adolescent concerns he is facing' (PL 410). Alternatively, the recommendation was sometimes based on a presumption that the defendant had already profited from previous carceral confinement. 'If he is released on probation on these charges, he could, perhaps, benefit from a supportive relationship with a male probation officer ... He expressed a desire to cease anti-social behaviour in order to avoid future incarceration. Although it is difficult to predict whether Mr. H. is sincere in this desire, at this time it would appear that his detention has had a deterrent effect and may well reduce future anti-social behaviour' (PL 282). For other METFORS patients, probation was offered as a critical testing-ground for evaluating the need for future incarceration. In Case 363, the subject was arrested for assault and petty trespassing during the term of a probation order arising out of an earlier sentence. Following the brief assessment at METFORS, the psychiatrist advocated a continuation of probation, while attaching qualifying conditions to this recommendation: '[A]t the present time he has not had [a] sufficient period of probation to accurately assess his need for detention. I would recommend that Your Honour consider strict conditions for bail and/or probation in the event he is convicted of these charges, with the clear idea that if he fails to keep the conditions he will be returned to a detention setting. This young man must be faced with the responsibility for his own behaviour and thus avoid projecting his difficulties onto the family' (PL 363).

Finally, these 'probation orders' were often conveyed by psychiatrists in an attempt to secure psychiatric treatment. For patients considered marginally disordered and minimally dangerous, clinical intervention could be virtually ensured through the enforcement of probation conditions. One such patient, remanded on a charge of 'Breaking and Entering,' was found to be already involved in a 'therapeutic relationship' with two private psychiatrists. The METFORS court letter read:

It is quite possible that this man's personality structure has some antisocial elements in it and he would need at this particular time in his life to have some special form of therapy. Inasmuch as he is currently in therapy with Drs. L. and F. it seems preferable to have him continue his association with them. If he were given probation and again according to him this is his first offence, then he should continue in therapy with the above-named doctors who can then monitor the situation properly to see when and if he needs inpatient treatment in any institution then this can be arranged. (PL 400)

In a similar case, the METFORS psychiatrist advised an extension of probation, by voicing a paradoxical blend of moral retributivism and therapeutic benevolence. The subject was a sixteen-year-old male, arrested for 'Possession Under' while on probation for an offence he had committed as a juvenile. The psychiatrist's 'lenient' recommendation was infused with a cascade of negative labels that together advanced an argument for psychiatric intervention:

His major complaint about himself was that he feels 'confused'. This is quite understandable in view of his experiences, his limited intelligence and his limited education ... If he receives further probation one of the conditions for his probation should be that he attend a psychiatric hospital of his own catchment area. This can be arranged by and through his probation officer. Presumably, if he did this he may be helped with his adolescent adjustment problems and instead of acting out in the anti-social fashion in which he has done, he may learn more appropriate ways of dealing with his frustration and his 'confusion.' (PL 568)

Psychiatric Detention
Thirty-three METFORS subjects were recommended for immediate in-patient status by the Brief Assessment Unit psychiatrists. This figure does not include the 193 persons who were referred to mental hospitals for the purpose of protracted assessment rather than treatment (see Chapter 4). In general, the diversion of criminal defendants into the mental health system presented few conceptual or procedural difficulties for the METFORS clinicians. By declaring patients to be both mentally disordered and dangerous, psychiatrists could initiate involuntary certification and therefore assume jurisdiction away from the courts. When accused persons manifested a 'displaying mode' (Pfohl 1978) – when they were floridly psychotic or delusional during their assessment – the psychiatrists simply transcribed their conduct and utterances into the court report. Apart from establishing the pathological disorder of defendants, these letters also provided a firm corner-stone for decisions about dangerousness, treatability, and the need for protracted assessment. Clinical reports that announced or advocated in-patient confinement were therefore replete with graphic accounts of madness.

Mr. I.'s talk was full of delusional material influenced by hallucinations. He talked a lot about having to make a gold cross and make a man with a gold heart in order to re-enact the scene of the crime concerning Christ who fell three times. His affect was flat and some of his conversation resembled what is proverbially called a word salad. He, in describing the incident with which he is charged, stated voices had told him to drive down [   ] Street ... Suddenly there was a song by Paul McCartney about him and as he passed a [record] shop he felt something special had to happen there. There were all kinds of messages coming to him ... This man is suffering from chronic paranoid schizophrenia. (PL 195)

He insisted that every time the Federal government wants to set an example they send him to hospital. He talked a lot about political football, the F.B.I., and the German flag; indeed his conversation was dominated by a series of delusions. There is no doubt in our minds that this man suffers from chronic paranoid schizophrenia. There is also no doubt in our minds that this man should be returned to the H. Psychiatric Centre ... from which he is alleged to have run away. (PL 324)

Mr. P. shows evidence of an acute psychotic mental illness. He was markedly suspicious accusing the examiners of being prejudiced against him. He claimed that he was Jehovah God and the devil at the same time. He was verbally abusive to all of the staff and exhibited threatening behaviour ... Mr. P.'s thinking was disjointed and grandiose ... Because Mr. P. requires immediate psychiatric attention, I have taken the liberty of certifying him to the Queen Street Mental Health Centre ... I hope this course of action is acceptable to Your Honour. I believe it is in the best interests of both the accused and the Court. (PL 022)

The BAU psychiatrist's referral to mental hospital was frequently accompanied by a declaration in the court letter concerning the subject's potential for dangerous behaviour. For example, one patient – a twenty-five-year-old male charged with 'Breaking and Entering' – received a diagnosis of 'undifferentiated schizophrenia,' and was certified to the Clarke Institute of Psychiatry in order to ensure his continued institutional detention. The psychiatrist wrote: 'On examination today it was difficult to obtain from this man a clear account of his present situation. He showed marked looseness of associations in his thinking and gave irrational and irrelevant replies to questions. It is possible that he is hallucinating at this time ... It is our opinion that this man represents a significant physical danger in the community and I believe his further detention is necessary. To facilitate his admission to the Clarke Institute I attach hereto a [certificate of involuntary admission]' (PL 222).

In a related case the BAU psychiatrist certified the defendant after establishing a causal relationship between delusional performance and dangerous propensity. '[H]e proceeded to tell us that he was God, that he had died on the operating table and returned to life and subsequently he knows exactly what is going to happen from day to day. He indicated that he was the first born of three siblings and his mother's name was Mary, giving him all the more reason to be God ... Mr. U. is certifiable under the Mental Health Act and I am enclosing ... an Involuntary Certificate for use by the Court ... It should be added that it is quite possible in his present state, believing that he is God and could do no wrong that he could be dangerous' (PL 406).

Lastly, hospitalization could be advocated for the overt purpose of exercising institutional control, when the defendant was apparently not amenable to clinical treatment. Case 547, for instance, involved a forty-one-year-old woman who had been romantically harassing her former employer over a period of several years, and who was on this occasion remanded to METFORS following a charge of 'Harassing Telephone Calls.' The BAU psychiatrist reported to the presiding judge that 'Miss W. suffers from what we call an encapsulated paranoid delusion. It looks as if she believes that her boss is in love with her and she has to act in accordance with this belief. This condition is notoriously difficult to treat with success.' Nevertheless, the psychiatrist was moved to recommend that the defendant be institutionalized in a mental hospital. '[I]n view of the relatively long time this has gone on, in view of the various methods that have been tried, including incarceration and fines ... we are suggesting that Miss W. be referred to and hooked up with the Queen Street Mental Health Centre' (PL 547). Following the METFORS brief assessment the subject was hospitalized at Queen Street for six weeks. The criminal charge was withdrawn by the court.

Fitness to Stand Trial

As indicated in Chapter 3, the METFORS psychiatrists found 16 per cent of their Brief Assessment Unit subjects to be unfit to stand trial. A further 11 per cent of accused persons were categorized as 'questionably fit.' It would appear generally that forensic psychiatrists experience little difficulty in assigning diagnoses of unfitness (Roesch and Golding 1980). 'Psychiatrists tell us that of all the various things courts ask them to do, unfitness is the easiest and quickest to assess' (Law Reform Commission of Canada 1976: 34). Moreover, research involving semi-structured assessment instruments (McGarry, Curran, Lipsitt, Lelos, Schwitzgebel, and Rosenberg 1974; Menzies, Webster, Roesch, Eaves, and Jensen 1984; Roesch, Webster, and Eaves 1984) has established that even laypersons are able to discriminate between fit and unfit defendants with considerable reliability and confidence. However, in contrast to the American context,[5] decisions about fitness in Canada are impeded by the absence of clear statutory criteria (Webster, Menzies, and Jackson 1982: 93–7). More than a decade ago, the Canadian Law Reform Commission offered the following guidelines: 'A person is unfit, if, owing to mental disorder: (1) he does not understand the nature or object of the proceedings against him, or (2) he does not understand the personal import of the proceedings, or (3) he is unable to communicate with counsel' (LRCC 1976: 14). These have yet to be formally incorporated into criminal or procedural law.

At a pre-trial level, fitness is the only clinical judgment that is legally mandated by the Canadian Criminal Code.[6] Given the vast majority of remanded subjects who are obviously fit according to both judicial and medical practitioners, it would appear that the issue of competency is regularly being used as a justification for obtaining clinical recommendations about dangerousness, treatability, and dispositional alternatives. Moreover, a finding of unfitness harbours a potential life sentence in a mental institution (Verdun-Jones 1981). Incompetent defendants are exposed to powerful control mechanisms, as they are indefinitely confined under the authority of a Lieutenant-Governor's Warrant[7] until their fitness to stand trial is 're-established.' Whereas ostensibly this issue evolved in jurisprudence as a protection against arbitrarily imposed criminal process, in practice competency decisions have over the years been effectively integrated into the prosecutorial machinery imposed on mentally disordered defendants (Coleman 1984; McGarry, Curran, Lipsitt, Lelos, Schwitzgebel, and Rosenberg 1974; Menzies 1985; Robitscher 1980; Schiffer 1978).

For persons found unfit to stand trial, the hospital becomes the carceral alternative to the prison. As a consequence, the unfit person is not 'diverted' within any true sense of the term. The individual is either rerouted into the mental health stream ... or the criminal trial is suspended until the accused can be rendered sufficiently fit to proceed with his defence ... [T]he assessment procedure has forfeited its original status as a defence-related mechanism; the majority of fitness cases are now referred by the courts and prosecutors ... The clinician, therefore, is increasingly dependent upon and engaged with the daily administration of criminal justice, rather than functioning simply as an agent responsible for protecting disordered persons from the full weight of the system. (Webster, Menzies, and Jackson 1982: 94–5)

In finding people unfit to stand trial, the METFORS psychiatrists clearly subscribed to the theory that such an outcome was in the best interests of criminal defendants. Court letters made repeated references to the welfare of accused persons, to their ability to 'inform counsel,' and to their anticipated performance during the trial proceedings. The following passages are typical of these accounts.

This man may not be fit to stand trial at this time because of the major mental illness schizophrenia. Although he appreciates the nature of the charges against him and the purpose of the criminal justice proceeding, his impairment in thinking may reduce his capacity to cooperate rationally with counsel. (PL 506)

Mr. B. showed evidence of delusional ideation stating that at times he has worked as a Russian spy, has killed a number of people, and has believed in the past that he is a billionaire ... Mr. B. does have a simple understanding of the nature of his charges and the potential consequences to these charges. However his major disturbance in thinking raises questions about his capacity to rationally cooperate with counsel in his own defense. (PL 374)

This is a cantankerous, demented, babbling old lady. She is also quite paranoid and accused me of being one of 'them' ... She is in need of long term hospitalization ... In my opinion she is also unfit to stand trial because she may be 'mute of malice' and she may be so uncooperative as to create quite a disturbance in the court scene. (PL 008)

For some patients a finding of unfitness was intimately related to the BAU psychiatrist's diagnosis of dangerousness. Such a linkage was established, for example, in the case of a seventy-three-year-old deaf pensioner accused of throwing lye in the face of his victim, causing minor burns. In the court letter the METFORS psychiatrist indicated that 'he is suffering from a mental illness which takes the form of a paranoid state. Apart from this he is mentally intact, considering his age and disability. I do believe he represents a significant level of dangerousness in the community because of his mental disturbance. For this reason I believe he is not fit to stand trial' (PL 098). Alternatively, a finding of unfitness could be delivered in the professed interests of the subject's own safety. 'This young man ... was confused in his thinking and delusional and was unable to give a true account of himself and his present situation ... He is presently suffering from an exacerbation of his mental illness and is not fit to stand trial ... I have arranged for his immediate admission to our Inpatient Unit here at METFORS. I am concerned about his welfare if he should return to the jail situation' (PL 448).

A related theme in these letters concerned the ability of defence lawyers to exercise constraint over unfit defendants. 'His mood was inappropriately cheerful and his stream of thought and his attitude and manner indicated to us that he is suffering from a major mental illness. We had no doubts in our mind that he is in a hypomanic state of manic depressive illness ... We felt at this time that Mr. N. may not be fit to stand trial because he may have difficulty concentrating on one topic at one time and his counsel may have difficulty in keeping him along one track' (PL 543). Finally, in marginal cases the psychiatrist's judgment about incompetency could be contingent on the anticipated complexity of the criminal proceedings. The unarticulated rider on these occasions appeared to be that the subject was fit to plead guilty but unfit to participate in an adversarial trial. The following recommendation was extracted from the psychiatrist's report on an 'undifferentiated schizophrenic' charged with 'Assault Causing Bodily Harm': 'Mr. V. is considered marginally fit to stand trial. By this I mean that he shows evidence of a mental disorder that may interfere with his ability to follow court proceedings. He is aware of his charges and his relationship to them. He understands the nature and meaning of an oath. He may have some difficulty instructing counsel based on this mental disorder. In the event of an uncomplicated procedure he would be considered fit' (PL 517).

Not Guilty by Reason of Insanity
The METFORS court letters rarely addressed the issue of criminal responsibility.[8] In only thirty-seven cases did the BAU psychiatrist refer to the subject's mental condition at the time of the alleged offence, usually to indicate summarily that (s)he was legally sane. Only four of 591 reports[9] argued that the defendant was not guilty by reason of insanity. Only five persons were found NGRI by the criminal court. Competency has clearly superseded criminal responsibility as the principal 'mental status' consideration confronting the forensic clinician (see Scheidemandel and Kanno 1969; Teplin 1984a; Verdun-Jones 1981). Owing in large part to legal and clinical difficulties in rendering retrospective judgments about the defendant's ability to 'appreciate the nature and quality' of the offence (Caplan 1984), and given the adversarial nature of the criminal proceedings on insanity, forensic psychiatrists are generally reluctant to volunteer their opinion on this issue (Hucker, Webster, and Ben-Aron 1981; Schiffer 1978). Notwithstanding the high profile of insanity in jurisprudential literature and public discourse, criminal responsibility is a relatively peripheral issue in medico-legal decision-making (Morris and Hawkins 1970: 176).

The few METFORS findings of 'not guilty by reason of insanity' were reserved for the most serious cases of first or second degree murder, where a conviction would result in a mandatory life sentence with no parole eligibility for ten to twenty-five years. Case 574 was illustrative of psychiatric reasoning associated with criminal responsibility. It was also indicative of the dissensus between clinic and court in the determination of this issue. A middle-aged man had been arrested for 'First Degree Murder' following the shooting death of a Toronto lawyer. A week after the arrest the subject was twice interviewed, over a period of almost five hours on successive days in the Brief Assessment Unit. The resulting five-page court report was the longest in the entire BAU sample. In the letter the METFORS psychiatrist itemized the informational sources that were relevant to his clinical judgment:

[T]he following materials were considered in arriving at the opinions below:
1. Psychological testing by Dr. D. and Dr. S., psychologists.
2. Physical examination by Dr. V., psychiatric resident.
3. Electroencephalogram, electrocardiagram, and skull x-rays.
4. Consultation with several police investigators with the Metropolitan Toronto Police Department, Homicide Unit.
5. Consultation with Mr. B., Crown Attorney, and Mr. Z., Defence Lawyer.
6. Consultation with Dr. A., psychiatrist and a review of his report to [the court].
7. Statement by the accused made [at the time of his arrest].
8. An interview with the accused's ex-wife.
9. Information from acquaintances and friends of [the accused] about his behaviour and conversation in the days prior to the alleged act of murder. (PL 574)

These varied sources of specialist knowledge were used to reinforce the scientific authority of the psychiatrist's ultimate determination. The defendant was diagnosed to be suffering from a 'paranoid personality disturbance, characterized by rigid thinking, hyper-sensitivity, a tendency to blame others for his own difficulties.' This depiction was extrapolated from three sources: (1) the subject's personal history: 'He noted that he observed a number of [soldiers] during the war who acted according to their own conscience in securing justice for their own principles, including killing those who disagreed. This experience may be relevant to Mr. O.'s alleged act of murder.' (2) Events precipitating the homicide: 'He felt unfairly persecuted ... He purchased a gun and some ammunition from a stranger in his shop. He described his motivation as needing to protect himself ... He stated that the victim contacted him by phone and threatened to ruin him and kill him. Since that time he felt himself in some danger and carried the loaded weapon with him on most occasions.' (3) The patient's demeanour during the BAU interview: 'His responses were overly detailed, complex and obsessive. He insisted on telling his story in his own way and refused to be directed in simple answers. He revealed considerable anger during the interview towards a number of lawyers with whom he had had "bad" experiences' (PL 574).

Despite this comprehensive review of psychiatric 'disturbance,' the METFORS psychiatrist concluded that the subject was legally sane at the time of the alleged offence.

He was clearly aware of the nature of his acts of carrying, pointing and shooting the gun at [the victim]. The purpose of the act was clear in his mind in that he wanted [the victim] dead ... Mr. O's coherent and complete statement made shortly after the act did not suggest a psychotic disturbance in thinking or mood. Rather, the statement reveals goal-directed behaviour consistent with anger and resentment, built up over several years ... Despite evidence of a paranoid personality disturbance, I do not find sufficient evidence that Mr. O.'s thinking reached a psychotic level at any time prior to, during, or after the alleged act of murder. In my opinion he was able to appreciate the nature and quality of the alleged act of murder and knew and understood that the alleged act was legally wrong ... All of the above data suggest that despite Mr. O.'s personality and longstanding and significant stress dating back several years, he was sane at the time of the alleged act of murder. (PL 475)

Following the METFORS assessment, the defendant was held in pre-trial correctional detention for seven months, and received a series of further evaluations from both prosecution and defence psychiatrists. He was ultimately found not guilty by reason of insanity after a jury trial, and was committed indefinitely under a Warrant of the Lieutenant-Governor to the Oak Ridge unit for the criminally insane at Penetang.

Dangerousness to Self

In only forty-seven cases (8.0 per cent) did the METFORS psychiatrist's court letter indicate that the subject was potentially suicidal or dangerous to him/herself (see Daley 1987). In fifteen of these reports this depiction was coupled with an attribution of dangerousness to others. When psychiatrists referred to the possibility of self-directed harm, the judgment was typically made in summary fashion; it cited prior suicide attempts or threats; and it was mobilized to endorse an extended in-patient assessment or involuntary certification.[10]

In contrast to their frequent ascriptions of dangerousness toward other persons, BAU psychiatrists appeared to be much more reticent about communicating a prediction of dangerousness to self. In fact, court letters were consistently used to dismiss the suicidal utterances elicited from criminal defendants, or to characterize these claims as pathological symptoms or manipulative gestures on the part of patients. For example, when a person charged with 'Second Degree Murder' announced to the assessment team that he wanted to die, this was transposed into the court letter as follows: 'There [were] no indications of depressive ideation, in particular of overt suicidal ideation, although he did indicate that, "I don't want to live ...," which might be construed as a suicidal preoccupation' (PL 494). Another individual had slashed his wrists in jail three days prior to the METFORS assessment. The psychiatrist wrote: 'Mr. J. has recently made a suicidal gesture in the detention centre. This gesture relates to his long standing depressive features, his manipulative personality and to his recent withdrawal from drugs ... Mr. J. is not a good candidate for bail and/or probation ... In the event he is incarcerated on the present charges he could, perhaps, benefit from some psychological assistance with his depression' (PL 344).

Evidence of prior suicide attempts could also be qualified by stressing the unreliability of the subject as an informant. 'He reported suicidal acts by hanging or jumping from a bridge some four years ago, and suicidal gestures by scratching his arms, "to get out of the hospital wing in jail", a few days ago. His social judgment appeared poor and there was no insight into any problems that he has ... He has self-inflicted scratch marks on his upper arm which he related in a provocative and manipulative manner. His report was scattered and appeared unreliable' (PL 493).

A related strategy for neutralizing subjects' suicidal accounts involved the solicitation of conflicting reports from other authorities. In Case 585 a male patient charged with 'Fraud' and 'False Fire Alarm' was labelled by the Brief Assessment Unit team as an 'inadequate personality disorder with hysterical and antisocial features,' and subsequently received nine months in prison and twenty-four months' probation for the offences. During the forensic interview, the subject claimed to have attempted suicide in his prison cell. A phone call to the correctional institution failed to corroborate his claim, and the incident became a salient item in the court letter: 'Mr. P. noted that he had *tried* to hang himself at the Don Jail on the evening prior to this examination. However, when we contacted that facility we learned that Mr. P. had handed the correctional officers a short rope and stated that he had *intended* to kill himself. Mr. P. has a history of manipulative behaviour and it is possible that much of his present distress is secondary to his desire to avoid responsibility for the present charges' (PL 585).

Dangerousness to Others
Psychiatrists cannot predict dangerousness to others. More than two decades of research have consistently documented the questionable role of dangerousness as a legitimate medico-legal concept (Bottoms 1977; Menzies 1986; Petrunik 1983; Pfohl 1978; Webster, Dickens, and Addario 1985); the gross inaccuracy of clinical projections about future violence (Frederick 1978; Hinton 1983; Webster, Hucker, and Ben-Aron 1985); the systematic tendency to overpredict assaultiveness (Monahan 1981; Quinsey 1979; Steadman and Cocozza 1974; Thornberry and Jacoby 1979); the failure of psychometric instruments substantially to improve upon clinical prognostications (Cocozza and Steadman 1976; Menzies, Webster, and Sepejak 1985a, b; Steadman 1973); and the general lack of correspondence between mental illness and dangerousness (Menzies and Webster 1987; Menzies, Webster, and Sepejak 1987; Mesnikoff and Lauterbach 1975; Rabkin 1979; Steadman 1981).

These findings are recurrent and unequivocal, and yet North American and European forensic psychiatrists continue to offer their professional judgments about the potential violence of mentally disordered criminal defendants. They do so because dangerousness remains an empowering (and profitable) issue for both clinical and judicial authorities. The forensic assessment is primarily concerned with the production of dispositional choices, and such options are always conditioned by the presence or absence of a potential threat posed by accused persons. Forensic psychiatrists predict dangerousness because, tacitly or overtly, this issue is on the discretionary agenda. The eradication of dangerousness from forensic decision-making could well render clinical assessments largely irrelevant to the pragmatic business of producing criminal court dispositions.

It was patently clear that dangerousness to others was a focal concern for the METFORS assessment team. Accused persons were declared to be dangerous to others in 139 of 591 Brief Assessment Unit letters. In 96 cases (16.2 per cent) the psychiatrist indicated to the court that the defendant was *not* dangerous; 62 letters (10.5 per cent) reported that the presence of dangerousness was unclear; and in only 294 cases (49.7 per cent) was the issue not addressed. Hence, in almost one-quarter of METFORS BAU assessments the criminal court judge received a direct clinical affirmation that the forensic subject was dangerous to others.

Accounts of dangerousness in court letters were designed to impress legal officials with the severity of the subject's condition, with the supposed pathological features of violence, and with the dire consequences to be anticipated if such persons were to be released from penal or medical confinement. Examples were abundant. 'He came across as if he were like a caged animal, full of all sorts of aggressive feelings within him ... [H]e is given to fits of violence' (PL 091); 'Mr. H. is potentially a very dangerous man. He would talk about slitting somebody's throat without batting an eye as if he were merely performing some very simple act' (PL 351). '[H]e has been charged from about age 11 with breaking and entering and setting fires to thirty-two houses as well as smoking dope and using Acid, Speed, and other street drugs ... He also had fights with teachers and had fooled around with guns ... He denies any homosexual experiences but has been approached on more than one occasion. In addition to all this he stated that he can drive and has driven without ever having had a license ... If all the stories he has told us are true then he is obviously quite a dangerous young man ... He probably can only be contained in a custodial setting' (PL 320).

These labels concerning dangerousness were yielded from a wide range of documentary sources in the Brief Assessment Unit. Psychiatrists had access to a seemingly infinite number of 'dangerous facts' that were selectively germane to a given forensic case. An individual's *denial* could be reported as an indication of potential dangerousness. '[W]hat is perhaps the worst factor involved here is that he does not perceive himself as dangerous and ... he sees his aggressive behaviour as acts of self-preservation' (PL 541); '[W]e consider this man an exceptionally poor treatment risk, especially also in view of the fact that he has had opportunities for the best treatment available. More ominous, however, is that he does not perceive himself as dangerous and is not concerned about his behaviour' (PL 542). Conversely, the subject's self-perception *as* dangerous could be incorporated into the clinical label. 'This man is considered to be a significant danger in the community. Moreover, he has indicated that he considers himself to be dangerous' (PL 394).

Psychiatrists might also focus on the physical stature of the defendant. 'Mr. R. is a big man. He is over 6 foot and he weighs 195 pounds and his talk is interspersed with many examples of him having been involved in violent acts ... [W]e were all convinced that this man is possibly quite dangerous' (PL 432). They might embrace previous designations by other legal authorities. 'According to police officers at 99 Division, Mr. A. is a grossly disturbed individual who "may be dangerous" ' (PL 180). Earlier recorded incidents could be cited to identify an irreversible violent career. '[A]t times he has been perceived by ... staff as hostile and threatening. Apparently one incident occurred when Mr. Y. was hospitalized in [a psychiatric] facility in which he seriously threatened a staff member by grabbing them around the throat. By Mr. Y.'s own admissions he is a dangerous individual when he "loses his temper". This long standing explosive character trait is not amenable to psychiatric treatment. Therefore, Mr. Y. is likely to continue to engage in aggressive behaviour in the future' (PL 513). Or, a dangerous label could be invoked through the deployment of remarkable 'insight' into the social conditions of deviance. 'He comes across as a man with a short fuse, a temper, and with a tendency to act out in an aggressive and violent fashion. The history of his activities, his association with [his common-law wife], and his involvement with alcohol, drugs and the particular job he has (a part-time roofer) hints to us that this man has existed on the fringe of society and is what has often been called by sociologists a marginal person ... We considered that under certain circumstances e.g., provocation and imbibing of alcohol he could be quite dangerous' (PL 401).

The METFORS psychiatrists were also prepared to translate mental illness into dangerousness, to speculate about future assaultiveness in the absence of palpable evidence, and to support their judgments with narrations of violence about which criminal charges had never been laid. In several cases, for example, a diagnosis of psychiatric pathology appeared to provide sufficient grounds in itself for imputing dangerousness to others. A thirty-five-year-old transsexual was described as follows: 'On examination he was flippant, joking, effeminate, and laughing in a seductive fashion ... His personality showed marked antisocial features with a fairly high level of aggression and indifference to the feelings of others. The psychological testing that was performed showed some schizophrenic features ... Basically he has a lot of aggression, which when mixed with his antisocial trends, makes him a significant danger in the community' (PL 070). Alternatively, a finding of non-dangerousness could be held up as a rare exception to the implicit association between violence and insanity. 'From a psychiatric viewpoint we could not elicit any indications of dangerousness in this man, despite his mental condition' (PL 530).

Prognostications about future violence could arise in the complete absence of verifiable data. In Case 170, the METFORS psychiatrist drew the following conclusion from the subject's failure fully to co-operate with the assessment process. 'On examination today this man was found to be highly demanding and uncooperative, becoming increasingly restless and hostile during the period of assessment. He could not answer questions to any extent ... I consider that he represents a significant potential for dangerousness in the community ..., although I was not able to establish any clear history about such abuse on this examination' (PL 170).

For other BAU patients the court letter might indicate a *potential* for violent behaviour in the future, conditional upon specified factors identified by the psychiatrist. 'Mr. E. does not appear to represent an acute danger to himself or the community at this time. In the event his present psychological defences do not protect himself against the underlying self-doubt and low self-esteem, he could be dangerous in the future' (PL 500).

Lastly, the METFORS psychiatrists sometimes attempted to substantiate their designations of dangerousness with data yielded from the clinical interview, which suggested involvement in criminal activities entirely unrelated to the current charges. In Case 291, the subject was remanded to METFORS, on a charge of failing to comply with a probation order, after discharging himself from the Lakeshore Psychiatric Hospital. In the clinical interview the patient disclosed that he had been involved in sexual activities with children during the term of his probation. The psychiatrist displayed no hesitation in relaying this confession in his court report to the presiding judge.

Mr. R. indicated that he has a past history of arrests for Indecent Assaults on male and female children. He also indicated that in the ten months while at Lakeshore Psychiatric Hospital as a condition of probation, he has been sexually involved with children. Mr. R. notes that his sexual urges increase when he drinks and that he has frequently left the Lakeshore Psychiatric Hospital grounds in order to drink in nearby taverns ... Mr. R. is a potentially dangerous individual because of his predilection to sexual involvement with children. It is my opinion that Mr. R. requires a closed setting ... I would recommend that he undergo a 30 day psychiatric assessment at the Oak Ridge unit at Penetang. This would allow the staff at that facility to assess his capacity to benefit from their programme. In the event that they did not feel that he was suitable for the facility, I do not believe that he should be released from detention. He is not a suitable individual for an open-door setting. (PL 291)

SUMMARY

Clinical court letters constitute the primary instrument for legitimizing forensic psychiatric assessments. In developing selective accounts of their labelling work, framed in constructs and discourse that are less therapeutic than legalistic, psychiatric experts succeed in regulating the flow of information to the criminal court. Their editorial strategies allow members to accentuate their expert status, while maintaining power to define the mental disorder and criminality of accused persons.

Socio-legal research on the attitudes of judicial authorities to forensic psychiatry – and on the relationship between recommendations and decisions concerning penal dispositions, fitness to stand trial, involuntary commitment, and dangerousness – has consistently demonstrated the tendency of court officials to relinquish their judgmental authority to psychiatric agents. The concordance between clinical prescriptions and juridical outcomes has often attained unanimity in these studies. Such results have been yielded under a variety of legal, institutional, and procedural conditions.

As with these earlier investigations, it was clear that sentencing prescriptions played a major role in the construction of METFORS decision-making, and in the relationship between the clinic and the criminal courts. For example, over two-thirds of court reports in the Brief Assessment Unit contained a specific dispositional recommendation. And these letters exerted a major impact. In more than three-quarters of cases where the psychiatrist prescribed a carceral disposition, the subject did indeed receive a term of imprisonment. Persons nominated in the BAU for probation tended to obtain probation. As well, almost 70 per cent of defendants recommended by psychiatrists for in-patient hospitalization (for either assessment or treatment) were acquitted, discharged, or received probation, compared with less than half of other groups.

A correspondingly high rate of agreement prevailed between judicial outcomes and the clinical recommendations issuing from in-patient letters for the 123 subjects remanded for protracted assessment at METFORS. Nine of ten persons recommended for imprisonment by in-patient psychiatrists were subsequently incarcerated by the court. Further, more than two-thirds of the forty-one subjects receiving in-patient recommendations for probation were given this sentence, and another 10 per cent received probation supplementary to a period of imprisonment.

This congruence could be largely attributed to the reportorial styles and strategies adopted by the METFORS psychiatrists. The court letters were fashioned to maximize control over subsequent judicial decision-making. They were relatively brief, standardized in format, and replete with conclusionary remarks that typically excluded the underlying inferential process. Psychiatrists were inclined to offer specific recommendations in these reports that could be directly incorporated by judges into the ensuing sentence. Letters were permeated with explicit and tacit claims to specialist knowledge which imparted a sense of technical authority to their medico-legal pronouncements. Finally, the documents functioned to amplify the negative ascriptions accumulated throughout the assessment process, providing judges with a concentrated, dramatic, and unambiguous depiction of the defendant's pathological and delinquent condition.

The METFORS psychiatrists enlisted these various factors to bridge the discrete worlds of the forensic clinic and the criminal court. The reports became their catalysts for transporting professional influence outside of METFORS and into the confines of the judicial process itself. By demonstrating the unique and essential nature of their legal contribution, they managed to play a role not only in the hospitalization and treatment of mentally ill defendants, but more directly in the routine adjudication of such mainstream criminal concerns as pre-trial detention, probation, dangerousness, and carceral confinement.

6

The Aftermath

Let your own discretion be your tutor: suit the action to the word, the word to the action.

WILLIAM SHAKESPEARE   *Hamlet* III, 2

All knowledge – like all ignorance – tends to be opportunistic when not critically scrutinized.

GUNNAR MYRDAL   *Against the Stream*

Knowledge itself is power.

FRANCIS BACON

SURVIVAL OF THE SANEST

This final chapter considers the clinical, legal, and institutional consequences of psychiatric assessments at the Metropolitan Toronto Forensic Service. The deviant careers of METFORS subjects did not end following their BAU remand and subsequent sanctioning by the criminal courts. To the contrary, for many patients the aftermath of forensic evaluation brought a seemingly endless series of confrontations with criminal justice and mental health officials.

The medico-legal system can be likened to a complex switching mechanism, in which defendants suspected of mental illness are continuously being shunted through an intricate network of interconnected tracks. MET-FORS was only one station in this longitudinal processing system. The forensic professionals in this study exercised extraordinary power to determine the future prospects of their subjects, and yet such power was always reflexive and incomplete, and it was mediated by the prior and future choices of other medico-legal officials. For their part, the 592 MET-FORS patients converged upon the BAU from a broad array of personal and institutional backgrounds, and they were subsequently propelled onto lines of carceral and therapeutic intervention that grew increasingly entangled across time and space. In order to place some perspective on the influence and permanence of the forensic classifications described in the first five chapters of this book, it is necessary to contextualize the activities of clinical professionals at METFORS, and to explore the ramifications of their work within the wider landscape of this penal-therapeutic enterprise.

Relationships between mental health and criminal justice institutions are governed by a kind of institutional symbiosis, through which 'bureaucracies with conscript clientele become real clients of one another, mutually dependent for referral of cases' (Friedenberg 1975: 2). As control is dispersed through increasingly wider reaches of interconnected systems, officials come to develop strategic patterns of accommodation, which permit knowledge and control practices to be piled up at points of convergence such as police information centres, prosecutors' offices, courthouses, medical record libraries, and forensic clinics (Berry 1975: 353). Therapeutic and penal agencies become 'loosely coupled systems' (March and Olsen 1976), linked by convoluted patterns of exchange and compliance as subjects and information are continually passed on through the organizational circuitry.

This worked-out institutional environment has particular implications for the professional activities of forensic clinicians. As earlier chapters have shown, the pre-trial classification work of medico-legal practitioners is largely governed by frankly legalistic perspectives and priorities. Although clinicians never entirely abandon their therapeutic identity, none the less they come to recognize that their participation in the criminal justice enterprise depends on recurrent demonstrations of an ability to engineer, or at least to enhance, the application of legal control. Forensic specialists occupy a precarious berth between legal and clinical obligations, and they work largely to resolve and reconcile the contradictions flowing from these competing allegiances. Psychiatric assessments for the court offer needed opportunities for the affirmation of medical competence, specialist knowledge, and virtuosity. Yet paradoxically, pre-trial remands also present poignant reminders of the clinician's fragile status within the medico-legal scheme of things.

For their part, judicial officials benefit greatly from the psychiatric injection of scientific legitimacy into carceral dispositions. Expert knowledge and technical know-how become fused with criminal sanctions because they justify punishment under the rubric of science, and because they diffuse the responsibility for legal control across a wide assortment of judicial and parajudicial agents. Recognizing the respective gains to be secured from such arrangements, courts and corrections officials endeavour to enlist satellite institutions that offer such 'expert' services. The result is a proliferation of classification, supervision, and treatment agencies that become interwoven with traditional criminal justice corridors:

Throughout the penal procedure and the implementation of the sentence there swarms a whole series of subsidiary authorities. Small-scale legal systems and parallel judges have multiplied around the principal judgment: psychiatric or psychological experts, magistrates concerned with the implementation of sentences, educationalists, members of the prison services, all fragment the legal power to punish ... [S]ubsidiary judges they may be, but they are judges all the same. The whole machinery that has been developing for years around the implementation of sentences, and their adjustment to individuals, creates a proliferation of the authorities of judicial decision-making and extends its powers of decision well beyond the sentence. (Foucault 1977: 21)

The present research provided an ideal opportunity to map the contours of such a 'transcarceral' system (Lowman, Menzies, and Palys 1987) as it conditioned the content and outcome of classification work at the Metropolitan Toronto Forensic Service. It was possible, through a two-year follow-up of the METFORS patient cohort, to observe the longitudinal courses of forensic careers as subjects encountered and were absorbed by successive waves of psycholegal control.

In particular, the follow-up component of this study was intended to shed some light on the relative accuracy and permanency of forensic judgments through the post-assessment lives of the BAU patients. Could the diagnoses and predictions of forensic experts be validated against the subsequent conduct and experiences of their subjects? And perhaps more central to the concerns of this book, to what extent did these initial medico-legal judgments survive the passage of time, and how did they contribute to patterns of medico-legal response in the following months and years? Given the increasing galvanization of therapy and punishment throughout the judicial apparatus, how were forensic labels sustained in later encounters with control agents, and how in turn did subsequent criminal sanctions function to enhance psychiatric definitions of reality? Was it possible to evaluate the relative significance of clinical judgments at METFORS within this wider field of legal and mental ordering? And what conclusions can be drawn about METFORS as a site and source of therapeutic and carceral control?

These questions are also fundamental to understanding the changing nature of social control in contemporary state society. As a number of socio-legal commentators have pointed out over recent years (Austin and Krisberg 1981; Cohen 1985; Foucault 1977; Garland 1985; Garland and Young 1983; Lowman, Menzies, and Palys 1987; Scull 1983; Turner 1987; Warren 1981), the application of legal control has become partially de-institutionalized with the advent of numerous ancillary agencies and with the growing confluence of institutions of social order such as criminal justice, welfare, and mental health. As boundaries become blurred, and as the practices and functions of various officials become increasingly inter-dependent and interchangeable, legal subjects – whether defined as criminals or dependants or mental patients or some combination of statuses – are apt to experience 'the control system' as a holistic enterprise with no fixed boundaries. Social control itself is likely to be felt as a recurrent, and often omnipresent phenomenon with no apparent end. Persons caught within the realm of such a transinstitutional system become identified with dual or multiple labels, which have simultaneous relevance for numerous organizations and agencies. Psychiatric and criminal justice institutions, and even the community, are not viewed as insulated entities, since each comes to exist as much for the perpetuation of the others as for its own survival. Transformations in carceral and therapeutic systems result in some fundamental mutations in the very substance of social control itself:

The transcarceral apparatus describes a cyclical practice that ... transcend[s] classical institutional boundaries, and in the process transform[s] political and cultural con-structions of criminality, madness, and other forms of deviance. The defective, the deranged, the dependent and the dangerous within the transcarceral enterprise, merge into an inclusive deviant category that is eligible for multiple applications of control. Technologies of surveillance, programmes of docility and registration, and organizational alliances have combined to fashion a new trade in deviance. (Lowman and Menzies 1986: 110)

The consequences are profound for the METFORS subjects and other forensic populations. Mentally disordered offenders resemble their clinical evaluators in being suspended between the parallel structures of criminal justice and mental health. Ironically, they are exposed to many of the same conflicts and contradictions. For a substantial proportion of forensic subjects, it becomes difficult (if not impossible) to escape the mutually energizing gravitational fields being exerted by carceral and therapeutic organizations. As subjects are shuttled back and forth over time between and among various 'loosely coupled' agencies, the phenomenon of legal control comes to take on cyclical features (Menzies 1987b). Judicial and medical interventions tend to multiply and to recur in accelerating bursts of surveillance and confinement. With increasingly sophisticated knowledge systems, computer profiling, and the general 'scientification' of control work (Ericson and Shearing 1986), old labels seldom disappear while new ones are systematically fused with existing deviant categories.

Pre-trial forensic clinics such as METFORS play an especially prominent role in these transinstitutional control mechanisms. As outlined in the following survey of their longitudinal careers, many of the METFORS subjects found themselves being repeatedly cycled through the Brief Assessment Unit and other psychiatric assessment agencies for periodic confirmations of their deviant status. Not only were these people exposed to an extraordinary intensity and range of medico-legal control in the two years following their initial forensic assessment, but it became apparent that in many cases METFORS and similar facilities were being recurrently used to activate and sustain deviant identities over the course of time.

By reviewing the post-assessment conduct and experiences of the patients in this study, this final chapter sets out then to assess the function of METFORS as a control catalyst, and as a springboard for deviant careers that continued into the immediate future and beyond. But more than this, such an analysis necessarily invites questions about the very nature of medico-legal control within the criminal justice – mental health complex; about strategies for containing and countering the authority of forensic professionals; and about the future of clinical assessment agencies such as METFORS within a constantly shifting carceral environment. These too will be considered.

THE OUTCOME CAREERS OF THE METFORS SUBJECTS

Surveying the Subsequent Conduct of 571 BAU Patients
As detailed in Chapter 1, the institutional and behavioural careers of the METFORS subjects were tracked over a two-year period following their initial remand to the Brief Assessment Unit. Data were compiled from a variety of institutional sources, including the Ontario Ministry of Correctional Services central registry, the Correctional Services Canada (Federal) files, Canadian Police Information Centre (CPIC) computer print-outs, the documents of the Toronto Coroner's Office, and the medical records from METFORS along with the six major forensic psychiatric hospitals within a 100-mile radius of Toronto. This information was assembled into a follow-up profile of each METFORS patient, which included all institutional contacts and confinements during the twenty-four months, as well as all officially reported incidents of criminal charges, events leading to hospitalization, misconducts during pre-sentence carceral detention or post-sentence imprisonment, and disruptive, assaultive, or self-injurious behaviour during hospitalization in psychiatric facilities. The follow-up sample comprised 571 subjects. Twenty-one persons exited from the analysis because they either died ($N = 10$) or left the country ($N = 7$), or because their names failed to appear on any of the follow-up documents ($N = 4$: see Appendix C).[1] Sample outcome profiles are presented in Appendix B.

The METFORS subjects registered a total of 2616 incidents during the two years subsequent to their brief assessment (mean = 4.58). Of the 571 patients, 423 were involved in at least one officially recorded incident. Among these transactions, 1658 occurred in the community (1322 leading to criminal charges and 326 to psychiatric hospitalizations), 535 were prison misconducts, and 423 involved in-hospital behaviour.

Out of the 2616 documented occurrences, 502 depicted overtly violent conduct (not including verbal threats) perpetrated by the METFORS patients. One-third of the cohort (191 out of 571 individuals)[2] exhibited assaultive behaviour during the follow-up period. The mean number of violent acts per subject was 0.88. The community was the context for 258 (51.4 per cent) of these violent incidents (213 resulting in criminal charges and 45 leading to psychiatric hospitalization). The remainder of the encounters were recorded in prison ($N = 106$) or hospital ($N = 138$).

A further 100 occurrences, involving 60 separate individuals, consisted of suicidal gestures or threats, or self-injurious behaviour. This translates into an average of 0.18 such incidents per individual across the entire cohort. Forty-three of these acts of self-directed violence occurred in the

FIGURE 6.1 Month-by-month follow-up of officially recorded incidents involving METFORS patients (N = 571; incidents during immediate METFORS in-patient assessments not included)

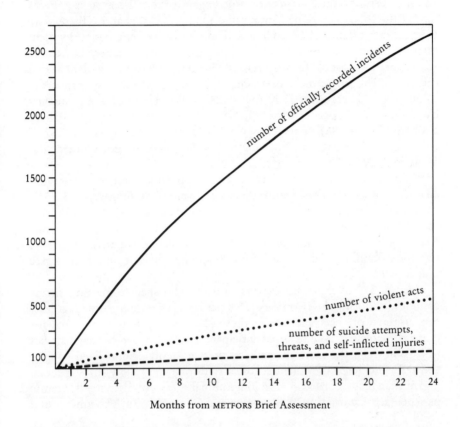

Months from METFORS Brief Assessment

community (all of them leading to mental institutionalization), three took place in prison, and the remainder were observed within psychiatric hospital walls.

Figure 6.1 presents a graphic depiction of the officially documented conduct of the METFORS subjects, charted monthly across the entire term of the follow-up research. Notably, the incidence of violent and other transactions is distributed in a virtual linear pattern throughout the course of the twenty-four months. There was no apparent tendency for the reported incidents to cluster at any point along the longitudinal continuum. Instead, registered violence, along with other manifestations of deviant conduct within either the community or institutional contexts, accumulated incrementally over the two-year period.

In Appendix F, a complete inventory is provided of all criminal charges and incarceration misconducts recorded against the 571 METFORS patients during the follow-up term. Among the 1332 criminal charges, there were 436 property offences, 267 'technical or administrative' charges, 213 violent offences against the person, 207 crimes against public order, 111 traffic violations, 82 alcohol- or drug-related charges, and 16 non-violent sexual offences.[3] The single most prevalent individual charge levied against the subjects was 'Theft under $200' ($N = 124$), followed in order of frequency by 'Failure to Appear' ($N = 86$), 'Willful Noncompliance with Bail or Probation' ($N = 86$), 'Possession over $200' ($N = 65$), 'Theft over $200' ($N = 62$), 'Breaking and Entering' ($N = 58$), and 'Liquor Control Act Violation' ($N = 53$).

Within the 'violent offences' category in Appendix F, the most common charges, with their associated frequencies, were 'Common Assault' (51), 'Assault Causing Bodily Harm' (48), 'Weapons Dangerous' (28), 'Robbery' (20), 'Assault Police' (14), 'Indecent Assault Female' (14), 'Assault While Resisting Arrest' (12), and 'Arson' (10). There were three arrests for rape, two for wounding, and one each for kidnapping, choking, and first-degree murder.

Overall, 312 of the 558 METFORS subjects who spent some time in the community during the two years (55.9 per cent) were charged with at least one criminal offence, and 126 of these (22.6 per cent) were arrested for crimes of violence. As one might anticipate from their correctional histories (see Table 1.1), the METFORS subjects were a highly criminalized cohort, and their incidence of violent criminality during the follow-up was much higher than that recorded in most longitudinal studies of discharged forensic patients (e.g. Quinsey 1979; Steadman and Cocozza 1974; Thornberry and Jacoby 1979).

The second half of Appendix F tabulates incarceration misconducts leading to prison disciplinary action during the twenty-four months following initial BAU assessment. In total, there were 535 such infractions, involving 151 imprisoned subjects. The overwhelming majority of these violations occurred in provincial institutions. There were 106 assaultive offences altogether, involving 65 of the 350 persons who were confined in prison at some stage during the two-year period. In relative terms, this meant that 43.1 per cent of imprisoned subjects engaged in at least one institutional violation, and 18.6 per cent committed or threatened to commit[4] one or more assaults. Apart from the 'assault' category, the other most prevalent

TABLE 6.1
Correlations among measures of outcome conduct

	INC	VIOL	CCV	IMV	HCV	IHV
INC	–	.654	.496	.473	.186	.330
VIOL		–	.618	.548	.310	.711
CCV			–	.255	−.003*	.083
IMV				–	.001*	.100
HCV					–	.117

Note: INC = incidents during follow-up, VIOL = violent incidents during follow-up, CCV = violent criminal charges during follow-up, IMV = violent incarceration misconducts during follow-up, HCV = violent incidents leading to hospitalization, IHV = violent incidents during hospitalization.
* Not significant at the 0.05 level.

prison misconducts, with their frequencies bracketed, were: 'Disobeying a lawful order' (120), 'Conducting oneself in a manner detrimental to the welfare of other inmates or the institutional programme' (80), 'Using gross, indecent or profane language' (58), 'Wilfully breaching or attempting to breach a regulation governing the conduct of inmates' (39), and 'Destroying or defacing government property' (28).

Next, Table 6.1 presents a correlation matrix among five indicators of follow-up violence (violent criminal charges, violent incarceration misconducts, assaults leading to hospitalization, assaultive behaviour during hospitalization, and total number of violent transactions), along with the total frequency of general incidents recorded against each subject during the two years. These correlations factored into two general components – criminal dangerousness and violence connected with psychiatric institutionalization. The number of criminal charges among the METFORS patients, for example, corresponded significantly with the number of violent incarceration misconducts, but associated only marginally with in-hospital assaultiveness, and not at all with pre-hospital violence. Similarly, persons who were assaultive in prison were somewhat more likely to display violent behaviour in hospital, but correctional misconducts were entirely unrelated to community behaviour leading to mental institutionalization. Stated differently, the METFORS patients who were physically aggressive in hospital were only slightly more likely than others to engage in violent crime on the street. Interestingly, the correlation between hospital and pre-hospital violence was only 0.117, suggesting that dangerous conduct in mental hospitals was not predictive of violence in any other institutional or community context.

Five main observations can be made, then, about the criminal and violent transgressions of METFORS patients throughout the twenty-four months following their initial assessment in the Brief Assessment Unit.

First, when compared with the subjects of other studies, this group was involved in an abundance of deviant and disruptive conduct during the outcome period. Out of the 571 subjects, 74 per cent registered at least one officially recognized incident in either the criminal justice or mental health system, 55 per cent were charged with criminal offences, and 33 per cent manifested overtly violent conduct. However, the vast majority of these assaults were relatively minor in nature – there were, for example, only three cases of rape, one armed robbery, and one murder.

Second, the majority of follow-up incidents ($N = 1658$) occurred in the community, compared with 535 in prison and 423 in psychiatric institutions. In contrast, there was a tendency for hospitals to record proportionately higher rates of assault than were manifest in either prisons or the community. This accords with recent findings (Cocozza, Melick, and Steadman 1978; Lowman, Menzies, and Palys 1987; Steadman and Felson 1984; Teplin 1984a) suggesting that violence in psychiatric institutions may be rising in response to the expanding role of the mental health system in containing criminal populations. Alternatively, the apparent 'dangerousness' of the forensic clientele in these hospitals may well be a function of differential surveillance and recording practices. The enhanced visibility of assaultiveness within the walls of such institutions, the particular organizational response to infractions, and associated context-specific features of transgression and reaction may be largely responsible for the recorded differences in officially registered violence among hospitals, prisons, and the community.

Third, there was no evidence that the dangerousness of METFORS patients was in any sense more pronounced during the short-term 'crisis period' immediately following their first arrest and remand to the Brief Assessment Unit. As Figure 6.1 indicates, the cumulative distribution of violent and other incidents displayed a linear uniformity of progression across the span of twenty-four months. This would appear to contradict speculation about the potentially greater validity of short-term predictions, based on arguments that dangerousness may be especially 'intense' in the days and weeks following initial institutionalization (Monahan 1981; see Teplin 1984a).

Fourth, the data revealed a trend toward the coincidence of assaultive and suicidal conduct within the subject population. Among the minority of METFORS patients who attempted or threatened suicide, or who physically harmed themselves (60, or 10.5 per cent of the cohort), a full 65 per cent also exhibited violent behaviour. However, given the low base rates of self-injurious conduct (see Daley 1987; Menzies, Corrado, Glackman, and Ryan 1987; Rosen 1954), this relationship would be virtually useless for the prediction of violence among suicidal forensic patients.

Fifth and last, the correlation matrix in Table 6.1 displayed a divergence between 'criminal' and 'psychiatric' dangerousness in the outcome careers of the METFORS subjects. Whereas violent criminal behaviour was significantly associated with assaultive prison misconducts, there was virtually no correlation between pre-hospital or in-hospital assaultiveness and violent conduct that precipitated criminal charges. In other words, one could not predict the dangerousness of subjects in the community, based upon their behaviour in psychiatric institutions. The different contexts were associated with qualitatively different institutional arrangements, and with apparently unrelated manifestations of dangerous misconduct.

Patterns of Institutional Confinement
During the two years following their forensic remand to the Brief Assessment Unit, the METFORS patients were subject to intensive patterns of institutionalization in both the criminal justice and the mental health system. For these people, the continuum of penality (Austin and Krisberg 1981; Foucault 1977; Garland 1985; Garland and Young 1983; Lowman, Menzies, and Palys 1987) was experienced as a recurrent series of confrontations with legal authorities, and as a seemingly endless cycle of confinements in penal and psychiatric institutions. Among the 571 patients, 349 (61.1 per cent) were sentenced to a total of 663 terms of imprisonment, for an average of 1.16 incarcerations across the entire cohort within only two years of the BAU assessment. Five people were imprisoned on five separate occasions, three individuals received six prison terms each, five were confined seven times, and one patient was sent to prison nine times overall. Altogether, the METFORS subjects incurred 2204 months of carceral confinement,[5] with a mean of 3.9 months per individual. This meant that about one-sixth of the patients' time during the subsequent two years was spent behind bars.

An analysis of hospital documents revealed that 281 members of the cohort (49.2 per cent) received a total of 592 in-patient admissions (averaging 1.04 per individual) over the course of the twenty-four months.[6] These included both voluntary admissions and formal certification, for purposes of both assessment and treatment, under the legislative authority of both the federal Criminal Code and the Ontario Mental Health Act. In total, 1145 patient-months were accumulated in mental institutions (an average of 2.0 months per subject).

In the aggregate, therefore, one out of every four months (or 25 per cent of the entire outcome term) was spent by subjects inside the walls of a correctional or psychiatric institution. Moreover, only 82 people in the entire cohort (14.4 per cent) escaped both carceral and therapeutic confinement. Of the remainder, 141 (24.7 per cent) were interned in both prison and hospital, 208 (36.4 per cent) were in prison only, and 140 (24.5 per cent) experienced only psychiatric institutionalization. Stated otherwise, among those subjects who were admitted as in-patients to mental hospitals during the two years following their METFORS BAU assessment, more than half were also sentenced to at least one term of imprisonment. For these people, the mental health system could scarcely be regarded as an alternative to prison.

Less intrusive modes of management and control were also a prominent feature of the 571 subjects' lives over the course of the two-year follow-up term. Of the 10,355 patient-months[7] passed in the community during the outcome period, 5584 months (53.9 per cent) were spent under the authority of a probation order.[8] As well, 160 of the subjects incurred a total of 223 out-patient or day-care referrals to psychiatric hospitals. This figure includes only the preliminary institutional referral – in many cases the out-patients were in virtually continuous contact with hospital personnel over the course of the follow-up period.

Finally, at the conclusion of the two-year outcome only 199 of 564 subjects (35.2 per cent) were under no form of confinement, supervision, or control.[9] Among the remainder, 198 (35.0 per cent) were on probation, 37 (6.5 per cent) in psychiatric institutions, 36 (6.4 per cent) in provincial prisons, 35 (6.2 per cent) in federal penitentiaries, 24 (4.2 per cent) in the community on bail, 15 (2.7 per cent) on psychiatric out-patient or day-care status, 11 (1.9 per cent) subject to parole or mandatory supervision, and 10 (1.8 per cent) held in pre-trial detention. Even after the passage of two years, the majority of METFORS subjects were still caught in the control orbit of medico-legal systems. Almost two-thirds of the people were subject to some form of therapeutic or carceral surveillance. More than one patient in five was still being held in prison or hospital.

In Table 6.2, the data on patient conduct and institutional experience are reconstructed, to generate an index of the relative incidence of violence and other behaviour per subject-year in the community, prisons, and hospitals. For all categories the number of officially registered incidents was

TABLE 6.2
Follow-up incidents by time spent in community, prison, and hospital

Location	Number of subjects in condition	Total months in condition	Type of incident	Number of subjects involved in incidents	Number of incidents	Mean incidents per subject/year
Community	538	10,355[a]	Recorded incidents	359	1,658	1.92
			Violent behaviours[b]	143	258	0.30
			Suicidal/self-injurious[c]	27	43	0.05
Criminal charges			Recorded incidents	312	1,332	1.54
			Violent behaviours[b]	126	213	0.25
			Suicidal/self-injurious[c]	0	0	0.00
Incidents leading to hospital			Recorded incidents	141	326	0.38
			Violent behaviours[b]	35	45	0.05
			Suicidal/self-injurious[c]	27	43	0.05
Prison	350	2,204	Recorded incidents	151	535	2.91
			Violent behaviours[b]	65	106	0.58
			Suicidal/self-injurious[c]	2	3	0.02
Hospital	281	1,145	Recorded incidents	122	423[d]	4.94[e]
			Violent behaviours[b]	64	138	1.45
			Suicidal/self-injurious[c]	33	54	0.57
All contexts	571	13,704	Recorded incidents	423	2,616	2.31[f]
			Violent behaviours[b]	191	502	0.44
			Suicidal/self-injurious[c]	60	100	0.09

a A slight overestimate of time spent in the community, since statistics on pre-trial remands in custody were unavailable. The 10,355 months in community include 5584 months spent by subjects on probation.
b Verbal threats of violence were not included.
c These included suicide attempts, threats, and self-inflicted injuries.
d For 121 subjects assessed immediately in the METFORS In-patient Unit (for a total of 118 months), only incidents involving violence or suicidal/self-injurious behaviour were coded.
e Calculated for a period of 1027 months (1145 less 118 months at METFORS where general incidents were not recorded).
f Calculated for a period of 13,586 months (13,704 less 118 months at METFORS where general incidents were not recorded).

divided by the number of patient-months spent in each context by all 571 subjects, then multiplied by a factor of 12 to arrive at the average frequency of annual occurrences per individual.

Substantial variations emerged among institutional and community settings. For example, psychiatric in-patients averaged 4.94 officially recorded incidents per annum (violent and otherwise), in contrast to 2.91 yearly misconducts among prison inmates and 1.92 occurrences in the community (1.54 leading to criminal charges, and 0.38 precipitating a contact with psychiatric authorities). These contextual differences were even more graphic when violent conduct only was considered. Hospital patients engaged in 1.45 'violent incidents' for every year of confinement, compared with an annual rate of 0.58 assaultive misconducts in prison and 0.30 violent occurrences in the community (for every six incidents in the latter category, five led to criminal charges and one to contact with psychiatric facilities). There was also a higher relative frequency of in-hospital suicidal or self-injurious conduct (0.57 per patient-year, versus 0.05 in the community and 0.02 in correctional settings). When these various rates were collapsed across all contexts, the overall annual incidence among the 571 METFORS subjects was 2.31 reported transactions, 0.44 occurrences of violent conduct, and 0.09 suicide attempts or self-induced injuries.

It would appear, then, that the 571 METFORS patients were especially 'dangerous' during their confinement in mental institutions. Yet it should be again noted that the majority of these in-hospital assaults were relatively transitory and innocuous in nature. In general, officially reported violence in mental hospitals was more frequent and less serious than violence on the streets. Assaults located in institutional settings were also more visible than community violence, and accordingly they were more susceptible to detection and reporting by authorities. The context-specific organization of official response may well be the primary determinant of these apparent differences in official rates of violence (see Bottomley and Coleman 1981; Ditton 1979; Lowman and Menzies 1986).

Forensic Roulette and the Phenomenon of Multiple Remands
The single most prominent feature of METFORS patient outcome careers was the recurrent imposition of forensic remands on a large proportion of the subject cohort. Of the 571 persons tracked over the two-year period, 138 (24.2 per cent) incurred a total of 229 subsequent in-patient or brief assessments (mean = 1.66 per repeat subject). These remands took place at either METFORS or other forensic agencies in southern Ontario. They

did *not* include the 193 immediate in-patient assessments associated with the original criminal charges (see Chapter 4) which were tabulated separately.

According to these figures, almost one Brief Assessment Unit subject in every four could expect at least one subsequent psychiatric remand from the criminal courts within the following two years. Seventeen of the METFORS patients were further assessed on three separate occasions; four persons received four follow-up evaluations; and two each were referred five and six times respectively during the twenty-four months. The median elapsed time between the original BAU assessment and the first subsequent remand was only 3.5 months (mean = 6.4). Clearly, the multiple forensic evaluation was an integral feature of the institutional experiences of METFORS patients. These repeated remands were commonplace, and they commonly took place within only a few months of their original Brief Assessment Unit appearance.

For courts and clinics alike, this proliferation of multiple remands was apparently condoned as a necessary response to changing individual patterns of psychopathology among forensic patients (see Soothill 1974). As the American Psychiatric Association has asserted, '[e]ven in consultation work, single or "one shot" examinations should be very much discouraged. Repeat remands allow the clinician to assess the patient in more than one environmental setting and aid in the distinguishing of situational contributions from characterological factors' (APA 1974: 32). This argument mirrors the medical model assumption that validity is an emergent product of recurrent imputations about mental disorder, criminality, and related pathological 'conditions.' It also implies that forensic labels are changeable, that subsequent medical classifications are largely autonomous from prior diagnoses.

In this section I will explore the implications of this reasoning, by examining the process of multiple remands as it affected the deviant careers of the METFORS patients. I argue that these repeated assessments function primarily to consolidate already existing labels and categories, and that they operate in the interests of justification rather than discovery (see Pfohl 1978). It will be seen that subsequent assessments provide retrospective legitimacy for prior medico-legal decisions – only rarely do they result in concrete revisions to diagnoses, identities, or institutional response.

In their justifications for invoking multiple remands at METFORS, the clinicians in this study frequently relied upon prior mental histories, linking these to the need for yet further psychiatric intervention into the lives of forensic patients. The subject in Case 252, for example, was originally remanded to the BAU in May 1978 after stealing a car. He received three weeks in prison for the offence. In August 1978 he was once again arrested for 'Theft Auto,' and remanded to METFORS. This time he was sentenced to three years' probation. After spending one month as an in-patient at the Lakeshore Psychiatric Hospital in Toronto, the subject was released, and proceeded to steal another car in November 1978, leading to yet another BAU assessment. On this appearance the METFORS psychiatrist requested and received from the court a Warrant of Remand mandating an extended evaluation in the facility's Inpatient Unit. The psychiatrist's letter to the presiding judge read: 'Because Mr. B. has been examined on three separate occasions at the METFORS Brief Assessment Unit as the result of three separate but similar incidents, it would appear that a more complete assessment may be of some assistance to the Court ... [I]t is clear that his antisocial behaviour has continued to date. This was noted in my report [in September] when I stated that, "without assistance, Mr. B.'s present lifestyle could recur in the future." ... It may be that the assessment will add little in resolving Mr. B.'s longstanding difficulties, nevertheless after 3 brief assessments I consider it appropriate that a full assessment be done in hospital' (PL3 252).

The subject was then confined in the METFORS Inpatient Unit for one month, and subsequently sentenced to six months' imprisonment (of which he served four months between January and May 1979). In October 1979, Mr. B. was again charged with Theft Auto! Two days later he found himself in the METFORS Brief Assessment Unit. As in all previous remands, the diagnosis was 'antisocial personality disorder.' He was returned to jail, received bail, and was still awaiting disposition when the study period ended.

For trouble cases of this kind, the circular process of reinstitutionalization could take on a momentum that led to further assessments, even when past diagnostic efforts had proved futile. In fact, evidence of prior clinical failures could actually be mustered to support recommendations for yet more medico-legal intervention. One forty-eight-year-old 'paranoid schizophrenic' had already received two brief assessments (both at MET-FORS) and four in-patient evaluations during the first fourteen months of the two-year outcome period. Following a further criminal charge – this time for 'Wilful Noncompliance With Terms of Probation' – he was again remanded to METFORS. On this visit (the seventh forensic contact in fourteen months), the METFORS psychiatrist certified the patient under the Ontario Mental Health Act in order to ensure still another in-patient remand (at the Queen Street Mental Health Centre), in a court letter that ironically seemed to provide ample testimony that no such compulsory assessment was needed:

Mr. J. had previously been seen in the Brief Assessment Unit at METFORS in August, 1978 and a letter was forwarded to [the judge] on that date.
In September, 1978 he was admitted to the Inpatient Unit at METFORS ...
In October, 1978 he was admitted to the Queen Street Mental Health Centre where he has been a patient on and off since 1956. A psychiatric report ... was forwarded to [the judge] by Dr. K.
In February, 1979 he was again seen in the Brief Assessment Unit and a copy of this letter is enclosed.

...

It is well documented that he suffers from chronic paranoid schizophrenia (my emphasis).

Our unanimous recommendation is that he be returned to the Queen Street Mental Health Centre for further assessment and treatment. At the end of his stay there a further report would be forwarded to the Court by Dr. K. and his staff. (PL3 330)

Even in the face of contradictory evidence, then, it was clearly possible for the METFORS clinicians to legitimize the repeated hospitalization of defendants for the purpose of forensic assessment. These patients became a recyclable commodity for distribution and consumption by medico-legal institutions. The subject populations in these agencies would decline substantially over time without the recurrent ingestion of a readily available pool of ongoing candidates for clinical assessment. Continued justification of scarce public resources and personnel, and official demonstrations of organizational utility, demanded that an identifiable population of forensic subjects be referred in periodic cycles for psychiatric evaluation.

Clinicians were also taking advantage of repeated remands to cement previous diagnoses of psychopathology and criminality, and to announce retrospectively the validity of earlier classifications. While subsequent decision-making was typically anchored in the categories of prior diagnoses, these new assessments could still have an additive effect on images of deviance that were being progressively built up around the subject's pivotal identity (Lofland 1969). Clinicians were able to mobilize each successive remand as a venue for the saturation of mental illness categories. The sheer volume of these characterizations, compiled chronologically, rendered them virtually impermeable to change.

In one typical case, the patient first arrived at METFORS on a charge of 'Indecent Telephone Calls.' At that time, the attending psychiatrist diagnosed the presence of schizophrenia and certified the subject to a closed ward at the Clarke Institute of Psychiatry in Toronto, where he spent the next twelve weeks. Four months after his release from hospital (having been sentenced to probation for the precipitating offence), he was arrested for 'Public Mischief' and 'Possession under $200,' and again remanded to the Brief Assessment Unit. The following is an excerpt from the psychologist's report on the occasion of this second remand:

During the interview situation Mr. R. was defiant and quietly insolent. Generally speaking, he refused to answer questions that were put to him, saying that he didn't know or repeating the same questions to one of the clinicians that was present. Essentially, he behaved in a hostile, challenging and passive-aggressive manner. Although he seemed genuinely disoriented with regard to his charges and the circumstances behind the present interview, it is unclear as to whether this disorientation is a reflection of a major mental illness or a function of his hostile and uncooperative attitude towards his assessment. I suspect that it is the latter ... It seems clear that this man, as well as having a history of a major mental illness, suffers from an explosive characterological disorder involving low impulse control, paranoid aggressivity and high potential for violent acting-out. I feel this man should be incarcerated in a maximum security mental health facility for further assessment and treatment. (POR2 467)

On the basis of this assessment, the subject was again remanded to the Clarke Institute, this time for three weeks, before being released on bail. Three months later, while still on bail, he was once more arrested on charges of 'Obscene Telephone Calls,' 'False Messages' and 'Being Unlawfully in a Dwelling House.' It was interesting to note the virtual interchangeability between the psychologist's reports yielded from these two brief assessments, which were chronologically separated by more than four months. Intervening events were apparently seen to corroborate the psychologist's earlier account of the patient's disorder, and this information was enlisted to establish retrospective validity:

During the interview, he gave signs of suffering from a major mental illness and having a personality disorder. That is, while he displayed loose associations, disorientation and tangentiality, he was also very hostile, passively and actively aggressive and highly manipulative mumbling his answers to questions in a monosyllabic manner, or not answering them at all. He often answered a question with another question. Initially, he refused to cooperate, but eventually did so to some extent when asked to leave. Even after this point, he supplied us with minimal information. It appears then that Mr. R. is a very angry, very disturbed young man, who suffers from a major mental illness in a basically antisocial personality. He has in the past spent much energy testing the limits and challenging authority. It seems that previous attempts of psychiatry to deal with his illness have failed. This factor, combined with his willful lack of regard for the rights of others, suggests that he may be suited at this time to proceed through the prison system. (POR3 467)

Following this assessment, the subject spent two weeks in jail, then was sentenced to one year of imprisonment, of which he served six months before being paroled. There were no further officially registered incidents during the final eight months from his parole date to the end of the two-year follow-up period.

Dangerousness was a central theme in subsequent assessments, as it was during the METFORS subjects' initial contacts with the pre-trial forensic system. In 27 out of 79 available court letters from *second* METFORS evaluations (34 per cent) the psychiatrist indicated to the judge that the individual was dangerous to others. Fifteen of 37 subjects on their *third* METFORS remand (41 per cent) were labelled as dangerous to others in the court letter. Subsequent forensic interviews appeared to evoke a hypersensitivity among clinicians to the potential for violence, given their subjects' failure to 'benefit' from previous contacts with psychiatry, and given these persons' apparent propensity for repeated entanglements with the law. Moreover, the METFORS classifiers were given the opportunity on these occasions to demonstrate longitudinal reliability in their evaluations of dangerousness, which seldom fluctuated from one remand to the next. Instead, the overall diagnostic pattern for most patients involved a progressive consolidation of apprehended potential for violence, as their personality 'structures' were seen to coagulate over the course of time.

For example, on his first appearance at METFORS, the subject in Case 080 was diagnosed as a 'chronic paranoid schizophrenic,' and was described as a 'very angry, uncommunicative, uncooperative man' (NR 080). On his return six months later following a subsequent arrest for indecent assault, the danger label had been much more firmly entrenched: 'Clinically, this man demonstrates much over-controlled hostility with very few internal controls. Very few individuals seen in the Brief Assessment Unit have impressed this examiner as being so imminently dangerous to others. It was this examiner's impression that if Mr. N. was allowed to continue the interview, he would have lashed out and hurt one or more people in the room' (POR2 080).

Another individual, on his third METFORS brief assessment (only seven months after the first), found his perceived dangerousness revised upwards, and his diagnosis modified from 'manic depressive' to 'paranoid,' after protesting his persecution at the hands of authorities. 'He says that he has spent 18 days in jail illegally and that we are coming into a police state. He says that judges and police are always after him and trying to push him into obtaining welfare and going into hostels. He says that his reputation has been badly damaged. He indicated that Dr. G.'s previous reports have been damaging to him.' (SWR3 481); 'All our staff agreed that he is suffering from Paranoid Psychosis ... [H]is behaviour is therefore difficult to control ... Under these circumstances, our recommendation therefore is that he be sent to the Oak Ridge Unit at Penetang for a further period of assessment and treatment' (PL3 481).

On only one occasion did the repeated assessment result in an apparent 'softening' of the initial psychiatric depiction. This case demonstrated the clinicians' ability to substitute psychiatric labels when they suspected that a radical discrepancy between original diagnoses and subsequent conduct might threaten professional legitimacy. Under these circumstances the experts were induced to modify their original ascription to sustain the credibility of their diagnosis. A nineteen-year-old black woman was initially assessed at the METFORS BAU in August 1978 on a charge of 'Theft Auto.' Throughout the brief assessment the subject displayed erratic behaviour, striking one of the correctional officers, openly masturbating in the holding cell, verbally abusing the staff members, slamming doors, and dousing one of the clinicians with a glass of milk. The Brief Assessment Unit psychiatrist arrived at a diagnosis of 'acute psychosis,' and certified her involuntarily to St Thomas Psychiatric Hospital where she was confined for a month.

Prior to the judicial disposition of the original charge, the subject was again arrested (for possession of marijuana) in late September 1978, and remanded to METFORS. This time she presented an entirely different profile to the clinical team. It became apparent that her earlier demeanour had been a product of drug use rather than functional psychosis as originally thought. The patient was re-diagnosed as an 'antisocial personality disorder' and classified as dangerous. Further, the psychiatrist reported that the subject's hospital stay had been directly responsible for curing her apparent psychotic disorder. The court letter read: 'At the time she was seen in August Dr. C. and the team diagnosed her as having an unspecified psychosis and needing inpatient management .. Today the picture is much improved, in that this young lady has improved considerably following her stay in the Whitby Psychiatric Hospital ... As far as her psychosis is concerned ... she has improved sufficiently to be now fit ... to receive whatever sentence the court may choose to dispense. ... We consider that she is possibly a dangerous young woman in that she can get herself involved in activities which can harm a lot of people. We also felt that her dangerousness can be increased with the use of drugs and alcohol most of which she has acknowledged she has used to a great extent despite her relatively tender years' (PL2 356).

Following this second BAU assessment the subject was placed on bail until further charges of 'Assault Police' and 'Contempt of Court'[10] were laid in June 1979, and she was again remanded to METFORS. By this time the 'psychosis' label had been thoroughly expunged from her forensic profile, and the patient's personality disorder, drug abuse, and dangerousness had become the defining framework for the assessment process:

Ms. T. shows no indications of a major mental illness at this time. Her examination at this time supports the diagnosis of a personality disorder of the explosive type with anti-social features. By this one means a recurrent pattern of low tolerance to frustration, impulsivity, and explosive outbursts both verbally and physically with minimal provocation with a tendency to appear in a normal or rational state in between explosive outbursts ... Ms. T. is considered to be a potentially explosive individual and at such times as she is undergoing an explosive outburst would be considered a danger to others. (PL3 356).

By emphasizing the periodicity of the patient's 'explosivity,' the psychiatrist artfully explained away the initial erroneous diagnosis as the product of 'bad timing,' and he simultaneously conveyed a symbolically powerful message to the criminal court about the subject's potential for assaultiveness. Ms T. was sentenced to two months' imprisonment for 'Contempt of Court,' and to four months' prison plus eighteen months' probation for 'Assault Police.'

Finally, on infrequent occasions the METFORS clinicians could themselves demonstrate a sensitivity to the inefficacy of multiple assessments; yet even here they tended to ascribe such difficulties to the recalcitrance of subjects, rather than to the eccentricities of psycholegal systems and officials. One patient was initially remanded to the Brief Assessment Unit on charges of 'Theft Under' and 'Assault with Intent to Resist Arrest.' He was diagnosed as a 'simple schizophrenic,' and recommended for a protracted evaluation because he 'presented a confusing picture during the examination' (PL 499). After spending seven weeks in the METFORS Inpatient Unit, he was returned to court and the criminal charges were withdrawn. Seven days later the subject was again charged, this time for 'Common Assault,' 'Theft Under,' and 'Public Mischief.' He was once more remanded by the court to MET-FORS for a brief assessment, where he refused to comply with the evaluation process. This time the psychiatrist wrote: '[I]n the interview situation ..., Mr. I. was totally mute and uncooperative and refused to answer any questions from anyone. This is despite the fact that he knew [the BAU psychologist] and indeed they had quite a therapeutic relationship for a fair period of time during his [earlier] stay in the METFORS Unit. It appears therefore that we have nothing further to add to the [earlier] letter' (PL2 499).

Through the following twelve months this subject was arrested on three more occasions, for theft, causing a disturbance and assorted liquor and motor vehicle violations. He was remanded for another forty-five-day hospitalization in the METFORS In-patient Unit, where his prior diagnosis of schizophrenia was again confirmed. He was sentenced to one month of incarceration after being returned to the court.

Finally, twenty months after the original BAU assessment, the man was charged with 'Theft,' 'Possession of Stolen Goods,' and 'Failure to Appear.' Predictably, he was again transferred to METFORS, where the BAU psychiatrist recommended carceral confinement, writing: 'Mr. I. is well known to us, having been an outpatient at our facilities on two occasions as well as receiving several outpatient psychiatric assessments. He shows clear evidence of schizophrenia ... Despite this man's psychiatric history, this man's antisocial behaviour is likely to persist whether he is actively mentally ill or not ... We would recommend that a period of incarceration in a correctional setting is indicated' (PL4 499). The subject was still awaiting sentencing at the end of the two-year follow-up period.

During some assessments the METFORS clinicians did at least indirectly acknowledge the diminishing returns of inappropriate psychiatric referrals. The second psychiatric letter in Case 121, written eighteen months after the original BAU appearance, was illustrative of remands that simply underlined prior recommendations: 'Mr. U. had been previously examined in our Brief Assessment Unit for the Court in June of 1978. At that time the final diagnosis was that of an explosive personality disorder complicated by drug dependence and he was not considered then to be a suitable candidate for psychiatric treatment despite obvious problems associated with his personality ... On examination almost the identical picture was found today as was reported by me in June of 1978' (PL2 121).

When repeated remands were seen to endanger the legitimacy of forensic officials and practices, members could sometimes even overtly reject the need for further evaluation. Following one patient's third METFORS assessment in seventeen months, the attending psychologist registered his frustration at the individual's intransigence, and advocated the long-term withdrawal of forensic services. The repeated recycling of this subject was seen by the writer as a function of individual pathology rather than institutional inertia: 'At the present time, the patient appears to have little to gain from exposure to clinical services. Certainly she has had ample opportunity in the past to engage herself in treatment. Accordingly, it is recommended that this woman not be returned for assessment for a period of several years' (POR3 044).

In summary, multiple assessments figured prominently in the institutional experiences of METFORS subjects. These subsequent forensic remands provided psychiatric and judicial authorities with an important resource for the reproduction and enhancement of labels about mental illness and criminality. They allowed a recycling of 'significant' knowledge between clinic and court, and in the process they were a catalyst for recurrent demonstrations of diagnostic validity. But apart from their legitimizing functions, subsequent forensic assessments added little to the stock of medico-legal knowledge about criminal defendants. Repeated remands usually resulted in simple reaffirmations of taken-for-granted labels and categories (Douglas 1971: 119). Over the course of time, the multiple assessments of METFORS subjects contributed to the truncation and distortion of their psycholegal reality.

Assessing the Validity of Clinical Prognostications
This section focuses on the accuracy of METFORS expert predictions about the future criminal, violent, and self-injurious behaviour of BAU subjects. As noted in Chapters 3 and 5, psycholegal predictions of future dangerousness to self (Daley 1987; Rosen 1954) and others (Ennis and Litwack 1974; Menzies 1986; Menzies, Webster, and Sepejak 1985a, b; Monahan 1981; Pfohl 1978; Webster and Menzies 1987; Warren 1979; Webster, Ben-Aron, and Hucker 1985) have proved to be notoriously imprecise. Even the most sophisticated research has failed to crack the 0.40 'sound barrier' correlation between statistical or clinical predictions and subsequent violent conduct (Menzies, Webster, and Sepejak 1985b; see Arthur 1971: 544;

Monahan 1981: 64–65; Sarbin 1986). Forensic decision-makers are unable to separate the populations of 'dangerous' or 'endangered' subjects from other groups with any degree of coherence or consistency (Conrad 1985). Moreover, these expert forecasts systematically err in the direction of overprediction, through the recurrent identification of potential criminality or violence in persons who present no such risk (Peay 1982; Steadman and Morrissey 1981). Even the American Psychiatric Association has long conceded the futility of clinical work in this area (APA 1974).

The forensic prediction of criminality and violence is beset with a variety of intractable problems. Apart from a few relevant factors such as age and prior violence (Steadman and Cocozza 1974; Thornberry and Jacoby 1979), most of the variables employed in these efforts are superfluous and have little predictive value. As Holt asserts, '[n]o matter how impressively high it is piled, garbage remains garbage' (1978: 12). Even worse, the low base rates of violence in most forensic populations militate against predictive accuracy. The most valid aggregate forecast is always that *no one* will be involved in future criminality or violence (Steadman 1981). Lastly, statistical prediction models fail to account for the 'social ecology of violence' (Geis and Monahan 1976; Steadman 1981). Deviant and dangerous behaviour is conditioned by a confusing and contradictory blend of social forces, contextual arrangements, transactions with potential victims, and a range of related environmental stimuli. Situations are even less amenable to prediction than are character 'traits' (Megargee 1976). Such transitory processes simply cannot be addressed adequately in medico-legal diagnoses, or in prediction equations yielded from prior events and the individual attributes of forensic subjects.

Yet, as the METFORS research has amply documented, the prediction of dangerousness and related deviant conduct continues to be a prominent feature of forensic classification work. Almost one-third of defendants arrived in the Brief Assessment Unit already earmarked as dangerous in the accompanying police report (Chapter 2); diagnostic activities in the BAU were systematically focused on the identification of potential violence (Chapter 3); more than 50 per cent of psychiatric letters requesting in-patient remands openly cited dangerousness as a clinical assessment issue (Chapter 4); and almost one patient in every four was classified as dangerous in METFORS letters distributed to the presiding court judge (Chapter 5).

These findings parallel a general movement throughout the medico-legal system toward a 'renaissance' of dangerousness (Bottoms 1977), and toward the increasing enlistment of clinical professionals to justify carceral or therapeutic detention on the basis of a presumed potential for future violence. Despite the impressive body of socio-legal evidence on the dangers of such trends, dangerousness prediction has become a fixed component of such widely diverse medico-legal practices as psychiatric referrals by police, the granting of bail, civil commitment proceedings, dangerous offender and sex psychopath determinations, parole hearings, mental hospital discharges, and even the decision to execute offenders convicted of capital crimes (Dix 1981; Hiday 1983; Petrunik 1983; Robitscher 1980; Shah 1978; Warren 1982).

The evaluation of dangerousness prediction at METFORS begins with a look at the relationship between METFORS patient attributes and subsequent conduct. Table 6.3 presents a series of bivariate statistics equating twenty-four background variables with three criterion measures: the total number of incidents officially recorded against each subject during the two-year outcome period, the number of violent incidents during follow-up, and the number of suicide attempts/threats/self-inflicted injuries. Included are only those t and F statistics that are significant at a 0.05 level or greater, and only those correlation coefficients above an absolute value of 0.10.

To begin, the subsequent self-inflicted injuries and suicidal gestures of METFORS patients were not highly correlated with their background characteristics. Only five of twenty-four variables were significantly associated with this outcome measure (previous suicide attempt, absence of prior violence, presence of hallucinations, depressed or psychotic behaviour in the BAU, and psychiatric diagnosis).

In contrast, a total of sixteen variables were related to the frequency of generally recorded incidents during follow-up, and fifteen to outcome violent occurrences. Only the latter variable is considered here in detail. Those background attributes with apparent relationship to violent outcome were: previous incarceration, prior violence, employment at arrest, juvenile court record, presence of hallucinations, presence of delusions, behaviour in the BAU, marital status, living status, diagnosis, level of drug use, age, number of prior convictions, years of education, and number of previous psychiatric hospitalizations. In contrast, the incidence of violence during the twenty-four month follow-up was *not* statistically dependent upon gender, prior suicide attempt, occupation, race, place of origin, court disposition, estimated IQ, or level of alcohol use.

In Table 6.4, variables from Table 6.3 displaying significant t and F statistics on the outcome violence criterion are disaggregated by category. According to the group means from t tests, the most frequent violent offenders during follow-up were those who: had a history of incarceration;

TABLE 6.3
Associations between background variables and two-year follow-up behaviour

	Number of recorded incidents			Number of violent incidents			Number of suicide threats/attempts/self-injuries		
	t	df	p	t	df	p	t	df	p
Gender	2.01	569	.045				4.23	569	<.001
Prior suicide attempt	3.04	569	.003	3.52	569	.001			
Previous incarceration	3.32	569	.001	5.47	569	.001	−2.00	569	.046
Prior violence	3.63	568	<.001	2.36	568	.018			
Employed at arrest	4.40	562	<.001	2.80	562	.005			
Juvenile court record	2.38	568	.018	3.15	568	.002			
Hallucinations				2.78	568	.006	3.04	568	.002
Delusions									
	F	df	p	F	df	p	F	df	p
Behaviour in BAU	7.77	5,564	<.001	9.98	5,564	<.001	2.74	5,564	.019
Occupation	5.03	3,558	.002						
Race									
Place of origin	5.40	5,565	<.001	3.69	5,565	.003			
Marital status	6.84	4,565	<.001	3.76	4,565	.005			
Living status									
Current charge	2.85	5,564	.015	2.49	5,564	.030	2.58	5,564	.025
Diagnosis									
Disposition									

	Pearson r	Pearson r
Estimated IQ		
Level of alcohol use		
Level of drug use	.225	.125
Age	-.206	-.114
Number of prior convictions	.169	.194
Years of education	-.114	-.188
Number of prior hospitalizations	.107	.150

Note: The *t* statistic was generated for dichotomous background variables, *F* for non-metric variables with three or more categories, and *r* for metric variables. Only significant results are shown for *t* and *F* statistics. Only Pearson coefficients above |.10| are included. *N* = 571.

TABLE 6.4
Significant breakdowns: total number of outcome violent incidents by background variables.

t Statistics

	No		Yes					
	Mean	N	Mean	N	t	df	p	
Previous incarceration	0.69	313	1.25	279	3.65	590	<.001	
Prior violence	0.54	307	1.40	285	5.71	590	<.001	
Employed at arrest	1.05	441	0.65	150	-2.25	589	.005	
Juvenile court record	0.80	423	1.27	162	2.98	583	.003	
Hallucinations	0.86	505	1.53	86	3.13	589	.002	
Delusions	0.85	450	1.29	141	2.46	589	.014	

Analysis of variance

	Mean	N	F	df	p	Beta/R
Behaviour in BAU			9.09	5,585	<.001	.268
Pleasant/co-operative	0.63	249				
Depressed/despondent	0.64	150				
Angry/hostile	1.70	74				
Psychotic/delusions	1.36	96				
Refused to co-operate	1.70	10				
Violent/acted out	2.91	12				

			Mean	N		
Marital status			3.52	5,586	.004	.171
Single	1.18	364				
Separated	0.89	72				
Divorced	0.50	52				
Widowed	0.90	10				
Cohabiting	0.31	38				
Married	0.43	56				
Living status			3.32	4,586	.011	.149
With parents	0.91	105				
With 2nd family/friends	0.48	117				
Alone	0.99	207				
No fixed address	1.35	125				
Institution	0.97	37				
Diagnosis			3.42	5,585	.005	.168
None–neurosis	0.43	90				
Psychosis	1.10	150				
Sex disorder	0.26	15				
Mental retardation/organic	1.51	37				
Alcohol/drugs	0.74	108				
Personality disorder	1.15	191				

had committed violence in the past; were unemployed at the time of arrest; had a juvenile court record; displayed hallucinations during the BAU assessment; and were considered delusional. Similarly, cell means from analysis of variance demonstrated a higher incidence of follow-up violence among those defendants who: acted out, were angry or hostile, or uncooperative while in the BAU; were unmarried at the time of the original assessment; had no fixed address or lived alone; and were diagnosed by psychiatrists as mentally retarded or organically disordered (those with sexual disorders, in contrast, recorded the lowest average incidence of outcome violence).

In general, the METFORS patients' propensity for future assaultiveness was associated with an array of clinical, legal, and demographic attributes. Yet no definitive patterns emerged from these analyses. Even the most powerful single predictor variables (prior violence, behaviour in the facility, number of previous convictions) could each explain only 5 or 6 per cent of the variance in levels of assaultiveness during the next two years. Such results were useless for the purpose of clinical prediction. The associations were simply too tenuous to merit incorporation into the individual case judgments of Brief Assessment Unit team members. Moreover, given the weak bivariate relationships demonstrated here between background and outcome variables, the generation of multivariate regression and discriminant equations based on even the best of these findings could only marginally enhance predictive efforts. Although a number of such procedures were attempted using violent follow-up incidents as the dependent variable, none was able to account for more than 12 per cent of the variance, and hence the results did not warrant further attention (see Menzies and Webster 1987; Menzies, Webster, and Sepejak 1985b).

The limitations of these background-outcome relationships are in accord with conclusions drawn from other studies. With the possible exception of Kozol, Boucher, and Garofalo (1972) researchers have been unanimous in finding little support for dangerousness predictions based on the demographic or medico-legal attributes of patients. The incorporation of such 'objective' indicators into forensic forecasts is a clear example of what Gottfredson (1971) has called a 'narrow band' process of decision-making. Models based on actuarial equations, and quantitative scores constructed from medico-legal criteria, have achieved little, other than to further legitimize an invalid practice. These endeavours are necessarily undermined by the very nature of medico-legal knowledge. Actuarial predictions of this kind naively attempt to relate the situational formulations of forensic clinicians to other distant past and future constructions produced indexically and reflexively by other enforcement officials, all under the rubric of objective statistical measurement. It is small wonder that such work consistently fails. As Diamond suggests, the marshalling of actuarial measures for clinical prediction becomes a dangerous justification for prognostications that are always intuitive, and usually wrong: '[I]t would be difficult for an objective observer to take such claims seriously if such pseudo-scientific descriptions had not been reiterated so often that they had become part of the accepted mythology of clinical practice' (Diamond 1974: 443).

Following this look at the relationship between METFORS patient characteristics and their officially recorded follow-up conduct, it remains to consider the accuracy of the actual clinical predictions offered by Brief Assessment Unit team members. With the use of the one-page summary forms completed independently by psychiatrists and other BAU members after each interview (See Appendix A, Chapters 1 and 3), a direct comparison between dangerousness predictions and subsequent violence was made possible. Whereas other research has also measured the accuracy of overt clinical predictions (cf. Kozol, Boucher, and Garofalo 1972; Mullen and Reinehr 1982; Steadman and Cocozza 1978; Steadman and Morrissey 1981), this study had the twin advantages of incorporating decision-making instruments designed solely for research purposes and of employing metric prediction variables (on a five-point scale: 1 = no; 2 = low; 3 = questionable; 4 = medium; 5 = high) instead of forced-choice 'yes/no' dichotomies.

The level of association between BAU predictions of dangerousness to others in future and both the total number of recorded follow-up incidents and the number of violent transactions was first measured for the five clinical occupations, by aggregating cases across all members of each profession. The resulting correlation coefficients are presented in Table 6.5. Clearly, none of the professions as a group was able to forecast the total number of follow-up incidents. In the specific prediction of violence, they fared only slightly better, with Pearson coefficients ranging from 0.18 (psychiatrists) to 0.05 (social workers). The prediction-outcome correlation attained by psychiatrists – the most 'successful' group – accounted for a meagre 3 per cent of explained variance for subsequent violent conduct. Subsequent violent conduct was apparently even less closely aligned with clinical predictions than it was with the background attributes of the METFORS subjects.

A corollary issue concerned the relative ability of individual Brief Assessment Unit clinicians to forecast the future violence of accused persons. As indicated in Table 6.5, the total number of registered outcome incidents

TABLE 6.5

Pearson correlation coefficients between clinical predictions and outcome conduct

	INC	VIOL	N
Psychiatrists	.064	.182	571
Psychiatrist 1	.033	.110	234
Psychiatrist 2	.012	.229	128
Psychiatrist 3	.145	.260	148
Psychiatrist 4	.022	.232	61
Psychologists	.090	.167	496
Psychologist 1	.042	.185	225
Psychologist 2	.070	.129	132
Psychologist 3	.118	.163	139
Social workers	−.034	.051	422
Social Worker 1	−.009	.045	357
Social Worker 2	−.097	.104	357
Social Worker 3	−.074	.335	37
Nurses	−.086	.071	569
Nurse 1	−.052	.069	492
Nurse 2	−.153	.240	31
Nurse 3	−.110	.387	13
Nurse 4	.343	.575	11
Correctional officers	.041	.146	546
Correctional Officer 1	.052	.149	58
Correctional Officer 2	.014	.103	74
Correctional Officer 3	.105	.144	22
Correctional Officer 4	−.010	.260	17
Correctional Officer 5	−.099	−.001	84
Correctional Officer 6	.125	.193	84
Correctional Officer 7	.219	.272	87
Correctional Officer 8	−.059	−.059	82

Note: Clinicians involved in fewer than ten assessments were excluded from the analysis. INC = number of recorded incidents during follow-up. VIOL = number of recorded violent incidents during follow-up.

was no more amenable to prediction by individuals than it had been by the aggregated professional groups, with only Nurse 4 ($r = 0.219$) and Correctional Officer 7 ($r = 0.219$) demonstrating any prognostic powers. For predictions of overtly violent occurrences, the variation of accuracy within each clinical discipline was minimal. For example, prediction-outcome coefficients for the four psychiatrists were respectively 0.110, 0.229, 0.260, and 0.232; Psychiatrist 1 alone departed marginally from the general performance level. While some minor variation was detected within other disciplines, these differences were relatively meaningless in real terms. Just three individuals (Social Worker 3, Nurse 3, and Nurse 4) were able to account for more than 8 per cent of the outcome variance in predicting patient violence. Only one cracked the 'forensic sound barrier' of 0.40 – Nurse 4, who participated in only eleven assessments, and whose seemingly impressive coefficient of 0.575 was most likely the result of sampling error.

Table 6.6 introduces one further nuance to the analysis, by tracing the changes in success rates of psychiatrists' predictions of violence as the outcome period was extended respectively from one month to three months, six months, one year, and finally the entire two years. This exercise illustrates the impact of changing base rates on predictive accuracy according to different lengths of follow-up.

The first section of Table 6.6 indicates that the Pearson correlations between psychiatrists' predictions and the frequency of later patient violence increased across each successive chronological stage, from 0.101 (one-month follow-up) to 0.182 (two-year follow-up). However, the relative improvement appeared to decline by the end of the first year following the BAU assessment, and psychiatrists were only marginally better at predicting violence over a period of two years as opposed to twelve months ($r = 0.182$ and 0.170 respectively).

These relative improvements in success rates over time were coincidental with changing patterns of hits, false positives, and false negatives. The second part of Table 6.6 collapses the original psychiatric predictions into two categories ('no/low' and 'medium/high'), and dichotomizes subjects into 'violent' and 'non-violent' classes for each of the five follow-up time segments. Results clearly show a dramatic increase in base rates of violence throughout the course of the longitudinal outcome term. After one month, only 25 of 571 METFORS subjects (5.0 per cent) had engaged in violent conduct. The subsequent frequencies were: 64 after three months (13.0 per cent), 97 after six months (19.7 per cent), 145 after one year (29.4 per cent), and 196 after two years (39.7 per cent).[11]

The relative distribution of accurate and erroneous predictions was closely associated with these changing base rates. The proportion of 'high hits' (confirmed predictions of violence) increased from 4 to 25 per cent. Similarly, 'false negatives' (invalid predictions of non-violence) rose from 1 to 15 per cent. In contrast, over 48 per cent of patients were 'low hits' after one month, compared with 34 per cent after two years. And the false positives (those incorrectly predicted to be violent) declined from 271 to 128. Expressed as a ratio, the absolute numbers of false positives incurred for each accurate prediction of dangerousness were as follows: 12.8 after

TABLE 6.6
Changes in accuracy of psychiatrists' predictions of violence by length of follow-up

	One month		Three months		Six months		One year		Two years	
Pearson correlations*										
Coefficient	.101		.103		.133		.170		.182	
Significance level	.008		.007		.001		<.001		<.001	
	No.	%	No.	%	No.	%	No.	%	No.	%
Cross-tabulations†										
False negatives	7	1.4	23	4.7	36	7.3	50	10.1	75	15.2
False positives	231	46.9	208	42.2	188	38.1	154	31.2	128	26.0
Low hits	237	48.1	221	44.8	208	42.2	194	39.4	169	34.3
High hits	18	3.6	41	8.3	61	12.4	95	19.3	121	24.5
Chi-square	4.00		4.80		6.80		17.67		15.67	
Significance level	.045		.028		.009		<.0001		<.0001	

* Psychiatrist prediction of dangerousness by number of violent incidents ($N = 571$).

† 2×2 table, 1 degree of freedom, $N = 493$.
For prediction variable: 'No' or 'Low' dangerousness = 1st category; 'medium' or 'high' dangerousness = 2nd category; 'unclear' responses were deleted.
For outcome variable: no violent incidents = 1st category; one or more violent incidents = 2nd category.

one month, 5.1 after three months, 3.1 after six months, 1.6 after one year, and 1.1 after two years.

The length of follow-up term thus had an obvious impact on the validity of clinical predictions about future violent occurrences among the METFORS patients. The accuracy of these predictions increased as the ratio of 'false positives' to 'high hits' diminished over time. None the less, these findings could hardly be offered as support for the validity of forensic predictions of dangerousness. To the contrary, even at the end of a full two years, within a subject population which perpetrated relatively high base rates of violence (compare Quinsey 1979; Soothill, Way, and Gibbens 1980; Steadman and Cocozza 1974; Thornberry and Jacoby 1979), there were more false positives than high hits. When the METFORS Brief Assessment Unit psychiatrists predicted that their patients would be dangerous in future, they were wrong more than half of the time. Conversely, 169 of 244 psychiatric predictions of 'no' or 'low' dangerousness in the BAU (69.3 per cent) were corroborated by patients who remained officially non-violent for a full two years after assessment. Even among a METFORS cohort that generated a 40 per cent base rate over twenty-four months, the best prediction was that *none* of these subjects would ever commit a violent act. This generic judgment would have resulted in 196 mistakes, compared with the 203 wrongful predictions of violence recorded by the Brief Assessment Unit psychiatrists.

WHAT IS TO BE DONE ABOUT FORENSIC ASSESSMENTS?

A number of strands may now be drawn together. This book has described the decision-making practices of forensic clinicians in assessing criminal defendants suspected of mental disorder. Psychiatrists and other mental health professionals at METFORS were in the business of applying deviant labels to accused persons. They were engaged by the courts primarily to assist in the criminal sentencing process. In their role as medico-legal classifiers, clinicians were only incidentally involved in the pursuit of therapeutic goals. Their main concentration was frankly legalistic, and the 592 forensic subjects processed at METFORS during 1978 were exposed to discretionary judgments that closely resembled those occurring at other stations along the criminal justice corridor. Even in the clinic, the careers of these people were being shaped by traditional penal models that relied on conceptions of responsibility, retribution, and moral order. Psychiatry, as a powerful system of knowledge, was used by medico-legal authorities as a catalyst for the deployment of legal control, for the scientification of criminal court decisions (Ericson and Shearing 1986), and for the mutual legitimation of clinical and judicial decision-makers.

The activities of the METFORS clinicians need to be contextualized within the wider domain of this criminal justice/mental health complex. Like all legal authorities, these psychiatric professionals were continuously adapting to an institutional environment from which they were only partially autonomous, and over which they could command at best a finite degree of understanding and control. Brief Assessment Unit and Inpatient team members were immersed within organizational surroundings that both facilitated and constrained their classification work. Much of what went on at METFORS was the outcome of clinical strategies developed to manage this institutional environment. Given their fragile connections to the criminal courts, and given their occupational objective to supply judges with legally relevant reports, members were justifiably concerned with maintaining legitimacy and accountability for judicial audiences.

Like organizational knowledge circulating throughout the crime control enterprise, the forensic documents produced by these clinicians were used to promote images of authority, expertise, and moral order. They systematically refracted the myriad identities of subjects and the intricate process of clinical assessment into routine and recognizable scripts that invoked desired legal outcomes. This distillation of psychiatric appearance into judicial reality was an ongoing feature of forensic decision-making at METFORS. Yet, as chronicled throughout this book, it was infused with conflict and contradiction.

Psychiatrists and other team members were constantly alert to the power of legal officials to reject, ignore, or otherwise neutralize their descriptions and explanations of pathology and criminality, in much the same fashion that the clinicians themselves were exercising editorial control over the accounts of patients. Judges and prosecutors still maintained their central command over the dispositional process. In order to fulfil judicial objectives and hence to assume their share of legal power that was being distributed outwards by the courts, forensic classifiers needed to tread a constantly shifting and treacherous course. On the one hand, they continually faced the prospect of forfeiting their usefulness for the projects of criminal authorities. On the other, in demonstrating legal relevancy they risked sacrificing their mental-health identity altogether.

However, in their strategies for maintaining an equilibrium between these opposing forces, forensic professionals at METFORS were able to tap a deep reservoir of resources that enhanced control over knowledge and subjects. They routinely expropriated the accounts of other officials such as the police, reproducing these in their own categories and discourse, and thereby assuming jurisdiction over medico-legal cases (Christie 1977). They subjected criminal defendants to mini-trials of deviant identity, compiling reports in which legal, psychiatric, and moral denunciations were effectively merged. They laid claim to expert knowledge about the causes of crime and the character of mental illness, couching their accounts in language tailored to exhibit the scientific trappings of their diagnostic practices. Liberal use was made of psychometric instruments which underscored the professed technical features of mental health labels. Informants were recruited from among the families and friends of subjects, in efforts to extend the diagnostic orbit beyond the walls of medico-legal institutions. Inpatients were placed under nearly continuous surveillance by line staff, and their conduct and utterances were selectively charted to cement already existing deviant categories. These depictions were presented to courts as the consensual products of scientific methodologies. Evidence of dispute and conflict was expunged from official documents and psychiatric letters, and the METFORS reports regularly prescribed punitive outcomes that were consistently endorsed by criminal judges. The labels applied by forensic classifiers displayed an extraordinary degree of resiliency and longevity throughout the course of the subsequent institutional careers of the 571 METFORS subjects. In the final analysis, despite their contradictory relationship to the legal apparatus, the clinicians in this study were eminently successful in applying these and other strategies to engineer desired results. As documented throughout this book, their forensic versions of reality were seldom either challenged or modified as the METFORS patients were longitudinally processed through the medico-legal complex.

Intrinsic to all of these organizational strategies was the overarching role of science as a power tool for the METFORS clinicians, and by extension for the legal system more generally (see Ericson and Shearing 1986; Gusfield 1981). Forensic professionals in this study were able to translate the idiom of science into a discourse that paralleled and intensified the authority of law. One of the remarkable features of classification work at METFORS was the reliance on scientific categories and discourse as both an ideological instrument for legitimacy and a pragmatic resource to bring off desired outcomes. Members were able to invoke claims to scientific knowledge and technologies as a strategy for establishing their own status and for securing the compliance of others in managing mental cases. They brandished scientific rationality as a modality of power, in the same sense that formal legal rationality is used elsewhere in the system to reinforce the control work of judicial and carceral authorities. Since they appeared to subscribe to benevolent mandates embodied in the medical model, and since their accounts were framed in the enabling language of psychiatry, clinicians were able to conceal the subjective, moralistic, and idiosyncratic features of their discretionary judgments. For their part, judges and other legal officials routinely endorsed these decisions, since they appeared to satisfy the twin criteria of scientific methodology and legal relevancy.

As this final chapter has described, the discourse of science was especially salient to clinical depictions of criminality and dangerousness at METFORS. Despite the legion of research attesting to the prognostic limitations of clinical decision-makers (Menzies 1986; Monahan 1981; Steadman and Cocozza 1974; Warren 1979; Webster, Ben-Aron, and Hucker 1985; Webster and Menzies 1987), the prediction of violence was and remains a focal objective in METFORS assessments. In the peculiar alchemy of forensic discretion, clinical authority is largely founded upon a task at which practitioners are alarmingly inept. Yet decisions about criminality and dangerousness continue. Prognostications about violence provide a powerful adhesive to the fractious relationship between clinics and courts. They permit a displacement of criminal causes from the structural and social ecology of violence to the individual pathology of violent offenders. They yield a justifying discourse for the containment and control of legal subjects, even when no prior violence has been observed. Most important, they incorporate the justifying rhetoric of medical science into judicial decisions about 'dangerous' persons, with the attendant implication that experts can reliably distinguish the dangerously disordered from the merely mad. As Foucault writes: 'What, then, is the role of the psychiatrist in legal matters? He is not an expert in responsibility, but an advisor on punishment; it is up to him to say whether the subject is "dangerous," in what way one should be protected from him, how one should interfere to alter him, whether it would be better to try to force him into submission or to treat him' (Foucault 1977: 22).

Through their reinforcement of traditional carceral values, forensic psychiatrists and allied clinicians have assisted in the circulation of many familiar themes in the public response to crime and violence. By professing special expertise in the identification and treatment of madness, criminality, and violence, mental health professionals have summoned forth a litany of positivistic ideals that advance the individualization of punishment and the primacy of social defence in the control culture.

With the decline of the 'therapeutic state' (Kittrie 1971) during the 1970s and 1980s, and with the attendant emergence of a 'post-therapeutic state' grounded in classical values of social order, deterrence, and retributive justice (Menzies and Boyd 1983), psychiatry has undergone a dramatic transformation in its relationship to the legal process. Forensic practitioners have become alienated from the rehabilitative ideal, and have instead become experts in the classification of criminals and the detection of pathology and danger. As documented throughout this book, the METFORS clinicians selectively invoked medical categories and criteria primarily as a strategic resource, to legitimize decisions that were essentially punitive in style and function. Their residual concern with curing mental illness was secondary to their preoccupation with public protectionism and legal sanctions.

For their part, the 592 METFORS subjects were the targets of a psycholegal control enterprise that tended to obscure the exculpatory features of mental illness. Their psychiatric pathologies were used as a rationale not for diminished responsibility or diversion out of the criminal justice system, but instead for intensified control initiatives that galvanized medical and legal ordering processes. Against the background of a converging metasystem of surveillance and constraint, forensic patients at METFORS and elsewhere have become the subjects of a crime control apparatus that paradoxically uses madness to demonstrate criminality, and therapy to extend and justify punishment. The medico-legal complex has itself become a truly Darwinian world in which only the sane can survive, at least as survival happens to be defined by those in power.

At the level of professional practice, disciplinary boundaries throughout the transcarceral system have become increasingly blurred (Lowman, Menzies, and Palys 1987), as judicial, health and welfare officials, helping and control agents, allies and adversaries have come to assume similar functions and to speak a common carceral language. With the explosion of technology and proliferation of communication networks, and with the accelerating movement of people and knowledge within and across control organizations, it is not surprising that authorities in various member institutions begin to think and act according to similar philosophies and goals. The professional survival of psychiatrists and other ancillary agents depends on their accommodation to control practices which are initially foreign, but which soon become accepted features of their everyday response to mentally disordered defendants. At METFORS these adaptations have enabled clinicians to legitimize their participation in the criminal justice system. They have simultaneously serviced the state's overall control enterprise by contributing to the general delivery of legal punishment. Their science, like law itself, is primarily *for* crime control (McBarnet 1981), and it is an internal constitutive ingredient of the carceral process: '[T]he practice of calling on psychiatric expertise ... means that the sentence, even if it is always formulated in terms of legal punishment, implies, more or less obscurely, judgments of normality, attributions of causality, assessments of possible changes, anticipations as to the offender's future. It would be wrong to say that all these operations give substance to a judgment from the outside; they are directly integrated in the process of forming the sentence' (Foucault 1977: 20).

But what is to be done about METFORS and the multitude of other psychiatric assessment agencies which currently dot the carceral landscape? Before addressing this question directly, it will be useful to summarize briefly the main features of forensic classification work that were revealed in this book. When taken together these research findings offer little support for the perpetuation of clinical assessments at METFORS in their present form. On the contrary, they represent a litany of forensic practices that contradict some basic canons of traditional medical ethics, and that violate numerous established criminal justice standards of utility, efficiency, and due process of law. These troubling clinical activities surfaced throughout the many stages of the forensic corridor, and they included the following:

1. In their arrests of the METFORS subjects, police officers routinely relied on uncorroborated records of mental disorder that were contained in the official files. Moreover, forensic assessments were frequently recommended in the text of arrest reports, since a remand to METFORS could enhance police objectives by invoking supplementary psychiatric interventions while leaving criminal court proceedings intact. (Chapter 2)

2. For their part, the police reports about METFORS subjects were systematically incorporated into the discretionary practices of Brief Assessment Unit clinical team members. Despite the questionable validity and inflammatory nature of police records – and despite the fact that such evidence had not yet been ruled admissible by the courts – clinicians were profoundly influenced by the content of these documents, and the forensic interview process itself often gravitated around issues first raised by the police. (Chapters 2 and 3)

3. Brief Assessment Unit decisions about fitness and dangerousness were only marginally related to the medical and legal attributes of forensic subjects. Significant inter-rater differences emerged, across disciplines and individuals, in the levels and kinds of pathology ascribed to their BAU patients. The METFORS evaluation itself appeared to be primarily governed by professional demands for legitimacy. It involved a moral ordering process. Clinicians invoked idiosyncratic judgments, cultural stereotypes, and endlessly recycled categories in order to deactivate subject resistance, to maintain a

united front, to devalue the moral currency and credibility of accused persons, and to uncover 'secret knowledge' that was ostensibly unavailable to their legal audiences. Finally, the consequences of these practices were almost always unfavourable to forensic patients. Clinicians functioned primarily as professional informants, who participated in the denunciation of criminal defendants for the enhancement of criminal punishment. The sheer volume of negative attributions applied to subjects was probably the single most prominent feature of classification work at METFORS. Only rarely did people exit the facility with a positive forensic diagnosis, and even more rarely did they escape with no label at all. (Chapter 3)

4. Standard criteria of due process that would adhere in the criminal courts were consistently diluted or ignored altogether during the conduct of METFORS assessments. Defence lawyers were seldom present. Since police and witnesses did not directly participate in the BAU interview, defendants were not able to confront their accusers in the interview setting. Nor did they have recourse to appeal a negative clinical evaluation. Subjects consistently provided pre-trial evidence about their crimes, often framed as overt confessions, and this evidence was frequently cited in psychiatric letters to the court. Even when persons were overtly psychotic to the point where the voluntariness of consent was in question, and even when they refused the interview altogether, judges received a psychiatric report. Particularly in the case of in-patient remands, referrals to METFORS engendered a substantial delay in criminal proceedings, which was often accompanied by a denial of bail. In the case of Inpatient Unit remands, this delay averaged a full five months. Finally, marginal levels of proof that could not justify conviction in a criminal court were often sufficient to invoke psychiatric accounts of mental disorder and dangerousness. (Chapters 1, 2 and 3)

5. Clinical assessments at METFORS frequently failed to add new information to the profiles of forensic patients. Instead they tended to reproduce already existing legal and medical categories, and to encase these within a psychiatric discourse designed to establish accountability and to legitimize expert decisions. Consequently, clinical interventions were oriented more to the distribution and consumption than to the production of medico-legal knowledge. (Chapters 3 and 4)

6. Similarly, protracted thirty- to sixty-day remands in the Inpatient Unit were not demonstrably superior to brief assessments in facilitating expert judgments about mental disorder, fitness, criminality, or dangerousness. Although clinicians advocated extended evaluations as a strategy for sharpening the diagnostic focus in trouble cases, in practice there was little evidence that length of assessment was in any way related to validity.

To the contrary, it appeared that the legitimacy needs of clinicians rather than the therapeutic needs of patients were the principal concern of in-patient assessments at METFORS. When team consensus could not be adequately forged in the BAU, or when members were unable to establish a credible diagnosis, defendants could find themselves the subjects of a lengthy pre-trial forensic confinement under conditions of medium security. (Chapter 4)

7. During the course of in-patient assessments at METFORS, social workers recruited a network of informants from among the families and friends of accused persons. These informants actively furnished a wealth of intimate details from the personal lives of subjects, which were used to reinforce psychiatric attributions of mental disorder and criminality. The materials yielded from these social work interviews were systematically transcribed into the final METFORS Inpatient Unit letters to the court. In those few instances where informants actively resisted the efforts of social workers to elicit such denunciations, their testimony was typically discounted, or they were denounced themselves as contributors and accessories to the subject's problems. (Chapter 4)

8. During their confinement in the METFORS Inpatient Unit on Warrants of Remand, accused persons were the targets of systematic surveillance efforts on the part of attending nurses and psychiatric assistants. The activities and utterances of forensic patients were selectively charted in the unit progress notes and other reports, in order to provide documentation for previously established psychiatric labels. These recording practices were systematically biased against defendants, as they concentrated almost exclusively on discrediting information that sustained forensic impressions of pathology and criminality. Only rarely did these materials refer to the more positive features of subjects' conduct and character. Further, defendants were regularly encouraged to discuss the circumstances of their alleged crimes prior to trial and without the presence of defence counsel. Selected passages from in-patient progress notes were frequently cited in the psychiatrist's final letter to the criminal court. (Chapter 4)

9. Forensic letters to criminal court judges, as drafted by the presiding METFORS psychiatrists, were severely truncated and refracted representations of classification work in the Brief Assessment and Inpatient units. These court reports were infused with knowledge claims about the expertise of clinical members, and with selective portrayals of subjects' past, present, and future identities. They were replete with references to alleged offences and other judicially relevant materials that had not been ruled admissible according to evidentiary rules. Moreover, despite the absence of a clear

legal mandate, psychiatrists consistently offered opinions about bail, dangerousness, carceral disposition, and other penal issues of paramount interest to the courts. (Chapter 5)

10. These psychiatric recommendations were recurrently incorporated into the dispositional decisions of presiding criminal court judges. The findings of this research were therefore consistent with a legion of earlier studies demonstrating the close correspondence between clinical and judicial practices in the allocation of legal sanctions. Criminal court judges were compliant with the medico-legal prescriptions of forensic professionals. They systematically applied rubber stamps to clinical recommendations on the subject of pre-trial and post-sentence penal confinement. In the absence of a mandate in law, the METFORS clinicians were presenting judges with sentencing recommendations prior to judicial findings of guilt. These arrangements between medical and judicial authorities demonstrated the willingness of judges to delegate authority to mental health workers, who themselves were not adverse to assuming a direct role in punishing offenders. (Chapter 5)

11. As revealed earlier in this chapter, over the course of the two-year follow-up many of the 571 METFORS subjects were exposed to cycles of control that propelled them repeatedly through carceral and therapeutic control institutions. Among every twenty remanded defendants, a full seventeen were either imprisoned or hospitalized or both during the twenty-four months subsequent to their initial METFORS assessment. Altogether there were 663 prison terms, 5584 months of probation supervision, 592 in-patient hospitalizations, and 223 out-patient or day-care referrals. Moreover, 65 per cent of persons were still under some form of containment or surveillance at the conclusion of the outcome study. Based on these findings, it is difficult to accept standard official arguments for the 'diversionary' function of pre-trial psychiatric assessments. To the contrary, these remands appeared to activate long-term patterns of institutional inclusion that were in practice being empowered and legitimized by forensic gatekeepers working in mental health facilities like METFORS. (Chapter 6)

12. Similarly, the most evocative feature of these follow-up institutional careers was the repeated mobilization of multiple remands at METFORS and other forensic agencies. One subject in every four was the recipient of at least one subsequent psychiatric assessment during the two-year outcome period. Yet it was apparent that such repeated remands added little of substance to the medical and legal profiles of forensic patients. Instead, these evaluations typically generated psychiatric reports that simply reinforced pre-existing categories and labels. In so doing, the repeat remand

was being employed primarily as a legitimation device to demonstrate the apparent longitudinal reliability of professional decisions. According to scientific standards of validity and utility, and legal standards of minimal required intervention, the majority of these multiple assessments were clearly unnecessary. (Chapter 6)

13. The subsequent violent conduct of METFORS subjects during the two-year follow-up period was extremely resistant to prediction efforts by the Brief Assessment Unit clinical team. With few meaningful exceptions, none of the forensic disciplines, or individual professionals within given disciplines, were able to account for more than 5 per cent of the variance in the incidence of patient violence throughout the subsequent twenty-four months. Nor was there any evidence to suggest that future dangerous behaviour could be predicted on the basis of actuarial data relating to the socio-demographic or medico-legal attributes of patients. On the contrary, few of the background variables demonstrated more than a weak association with the subsequent violent conduct perpetrated by the 571 METFORS subjects, and those attributes with some degree of explanatory value tended to be criminal justice variables (for example, prior violence) with little psychiatric relevance. These findings are particularly damaging to the legitimacy of pre-trial forensic assessments at METFORS, given the high profile of dangerousness predictions both in the original justifications for psychiatric referrals and in clinical documents supplied to the criminal courts. (Chapter 6)

Taken in their entirety, these observations describe the systematic compromise of therapeutic ideals and legal protections against the overall mandate of crime control at the Metropolitan Toronto Forensic Service. This is hardly an encouraging scenario. As an extension of the judicial apparatus, METFORS is clearly in the 'service' of the state's legal ordering process, instead of the thousands of accused persons who have been psychiatrically assessed over the past decade. Again and again, criminal defendants have emerged from the Brief Assessment and Inpatient Units in worse condition than they entered, as measured by their prospects for freedom, by their identities as criminal or psychiatric deviants, and by their vulnerability to the interventions of carceral and therapeutic control agents.

It remains to be considered whether the practices described in this book can be regulated to represent the needs of patients better, and to reflect basic medical and legal standards of conduct. Can the activities of METFORS clinicians be modified and monitored, to ensure conformity with the agency's stated role as a psychiatric diversion service designed to *protect* mentally disordered accused persons? More generally, can medico-legal reforms be introduced to establish clear policies and powers for mental health workers and to ensure their autonomy from the punitive objectives of criminal justice? Is there a way to preserve the structural integrity of METFORS and the professional powers of its members, while reassessing its role within the state's crime control enterprise?

Whatever the envisioned benefits of forensic reform through the application of revised procedural standards or the policing of clinical activities (see Thompson 1975), psychiatrists and other medico-legal professionals are largely immune from such remedial efforts to confine their discretionary power. In practice, members can easily evade such apparent constraints, and in reworking the enabling features of law can even further legitimize and hence amplify their control over mentally disordered defendants. Institutional norms, evidentiary standards, and procedural safeguards can be mobilized to exert only a minimal level of regulation in a forensic agency like METFORS, where decision-making is largely inductive, contextual, independent of external rules, and invisible to legal audiences. The extraordinary discretionary latitude exhibited by the forensic clinicians in this study, despite the constellation of medical standards and procedural rules within which they ostensibly operated, is ample testimony to their relative autonomy from such formal guidelines. More law and heightened vigilance do not necessarily exact greater compliance from forensic or any other criminal justice authorities.

It would be convenient to defuse this tension by prescribing a variety of revisionist measures, including better training for member clinicians, the mandatory attendance of defence counsel during METFORS assessments, the standardization of clinical decisions and recommendations, greater communication between clinic and court, stricter rules of evidence, ethical codes of procedure, rights to appeal, and so forth. But a restricted reformist approach of this kind can have little impact in a forensic network that effectively absorbs such formal remedies, collapsing them into public demonstrations of the system's inherent benevolence, capacity for change, and adherence to the rule of law. At best, proposals aimed at institutionalizing legality may be viewed by psychiatric and judicial authorities as potentially corrosive to the interests of their organization, and hence will be defused or ignored. At worst, they will be selectively incorporated into superficial and chimeric reform, and mobilized to further legitimize an overall forensic control structure that resists fundamental change.

Under these conditions, the only appropriate destructuring strategy must involve a wholesale abolition of pre-trial clinical assessments for the criminal courts. Given the institutional limitations of legal reform, and given structured resistance to remedial measures aimed at curbing professional power, the option of discontinuing forensic remands must now be seriously contemplated. This book has revealed few justifications for the maintenance of current medico-legal practices. Outside of their role in facilitating criminal sanctions and legitimizing judicial and mental health authorities, these clinicians furnish little of substance to the understanding of psychopathology or criminality. Neither do they discernibly improve the life conditions of their subjects, nor soften the impact of criminal sanctions. Their principal function is to enhance the scope and intensity of the state's crime control apparatus, and it is only in this capacity that their work can be assessed favourably.

The abolition of pre-trial psychiatric remands would activate a number of immediate and long-term effects throughout the reaches of the medico-legal corridor. It would immediately streamline the judicial pathways for thousands of criminal defendants annually, while accelerating the judicial process, imposing some limits on unnecessary psycholegal confinement, and reducing fiscal expenditures. It would eliminate at least one salient organizational context for the various breaches of medical standards and due process of law that were charted in this study. It would shift the allegiances and activities of clinical disciplines to other realms, and with sufficient institutional support it might signal the return of forensic psychiatry to more therapeutic pursuits outside of the carceral system altogether. It would reduce the possibility that legal subjects could be confined or monitored on the basis of ambiguous psychiatric categories or suspected mental illness. It would deny a critical source of legitimacy to criminal court judges, whose sentencing decisions might be less infused with psychiatric discourse and categories. In the broadest context it would destabilize the collusive arrangements that have evolved between clinics and courts over the course of the past half-century, and in so doing it would represent a significant reversal in the overall proliferation of transcarceral networks, along with their recurrent patterns of cyclical control over criminal and mentally disordered populations.

On a realistic plane, the achievement of any genuine moratorium within the near future is at best a remote prospect, given the extraordinary investment of capital, people, and ideas in the present medico-legal enterprise. Destructuring programs are slow to gain currency or legitimacy when the entire physics of control systems is oriented towards policies of expansion rather than retraction. Abolitionist ideas are particularly unpopular within the law-and-order politics of the late 1980s. In the area of psychiatry and law, such proposals are doubly suspect as assaults on both the legal sanctity of criminal justice and the scientific authority of the medical model.

Still the eradication of forensic assessments is an objective worthy of pursuit, and such a course has authentic long-term possibilities. An abolitionist agenda must begin with efforts to expose carceral institutions and coercive practices to public view. This book has represented an attempt to unveil one such hidden corridor in the architecture of forensic justice. By casting light on clinical practices that are almost always obscured under the shadow of law, this and similar studies can generate useful knowledge for the enlightenment and enpowerment of counter-control measures.

What we have seen is a virtual microcosm of the knowledge-power systems that dominate systems of state authority in the latter half of this century. The classification work of METFORS experts was designed to service the crime control enterprise of which they were a part. Moreover, their efforts functioned to expand and intensify the power of forensic psychiatry as a discipline, by demonstrating its ongoing contribution to the ordering of legal subjects. Through the juridification of the mental health professions, and more generally through the fusion of therapeutic and carceral control systems, power has accumulated at the borderland between psychiatry and law.

Psychiatric assessments of pathology and criminality are used to energize a symbiotic forensic system that reproduces legal order across a wide band of civil and state institutions. The imputational practices of professional classifiers in this study benefited the state's control enterprise, by trading in deviant images that situated the causes of crime in the hearts and minds of flawed individuals instead of the socio-political machinery of a flawed society. The METFORS professionals were able to circulate powerful blends of medical, moral, and legal knowledge that enveloped the identities of accused persons, and left them open to recurrent interventions by carceral and therapeutic agents. They applied scientific and technological legitimacy to their own classification work, and more importantly to the judicial punishments that were imposed on criminal defendants. At the crossroads between medicine and law, the pre-trial forensic assessment has become a site for the dual enhancement of psychiatric and legal control over marginal citizens, and in the process it helps to reproduce and expand the ordering projects of the modern state.

As at present constituted, the pre-trial classification work of clinical experts cannot be justified on medical, moral, or legal grounds. METFORS, like other forensic assessment agencies, has become the venue for a range of control practices that violate basic therapeutic standards and due process criteria, and that remain generally hidden from public and legal scrutiny. Beneath their mental health facade, forensic clinicians are professionally in the employ of the state's carceral industry, and in the business of meting out punishment to persons accused of breaking the law. Clearly this kind of punitive function is beyond both clinical competence and legal tolerance. If there is a role to be played by mental health workers in correctional systems, it is in the defence of sick people, the humanization of criminal justice, the presentation of alternatives to penal intervention, and the general blunting of legal control. Yet in the history of forensic psychiatry, there has been little demonstration that mental health workers are capable of such a counter-control posture while they continue to operate within the realm of criminal justice.

Given the lack of such evidence in clinical practice and socio-legal research, the pre-trial psychiatric assessment must simply be abolished. In the final analysis, a moratorium on forensic remands has become the only feasible option for the demystification of psycholegal activities, for the restoration of therapeutic justice, for the control of professional conduct, and for the provision of some measure of legal protection to mentally disordered persons in conflict with the law.

BAU Psychiatric Assessment Summary Form

PATIENT'S NAME   ( )

RATER'S NAME   ( )

REFERRING JUDGE   ( )

FORM ( )   (1)   MARITAL STATUS   s(1) m(2) cl(3) d(4) s(5) w(6) (10)

( ) ( ) ( ) ( )   (2)   REFERRING COURT   (1)   (2)   (3)   (4)   (5)   (11)

AGE   ( ) ( )   (7)   BAU ASSESS. DATE   D( )( )   M( )( )   Y( )( )   (12)

GENDER   (m) (f) (9)

CHARGES: 1. _____ ( )( ) (18)   3. _____ ( )( ) (22)

           2. _____ ( )( ) (20)   4. _____ ( )( ) (24)

HISTORY:	No	UC	Yes	NA	Mixed	
Previous Out-patient Hospital Experience	(1)	(2)	(3)			(26)
Previous In-patient Hospital Experience	(1)	(2)	(3)			(27)
Previous Charges	(1)	(2)	(3)			(28)
Previous Time in Prison (Post-sentence)	(1)	(2)	(3)			(29)

PSYCHIATRIST'S OPINION:						
Fit to be Granted Bail at Present	(1)	(2)	(3)			(30)
Fit to Stand Trial at Present	(1)	(2)	(3)			(31)
Fit to Receive Sentence at Present	(1)	(2)	(3)			(32)
Patient Mentally Disordered at Present	(1)	(2)	(3)			(33)
Certifiable at Present	(1)	(2)	(3)			(34)
Certified at Present	(1)		(3)	(4)		(35)

In-patient Hospital Treatment Needed Now	(1)	(2)	(3)			(36)
Further Analysis of Patient Needed Now	(1)	(2)	(3)			(37)
Out-patient Care Required	(1)	(2)	(3)			(38)
Custodial Setting Required	(1)	(2)	(3)			(39)
Co-operation in Treatment Likely in Future	(1)	(2)	(3)			(40)
Presented Honest Picture of Self	(1)		(3)		(5)	(41)

DANGEROUSNESS:	No	Low	UC	Med	Hi	
Dangerous to Self at Present	(1)	(2)	(3)	(4)	(5)	(42)
Dangerous to Others at Present	(1)	(2)	(3)	(4)	(5)	(43)
Probably Dangerous to Self in Future	(1)	(2)	(3)	(4)	(5)	(44)
Possibly Dangerous to Others in Future	(1)	(2)	(3)	(4)	(5)	(45)
Dangerousness Increased under Drugs/ Alcohol	(1)	(2)	(3)	(4)	(5)	(46)

If 'Medium,' 'High,' or 'Unclear' under 42–46:

Dangerousness Related to Psychiatric Disorder	(1)	(2)	(3)	(4)	(5)	(47)
Danger Related to Sociocultural Enhancement	(1)	(2)	(3)	(4)	(5)	(48)
History of Institutionalization	(1)	(2)	(3)	(4)	(5)	(49)
Unfortunate Experiences as a Child	(1)	(2)	(3)	(4)	(5)	(50)
Has Long History of Aggressive Behaviour	(1)	(2)	(3)	(4)	(5)	(51)
Client Perceives Self as Aggressive	(1)	(2)	(3)	(4)	(5)	(52)
Client Concerned Regarding Aggressive Behaviour	(1)	(2)	(3)	(4)	(5)	(53)

Type of Dangerousness:

Angry Aggression (Responds with Aggression to Wide Range of Social Stimuli)	(1)	(2)	(3)	(4)	(5)	(54)
Hostility–Attitude (Negative Reaction to Behaviour and Motives of Others)	(1)	(2)	(3)	(4)	(5)	(55)
Control over Aggressive Tendencies	(1)	(2)	(3)	(4)	(5)	(56)

Short-Lived, Unpredictable, Transitory
   Anger/Rage   (1)   (2)   (3) (4)   (5)   (57)

PSYCHIATRIC CLASSIFICATION(S):   1. ( ) ( ) ( ) : ( ) ( )   (58)
                                   2. ( ) ( ) ( ) : ( ) ( )   (63)
                                   3. ( ) ( ) ( ) : ( ) ( )   (68)

STAGE OF ASSESSMENT: 1 = Pre-trial; 2 = During Trial; 3 = Pre-sentence

PSYCHIATRIST'S RECOMMENDATIONS: _____

Sample Follow-up Profiles for BAU Subjects

CASE 326

Date of BAU assessment: August 9, 1978
Subject: 48-year-old white male, born in Hungary
Original charges: Assault Bodily Harm; Weapons Dangerous
BAU diagnosis: Habitual Excessive Drinking
Assessments of dangerousness by BAU clinicians:

Psychiatrist	High
Psychologist	High
Social Worker	Medium
Nurse	(not present)
Correctional Officer	High

Court disposition: Six Months' Prison
Outcome status and incidents:

September 18/78 to January 16/79: Served 121 days of 6-month sentence for original charges.

January 17/79: Criminal charges for Liquor Control Act Violation (3 counts).

January 18/79 to February 5/79: Sentenced to 30 days in prison for liquor offences; served 19 days.

No further contacts or incidents.

CASE 008

Date of BAU assessment: January 24, 1978
Subject: 58-year-old white woman, born in Nova Scotia
Original charges: Fraud

BAU diagnosis: Paranoid Psychosis (Unfit to Stand Trial)
Assessments of dangerousness by BAU clinicians:

Psychiatrist   High
Psychologist   Unclear
Social Worker   (not present)
Nurse   Unclear
Correctional Officer No

Court disposition: Charges Withdrawn
Outcome status and incidents:

February 1/78 to March 30/78: In-patient assessment at Queen Street Mental Health Centre on original charge, referred by court on a Warrant of Remand.

April 1/78: Original charge (fraud) withdrawn by court.

April 19/78 to June 12/78: Involuntary in-patient at Queen Street Mental Health Centre. Brought to hospital by police after attempting to use stolen credit cards. Aggressive with admitting doctor, who certified subject.

October 16/79 to January 10/80: Queen Street Mental Health Centre in-patient. Was admitted after jumping in front of moving vehicles. Went AWOL for 5 days in December before being returned to hospital.

January 20/80 to study end (January 23/80): Queen Street day-care patient.

CASE 160

Date of BAU assessment: April 5, 1978
Subject: 49-year-old white male, born in southern Ontario
Original charges: Theft under $200
BAU diagnosis: Anti-Social Personality Disorder; Epilepsy
Assessments of dangerousness by BAU clinicians:

Psychiatrist   No
Psychologist   (not present)
Social Worker   No
Nurse   No
Correctional Officer Medium

Court disposition: Two Months' Prison
Outcome status and incidents:

April 7/78 to May 18/78: In prison on original charge.

August 19/78: Charged with Impaired Driving and Possession under $200.

October 20/78: Sentenced to 12 months' prison for August 19/78 charges. Served 8 months of sentence, was released on June 21/79.

May 11/79: Three incarceration misconducts: wilfully damaged property not owned by the inmate; created or incited a disturbance likely to endanger the security of the institution (×2).

July 9/79: Charged with Weapons Dangerous and Theft under $200. Charges withdrawn by the court.

September 10/79: Charged with Public Mischief and Liquor Control Act Violation.

September 27/79 to October 17/79: Sentenced to 31 days' prison for September 10/79 charges. Served 21 days of sentence.

October 10/79: Incarceration misconduct: had contraband in possession or participated in an attempt to bring contraband in or take contraband out of the institution.

October 23/79: Charged with Theft under $200 and Liquor Control Act Violation.

October 29/79 to December 29/79: Sentenced to 3 months' prison for October 23/79 charges. Served 62 days of sentence.

February 12/80: Charged with Possession Under $200.

February 12/80 to March 1/80: Sentenced to 30 days' prison and served 19 days.

CASE 263

Date of BAU assessment: May 23, 1978
Subject: 24-year-old white male, born in southern Ontario
Original charges: Unlawfully at Large
BAU diagnosis: Anti-Social Personality Disorder; Explosive Personality Disorder
Assessments of dangerousness by BAU clinicians:

Psychiatrist	High
Psychologist	High
Social Worker	High
Nurse	High
Correctional Officer	High

Court disposition: Twelve Months' Probation
Outcome status and incidents:

May 24/78 to November 6/78: Served remainder of a previous 15-month sentence in prison.

July 10/78: Two incarceration misconducts: made a gross insult directed at a person; took to the inmate's use property without the consent of the rightful owner of the property.

September 27/78: Incarceration misconduct: took to the inmate's own use property without the consent of the rightful owner of the property.

November 10/78: Charged with Theft Over $200 and Possession Over $200 (×2).

December 15/78 to January 19/79: Sentenced to 53 days' prison for the November 10 Theft Over charge (Possession Over charge withdrawn). Served 36 days of sentence.

March 1/79: Five criminal charges: Robbery with Violence, Weapons Dangerous, Escape, Possession over $200 (×2).

May 18/79: Sentenced to 8 years' federal prison for March 1 charges.

May 24/79 to June 29/79: Confined to regional classification centre.

June 29/79 to December 13/79: Transferred to medium-security institution.

December 13/79 to study end (May 22/80): Transferred to maximum-security penitentiary.

CASE 469

Date of BAU assessment: October 23, 1978
Subject: 20-year-old white male, born in Toronto
Original charges: Assault Police
BAU diagnosis: Paranoid Schizophrenia (Fit to Stand Trial)
Assessments of dangerousness by BAU clinicians:

Psychiatrist	Medium
Psychologist	High
Social Worker	Medium
Nurse	Unclear
Correctional Officer	Unclear

Court disposition: Twelve Months' Probation
Outcome status and incidents:

November 16/78 to November 15/79: On probation for original charge.

January 3/79: Drop-in at Clarke Institute of Psychiatry, complained of depression.

January 25/79 to February 22/79: Involuntary in-patient at Whitby Psychiatric Hospital. Certified by psychiatrist. Using vulgar language, clenching fists, spitting, banging walls.

February 24 to 26/79: Whitby Hospital patient. Had no place to stay. Uncooperative while in hospital.

March 8/79: Drop-in at Clarke Institute of Psychiatry. Received medication. Spoke angrily, inappropriate giggling.

March 15/79 to April 26/79: Whitby Hospital in-patient. Brought in by police. Had no place to stay. Uncooperative.

November 14/79: Charged with Uttering and Possession Under $200.

November 16/79: Received suspended sentence for November 14/79 charges.

December 14/79: Drop-in at Clarke Institute of Psychiatry. Inability to eat or sleep properly.

December 14 to 18/79: Whitby Hospital in-patient. Self-admission. 'Clowning around' during stay.

February 24/80: Drop-in at Clarke Institute of Psychiatry. Marked thought disorder, paranoid ideation, not eating, had been living on street for the previous two weeks.

March 16/80: Charged with Assault Causing Bodily Harm and Breach of Recognizance. Charges withdrawn on April 25/80.

March 31/80 to May 16/80: Transferred from jail to Whitby Hospital. Had attacked other inmates while in jail. Smashed windows and cut fingers during hospitalization.

October 21/80 to study end (October 22/80): Whitby Hospital in-patient. Referred to hospital for problem coping on the street. Felt like hurting other people. Waving arms wildly.

(Seven days after end of two-year follow-up period, subject was transferred to the Oak Ridge maximum-security unit at Penetang.)

CASE 479

Date of BAU assessment: October 26, 1978
Subject: 18-year-old white male, born in southern Ontario
Original charges: Weapons Dangerous
BAU diagnosis: Personality Disorder – Unspecified
Assessments of dangerousness by BAU clinicians:
  Psychiatrist   Medium
  Psychologist   (not present)
  Social Worker   Medium
  Nurse   (not present)
  Correctional Officer Medium
Court disposition: Prison 39 days and Probation 20 Months
Outcome status and incidents:
  October 28/78 to November 23/78: In prison serving sentence for original charge.
  November 23/78 to July 22/80: On probation for original charge.

March 21/79: Charged with Trafficking Narcotics, Trafficking in Restricted Drugs, Possession of Narcotics, and Common Assault.

April 17/79: Released on bail for March 21/79 charges.

June 26/79: Charged with Fraud Transportation and Assault Police. Bailed on same day.

May 23/80: Charged with Failure to Appear, Theft Under $200, Wilful Non-compliance with Probation/Bail Terms, and Assault Police.

May 29/80: Assessed in METFORS BAU.

July 18/80: Released on bail.

October 24/80: Admitted as in-patient to Queen Street Mental Health Centre. Had been abusing drugs. Had attacked a man who he believed was following him. Homicidal. Had been following and observing his former child worker and on one occasion had a 38-caliber gun in his possession. Claimed he had been sexually abused at the age of 6 years by the worker. Attempted to escape from the hospital. Angry, agitated, pounded fists on chair, yelled obscenities.

October 25/80 (study end): In hospital, and awaiting disposition of several charges.

CASE 064

Date of BAU assessment: March 30, 1978
Subject: 19-year-old white male, born in Toronto
Original charges: Robbery
BAU diagnosis: Moderate Mental Retardation; Recommended for In-patient Assessment
Assessments of dangerousness by BAU clinicians:
  Psychiatrist   Unclear
  Psychologist   Medium
  Social Worker   Low
  Nurse   High
  Correctional Officer High
Court disposition: Three Months' Prison and 18 Months' Probation
Outcome status and incidents:
  April 5 to 14/78: In-patient on Warrant of Remand in METFORS Inpatient Unit.
  May 3/78: Charged with Common Assault while on bail.
  May 9/78: Charged with Assault Causing Bodily Harm, Common Assault, and Causing a Disturbance while on bail.

May 12 to 29/78: Lakeshore Psychiatric Hospital in-patient. Referred from jail and certified. In jail had torn clothes, damaged cell, was extremely upset. Discharged to custody of police on May 29/78.

May 29 to August 14/78: In jail awaiting court disposition.

August 10/78: Assessed in METFORS BAU.

August 14/78: Sentenced to 3 months' prison and 18 months' probation for original charge, plus May 3/78 and May 9/78 charges.

September 14/78: Incarceration misconducts: neglected performing work or duty assigned to him; used foul, indecent, or profane language.

October 14/78: Released from prison.

October 14/78 to study end (March 29/80): On probation.

October 31/78: Charged with Arson and Weapons Dangerous.

November 2/78: Transferred to Oak Ridge maximum-security unit at Penetang and certified. Arson and Weapons Dangerous charges later dropped.

November 2/78 to study end (March 29/80): Involuntary patient at Penetang. The following incidents were recorded: hit co-patient with cup; punched co-patient in the head; struck staff member; attempted to hit staff member with broom handle; kicked co-patient in leg; generally very verbally abusive; threatening, taunting, screaming; spitting and hard to get along with.

CASE 534

Date of BAU assessment: November 17, 1978
Subject: 19-year-old white male, born in Scotland
Original charges: Robbery
BAU diagnosis: Anti-Social Personality Disorder
Assessments of dangerousness by BAU clinicians:

Psychiatrist	Medium
Psychologist	High
Social Worker	(not present)
Nurse	Unclear
Correctional Officer	High

Court disposition: 21 Months' Prison and 24 Months' Probation
Outcome status and incidents:

November 21/78 to January 14/80: In prison for original robbery offence. Following misconducts during incarceration:

January 3/79: Conducted self in a manner detrimental to the welfare of other inmates or the institutional program.

February 5/79: Used foul, indecent, or profane language.

March 5/79: Conducted self in a manner detrimental to the welfare of other inmates or the institutional program (×2). Attacked or threatened to attack another person within the institution.

June 22/79: Left cell, place of work, or other appointed place without authority.

June 28/79: Wilfully breached or attempted to breach a regulation governing the conduct of inmates (×2).

July 3/79: Wilfully breached or attempted to breach a regulation governing the conduct of inmates.

August 17/79: Wilfully breached or attempted to breach a regulation governing the conduct of inmates.

September 5/79: Created or incited a disturbance likely to endanger the security of the institution.

September 20/79: Wilfully disobeyed a lawful order of an officer. Committed or threatened to commit an assault upon another person.

October 1/79: Had contraband in his possession or participated in an attempt to bring contraband in or take contraband out of the institution.

January 3/80: Wilfully disobeyed a lawful order of an officer (×2). Committed or threatened to commit an assault upon another person (×2).

January 14/80: Released from prison, on probation to end of follow-up.

April 16/80 to study end (November 16/80): Out-patient at Clarke Institute of Psychiatry. Referred by probation officer for assessment to determine suitability for treatment. Poor hygiene, violent and disrespectful behaviour. Verbally abusive. Tantrums.

July 18/80: Charged with Second Degree Murder.

September 11/80: Received bail on Murder charge.

September 26/80: Drop-in at Clarke Institute of Psychiatry. Referred by lawyer. Despondent, disoriented, frustrated. Lawyer concerned he might do something foolish and be sent back to jail.

November 16/80 (study end): Still on bail awaiting trial for murder charge.

APPENDIX C

Cases Deleted from Two-Year Follow-up

CASE NUMBER	DATE OF ASSESSMENT	REASON FOR DELETION
027	23 February 1978	Returned to India.
086	2 March 1978	Suicided. Jumped off a bridge on 29 July 1978.
107	27 June 1978	Suicided.
123	28 June 1978	Died on 13 December 1979. Accident in home (electrocution).
163	7 April 1978	No data in either provincial or federal records.
248	3 May 1978	Died on 3 April 1979 from an epileptic seizure.
258	16 May 1978	Returned to a mental hospital in the United States.
276	31 July 1978	Died in a car crash on 16 November 1978.
294	4 July 1978	Died accidentally at home from an overdose of analgesics.
307	7 July 1978	No data in either provincial or federal records.
313	11 July 1978	Died on 19 December 1978 from aspiration of stomach contents.

253 Cases Deleted from Two-Year Follow-up

CASE NUMBER	DATE OF ASSESSMENT	REASON FOR DELETION
319	18 July 1978	Died on 6 June 1978 from coronary artery insufficiency and fibrosis.
324	1 August 1978	Deported to a mental hospital in the United States.
325	30 August 1978	Deported to a mental hospital in the United States.
348	25 August 1978	Returned to family in Florida.
361	16 August 1978	Died accidentally on 12 February 1979. Electrocuted while working in a car wash.
365	10 August 1978	Returned to parents in Florida.
390	11 September 1978	Suicided on 3 December 1978 by jumping off a bridge.
392	8 September 1978	No provincial or federal data.
433	3 October 1978	Returned to India.
570	14 December 1978	No provincial or federal data.

APPENDIX D

Characteristics of METFORS Patients

PLACE OF ORIGIN

Toronto		217
Canada – Other		202
Southern Ontario	70	
Nova Scotia	30	
Northern Ontario	23	
Newfoundland	22	
New Brunswick	16	
Quebec	15	
British Columbia	7	
Manitoba	7	
Alberta	5	
Saskatchewan	4	
Prince Edward Island	3	
United States		16
Great Britain		24
England	13	
Scotland	10	
Wales	1	
Europe		83
Italy	13	
Poland	12	
Yugoslavia	11	
Hungary	8	
Greece	7	
Portugal	6	

Austria	4	
West Germany	4	
Czechoslovakia	3	
Bulgaria	3	
Spain	3	
Soviet Union	2	
Switzerland	2	
Malta	2	
Ukraine	2	
Cyprus	1	
Caribbean–South America		28
Jamaica	16	
Guyana	5	
Trinidad	2	
Grenada	1	
Saint Vincent	1	
Brazil	1	
Peru	1	
Ecuador	1	
Asia		9
India	6	
Hong Kong	1	
Korea	1	
Philippines	1	
Africa–Mediterranean		7
Lebanon	2	
Israel	1	
Egypt	1	
Kenya	1	
Ghana	1	
South Africa	1	
TOTAL		586
MISSING CASES		6

CRIMINAL CHARGES PRECIPITATING ASSESSMENT

	First charge*	Second charge
Violent Offences vs. Person	259	100
Assault Causing Bodily Harm	52	13
Weapons Dangerous	46	41
Common Assault	34	11
Robbery	29	3
Wounding	16	2
Attempted Murder	12	
Indecent Assault – Female†	10	
Arson‡	9	
Armed Robbery	6	
Criminal Negligence – Motor Vehicle	6	2
Indecent Assault – Male†	5	
Assault – Police	5	13
Assault – Intent to Resist Arrest	5	8
Rape	5	
First Degree Murder	4	
Second Degree Murder	2	
Attempted Rape	2	
Dangerous Driving	2	4
Forcible Seizure	2	2
Abduction	2	1
Kidnapping	1	
Assault – Attempt to Disfigure	1	
Choking	1	
Causing Injury with Intent	1	
Administer a Noxious Substance	1	
Property Offences	148	84
Breaking and Entering	43	8
Theft under $200	33	7
Theft over $200	18	12
Possession Over $200	10	14
Unlawfully in Dwelling Place	7	2
Fraud	6	4

	First charge*	Second charge
Fraud Accommodation	5	3
Attempted Break and Enter	4	
Fraud Transportation	3	1
False Pretences	3	3
Possession Under $200	3	15
Theft from Mails	3	2
Uttering	3	2
Theft of Credit Card	3	2
Attempted Theft	2	
Attempted Fraud	1	
Forgery	1	3
Possession of Housebreaking Tools		6
Offences against Public Order	131	61
Mischief to Private Property	31	7
Public Mischief	17	9
Causing a Disturbance	16	4
Arson‡	15	
Threatening	12	7
Trespassing	5	4
Possession of Restricted Weapon	4	3
Threatening Telephone Calls	4	1
Watch and Beset	4	
Pointing a Firearm	3	2
Intimidation	3	3
Harassing Telephone Calls	3	
False Fire Alarm	2	4
Common Nuisance	2	
Wilful Damage	2	
Carry a Concealed Weapon	1	11
Dangerous Use of Firearm	1	2
Obstruct Police	1	1
Loitering	1	1
Nuisance of Flies–Cockroaches	1	1
Counselling to Commit an Offence	1	
False Messages	1	
Prowl By Night	1	
Careless Storage of Firearms		1

	First charge*	Second charge
Sexual Offences	33	12
Indecent Assault – Female†	14	3
Indecent Assault – Male†	7	1
Indecent Exposure	4	
Incest	3	
Indecent Act	2	1
Soliciting	2	
Bestiality	1	
Gross Indecency		4
Carnal Knowledge		3
Technical–Administrative Offences	14	53
Failure to Comply	9	21
Unlawfully at Large	3	
Escape Lawful Custody	1	
Breach of Recognizance	1	
Failure to Appear		30
Breach of Parole		3
Drug Offences	4	2
Possession of Marijuana	2	2
Trafficking in Cocaine	1	
Trafficking in PCP	1	
Traffic Offences	2	6
Impaired Driving	2	
Driving While Licence Suspended		3
Refusing a Breathalyser Test		1
Failure to Remain		1
Breach Highway Traffic Act		1

* $N = 591$ (missing data for one case)

† Categorized as a 'Sexual Offence' if no violence was employed in the commission. Otherwise classified as a 'Violent Offence against Persons.'

‡ Categorized as an 'Offence against Public Order' if no personal injury was threatened or sustained. Otherwise classified as a 'Violent Offence against Persons.'

DIAGNOSTIC CLASSIFICATIONS OF METFORS PATIENTS

	First diagnosis	Second diagnosis
Psychoses	151	4
Schizophrenic Illnesses		
Paranoid Schizophrenia	32	
Chronic Undifferent. Schizophrenia	25	
Undifferent.–Unspecified Schizophrenia	14	
Latent–Residual Schizophrenia	11	2
Acute Schizophrenic Reaction–Episode	10	
Chronic Paranoid Schizophrenia	8	
Simple Schizophrenia	6	1
Acute Paranoid Schizophrenia	3	
Schizoaffective Schizophrenia	3	
Catatonic Schizophrenia	2	
Incipient Schizophrenia	1	
Involutional Paraphrenia	1	
Mood Disorders		
Manic-Depressive Psychosis–Manic	12	
Manic-Depressive Psychosis–Bipolar	3	
Hypomania	2	
Drug-Related Psychoses		
Alcohol Psychosis	3	
Amphetamine Psychosis	2	
Alcohol Psychosis – Paranoid	1	
General Psychoses		
Unspecified Psychosis	5	
Paranoid State	5	
Schizoaffective Psychosis	2	
Reactive Paranoid Psychosis	1	
Personality Disorders	201	51
Antisocial	85	14
Unspecified	39	11
Explosive	19	6
Inadequate	13	5
Immature	12	3
Schizoid	9	3

	First diagnosis	Second diagnosis
Paranoid	7	2
Hysterical	3	1
Dyssocial	3	
Adolescent	3	
Passive Aggressive	2	1
Passive Dependent	1	1
Narcissistic	1	1
Obsessive Compulsive	1	
Affective	1	
Cyclothymic	1	
Mixed	1	
Masochistic		1
Impulse Disorder		1
Anhedonia		1
Sexual Disorders	15	9
Heterosexual Pedophilia	6	3
Sexual Deviation – Unspecified	3	1
Homosexual Pedophilia	2	1
Exhibitionism	2	
Homosexual Pedophilia – Sadism	1	1
Incest	1	
Bisexuality		1
Transsexualism		1
Transvestism		1
Mental Retardation	15	18
Chronic Alcoholism	27	5
Habitual Excessive Drinking	25	9
Alcoholism–Alcohol Addiction	13	12
Episodic Alcoholism	13	7
Episodic Excessive Drinking	6	8
Drug Abuse–Dependence		
Unspecified	9	11
Multiple	7	9
Solvents	1	3
Amphetamines	1	2

	First diagnosis	Second diagnosis
Heroin	1	2
Barbiturates	1	1
Cannabis	1	1
Narcotics	1	
Hallucinations	1	
Mild Tranquillizers	1	
Cocaine		1
Situational–Reactive	78	16
Situational Disturbance – Maladjustment	26	3
Reactive Depression	19	7
Adjustment Reaction of Adolescence	16	1
Depressive Neurosis	13	4
Institutional Neurosis	1	1
Anxiety Neurosis	1	
Hypochondriacal Neurosis	1	
Chronic Depression	1	
Stammering and Stuttering	1	
Organic Dysfunction	11	5
Organic Brain Syndrome	7	2
Epilepsy	2	3
Senile Dementia	1	
Paranoid State – Senility	1	
NO MENTAL ILLNESS	8	
NO PSYCHIATRIC DIAGNOSIS	4	
MISSING DATA	1	

APPENDIX E

Psychological Tests Administered at
METFORS

	BRIEF ASSESSMENT UNIT (N = 592)	IN-PATIENT UNIT (N = 123)
Minnesota Multiphasic Personality Inventory	210	66
Zung Depression Scale	30	2
Rorschach	28	49
Saks Sentence Completion Test	26	42
Wechsler Adult Intelligence Scale	18	45
METFORS Questionnaire	12	11
Bender Visual-Motor Gestalt	9	27
Raven's Progressive Matrices	6	9
Thematic Apperception Test	2	32
Draw-a-Person	1	2
IPAT Culture-Fair Test of Intelligence	1	0
Benton Visual Retention Test	0	2
TOTAL TESTS ADMINISTERED	343	287

Incidents Recorded during Two-Year Follow-up

CRIMINAL CHARGES

Violence against Persons	213	Unlawfully in Dwelling Place	9
Common Assault	51	Forgery	8
Assault Bodily Harm	48	False Pretences	7
Weapons Dangerous	28	Fraud Transportation	7
Robbery	20	Fraud Accommodation	5
Assault Police	14	Take Vehicle without Consent	5
Indecent Assault – Female	14	Possess. Housebreak. Tools	4
Assault Resisting Arrest	12	Illegal Use Credit Card	1
Arson	10	Theft Telecommunication	1
Rape	3		
Crim. Neglig. – Bodily Harm	3	*Sexual Offences*	16
Wounding	2	Indecent Act	8
First Degree Murder	1	Indecent Exposure	3
Choking	1	Procuring	2
Indecent Assault – Male	1	Found in Bawdy House	2
Armed Robbery	1	Carnal Knowledge	1
Crim. Neg. – Motor Vehicle	1		
Kidnapping	1	*Alcohol/Drug Offences*	82
Forcible Confinement	1	Liquor Control Act Violation	53
Abduction	1	Possession Narcotics	16
		Trafficking in Narcotics	13
Property Offences	436		
Theft under $200	124	*Offences vs. Public Order*	207
Possession over $200	65	Mischief Private Property	46
Theft over $200	62	Causing Disturbance	27
Breaking and Entering	58	Public Mischief	23
Possession under $200	48	Wilful Damage	18
Uttering	12	Provincial Statutes – Other	17
Fraud	11	Carrying Concealed Weapon	11
Attempted Theft	9	Municipal By-laws	10

Possession Restricted Weapon	7
Loitering	6
Impersonation	5
Threatening	5
False Fire Alarm	5
Obstructing Police	4
Obstructing Justice	4
Intimidation	4
Federal Statutes – Other	4
Dangerous Use Firearm	2
Harassment	2
Common Nuisance	2
Threatening Phone Calls	1
False Messages	1
Prowl by Night	1
Contempt of Court	1
Conspiracy to Commit Offence	1

Failure to Comply with Recognizance	31
Escape Lawful Custody	24
Provincial Parole Violation	13
National Parole Violation	11
Revocation of Probation	3
Unlawfully at Large	3
Acknowledge Bail Falsely	2

Traffic Offences	111
Breach Highway Traffic Act	34
Impaired Driving	25
Drive over 80 mg Alcohol	19
Drive While Licence Suspended	17
Dangerous Driving	10
Failing to Remain	6

TOTAL NUMBER OF OFFENCES	1332

Technical–Administrative Offences	267
Failure to Appear	94
Wilful Non-compliance with Bail or Probation	86

NOTE: Multiple counts of same offence were excluded. Arson and Indecent Assault were classified as violent.

INCARCERATION MISCONDUCTS

Sub-section	Offence type	Number of infractions
Ontario Ministry of Correctional Services Regulation 166 (effective to April 1979)		
23-A	Neglected performing work or duty assigned	18
23-B	Used foul, indecent, or profane language	31
23-C	Had in possession unauthorized articles	15
23-D	Disobeyed a lawful order given by an employee	55
23-E	Smuggled or attempted to smuggle an article either into or out of the institution	4
23-F	In an unauthorized place or left the limits of the institutional confines without being escorted or without express authority	8
23-G	Conducted self in a manner detrimental to the welfare of other inmates or the institutional program	80
23-H	Attacked or threatened to attack another person	66
23-I	Caused or conspired to cause a disturbance or riot	3
23-J	Destroyed or defaced government property	8

Ontario Ministry of Correctional Services Regulation 243/79
(implemented May 1979)

28-1-A	Wilfully disobeyed a lawful order of an officer	65
28-1-B	Committed or threatened to commit an assault upon another person	38
28-1-C	Made a gross insult directed at any person	27
28-1-D	Took for the inmate's own use property without the consent of the rightful owner	4
28-1-E	Wilfully damaged property not owned by the inmate	20
28-1-F	Had contraband in possession or participated in an attempt to bring contraband in or take contraband out of the institution	17
28-1-G	Created or incited a disturbance likely to endanger the security of the institution	16
28-1-H	Escaped, attempted to escape, or was unlawfully at large from the institution	2
28-1-I	Left cell, place of work, or other appointed place without authority	5
28-1-L	Committed or attempted to commit an indecent act	1
28-1-M	Gave counsel to or aided and abetted another inmate to do an act in violation of this regulation	2
28-1-N	Wilfully breached or attempted to breach a regulation governing the conduct of inmates	39
28-1-O	Wilfully breached or attempted to breach a term or condition of a temporary absence	5

FEDERAL PENITENTIARY MISCONDUCTS

Assault on inmate	2
Cell fire	2
Possession of contraband	2

Notes

1 Since the completion of this study, the composition of multidisciplinary teams on the Brief Assessment Unit has been altered in response to the re-alignment of clinical staff. Beginning in 1982, psychologists and social work-ers have been excluded from the process, and instead they currently focus their attention primarily on Inpatient Unit evaluations. BAU assessments are currently conducted by psychiatrists, nurses, and correctional officers.

2 The following tables provide a frequency distribution of individual BAU clini-cians according to the number of patients assessed by each member:

Psychiatrists			Psychologists		
Psychiatrist 1	243	41.0%	Psychologist 1	243	46.7%
Psychiatrist 2	134	22.6%	Psychologist 2	136	26.2%
Psychiatrist 3	152	25.7%	Psychologist 3	141	27.1%
Psychiatrist 4	63	10.5%	None	72	
Social Workers			Nurses		
Social Worker 1	380	85.0%	Nurse 1	513	86.7%
Social Worker 2	28	6.3%	Nurse 2	31	5.2%
Social Worker 3	39	8.7%	Nurse 3	7	1.2%
None	145		Nurse 4	9	1.5%
			Nurse 5	13	2.2%
			Nurse 6	7	1.2%
			Nurse 7	12	2.0%

Correctional Officers		
Correctional Officer 1	1	0.2%
Correctional Officer 2	9	1.6%
Correctional Officer 3	5	0.9%

Correctional Officer 4	59	10.5%
Correctional Officer 5	81	14.4%
Correctional Officer 6	8	1.4%
Correctional Officer 7	23	4.1%
Correctional Officer 8	17	3.0%
Correctional Officer 9	86	15.3%
Correctional Officer 10	9	1.6%
Correctional Officer 11	88	15.6%
Correctional Officer 12	94	16.7%
Correctional Officer 13	1	0.2%
Correctional Officer 14	82	14.6%
None	29	

3 As indicated in a 1980 review of METFORS for the attorney-general of Ontario, written by Alan Mewett: 'The Order in Council is remarkable in its brevity. It merely implements a new psychiatric service to be known as METFORS, located at the Queen Street Mental Health Centre and provides for the establishment of the Board. Nothing is said about the purpose and objects of METFORS, nor is anything spelled out about the complicated relationship between METFORS and the Clarke Institute. Nothing is said about the budgetary arrangements beyond the fact that the Attorney-General is to provide the funds that are to be administered through the Ministry of Health. It is only because of the interest and good will on the part of all persons involved that METFORS has achieved such signal success' (Mewett 1980: 4).

4 This turned out to be an overestimate, by some 500 per cent, of the Brief Assessment Unit's caseload over the ensuing decade. After four years, the number of patients assessed annually stabilized at a rate of 500 to 600 (although in 1986 the rate experienced a sudden increase to nearly 800: METFORS Annual Reports).

5 The three major pre-trial detention facilities in Toronto are the Toronto West Detention Centre, the Toronto East Detention Centre, and the Toronto Jail (otherwise known as the Don Jail).

6 This included multiple assessments of single individuals. Refer to subsequent sections of this chapter.

7 There has been considerable controversy about the 'voluntary' and 'informed' nature of the forensic patient's 'consent' (see Schiffer 1978; Verdun-Jones 1981). In the United States, several commentators have suggested that the forensic assessment represents an abuse of the subject's constitutional right against self-incrimination. Schiffer, in the Canadian context, recommends a Miranda-like warning prior to the commencement of a pre-trial

psychiatric examination (1978: 49–50). Given the relatively high frequency of psychiatric pathology among pre-trial forensic populations, it is doubtful that consent is either voluntary or informed in a substantial proportion of cases. This problem is exacerbated by the fact that virtually all patients discuss their alleged offences during the course of the interview (Butler and Turner 1980), and that clinicians are not considered 'persons in authority' under Canadian law, removing the protection of professional privilege from confessions extracted during assessments (Verdun-Jones 1981: 384–7).

8 Only a minority of defendants had retained counsel prior to their appearance at METFORS, and lawyers were virtually never present during the interview itself (Webster, Menzies, and Jackson 1982: 76).

9 Section 16 of the Canadian Criminal Code states:

'(1) No person shall be convicted of an offence in respect of an act or omission on his part while that person was insane.

(2) For the purposes of this section, a person is insane when the person is in a state of natural imbecility or has disease of the mind to an extent that renders the person incapable of appreciating the nature and quality of an act or omission or of knowing that an act or omission is wrong.

(3) A person who has specific delusions, but is in other respects sane, shall not be acquitted on the ground of insanity unless the delusions caused that person to believe in the existence of a state of things that, if it existed, would have justified or excused the act or omission of that person.

(4) Every one shall, until the contrary is proved, be presumed to be and to have been sane.'

Section 614 reads:

'(1) Where, on the trial of an accused who is charged with an indictable offence, evidence is given that the accused was insane at the time the offence was committed and the accused is acquitted,

(a) the jury, or

(b) the judge or provincial court judge, where there is no jury, shall find whether the accused was insane at the time the offence was committed and shall declare whether he is acquitted on account of insanity.

(2) Where the accused is found to have been insane at the time the offence was committed, the court, judge or provincial court judge before whom the trial was held shall order that he be kept in strict custody in the place and in the manner that the court, judge or provincial court judge directs, until the pleasure of the lieutenant governor of the province is known.'

(See Schiffer 1978; Hucker, Webster, and Ben-Aron 1981.)

10 *International Classification of Diseases, Ninth Revision* (ICDA-9): *Manual of*

the International Statistical Classification of Diseases, Injuries, and Causes of Death. Adopted by the 29th World Health Assembly (Geneva: World Health Organization 1977)

11 The month-by-month breakdown of Brief Assessment Unit cases appeared as follows:

January	17	2.9%	July	56	9.5%
February	45	7.6%	August	57	9.6%
March	38	6.4%	September	49	8.3%
April	53	9.0%	October	59	10.0%
May	56	9.5%	November	63	10.6%
June	58	9.8%	December	41	6.9%

12 In addition to METFORS, the six major hospitals included in the study were: Queen Street Mental Health Centre, the Clarke Institute of Psychiatry, Lakeshore Psychiatric Hospital (which closed in 1979, part of the way through the follow-up study), Whitby Psychiatric Hospital, St Thomas Psychiatric Hospital, and the Oak Ridge Unit at Penetanguishene Mental Health Centre.

13 According to the 'two-year rule' in Canada, persons sentenced to imprisonment for less than two years serve their term in a provincial institution. Those receiving prison sentences of two years or longer are confined in a federal penitentiary. Section 731 of the Canadian Criminal Code reads:
'(1) Except where otherwise provided, a person who is sentenced to imprisonment for
  (a) life,
  (b) a term of two years or more, or
  (c) two or more terms of less than two years each that are to be served one after the other and that, in the aggregate, amount to two years or more,
shall be sentenced to imprisonment in a penitentiary.'

14 Cases with missing data on any variable were excluded from Figure 1.1 on a casewise basis.

15 The fully delineated statuses of METFORS subjects at the commencement of the study were as follows:

No Correctional Status	307	52.0%
Probation	106	18.0%
Bail	98	16.6%
Parole	16	2.7%
Prison	7	1.2%
Probation and Parole	3	0.5%
Probation and Bail	28	4.7%
AWOL–Outstanding Warrant	25	4.2%

16 The length of time between Brief Assessment Unit appearance and final sentence ranged from 1 to 1001 days.

17 At the conclusion of the two-year follow-up, the full breakdown of institutional status among subjects is given below:

Absolute Release	199	35.2%
Probation	198	35.0%
Hospital	37	6.5%
Provincial Prison	36	6.4%
Federal Prison	35	6.2%
Bail	24	4.2%
Out-patient Care	15	2.7%
Parole	11	1.9%
Remand in Detention	10	1.8%

18 Throughout the discussion in this and subsequent chapters, all identities of subjects and officials are disguised, and where necessary institutional and place-names are changed to ensure confidentiality. Case identification numbers referred to in this book do not correspond to the actual medical record numbers of patients. They are assigned randomly within each month rather than in any sequential order. The METFORS patients are referred to with the use of a fictional first or second initial. All dates for an individual case are moved systematically forward or backward (i.e., by the same number of days and/or months for each reference to that case), in order to permit an accurate rendition of outcome experiences.

19 The police and METFORS documents are referenced in subsequent chapters according to the source of the cited material and the record number of the case (e.g., PR 104, IPN 458). The abbreviated sources are as follows:

PR	Arresting police officer report
NR	Brief Assessment Unit nurse's report
SWR	Brief Assessment Unit social worker's report
POR	Brief Assessment Unit psychologist's report
COR	Brief Assessment Unit correctional officer's report
PL	Brief Assessment Unit psychiatrist's court letter
INR	METFORS Inpatient Unit nurse's report
ISWR	METFORS Inpatient Unit social worker's report
IPOR	METFORS Inpatient Unit psychologist's report
IPL	METFORS Inpatient Unit psychiatrist's court letter
NR2	Nurse's report: first subsequent METFORS assessment
PL3	Psychiatrist's court letter: second subsequent METFORS assessment

and so on. Excerpts from all records are reproduced in this book as they appeared in the original, with the exception of changes in names, times, and locations to ensure confidentiality, and minor corrections in spelling and grammar. Errors of syntax, along with major grammatical or stylistic deficiencies, are retained in all citations from these documents.

20 The procedural law concerning pre-trial release is articulated in section 515 of the Canadian Criminal Code. The relevant subsections are indicated below:

'(1) Subject to this section, where an accused who is charged with an offence ... is taken before a justice the justice shall, unless a plea of guilty by the accused is accepted, order, in respect of that offence, that the accused be released on his giving an undertaking without conditions, unless the prosecutor, having been given a reasonable opportunity to do so, shows cause, in respect of that offence, why the detention of the accused in custody is justified or why an order under any other provision of this section should be made ...

(10) For the purposes of this section, the detention of an accused in custody is justified only on either of the following grounds:

(a) on the primary ground that his detention is necessary to ensure his attendance in court in order to be dealt with according to law; and

(b) on the secondary ground (the applicability of which shall be determined only in the event that and after it is determined that his detention is not justified on the primary grounds referred to in paragraph (a)) that his detention is necessary in the public interest or for the protection or safety of the public, having regard to all the circumstances including any substantial likelihood that the accused will, if he is released from custody, commit a criminal offence or an interference with the administration of justice.'

21 This referred to the subject's practice of pitching tents in front of government and newspaper buildings as a form of protest.

CHAPTER 2: Opening the Door: Police Encounters with the METFORS Patients

1 The relevant section of the Ontario Mental Health Act reads as follows: 'Where a constable or other police officer observes a person,

(a) apparently suffering from mental disorder; and

(b) acting in a manner that in a normal person would be disorderly;

the officer may, if he is satisfied that,

(c) the person should be examined in the interests of his own safety or the safety of others ...

take the person to an appropriate place where he may be detained for medical examination. Where in addition the constable or other peace officer is of the opinion that the person is apparently suffering from mental disorder of a nature or quality that likely will result in,

    (d) serious bodily harm to the person;

    (e) serious bodily harm to another person; or

    (f) imminent and serious physical impairment of the person,

and that it would be dangerous to proceed under [any other section], the constable or other peace officer may take the person in custody to an appropriate place for assessment by a physician.'

2 See note 20, Chapter 1.

3 This practice is fraught with serious ethical problems, since the forensic clinicians are working with police materials, including alleged confessions, that have not yet been ruled admissible by the criminal court.

4 Section 518.1 of the Canadian Criminal Code establishes the conditions for the show cause hearing:

'(1) In any proceedings under Section 515,

    (a) the justice may, subject to paragraph (b), make such inquiries, on oath or otherwise, of and concerning the accused as he considers desirable;

    (b) the accused shall not be examined or cross-examined by the justice or any other person respecting the offence with which he is charged, and no inquiry shall be made of him respecting that offence;

    (c) the prosecutor may, in addition to any other relevant evidence, lead evidence

        (i) to prove that the accused has previously been convicted of a criminal offence,

        (ii) to prove that the accused has been charged with and is awaiting trial for another criminal offence,

        (iii) to prove that the accused has previously committed an offence under section 145 [i.e., 'Unlawfully at large'], or

        (iv) to show the circumstances of the alleged offence, particularly as they relate to the probability of conviction of the accused;

    (d) the justice may take into consideration any relevant matters agreed on by the prosecutor and the accused or his counsel; and

    (e) the justice may receive and base his decision on evidence considered credible or trustworthy by him in the circumstances of each case.'

(Refer to Note 20, Chapter 1.)

5 Disaggregated by month, the frequencies of completed police reports, recommendations for psychiatric assessment, and references to METFORS are as follows:

	Police report available	Remand recommended	METFORS indicated
January	17	3	0
February	39	8	0
March	33	12	0
April	46	16	0
May	45	24	2
June	56	18	0
July	48	18	1
August	52	15	0
September	41	17	4
October	45	19	2
November	53	26	4
December	29	16	2

6 Emergency Task Force.

7 The subject had been an in-patient at METFORS prior to the opening of the Brief Assessment Unit. The Inpatient Unit began receiving patients four months earlier than the BAU (see Chapter 1).

8 During the course of the two-year follow-up study, at least, this recommendation for castration was not carried out.

CHAPTER 3: The Forensic Corridor I: The METFORS Brief Assessment Unit

1 Of 591 BAU subjects for whom data were available, 86 (14.6 per cent) were described by clinicians to be actively hallucinating on the unit, and 141 (23.9 per cent) were diagnosed as delusional.

2 In constructing this three-category variable, subjects were coded as 'violent' if the first, second, or third charge involved violence against persons. If not violent, persons were categorized as 'property offenders' if the first, second, or third charge fell into the latter classification. All remaining patients were coded as 'other.'

3 The beta coefficient is a multiple regression equivalent to Pearson's r, in this case measuring the zero-order correlation between type of charge and predictions of dangerousness.

4 There were few differences in the background characteristics and subsequent experiences of the METFORS subjects assessed by the four different psychiatrists. Of twenty-seven variables disaggregated across the BAU psychiatrists, only two displayed statistically significant differences: Estimated IQ ($p = 0.04$) and Level of Alcohol Use ($p = 0.049$). All other tests of association were non-significant.

5 In this case the subject had two earlier convictions, and had received a sentence of probation on each occasion.

CHAPTER 4: The Forensic Corridor II: The METFORS Inpatient Unit

1 In 1978, almost 2 per cent of defendants in the Toronto provincial court system (686 out of 36,234) were remanded to the Brief Assessment Unit. These assessments include multiple remands of the same defendants (see Chapter 1). Similarly, the 36,234 court cases include multiple adjudications of single accused persons.

2 This ratio excludes eighteen persons who were involuntarily certified by the BAU psychiatrist under the provisions of the Ontario Mental Health Act, and who were therefore diverted at least temporarily outside of the court's jurisdiction.

3 Once again, this figure excludes the eighteen subjects who were involuntarily certified to hospital by the BAU psychiatrist (see note 2 above).

4 In another such case a woman arrived in the Brief Assessment Unit charged with 'Fraud Transportation.' The subject refused to communicate with staff during her confinement on the unit. As the BAU psychologist reported: 'Ms. J. was uncooperative and angry when asked to participate in an interview. Subsequent tries to interview her met with further resistance. Her behaviour when not being approached by others was observed to be quiet. The behaviour observed did not indicate that she was in any way agitated or suffering from active hallucinations' (POR 258). In contrast, the psychiatrist interpreted the patient's resistance to be indicative of possible mental illness, writing that 'this woman appeared to be very angry at whatever was going on in her own head.' He suggested to the judge that an in-patient assessment might succeed in breaking down the subject's defences: 'As a result of today's interviews it is impossible to state definitively whether she is fit to stand trial or whether she is fit to be granted bail or whether she is or is not dangerous ... [I]f Your Honour so wishes we can accept her on the Inpatient Unit on a Warrant of Remand for a period not exceeding 30 days. As you are aware it would be difficult for her to remain uncooperative for a period of 30 days in a hospital setting such as exists on the Inpatient Unit' (PL 258).

5 The majority of research on the social organization of mental institutions has adopted an ethnographic or participant observational method (e.g. Barry 1971; Braginsky, Braginsky, and Ring 1969; Brandt 1975; Goffman 1961; LeBar 1973; Perrucci 1974; Rosenhan 1973; Townsend 1976). This literature deals with such interrelated topics as the hierarchical and bureaucratic structure of the psychiatric hospital; the 'caste system' that develops among

professionals, line staff, and inmates (Perrucci 1974; Rosenhan 1973); the socialization of individuals into the patient role (Brandt 1975); and the 'secondary adjustments' by which inmates attempt to neutralize the control efforts of the total institution and its caretakers (Goffman 1961).

6 The use of compliance strategies was not restricted to the line staff. In the case of a male in-patient charged with 'Breaking and Entering,' the presiding psychiatrist attempted to secure the subject's co-operation by pointing out the consequences of a negative assessment. The psychiatrist's progress notes read: 'Refused to converse today. Declined to go to interview room. Insisted he didn't have to answer our questions or to co-operate. Acknowledged he has no lawyer. Doesn't intend to obtain counsel until a trial date is set. Plans to plead guilty. Thinks he will get probation or at most 2–3 months sentence ... I pointed out to him that if he is found to be unfit to stand trial by the court that his plans to plead guilty are meaningless. Endeavoured to suggest to him that the outcome of this assessment is very important for him [and that] the consequences of being found unfit would be very grave (meaning indeterminate custody at a closed psychiatric setting such as Penetang). Reinforcing this reality upon him might be one way of getting Mr. R. to open up and communicate more' (IPN 381).

7 Among the 122 METFORS in-patients for whom records were available, there were eight aggressive incidents directed toward staff members (all of a minor nature, including spitting and throwing water), twelve fights involving two patients each, and sixteen minor assaults upon other patients. In no instance was medical attention required beyond first aid. There were nine self-directed injuries, including two serious suicide attempts (by strangulation) committed by the same subject within a single week.

CHAPTER 5: The Forensic Corridor III: Sentencing the METFORS Patients

1 *R. v. Morrison*, Ontario Supreme Court (1983). Refer to Webster, Dickens, and Addario (1985: xiv).

2 In four of the 592 BAU cases, the court disposition was unknown. In one case, the disposition was unknown and the psychiatrist's letter to the court was missing. Consequently the analyses of recommendations and dispositions are based on the remaining 587 cases.

3 Psychiatrists routinely registered their indignation when judges failed to act upon their recommendations for custodial confinement or hospitalization. In Case 181, for example, the BAU psychiatrist requested a Warrant of Remand for a fifty-five-year-old male charged with 'Mischief to Private Property.' In spite of the psychiatrist's appearance in court to support this request, the

court denied the application and granted bail to the subject. In his follow-up report, the psychiatrist wrote: 'Appeared in Court [   ] today. Decision to grant bail, not to admit to METFORS. One question the Court does not understand is that a person may not be psychotic or certifiable but still in need of further evaluation re. his mental state and his dangerousness.' As it turned out, the charges in this case were later dropped. In Case 042 the psychiatrist again recommended denial of bail and an in-patient assessment for a subject charged with 'Common Assault.' Once again the court released the defendant on bail. The psychiatrist wrote as an addendum to his original BAU letter: 'The patient's lawyer has called to say that the judge has ordered that this man see me on an outpatient basis!! Further, the case has been put off [for two months]. Man is out on bail!!!' (PL 042).

4 Following this BAU evaluation, the subject spent one month as an in-patient at the Clarke Institute of Psychiatry on a Warrant of Remand. The charges were withdrawn by the court four months after the original METFORS assessment.

5 In *Dusky v. United States* 362 U.S. 402 (1960), the Supreme Court held: 'It is not enough for the district judge to find that "the defendant is oriented to time and place and has some recollection of events," but that the test must be whether he has sufficient present ability to consult with his lawyer with a reasonable degree of rational understanding – and whether he has a rational as well as factual understanding of the proceedings against him.' See Roesch and Golding (1980).

6 Fitness to stand trial is the only issue which forensic clinicians are legally mandated to address during pre-trial assessments under Canadian law (see Schiffer 1978; Webster, Menzies, and Jackson 1982).

7 Section 617 of the Canadian Criminal Code provides for the disposition of persons found unfit to stand trial:
'(1) Where an accused is, pursuant to this Part, found to be insane, the lieutenant governor of the province in which he is detained may make an order
(a) for the safe custody of the accused in a place and manner directed by him; or
(b) if in his opinion it would be in the best interest of the accused and not contrary to the interest of the public, for the discharge of the accused either absolutely or subject to such conditions as he prescribes.
(2) An accused to whom paragraph (1)(a) applies may, by warrant signed by an officer authorized for that purpose by the lieutenant governor of the province in which he is detained, be transferred for the purposes of his rehabilitation to any other place in Canada specified in the warrant with the consent of the person in charge of that other place.'

Section 619 sets the conditions for the review and release of unfit defendants.

'(1) The lieutenant governor of a province may appoint a board to review the case of every person in custody in a place in that province by virtue of an order made pursuant to section 617 ...

(2) The board shall consist of not less than three and not more than five members of whom one member shall be designated chairman by the members of the board, if no chairman has been designated by the lieutenant governor.

(3) At least two members of the board shall be duly qualified psychiatrists entitled to engage in the practice of medicine under the laws of the province for which the board is appointed, and at least one member of the board shall be a member of the bar of the province.

(5) The board shall review the case of every person referred to in subsection (1)

(a) not later than six months after the making of the order referred to in that subsection relating to that person, and

(b) at least once in every twelve month period following the review required pursuant to paragraph (a) so long as the person remains in custody under that order, and forthwith after each review the board shall report to the lieutenant governor setting out fully the results of such review and stating

(c) where the person in custody was found unfit on account of insanity to stand trial, whether, in the opinion of the board, that person has recovered sufficiently to stand trial ...

(f) any recommendations that it considers desirable in the interests of recovery of the person to whom such review relates and that are not contrary to the public interest.'

8 For a summary of Canadian criteria and procedures concerning criminal responsibility and insanity at the time of committing the offence, see note 9 in Chapter 1. Section 619 provides for the review of persons found not guilty by reason of insanity. For example, Section 619 (5d) reads: 'After each review the board shall report to the lieutenant governor setting out fully the results of the review and stating, where the person in custody was found not guilty on account of insanity, whether, in the opinion of the board, that person has recovered and, if so, whether in its opinion it is in the interest of the public and of that person for the lieutenant governor to order that he be discharged absolutely or subject to such conditions as the lieutenant governor may prescribe.'

9 One psychiatric letter was missing from the research files, leaving a sample of 591 for these analyses.
10 Dangerousness to self is one of the criteria for involuntary certification in the province of Ontario (Ontario Mental Health Act, section 13–3b).

CHAPTER 6: The Aftermath

1 The twenty-one subjects deleted from the outcome study were not substantially different from other persons when compared on a range of socio-demographic, legal, and clinical variables. Those individuals expunged from the analysis, because they died ($N = 10$) or left the country ($N = 7$) during the follow-up period, or because they failed to appear in any institutional data bases ($N = 4$), appeared to depart from the norm on only five variables. They were slightly older than other subjects (mean age of 36), they had more prior psychiatric hospitalizations (mean = 3.6) and more previous convictions (mean = 3.33) – although they averaged only 0.33 prior convictions for crimes of violence. Finally, the excluded subjects were more likely to be diagnosed as psychotic (11 of 21), and to have no fixed address at the time of their arrest (8 of 21).
2 This figure does not include five subjects who displayed assaultive conduct during their immediate in-patient assessment at METFORS.
3 Multiple counts of the same offence were not included. Arson, indecent assault, and robbery were all coded as violent incidents.
4 For incarceration misconducts, no distinction was made in the official records between threatened and completed assaults. See Appendix F.
5 The figure of 2204 months spent in prison by the METFORS subjects was arrived at by determining the number of days of confinement for each individual, aggregating across the entire cohort, and dividing by 30.5. Systematic data were not available on the amount of time spent by subjects in pre-trial carceral detention.
6 These admissions included immediate in-patient assessments following the initial Brief Assessment Unit examination at METFORS.
7 The 10,355 months logged in the community represent something of an overestimate, since data were not available on the proportion of outcome periods spent in pre-trial detention.
8 There was no systematic information on the amount of time spent by subjects on parole during the two-year follow-up.
9 For seven of the 571 METFORS patients, data were not available on their status at the conclusion of the twenty-four-month outcome period.

10 The 'Contempt of Court' charge arose after the subject had thrown a shoe at the provincial court judge who was trying her case. As the METFORS social worker's report read: 'She stated that she got so angry in court because the judge would not make the call to find out what she was saying was true and she threw a shoe at him. She made a point of stating that it wasn't her own shoe because she was afraid that he would not give it back' (swr3 356).

11 These base rates of outcome violence differ from those reported earlier in this chapter ($N = 191$, or 34 per cent), because for the present analysis 'questionable' decisions by the clinicians are being excluded, and assaultive occurrences in the METFORS Inpatient Unit are being added to the profiles.

References

Allen, Hilary. 1987. *Justice Unbalanced: Gender, Psychiatry and Judicial Decisions*. Milton Keynes, UK: Open University Press

Allodi, R., and R. Montgomery. 1975. 'Mentally abnormal offenders in a Toronto jail.' *Canadian Journal of Criminology and Corrections* 17: 227–83

American Psychiatric Association. 1974. *Clinical Aspects of the Violent Individual*. Washington, DC

Angrist, Shirley, Mark Lefton, Simon Dinitz, and Benjamin Pasamanick. 1968. *Women after Treatment: A Study of Former Mental Patients and Their Normal Neighbours*. New York: Appleton

Arkes, Harold, and Kenneth R. Hammon (eds). 1986. *Judgment and Decision Making: An Interdisciplinary Reader*. New York: Cambridge University Press

Arthur, R. 1971. 'Success is predictable.' *Military Medicine* 136: 539–45

Austin, James, and Barry Krisberg. 1981. 'Wider, stronger and different nets: The dialectics of criminal justice reform.' *Journal of Research in Crime and Delinquency* 18, 1 (January): 165–96

Baldwin, J., and S. McConville. 1977. *Negotiated Justice: Pressures on Defendants to Plead Guilty*. London: Martin Robertson

Barry, Anne. 1971. *Bellevue is a State of Mind*. New York: Harcourt Brace Jovanovich

Bazelon, David L. 1975. 'A jurist's view of psychiatry.' *Journal of Psychiatry and Law* 3: 175–90

Bearcroft, John S., and Mary D. Donovan. 1965. 'Psychiatric referrals from courts and prisons.' *British Medical Journal* 2: 1519–23

Becker, Howard S. 1963. *Outsiders: Studies in the Sociology of Deviance*. New York: Free Press

Benson, Douglas, and John A. Hughes. 1983. *The Perspective of Ethnomethodology*. London: Heinemann

Berger, Peter L., and Thomas Luckmann. 1967. *The Social Construction of Reality: A Treatise in the Sociology of Knowledge*. Garden City NY: Doubleday

Berki, R.N. 1986. *Security and Society: Reflections on Law, Order and Politics*. London: J.M. Dent and Sons

Berry, J.J. 1975. 'Deviant categories and organizational typing of delinquents.' In F. James Davis and Richard Stivers (eds), *The Collective Definition of Deviance*. New York: Free Press

Bittner, Egon. 1967. 'Police discretion in emergency apprehension of mentally ill persons.' *Social Problems* 14: 278–92

Blum, Allen F., and Peter McHugh. 1971. 'The social ascription of motives.' *American Sociological Review* 36 (February): 98–109

Blumberg, Abraham. 1967. *Criminal Justice*. Chicago: Quadrangle Press

Blumer, Herbert. 1969. *Symbolic Interactionism: Perspective and Method*. Englewood Cliffs, NJ: Prentice-Hall

Bohme, Gernot, and Nico Stehr (eds). 1986. *The Knowledge Society. Sociology of the Sciences Yearbook*. Vol.10. Dordrecht: Reidel

Bohmer, Carol E.R. 1973. 'Judicial use of psychiatric reports in the sentencing of sex offenders.' *Journal of Psychiatry and Law* 1: 223–42

– 1978. 'Bad or mad: The psychiatrist in the sentencing process.' *Journal of Psychiatry and Law* 4, 1 (Spring): 23–48

Bonnie, Richard J., and Christopher Slobogin. 1980. 'The role of mental health professionals in the criminal process: The case for informed consent.' *Virginia Law Review* 66, 3 (April): 427–522

Botterell Committee. 1972. *Report of the Committee on the Health Care System in the Ministry of Corrections*. Ontario Ministry of Correctional Services, Toronto

Bottomley, A. Keith. 1973. *Decisions in the Penal Process*. London: Martin Robertson

Bottomley, A. Keith, and C.A. Coleman. 1981. *Understanding Crime Rates: Police and Public Roles in the Production of Official Statistics*. Farnborough, UK: Saxon House

Bottoms, Anthony E. 1977. 'Reflections on the renaissance of dangerousness.' *The Howard Journal of Penology and Crime Prevention* 16, 2: 70–96

Bowden, Paul. 1978. 'Men remanded into custody for medical reports: The selection for treatment.' *British Journal of Psychiatry* 132: 320–31

Boyd, Barry A. 1964. 'Our jails and the psychiatric examination and treatment of the disturbed offender.' *Canadian Journal of Corrections* 6: 477–9

Boyd, Neil. 1980. 'Ontario's treatment of the "criminally insane" and the "potentially dangerous": The questionable wisdom of procedural reform.' *Canadian Journal of Criminology* 20: 151–67

Braginsky, Benjamin M., Dorothea D. Braginsky, and Kenneth Ring. 1969. *Methods of Madness: The Mental Hospital as a Last Resort*. New York: Holt, Rinehart and Winston

Brandt, Anthony. 1975. *Reality Police: The Experience of Insanity in America*. New York: Morrow

Burke, Kenneth. 1945. *A Grammar of Motives*. Englewood Cliffs, NJ: Prentice-Hall

Butler, Brian T., and R. Edward Turner. 1980. 'The ethics of pre-arraignment psychiatric examinations: One Canadian viewpoint.' *Bulletin of the American Academy of Psychiatry and Law* 6: 368–404

Campbell, I.G. 1981. 'The use and efficacy of psychiatric presentence reports.' *Australia and New Zealand Journal of Criminology* 14: 67–82

Caplan, Lincoln. 1984. *The Insanity Defense and the Trial of John W. Hinckley Jr.* Boston: Godine

Carlen, Pat. 1974. 'Remedial routines for the maintenance and control of magistrates' courts.' *British Journal of Law and Society* 1: 101–17

– 1976. *Magistrates' Justice*. London: Martin Robertson

Castel, Robert, Francoise Castel, and Anne Lovell. 1982. *The Psychiatric Society*. New York: Columbia University Press

Chan, J.B.L., and Richard V. Ericson. 1981. *Decarceration and the Economy of Penal Reform*. Toronto: University of Toronto Centre of Criminology

Christie, Nils. 1977. 'Conflicts as property.' *British Journal of Criminology* 17: 1–15

Cicourel, Aaron V. 1968. *The Social Organization of Juvenile Justice*. London: Heinemann

Clausen, John A., and Marian Radke Yarrow (eds). 1955. 'The impact of mental illness on the family.' *The Journal of Social Issues* 11 (entire issue)

Cockerham, William C. 1981. *Sociology of Mental Disorder*. Englewood Cliffs, NJ: Prentice-Hall

Cocozza, Joseph J., Mary E. Melick, and Henry J. Steadman. 1978. 'Trends in violent crime among ex-mental patients.' *Criminology* 16: 317–34

Cocozza, Joseph J., and Henry J. Steadman. 1976. 'The failure of psychiatric predictions of dangerousness: Clear and convincing evidence.' *Rutgers Law Review* 29: 1084–1101

Cohen, Stanley. 1972. *Folk Devils and Moral Panics*. Suffolk: Paladin

– 1979. 'The punitive city: Notes on the dispersal of social control.' *Contemporary Crises* 3: 333–63

- 1985. *Visions of Social Control: Crime, Punishment and Classification.* Cambridge, UK: Polity Press

Coleman, Lee. 1984. *The Reign of Error: Psychiatry, Authority, and Law.* Boston: Beacon

Conrad, John P. 1985. *The Dangerous and the Endangered.* Lexington: Lexington Books

Daley, M.E. 1987. 'The clinical prediction of dangerousness to self: A six-year follow-up of 283 forensic cases.' Unpublished MA thesis, University of Toronto Centre of Criminology

Davis, Kenneth Culp. 1971. *Discretionary Justice: A Preliminary Inquiry.* Urbana: University of Illinois Press

Davis, Nanette J. 1975. *Sociological Constructions of Deviance: Perspectives and Issues in the Field.* Dubuque: William C. Brown

de Berker, P. 1960. 'State of mind reports: The inadequate personality.' *British Journal of Criminology* 1: 6–20

Dell, Susan, and T.C.N. Gibbens. 1971. 'Remands of women offenders for medical reports.' *Medicine, Science and the Law* 11: 117–27

Denzin, Norman K. 1978a. *The Research Act: A Theoretical Introduction to Sociological Methods.* 2nd ed. New York: McGraw-Hill

- 1978b. *Sociological Methods: A Sourcebook.* 2nd ed. New York: McGraw-Hill

Diamond, Bernard L. 1974. 'The psychiatric prediction of dangerousness.' *University of Pennsylvania Law Review* 123: 439–52

Ditton, Jason. 1979. *Contrology: Beyond the New Criminology.* London: Macmillan

Dix, George. 1981. 'Expert prediction testimony in capital sentencing: Evidentiary and constitutional considerations.' *American Criminal Law Review* 19, 1: 1–48

Donzelot, Jacques. 1979. *The Policing of Families.* New York: Pantheon

Douglas, Jack. 1970. *Deviance and Respectability.* New York: Basic Books

- 1971. *Understanding Everyday Life.* London: Routledge Kegan Paul

Ellul, Jacques. 1975. 'Technological morality.' In F. James Davis and Richard Stivers (eds), *The Collective Definition of Deviance.* New York: Free Press

Emerson, Joan P. 1970. 'Nothing unusual is happening.' In Tamotsu Shibutani (ed.) *Human Nature and Collective Behavior.* Englewood Cliffs, NJ: Prentice-Hall

Emerson, Robert M. 1969. *Judging Delinquents: Context and Process in Juvenile Court.* Chicago: Aldine

- 1983. 'Holistic effects in social control decision-making.' *Law and Society Review* 17, 3: 425–55

Ennis, Bruce J., and Thomas R. Litwack. 1974. 'Psychiatry and the presumption of expertise: Flipping coins in the courtroom.' *California Law Review* 62: 693–752

Ericson, Richard V. 1975. *Criminal Reactions: The Labelling Perspective*. Farnborough, UK: Saxon House

– 1976. 'Penal psychiatry in Canada: The method of our madness.' *University of Toronto Law Journal* 26: 17–27

– 1981. *Making Crime: A Study of Detective Work*. Toronto: Butterworths

– 1982. *Reproducing Order: A Study of Police Patrol Work*. Toronto: University of Toronto Press

Ericson, Richard V., and Patricia M. Baranek. 1982. *The Ordering of Justice: A Study of Accused Persons as Dependants in the Criminal Process*. Toronto: University of Toronto Press

Ericson, Richard V., Patricia M. Baranek, and Janet B.L. Chan. 1987. *Visualizing Deviance: A Study of News Organization*. Toronto: University of Toronto Press

Ericson, Richard V., and Clifford D. Shearing. 1986. 'The scientification of police work.' In Gernat Bohme and Nico Stehr (eds), *The Knowledge Society*. Sociology of the Sciences Yearbook, vol.10. Dordrecht: Reidel

Faulk, M., and R.A. Trafford. 1975. 'Efficiency of medical remands.' *Medicine, Science and the Law* 15: 4–11

Feeley, Malcolm M. 1979. *The Process Is the Punishment: Handling Cases in a Lower Criminal Court*. New York: Russell Sage

Forst, Martin L. 1980. 'The psychiatric evaluation of dangerousness in two trial court jurisdictions.' *Bulletin of the American Academy of Psychiatry and the Law* 8: 98–110

Foucault, Michel. 1977. *Discipline and Punish: The Birth of the Prison*. New York: Vintage Books

Fox, Richard W. 1978. *So Far Disordered in Mind: Insanity in California 1870–1930*. Berkeley: University of California Press

Fox, Richard, and Patricia Erickson. 1972. *Apparently Suffering from Mental Disorder*. Toronto: University of Toronto Centre of Criminology

Frederick, Calvin J. (ed.). 1978. *Dangerous Behavior: A Problem in Law and Mental Health*. Washington, DC: U.S. Government Printing Office

Freidson, Eliot. 1961. *Patients' Views of Medical Practice*. New York: Russell Sage

– 1966. 'Disability as social deviance.' In Marvin B. Sussman (ed.), *Sociology and Rehabilitation*. Washington, DC: American Sociological Association

Friedenberg, Edgar Z. 1975. *The Disposal of Liberty and Other Industrial Wastes*. New York: Doubleday

Garfinkel, Harold. 1956. 'Conditions of successful degradation ceremonies.' *American Journal of Sociology* 61 (March): 420–4

– 1967. *Studies in Ethnomethodology.* Englewood Cliffs, NJ: Prentice-Hall

Garland, David. 1985. *Punishment and Welfare: A History of Penal Strategies.* Aldershot: Gower

Garland, David, and Peter Young (eds). 1983. *The Power to Punish: Contemporary Penality and Social Analysis.* London: Heinemann

Geertz, Clifford. 1983. *Local Knowledge.* New York: Basic Books

Geis, Gilbert and John Monahan. 1976. 'The social ecology of violence.' In T. Lickona (ed.), *Moral Development and Behavior: Theory, Research and Social Issues.* Toronto: Holt, Rinehart and Winston

Geller, Jeffrey L., and Eric D. Lister. 1978. 'The process of criminal commitment for pretrial psychiatric examination: An evaluation.' *American Journal of Psychiatry* 135, 1 (January): 53–60

Gibbens, T.C.N., K.L. Soothill, and P.J. Pope. 1977. *Medical Remands in the Criminal Court.* Oxford: Oxford University Press

Giddens, Anthony. 1976. *New Rules of Sociological Method.* Hutchinson

– 1979. *Central Problems in Social Theory: Action, Structure and Contradiction in Social Analysis.* London: Macmillan

Gigeroff, Alex K. 1964. 'The evolution of Canadian legislation with respect to homosexuality, pedophilia and exhibitionism.' Fourth Annual Conference on Delinquency and Criminology, Montreal, 19 November

Glaser, Barney G., and Anselm L. Strauss. 1967. *The Discovery of Grounded Theory: Strategies for Qualitative Research.* Chicago: Aldine

Goffman, Erving. 1961. *Asylums: Essays on the Social Situation of Mental Patients and Other Inmates.* Garden City, NY: Doubleday

– 1981. *Forms of Talk.* Philadelphia: University of Pennsylvania Press

– 1983. 'The interaction order." *American Sociological Review* 48, 1 (February): 1–17

Gostin, Larry O. 1977. *A Human Condition.* Vol.I: *The Law Relating to Mentally Abnormal Offenders.* London: MIND (National Association for Mental Health)

– 1979. 'The merger of incompetency and certification: The illustration of unauthorized medical contact in the psychiatric context.' *International Journal of Law and Psychiatry* 2, 2: 127–68

Gottfredson, Don C. 1971. 'Assessment of Methods.' In Leon Radzinowicz and Marvin E. Wolfgang (eds). *Crime and Justice.* Vol. 3. New York: Basic Books

Gouldner, Alvin W. 1976. *The Dialectic of Ideology and Technology.* New York: Oxford University Press

Gove, Walter R., and Patrick Howell. 1974. 'Individual resources and mental hospitalization: A comparison and evaluation of the societal reaction and psychiatric perspectives.' *American Sociological Review* 39: 86–100

Gray, Kenneth G. 1952. 'Psychiatric examinations for the courts.' *Chitty's Law Journal* 2: 151–4

Greenland, Cyril, and Ellen M. Rosenblatt. 1972. 'Remands for psychiatric examination in Ontario, 1969–70.' *Canadian Psychiatric Association Journal* 17: 387–401

Gusfield, Joseph R. 1981. *The Culture of Public Problems: Drinking-Driving and the Symbolic Order.* Chicago: University of Chicago Press

Habermas, Jürgen. 1970. *Knowledge and Human Interests.* London: Heinemann

– 1975. *Legitimation Crisis.* Boston: Beacon Press

Hall, Stuart, Chas Critcher, Tony Jefferson, John Clarke, and Brian Roberts. 1979. *Policing the Crisis: Mugging, the State, and Law and Order.* London: Macmillan

Halpern, C.R. 1975. 'Use and misuse of psychiatry in competency examination of criminal defendants.' *Psychiatric Annals* 5: 8–69

Handel, Warren. 1982. *Ethnomethodology: How People Make Sense.* Englewood Cliffs, NJ: Prentice-Hall

Hawkins, Keith. 1981. 'The interpretation of evil in criminal settings.' In H. Laurence Ross (ed.), *Law and Deviance.* Beverly Hills: Sage

Hawkins, Richard, and Gary Tiedeman. 1975. *The Creation of Deviance: Interpersonal and Organizational Determinants.* Columbus, OH: Charles E. Merrill

Henn, Fritz A., Marijan Herjanic, and Robert H. Vanderpearl. 1977. 'Forensic psychiatry: Anatomy of a service.' *Comprehensive Psychiatry* 18, 4 (August): 337–45

Henry, Stuart. 1983. *Private Justice: Towards Integrated Theorising in the Sociology of Law.* London: Routledge and Kegan Paul

Hiday, Virginia Aldigé. 1977. 'Reformed commitment procedures: An empirical study in the courtroom.' *Law and Society Review* 11: 651–66

– 1981. 'Court discretion: application of the dangerousness standard in civil commitment.' *Law and Human Behavior* 5, 4: 275–89

– 1983. 'Judicial decisions in civil commitment: Facts, attitudes and psychiatric recommendations.' *Law and Society Review* 17, 3: 517–30

Hinton, John W. (ed.). 1983. *Dangerousness: Problems of Assessment and Prediction.* London: Allen and Unwin

Hochstedler, Ellen. 1986. 'Criminal prosecution of the mentally disordered.' *Law and Society Review* 20: 279–92

Hogarth, John. 1971. *Sentencing as a Human Process.* Toronto: University of Toronto Press

Holt, R. 1978. *Methods in Clinical Psychology.* Vol.2: *Prediction and Research.* New York: Plenum

Horwitz, Allan V. 1977. 'Social networks and pathways into psychiatric treatment.' *Social Forces* 56: 86–106

– 1982. *The Social Control of Mental Illness.* New York: Academic Press

Hucker, Stephen J., Christopher D. Webster, and Mark H. Ben-Aron (eds). 1981. *Mental Disorder and Criminal Responsibility.* Toronto: Butterworths

Hughes, Everett C. 1958. *Men and Their Work.* New York: Free Press

Hutchinson, H.C., M.D. Tuchtie, K.G. Gray, and D. Steinberg. 1964. 'A study of the effects of alcohol on mental functions.' *Canadian Psychiatric Association Journal* 9, 1: 17–25

Imershein, Allen W., and Ronald L. Simons. 1976. 'Rules and exemplars in lay and professional psychiatry: An ethnomethodological comment on the Scheff-Gove controversy.' *American Sociological Review* 41, 3 (June): 559–63

Ingleby, David (ed.). 1981. *Critical Psychiatry: The Politics of Mental Health.* Harmondsworth: Penguin Books

Jablon, N.C., R.L. Sadoff, and M.S. Heller. 1970. 'A unique forensic diagnostic hospital.' *American Journal of Psychiatry* 126: 1663–7

Jackson, Margaret A. 1978. 'An examination of court remands for psychiatric assessment: Factual and theoretical considerations.' Unpublished MA thesis, University of Toronto Centre of Criminology

Jobson, Keith B. 1969. 'Commitment and release of the mentally ill under criminal law.' *Criminal Law Quarterly* 11: 186–203

Johnson, Terence J. 1972. *Professions and Power.* London: Macmillan

Kadish, Mortimer R., and Sanford H. Kadish. 1973. *Discretion to Disobey: A Study of Lawful Departures from Legal Rules.* Stanford: Stanford University Press

Kadushin, Charles. 1969. *Why People Go to Psychiatrists.* New York: Atherton

Kahneman, Daniel, Paul Slovic, and Amos Tversky (eds). 1982. *Judgment under Uncertainty: Heuristics and Biases.* New York: Cambridge University Press

Kittrie, Nicholas N. 1971. *The Right to Be Different: Deviance and Enforced Therapy.* Baltimore: Johns Hopkins Press

Klein, John F. 1976. 'The dangerousness of dangerous offender legislation: Forensic folklore revisited.' *Canadian Journal of Criminology and Corrections* 18 (April): 109–23

Konečni, Vladimir J., Erin Maria Mulcahy, and Ebbe B. Ebbeson. 1980. 'Prison or mental hospital: Factors affecting the processing of persons suspected of being "mentally disordered sex offenders." ' In P. Lipsett and B.D. Sales (eds), *New Directions in Psycholegal Research.* New York: Van Nostrand Reinhold

Kozol, Harry L., Richard J. Boucher, and Ralph F. Garofalo. 1972. 'The diagnosis and treatment of dangerousness.' *Crime and Delinquency* 18 (October): 371–92

Kunjukrishnan, Reghuvaran. 1979. '10 year survey of pretrial examinations in Saskatchewan.' *Canadian Journal of Psychiatry* 24, 7 (November): 683–9

Laczko, A.L., J.R. James, and L.B. Alltop. 1970. 'A study of four hundred and thirty-five court referred cases.' *Journal of Forensic Science* 15: 311–22

Laing, R.D., and Aaron Esterson. 1964. *Sanity, Madness and the Family*. London: Tavistock

Law Reform Commission of Canada. 1976. *A Report to Parliament. Mental Disorder in the Criminal Process*. Ottawa: Queen's Printer

LeBar, Frank M. 1973. *Segregative Care in an Institutional Setting: The Ethnography of a Psychiatric Hospital*. New Haven: Human Relations Area Files

Leiter, Kenneth. 1980. *A Primer on Ethnomethodology*. New York: Oxford University Press

Lerman, Paul. 1982. *Deinstitutionalization and the Welfare State*. New Brunswick, NJ: Rutgers University Press

Levy, Harold J. 1980. 'Mental at gaol.' *Criminal Lawyer's Association Newsletter* (November): 1–7

Linn, Erwin. 1961. 'Agents, timing, and events leading to mental hospitalization.' *Human Organization* 20: 92–8

Lofland, John. 1969. *Deviance and Identity*. Englewood Cliffs, NJ: Prentice-Hall

Lowman, John, and Robert J. Menzies. 1986. ' "Out of the fiscal shadow": Carceral trends in Canada and the United States.' *Crime and Social Justice* 26 (Fall/Winter): 95–115

Lowman, John, Robert J. Menzies, and T.S. Palys (eds). 1987. *Transcarceration: Essays in the Sociology of Social Control*. Aldershot: Gower

Macdonald, J.M. 1976. *Psychiatry and the Criminal: A Guide to Psychiatric Examination for the Criminal Courts*. 3rd. ed. Springfield: Charles C. Thomas

Madden, Patrick G. 1978. 'A description of an Ontario jail population.' Unpublished paper, Ontario Ministry of Correctional Services, Toronto

Manning, Peter K. 1977. *Police Work*. Cambridge: M.I.T. Press

– 1979. 'The social control of police work.' In Simon Holdoway (ed.), *The British Police*. London: Edward Arnold

March, J., and J. Olsen. 1976. *Ambiguity and Choice in Organizations*. Oslo: Universitetsforlaget

Matthews, Arthur. 1970. 'Observations on police policy and procedures for emergency detention of the mentally ill.' *Journal of Criminal Law, Criminology, and Police Science* 61: 283–95

Matza, David. 1969. *Becoming Deviant*. Englewood Cliffs, NJ: Prentice-Hall

McBarnet, Doreen. 1979. 'Arrest: The legal context of policing.' In Simon Holdoway (ed.), *The British Police*. London: Edward Arnold

– 1981. *Conviction: Law, the State, and the Construction of Justice*. London: Macmillan

McCabe, Sarah, and Frank Sutcliffe. 1978. *Defining Crime: A Study of Police Decisions*. Oxford: Basil Blackwell

McGarry, A. Louis. 1971. 'The fate of psychotic offenders returned for trial.' *American Journal of Psychiatry* 127: 1181–84

McGarry, A.L., W.J. Curran, P.D. Lipsitt, D. Lelos, R.K. Schwitzgebel, and R.H. Rosenberg. 1974. *Competency to Stand Trial and Mental Illness*. Washington, DC: U.S. Government Printing Office

McKnight, C.K., J.W. Mohr, R.E. Quinsey, and J. Erochko. 1964. 'Mental illness and homicide, Oakridge project.' Fourth Research Conference on Delinquency and Criminology, Montreal, 19 November

McMahon, Maeve, and Richard V. Ericson. 1987. 'Rethinking decarceration: Trends in sentencing and corrections in Ontario, 1951–1984.' Report to the Ontario Ministry of Correctional Services, University of Toronto Centre of Criminology

McMain, Shelley, Christopher D. Webster, and Robert J. Menzies. 1987. 'Without end: Six years in the post-assessment lives of forensic patients.' Paper presented at the Annual Meetings of the American Society of Criminology, Montreal, 12 November

McRuer, J. 1958. *Report of the Royal Commission on the Criminal Law Relating to Criminal Sexual Psychopaths*. Ottawa: Queen's Printer

Megargee, Edwin I. 1976. 'The prediction of dangerous behavior.' *Criminal Justice and Behavior* 3, 1 (March): 3–22

Megargee, Edwin I., and Martin J. Bohn. 1979. *Classifying Criminal Offenders: A New System Based on the MMPI*. Beverly Hills: Sage

Menzies, Robert J. 1982. 'Explaining decarceration: Some thoughts on the balkanization of social control.' Meeting of the Society for the Study of Social Problems, San Francisco, September

– 1985. 'Psychiatric sentencing: The impact of forensic assessments on criminal court dispositions.' American Society of Criminology Annual Meeting, San Diego, November

– 1986. 'Psychiatry, dangerousness and legal control.' In Neil Boyd (ed.), *The Social Dimensions of Law*. Toronto: Prentice-Hall

– 1987a. 'Psychiatrists in blue: Police apprehension of mental disorder and dangerousness.' *Criminology: An Interdisciplinary Journal* 25, 3 (August): 901–25

– 1987b. 'Cycles of control: The transcarceral careers of forensic patients.' *International Journal of Law and Psychiatry* 10, 3: 233–49

Menzies, Robert J., Raymond R. Corrado, William Glackman, and Karen Ryan. 1987. *A Seven-Year Survey of Disruptive and Self-Injurious Conduct among Inmates of a Youth Detention Centre.* Report to the Solicitor General of Canada. Burnaby, BC: Simon Fraser University Criminology Research Centre

Menzies, Robert J., and Christopher D. Webster. 1987. 'Violence and mental illness.' Chapter 7 in Marvin E. Wolfgang and Neil A. Weiner (eds), *Pathways to Criminal Violence.* Beverly Hills: Sage

Menzies, Robert J., Christopher D. Webster, Brian T. Butler, Frederick A.S. Jensen, and R. Edward Turner. 1980. 'The parameters of psychiatric decision-making: Clinical and legal determinants of forensic assessments.' Annual Meeting of the Canadian Psychiatric Association, Toronto, September

Menzies, Robert J., Christopher D. Webster, Brian T. Butler, and R. Edward Turner. 1980. 'The outcome of forensic assessments: A study of remands in six Canadian cities.' *Criminal Justice and Behavior* 7 (December): 471–80

Menzies, Robert J., Christopher D. Webster, Brian T. Butler, R. Edward Turner, and Frederick A.S. Jensen. 1978. 'An analysis of the development and process of the METFORS Brief Assessment Unit.' METFORS Working Paper No. 7, Toronto

Menzies, Robert J., Christopher D. Webster, and Margaret A. Jackson. 1981. 'Legal and medical issues in forensic psychiatric assessments.' *Queen's Law Journal* 7, 1 (Fall): 3–40

Menzies, Robert J., Christopher D. Webster, Ronald Roesch, Derek Eaves, and Frederick A.S. Jensen. 1984. 'The Fitness Interview Test: A semi-structured instrument for assessing competency to stand trial, with a proposal for its implementation.' *Medicine and Law: An International Journal* 3, 2 (March): 151–62

Menzies, Robert J., Christopher D. Webster, and Diana S. Sepejak. 1985a. 'The dimensions of dangerousness: Evaluating the accuracy of psychometric predictions of violence among forensic patients.' *Law and Human Behavior* 9, 1 (Spring): 35–56

– 1985b. 'Hitting the forensic sound barrier: Predictions of dangerousness in a pre-trial psychiatric clinic.' In Christopher D. Webster, Stephen J. Hucker, and Mark H. Ben-Aron (eds), *Dangerousness: Probability and Prediction, Psychiatry and Public Policy.* New York: Cambridge University Press

– 1987. 'The dimensions of dangerousness: Evaluating the accuracy of psychometric predictions of violence among forensic patients.' Clarke Institute of Psychiatry Annual Research Prize Lecture, Toronto, 22 April

Mesnikoff, A., and G. Lauterbach. 1975. 'The association of violent dangerous behavior with psychiatric disorders: A review of the literature.' *Journal of Psychiatry and Law* 3: 415–45

Metropolitan Toronto Forensic Service (METFORS). Annual Reports, 1977–86

Mewett, Alan. 1980. *Evaluation of the Metropolitan Toronto Forensic Service.* Report to the Ontario Ministry of the Attorney General, Toronto

Mischel, W. 1965. *Personality and Assessment.* New York: John Wiley and Sons

Mnookin, R., and L. Kornhauser. 1979. 'Bargaining in the shadow of the law: The case of divorce.' *Yale Law Journal* 88: 950–97

Mohr, J.W., R.E. Turner, and J.R.B. Jerry. 1964. *Pedophilia and Exhibitionism.* Toronto: University of Toronto Press

Monahan, John. 1981. *Predicting Violent Behavior: An Assessment of Clinical Techniques.* Beverly Hills: Sage

Monahan, John, Cynthia Caldeira, and Herbert D. Friedlander. 1979. 'Police and the mentally ill: A comparison of committed and arrested persons.' *International Journal of Law and Psychiatry* 2: 509–18

Morris, Norval, and Gordon Hawkins. 1970. *The Honest Politician's Guide to Crime Control.* Chicago: University of Chicago Press

Mullen, J.M., and R.C. Reinehr. 1982. 'Predicting dangerousness of maximum security mental patients.' *The Journal of Psychiatry and Law* 10: 223–31

Murphy, Gerald. 1986. *Special Care: Improving the Police Response to the Mentally Disabled.* Washington, DC: Police Executive Research Forum

Parker, E., and G. Tennent. 1979. 'The 1959 Mental Health Act and the mentally abnormal offender: A comparative study.' *Medicine, Science and the Law* 19: 29–38

Peay, Jill. 1982. ' "Dangerousness" – Assumption or description?' In P. Feldman (ed.), *Developments in the Study of Criminal Behaviour*, vol. 2: *Violence.* Chichester, UK: Wiley

Perrucci, Robert. 1974. *Circle of Madness: On Being Insane and Institutionalized in America.* Englewood Cliffs, NJ: Prentice-Hall

Petrunik, Michael. 1983. 'The politics of dangerousness.' *International Journal of Law and Psychiatry* 5: 225–46

Pfeiffer, Eric, Richard B. Eisenstein, and E. Gerald Dobbs. 1967. 'Mental competency evaluation for the federal courts: 1. Methods and results.' *The Journal of Nervous and Mental Disease* 144: 320–28

Pfohl, Stephen J. 1978. *Predicting Dangerousness: The Social Construction of Psychiatric Reality.* Lexington, MA: Lexington Books

– 1979. 'From whom will we be protected? Comparative approaches to the assessment of dangerousness.' *International Journal of Law and Psychiatry* 2: 55–79

Polanyi, Michael. 1958. *Personal Knowledge.* London: Routledge Kegan Paul

Prins, Herschel. 1976. 'Remands for psychiatric reports.' *Medicine, Science and the Law* 16: 129–38

Quinney, Richard. 1970. *The Social Reality of Crime.* Boston: Little, Brown

Quinsey, Vernon L. 1979. 'Assessments of the dangerousness of mental patients held in maximum security.' *International Journal of Law and Psychiatry* 2: 389–406

Rabkin, J.G. 1979. 'Criminal behavior of discharged mental patients: A critical appraisal of the research.' *Psychological Bulletin* 86: 1–27

Ranson, Stewart, Bob Hinings, and Royston Greenwood. 1980. 'The structuring of organizational structures.' *Administrative Science Quarterly* 25 (March): 1–17

Robitscher, Jonas B. 1980. *The Powers of Psychiatry*. New York: Houghton Mifflin

Rock, Ronald, Marcus Jacobson, and Richard Janopaul. 1968. *Hospitalization and Discharge of the Mentally Ill*. Chicago: University of Chicago Press

Roesch, Ronald, and Stephen L. Golding. 1978. 'Legal and judicial interpretation of competency to stand trial statutes and procedures.' *Criminology* 16: 420–9

– 1980. *Competency to Stand Trial*. Urbana: University of Illinois Press

Roesch, Ronald, Christopher D. Webster, and Derek Eaves. 1984. *The Fitness Interview Test: A Method for Examining Fitness to Stand Trial*. Toronto and Burnaby: University of Toronto Centre of Criminology and Simon Fraser University Criminology Research Centre

Rollin, Henry R. 1969. *The Mentally Abnormal Offender and the Law*. London: Pergamon

Rosen, A. 1954. 'Detection of suicidal patients: An example of some limitations in the prediction of infrequent events.' *Journal of Consulting Psychology* 18: 397–403

Rosenhan, David L. 1973. 'On being sane in insane places.' *Science* 179: 250–8

Roth, Julius. 1977. 'Some contingencies of the moral evaluation and control of clients.' *American Journal of Sociology* 77 (October): 830–56

Rothman, David J. 1980. *Conscience and Convenience: The Asylum and Its Alternatives in Progressive America*. Boston: Little, Brown

Sampson, Harold, Sheldon Messinger, and Robert Towne. 1964. *Schizophrenic Women: Studies in Marital Crisis*. New York: Atherton

Sarbin, Theodore R. 1986. 'Prediction and clinical inference: Forty years later.' *Journal of Personality Assessment* 50, 3: 362–9

Schatzman, Leonard, and Anselm L. Strauss. 1973. *Field Research: Strategies For a Natural Sociology*. Englewood Cliffs, NJ: Prentice-Hall

Scheff, Thomas J. 1966. *Being Mentally Ill: A Sociological Theory*. Chicago: Aldine

– 1972. 'Screening mental patients.' In Earl Rubington and Martin S. Weinberg (eds), *Deviance: The Interactionist Perspective*. New York: Macmillan

– 1975. 'Social conditions for rationality: How urban and rural courts deal with the mentally ill.' In F. James Davis and Richard Stivers (eds), *The Collective Definition of Deviance*. New York: Free Press

Scheidemandel, D., and C. Kanno. 1969. *The Mentally Ill Offender: A Survey of Treatment Programs*. Washington, DC: A.P.A. Joint Information Service

Schiffer, Marc E. 1978. *Mental Disorder and the Criminal Trial Process*. Toronto: Butterworths

Schrieber, Aaron M. 1970. 'Indeterminate therapeutic incarceration of dangerous criminals: Perspectives and problems.' *Virginia Law Review* 56: 602–34

Schur, Edwin M. 1971. *Labelling Deviant Behavior: Its Sociological Implications*. New York: Harper and Row

– 1980. *The Politics of Deviance: Stigma Contests and the Uses of Power*. Englewood Cliffs, NJ: Prentice-Hall

Schutz, Alfred. 1964. *Collected Papers II. Studies in Social Theory*. The Hague: Martinus Nijhoff

Scull, Andrew T. 1983. *Decarceration. Community Treatment and the Deviant – A Radical View*. 2nd ed. Englewood Cliffs, NJ: Prentice-Hall

Segal, S.P., and U. Aviram. 1978. *The Mentally Ill in Community-Based Sheltered Care: A Study of Community Care and Social Integration*. New York: John Wiley

Sepejak, Diana S., Robert J. Menzies, Christopher D. Webster, and Frederick A.S. Jensen. 1983. 'Clinical predictions of dangerousness: Two-year follow-up of 408 pre-trial forensic cases.' *Bulletin of the American Academy of Psychiatry and the Law* 11, 2 (Summer): 171–81

Shah, Saleem A. 1975. "Dangerousness and civil commitment of the mentally ill: Some public policy considerations.' *American Journal of Psychiatry* 132: 501–5

– 1978. 'Dangerousness – a paradigm for exploring some issues in law and psychology.' *American Psychologist* 33 (March): 224–38

Shover, Neil. 1974. ' "Experts" and diagnosis in correctional agencies.' *Crime and Delinquency* 20, 4 (October): 347–58

Silverman, David. 1970. *The Theory of Organizations: A Sociological Framework*. London: Heinemann

Simpkin, Mike. 1979. *Trapped within Welfare: Surviving Social Work*. London: Macmillan

Skolnick, Jerome H. 1966. *Justice Without Trial: Law Enforcement in Democratic Society*. New York: John Wiley and Sons

Soothill, Keith L. 1974. 'Repeated medical remands.' *Medicine, Science and the Law* 14: 189–99

Soothill, Keith L., C.K. Way, and T.C.N. Gibbens. 1980. 'Subsequent dangerousness among compulsory hospital patients.' *British Journal of Criminology* 20: 289–95

Sparks, Richard F. 1966. 'The decision to remand for mental examination.' *British Journal of Criminology* 6: 6–26

Steadman, Henry J. 1973. 'Some evidence on the inadequacy of the concept and determination of dangerousness in law and psychiatry.' *Journal of Psychiatry and Law* 1 (Winter): 409–26

– 1979. *Beating a Rap? Defendants Found Incompetent to Stand Trial.* Chicago: University of Chicago Press

– 1981. 'Special problems in the prediction of violence among the mentally ill.' In J.R. Hays, T.K. Roberts, and K.S. Solway (eds), *Violence and the Violent Individual.* New York: SP Medical and Scientific Books

Steadman, Henry J., and Joseph J. Cocozza. 1974. *Careers of the Criminally Insane: Excessive Social Control of Deviance.* Lexington, MA: Lexington Books

– 1978. 'Psychiatry, dangerousness, and the repetitively violent offender.' *Journal of Criminal Law and Criminology* 69 (Summer): 226–31

Steadman, Henry J., and Richard B. Felson. 1984. 'Self-reports of violence: Ex-mental patients, ex-offenders, and the general population.' *Criminology* 22, 3 (August): 321–42

Steadman, Henry J., and Joseph P. Morrissey. 1981. 'The statistical prediction of violent behavior: Measuring the costs of a public protectionist versus a civil libertarian model.' *Law and Human Behavior* 5, 4: 263–74

Stokes, R.E., and R.E. Turner. 1964. 'The dangerous patient-offender.' 4th Annual Research Conference on Delinquency and Criminology, Montreal, 19 November

Stone, Alan A. 1978. 'Comment. The process of criminal commitment for pre-trial examination: An evaluation.' *American Journal of Psychiatry* 135: 61–3

Strauss, Anselm L. 1978. *Negotiations: Varieties, Contexts, Procedures, and Social Order.* San Francisco: Jossey-Bass

Sudnow, David. 1965. 'Normal crimes: Sociological features of the penal code in a public defender's office.' *Social Problems* 12: 255–72

Szasz, Thomas S. 1956. 'Some observations on the relationship between psychiatry and the law." *American Medical Association Archives of Neurology and Psychiatry* 75: 277–313

Tacon, T.A. 1979. 'A question of privilege: Valid protection or destruction of justice?' *Osgoode Hall Law Journal* 17 (August): 332–54

Teplin, Linda A. 1984a. *Mental Health and Criminal Justice.* Beverly Hills: Sage

– 1984b. 'Criminalizing mental disorder: The comparative arrest rate of the mentally ill.' *American Psychologist* 39, 7 (July): 794–803

Thompson, E.P. 1975. *Whigs and Hunters: The Origin of the Black Act*. London: Allen Lane

Thornberry, Terence P., and Joseph E. Jacoby. 1979. *The Criminally Insane: A Community Follow-up of Mentally Ill Offenders*. Chicago: University of Chicago Press

Townsend, John Marshall. 1976. 'Self-concept and the institutionalization of mental patients.' *Journal of Health and Social Behavior* 17: 268–71

Tucker, Charles. 1972. 'Societal reactions and mental illness: An examination of police behavior.' Unpublished paper. Cited in Walter R. Gove (ed.), *The Labeling of Deviance*, 2nd ed., pp. 62–3. Beverly Hills: Sage

Turner, Bryan S. 1987. *Medical Power and Social Knowledge*. Beverly Hills: Sage

Turner, R. Edward. 1960. 'The forensic clinic, Toronto.' *Criminal Law Quarterly* 20: 437–48

– 1966. 'Forensic psychiatry and criminology in Canada.' *Excerpta Medica: International Congress Series #150. Proceedings of the Fourth World Congress of Psychiatry*, Madrid, 5–11 September

– 1980. 'Service note: The development of forensic services at the Metropolitan Toronto Forensic Clinic.' *Canadian Journal of Criminology* 20: 200–09

Turner, R.E., H.E. Hutchinson, and L. O'D. Williams. 1958. 'The forensic clinic in the Toronto Psychiatric Hospital.' *Canadian Journal of Corrections* 1, 1: 7–14

Vann, Carl R. 1965. 'Pre-trial determination and judicial decision-making: An analysis of the use of psychiatric information in the administration of criminal justice.' *University of Detroit Law Journal* 43: 13–33

Verdun-Jones, Simon N. 1981. 'The doctrine of fitness to stand trial in Canada: The forked tongue of social control.' *International Journal of Law and Psychiatry* 4: 363–89

Waegel, William B. 1981. 'Case routinization in investigative police work.' *Social Problems* 28, 3 (February): 263–75

Walker, Nigel D., and Susan McCabe. 1973. *Crime and Insanity in England*. Vol. 2. Edinburgh: Edinburgh University Press

Warren, Carol A.B. 1977. 'Involuntary commitment for mental disorder: The application of California's Lanterman-Petris-Short Act.' *Law and Society Review* 11: 629–50

– 1979. 'The social construction of dangerousness.' *Urban Life* 9 (October): 303–11

– 1981. 'New forms of social control: The myth of deinstitutionalization.' *American Behavioral Scientist* 24, 6 (July/August): 724–40

– 1982. *The Court of Last Resort: Mental Illness and the Law*. Chicago: University of Chicago Press

Watson, Gordon, John Rich, and Kenneth G. Gray. 1957. 'A study of forensic cases.' *The Journal of Social Therapy* 3, 2: 105–19

Webster, Christopher D., Mark H. Ben-Aron, and Stephen J. Hucker (eds). 1985. *Dangerousness: Probability and Prediction, Psychiatry and Public Policy.* New York: Cambridge University Press

Webster, Christopher D., Brian T. Butler, R. Edward Turner, Margaret A. Jackson, and Robert J. Menzies. 1978. 'Psychiatric assessment of mentally disordered offenders in Canada.' 2 vols. Toronto: METFORS Working Papers 10 and 11

Webster, Christopher D., Bernard M. Dickens, and Susan M. Addario. 1985. *Constructing Dangerousness: Scientific, Legal and Policy Implications.* Toronto: University of Toronto Centre of Criminology

Webster, Christopher D., and Robert J. Menzies. 1987. 'The clinical prediction of dangerousness.' Chapter 9 in David N. Weisstub (ed.), *Law and Mental Health: International Perspectives*, vol.3. New York: Pergamon

Webster, Christopher D., Robert J. Menzies, and Margaret A. Jackson. 1982. *Clinical Assessment before Trial: Legal Issues and Mental Disorder.* Toronto: Butterworths

Webster, Christopher D., Robert J. Menzies, Brian T. Butler, and R. Edward Turner. 1982. 'Forensic psychiatric assessment in selected Canadian cities.' *Canadian Journal of Psychiatry* 27, 6 (October): 455–62

Wegner, Dennis L., and C. Richard Fletcher. 1969. 'The effect of legal counsel on admissions to a state mental hospital: A confrontation of professions.' *Journal of Health and Social Behavior* 10 (March): 66–72

Wexler, D.B., S.E. Scoville, et al. 1971. 'The administration of psychiatric justice: Theory and practice in Arizona.' *Arizona Law Review* 13: 1–259

Williams, Wright, and Kent S. Miller. 1981. 'The processing and disposition of incompetent mentally ill offenders.' *Law and Human Behavior* 5, 4 (1981): 245–61

Woodside, Moya. 1976. 'Psychiatric referrals for Edinburgh courts.' *British Journal of Criminology* 16, 1 (January): 20–37

Yarrow, Marian Radke, Charlotte Green Schwartz, Harriet S. Murphy, and Leila Calhoun Deasy. 1955. 'The psychological meaning of mental illness in the family.' *The Journal of Social Issues* 11: 12–24

Young, Frank. 1965. *Initiation Ceremonies.* Indianapolis: Bobbs-Merrill

Yuille, John. 1986. *Police Selection and Training: The Role of Psychology.* The Hague: Martinus Nijhoff

Zimmerman, Don C. 1974. 'Fact as practical accomplishment.' In Roy Turner (ed.), *Ethnomethodology: Selected Readings.* Harmondsworth: Penguin

Name Index

Subject Index

alcohol use/abuse: case description, 155, 174; dangerousness and, 88–9, 91–2; drug consumption and, 38; research on mental functions and, 18

assault, case description, 69, 71, 76, 118

assessment: abolition of pre-trial clinical, 237–40; accused persons awaiting trial for, 19, 21; brief, 24, 27; 'catch-22' situations and, 151–3, 174; contradictory evidence and, 209; criteria for, 7; cultural stereotypes and, 110–12, 116; dangerousness and, 10, 15; discovery as, 7, 12, 80–1, 134, 207, 233; discretionary justice and, 10, 93–4; dispositional recommendations and, 10–11, 168; faulty, 151; fitness/competency and, 10; follow-up (2 years after) to, 15; in-patient (protracted), 24, 27, 125–7, 148; judicial disposition and, 26; labelling and, 7, 93–4; patient characteristics and, 27, 89–91; police account and, 117; psychiatric, 7, 93–4, 104; quantity of case information and, 123; restatement of old knowledge as, 7, 12, 80–1, 134, 207, 233; treatment

recommendations and, 11; type of legal charge and, 89, 116–18, 133; types of (3 specific), 148

bail: denial of, 123, 233; fitness for, 26–7, 44, 65, 85, 124, 173–6, 217; in-patient assessments and, 123, 233

Bender Gestalt, 47, 134, 136–7

bestiality, case description, 72–3

Botterell Report, 19, 20

brief assessment in hospital setting. See METFORS Brief Assessment Unit

Brixton prison hospital, 160–1

Canadian Criminal Code, 21–3, 25, 122, 130, 181, 204, 269n, 270n, 272n, 273n, 277n, 278n

Canadian Penitentiary Headquarters, 29

Canadian Police Information Centre (CPIC), 29, 198

civil commitment: dangerousness prediction and, 217; due process and, 123–4; fitness to stand trial and, 161; judicial endorsements of psychiatric assessments and, 125, 130, 160–8; legislation, 57; mental illness and,